# the SEX LIVES of AUSTRALIANS

## A HISTORY

### FRANK BONGIORNO

Black Inc.

Published by Black Inc.,
an imprint of Schwartz Publishing Pty Ltd
37–39 Langridge Street
Collingwood VIC 3066 Australia
email: enquiries@blackincbooks.com
www.blackincbooks.com

The National Library of Australia Cataloguing-in-Publication entry:

    Bongiorno, Frank, 1969- author.

    The sex lives of Australians : a history / Frank Bongiorno.

    2nd edition.

    9781863957076 (pbk)
    9781921870668 (ebook)

    Includes index.

    Australians--Sexual behavior--History. Australians--Sexual behavior--Political
    aspects. Social change--Australia--History. Australians--Social life and cus-
    toms--History.

    306.70994

Cover design by Peter Long
Book design by Thomas Deverall
Typeset by Duncan Blachford

Printed in Australia by Griffin Press an Accredited ISO AS/ NZS 14001:2004 Environmental Management System printer.

*The Sex Lives of Australians* won the 2013 ACT Book of the Year Award and was shortlisted for the Australian History Prizes in the 2013 Prime Minister's Literary Awards and the 2013 NSW Premier's History Awards.

**PRAISE FOR *THE SEX LIVES OF AUSTRALIANS***

'Remarkable and highly readable.'—Michael Kirby

'A great book, a compound of wit and tragedy, as you'd expect from the subject matter, plus wide learning and common sense.' —Alan Atkinson, author of *The Europeans in Australia*

'*The Sex Lives of Australians* is such a treasure trove that it is hard to do it justice ... a work of real significance that makes a fresh contribution to understanding our culture.'—*The Australian*

'This is highly readable, serious history about our most intimate yet most culturally sensitive selves.'—*The Canberra Times*

'A fascinating tale.'—*Sydney Morning Herald*

'An engaging book ... both educational and entertaining.' —*Daily Telegraph*

'Entertaining, enlightening, infuriating and frequently hilarious. Highly recommended.'—*MX Sydney*

'Engaging, open-minded and humorous.'—*Bookseller+Publisher*

'The panel considered that *The Sex Lives of Australians: A History* was elegantly written with a strong narrative, offering readers an intelligent, accessible and balanced account of the changing attitudes and experiences of Australians since European settlement.' —Judges' comments from the 2013 ACT Book of the Year Award

# Contents

*For Nicole*

# Foreword

## *The Hon. Michael Kirby* AC CMG*

This remarkable and highly readable book offers a cornucopia of sexual tales from history. It holds up a mirror to Australian society and describes the sexual lives of its people from the first penal settlement in 1788 to the present times.

The book starts with stories of the sex-deprived convicts, mostly men, arriving in the Antipodean world. The advent of the first boatloads of disempowered women is recounted, as is the very vulnerable condition of the Indigenous people and the so-called half-castes that sprang from sexual unions with them. It proceeds through the early colonial age of repression, of harsh laws, of capital crimes and the cult of mateship. Captain Moonlite, the bushranger, strides boldly across the stage with his male lover. He and the Kelly Gang contributed to a panic over sodomites: the moral enemies of Australian society. The opening of the Victorian age sees reflections in the Australian colonies of many of the controversies that beset England and America at the same time: scandals in high places; hypocrisy in public and private conduct; patriarchal attitudes to 'ladies'; harsh sexual censorship; backyard abortions; the early controversial ventures into birth control; the plight of 'fallen women'; and the ever-present quest for social, racial and religious 'purity'.

Even masturbation deeply disturbed many of the leaders of Victorian society. Spilling of the seed was regarded as a serious sin and it was a

---

* Justice of the High Court of Australia (1996–2009), President of the International Commission of Jurists (1995–98); Laureate of the UNESCO Prize for Human Rights Education (1998); Australian Human Rights Medal (1991).

topic for endless debate and solemn instruction, mostly addressed to the young.

By the end of the nineteenth century, sadomasochism had put in an appearance, including by the gifted composer Percy Grainger. So had cases of cross-dressing. Venereal disease was literally on many people's lips. And with the start of World War I, a large cohort of young Australian men ventured overseas to discover, for the first time, the brothels of Cairo and Paris, before they were marched off to Gallipoli and the Somme, to die in the empire's battles. Our soldiers and their cousins from New Zealand proved shockingly sexual for the stern British commanders. Merrily they sang the song, 'How're they going to keep him down on the farm, after he's seen Paree?' Sexual internationalism had well and truly arrived.

The postwar era and the Great Depression brought the return of countless controversies in Australia over nudity, erotica, supposed clitoral nymphomania and that old recurring anxiety over masturbation.

But soon, the very existence of the nation was in danger. World War II brought 'factory girls' and many young men freed from the suburbs and farms, facing the possibility of death and determined to savour the joys of life, whilst they had it. The clientele for sex in Australia included some of the Yankee soldiers, a number of them black: exposing Australian women to the unaccustomed attractions of racial variation, not often seen in the era of White Australia.

When the Yanks went home, wartime austerity gave way to cautious national prosperity in the '50s and '60s. 'Heavy petting', 'car sex', bodgies and widgies, rock 'n' roll and other dastardly threats made their appearance. Lady Chatterley and Billy Graham take their bows in this Act of the drama, although not necessarily together.

And, as if this were not enough, the era of permissiveness gave way to a sexual revolution. The contraceptive pill saw women liberated from pregnancy. Naturally, religious leaders denounced the consequences, declaring them to be an end to civilisation. Their worst fears seemed to be realised, not only by the promiscuity of healthy young heterosexual Australians shamelessly 'living in sin', but also by an increasing cohort of gay advocates, after Dennis Altman, who outrageously refused to be ashamed of their 'perversion'. Increasingly, this 'queer' minority even began demanding equal legal rights – including (horrors) the right to marriage equality and civil recognition and acceptance of their intimate long-term relationships.

Although, by the current age, the denunciation of masturbation appears, at last, to have abated in the litany of Australia's national anxieties, new sources of stigma and discrimination appeared in the past twenty years to agitate the national psyche.

Just when sexual freedom was tasted for the first time, including among the previously demonised sexual minorities, a strange new retrovirus appeared, apparently out of Africa, to sweep the world. Cunningly it chose penetrative sexual intercourse as its major portal of entry. Whereas in Africa and Asia, the major impact of this virus was on heterosexuals, in Australia, as in other Western societies, the newly liberated communities of gay men felt the heaviest burden. With the virus came a groundswell of new fear and loathing.

To prove that attitudes to sexual activity are cyclical, and partly political, some Australian politians, taking their lead from America, saw votes to be had in whipping up new hostility. A huge media-driven campaign of fear was raised against paedophiles, often causing confusion in the public perception of homosexuals. Continuous campaigns were waged to tap religion-fuelled fears of relationship recognition for sexual minorities. The success of such campaigns can be measured by their impact on recent elections in Australia, as in the United States. Fear, whether on the ground of gender, race or sexuality, is always a potent weapon for demagogues.

The social value of this book is that it helps us to understand the debates and controversies that arise for contemporary Australians, by recognising their links to the same forces that had to be faced and overcome in earlier times. By knowing more about our past in this regard, Australians may become wiser and more accepting of sexual differences at present and in the future. And less willing to jump on the bandwagons so regularly rolled out by politicians and the media when the electoral cycle makes its recurrent appearances. As well, this book reveals a large unwritten story of the burden that repressive laws and attitudes have placed on millions of human beings. They have been cast into a well of loneliness by an enforced celibacy, often advocated by religious leaders. Yet now we have reached a time where the joy and fulfilment of a happy sexual life is often possible. And increasing millions will demand it, for it is central to a happy life, good health and personal fulfilment.

In this sense, this book is a story of the journey of one country, through repression and violence to truth and greater freedom. The journey to larger acceptance and peace is by no means over. But, as the author shows, it has well and truly begun.

*Michael Kirby*
Sydney
27 March 2012

# Introduction

Modern times can be unsettling. Men and women live without shame in de facto relationships. Sex outside marriage is treated as unexceptional. Men have sex with men, and women with women. People born into one gender live their lives as the other. Some enjoy whipping; others like being whipped. Parents worry about what their children get up to when out of their sight, fearing corruption from sexual predators, pornography or bad associates. Moralists panic about where all of this is leading, and it can sometimes seem that 'anything goes'.

This book is an account of the sex lives of Australians since the earliest years of European settlement. All of the behaviour so far described happens in our own times; it has also occurred over the last couple of centuries, revealing a sexual variety in the past hardly less rich than in the present. The nine chapters to come follow a rough chronology from 1788. Chapter 1 shows what happened to moral and sexual attitudes, codes and practices formed in Britain when they were translated to a convict settlement on the other side of the globe, one whose demography, society, political authority and material life diverged from those at home. Chapter 2 focuses on the Victorian era, and notably the quest for 'normality' and 'respectability' when the very conditions of colonial life seemed to militate against them. Chapter 3 deals mainly with the late nineteenth- and early twentieth-century decline in the birthrate, and the role it played in focusing attention on female sexuality. Chapter 4, which is concerned with the years either side of Federation, examines changing expectations and realities of male sexual conduct. In both chapters 3 and 4, we see the increasing entanglement of sexuality with ideas about race and nation. Chapters 5, 6 and 7 examine the period from 1914 to 1960, an era of global war and depression that saw growing recognition of sexuality as a driver of human behaviour while linking it with the promise of modernity. These hopes and expectations, however, continued to fall unequally on women and men, blacks and whites, gays and straights. The final two chapters – 8 and 9 – pursue the story of sexual revolution and counter-revolution from 1960 to the present.

We live in times where the past can seem an especially uncertain guide to how to act in the present – and perhaps no more so than in sexual matters. For instance, the debates across the twentieth century about sex censorship can appear arcane and even trivial when set beside the issues raised by the ubiquity and accessibility of sex on the internet. Yet the patterns of contemporary debate about this issue will not be entirely new to anyone familiar with the longer history of sexuality in Australia. Should governments introduce mandatory internet filtering to protect children, or is it rather the responsibility of parents to attend to such matters? What role should schools play? Will the government's efforts to block offensive content succeed, or will this simply encourage more furtive and ingenious efforts to evade prohibitions? At what point is the state justified in interfering with my right to pursue my own tastes, on the internet as elsewhere, so long as they do not interfere with the rights of others?

History provides no clear guide to answering any of these questions, but it at least offers the insight that the issues they raise are not completely novel. At the same time, it reminds us that sexual rights we now take for granted were often fought over with great tenacity. It would be easier to accept the arguments against same-sex marriage if so many of them did not bear such a remarkable resemblance to those once regularly advanced against the decriminalisation of homosexual behaviour.

Debate over matters of this kind is sometimes presented as less important than 'mainstream' issues such as the economy, a diversion from what politics should really be about. Political parties endorse this view by offering a 'conscience vote' on them, as if they are fundamentally different from the vast range of policy issues that, depending on how they are handled politically, either add to, or subtract from, the sum total of human suffering.

The question of how societies organise sexuality is not, however, a singularly personal or private issue but a fundamentally social and political one. The rules on sex in Australia have affected the very substance of people's lives, shaping and even deciding their chances of personal happiness, social acceptance and economic security. The legal regulation of sex has determined whether people went free, or to prison, or to the gallows. Even in fairly recent times, what governments, doctors and churches have done, or not done, has influenced whether people lived or died.

The British historian Jeffrey Weeks suggests that in its exposure of 'the sexual and moral diversity of the past', the history of sexuality might 'lead us to be a little more accepting of the diversity of the present'.[1] Even at the individual level, history can be liberating. A young Australian homosexual in the 1950s, having read a book 'that portrayed male homosexuality in ancient Greece as ... general and accepted as completely normal', as a result felt 'more at ease' about his own 'condition'.[2]

In these circumstances, it would be easy from our perspective to celebrate a story of unfolding freedom and progress, one in which ever fewer have been made to suffer for their sexual behaviour or orientation. I will present a much more nuanced, contested and uneven history. In that respect, if in no other, the story of the future is very likely to resemble that of the past.

# CHAPTER 1

# Founding Sexualities

***'Such a Crime Could Not Be Passed with Impunity'***
At 8 o'clock in the morning on St Patrick's Day in 1795, Mary Hartley, a sixteen-year-old Irish convict, arrived at the house of Thomas Cotterill, a former marine farming at the Field of Mars, in what is now the Sydney suburb of East Ryde. The 'house' was a grog shop, its supplies recently replenished by the arrival of some brandy from the Cape of Good Hope. Two men were with Hartley; the group had come to buy liquor, as had others, and the place was quickly occupied by a rowdy company of men.

Cotterill allowed Hartley, who was affected by alcohol but not insensible, to rest on his bed. While he was distracted, however, some other men in the house made for the bedroom. Cotterill later testified that he had caught one man, and then another, between Hartley's legs, but that he managed to ward them off. When he left the house to get more liquor from a nearby barn, some guests overpowered the man Cotterill had charged with looking after Hartley, and they dragged her from the house.

There were contradictions in the evidence later offered in court, but it is clear that Hartley was viciously gang-raped. She had early warning of her fate when she heard one man, John Anderson, 'say that he would have a grinding mill, to grind the fine corn. That having heard that expression before in Sydney, she understood by it, that a number would lay with one woman and use her as they liked'. Once they had reached the field, the men then laid her on her back and while two of them, Morgan Brian and Joseph Dunstill, opened her legs, two others held her hands and another covered her mouth. She claimed to have then been raped by sixteen men, twice each, although only six – a mixed cohort of convicts and ex-convicts – would come to trial. (Another witness later testified that Mary said she had been raped by forty men twice over.) Brian, she recalled, had said, 'kill the whore at once and there will be no more to do with her' while another man 'came and calling her bitch, bade her get up, not to lay there, they ought to have killed her'. Even after she left Cotterill's with two men – perhaps her original companions – she was followed by Brian and another man, John Hyams, and raped again. Her face covered in scratches, she later encountered the surgeon Thomas Arndell, to whom she told her story. He arranged for her admission to hospital, where she was unable to leave her bed without help for a fortnight.[1]

In the early years of our own century, media commentators deemed contrary to Australian values some 'pack-rapes' carried out by 'Muslim' youths just a few miles from the cornfield where Mary was assaulted that morning.[2] It took an historian, Graham Willett, to point out that even the term 'pack-rape' itself was of Australian coinage. 'Suddenly,' he said in a letter to a newspaper, 'we are forced to think about this kind of behaviour not as some recent and alien intrusion into our way of life, but as an integral part of Australian history, dating back to the unloading of the first convict ships'.[3] Willett was right that pack-rape had occurred from the earliest years of British settlement in Australia. All the same, the disgust that Mary's experience induced in some colonial men suggests that it was probably not a common offence. The authorities were certainly determined that the rapists should pay a price, that 'such a crime could not be passed with impunity', as Judge-Advocate David Collins remarked.[4] So, although the men were initially found not guilty, and despite the legal principle of jeopardy which is supposed to prevent anyone being tried twice for the same crime, they were retried on a lesser charge of assault, convicted and sentenced to several hundred lashes each.

Some historians have been all too eager to present rape as a foundational sexual experience of both white and black women in colonial Australia. Popular histories by Robert Hughes and Thomas Keneally have suggested, without evidence, that the initial landing of the female convicts in Sydney on 6 February 1788 was marked by their rape or attempted rape. These happenings are presented as part of an 'orgy' or 'great Sydney bacchanal'.[5] The reality was certainly more prosaic. Encouraged by the Governor himself, convict settlers married from the earliest days of the colony. Others formed households and de facto relationships that had customary standing as a marriage-like bond. Officials, marines and sailors took mistresses from among the convicts but children born out of wedlock were often acknowledged and provided for. Women were vulnerable to rape – including gang-rape – not least because they formed a minority in a colony where single men were preponderant. But despite the resilient stereotype of the convict woman as a 'whore', men valued such women for their skills, companionship and sexuality. As in other times and places, powerful men sometimes became infatuated, and they were occasionally willing to risk careers and reputations in pursuit of convict women. Within the constraints of a patriarchal society, women too made their choices, and they used their sexuality as a source of power in their dealings with men.[6]

## A Colonial Sexual Economy

Australia was first settled as a penal colony in 1788, at a time when some long-standing ideas about sex, gender and the body were being radically transformed.[7] In some ways, this means Australian sex was born 'modern'. By the late eighteenth century, scientific opinion was coming to accept a view of men's and women's bodies and minds as fundamentally different from each other. Medical opinion increasingly rejected the ancient idea that men and women had the same genitals, only that the greater heat of the male body caused men's to protrude. Women's possession of ovaries now came to define their sex, where once these had been treated as the female equivalent of the testes.[8]

These changes were accompanied by a decline in Britain in the average age of marriage over the course of the eighteenth century – from the late to the mid-twenties – a transition that some historians have attributed to economic factors such as rising wages and others to changes in sentiment and culture. There was also an increasing frequency of penetrative sex among young unmarried people. Where courting had once been dominated by various forms of petting short of full intercourse, sex was by the end of the eighteenth century coming to mean the penetration by the penis of the vagina. A true man was someone who desired and penetrated women. A respectable man would eventually settle with one woman, confine his penetration to her, and use his healthy semen to father vigorous children. Meanwhile, the sexual double standard ensured that while a true woman allowed herself to be penetrated, if she was virtuous she would only do so within marriage and with a natural feminine restraint, rather than the greater passion associated with women's sexual behaviour in the early modern period. Sex was also to be for the fulfilment of her essential purpose in life, motherhood. Where in the early modern period moderate female sexual pleasure was understood as a prerequisite for procreation, this idea was in decline by the late eighteenth century. Varieties of sexual behaviour that did not conform to these basic norms – masturbation, sex between men, sex between women, sex between humans and animals, even female aggression towards men – were not only sinful, but unnatural. As divisions between the bodies, minds and souls of the sexes became more sharply defined in western thought, so too did the boundaries between acceptable and unacceptable sexual behaviour.[9]

The development of this basic sexual economy was well advanced by the time the First Fleet sailed into Sydney Cove. Yet if we examine the very early colonial period – the half-century or so before Victoria came to the throne – there are few indications that the erotic behaviour of either free or unfree settlers was understood as a strong indication of the character of an individual or society. The early colonial state did not set the control of the 'sexual' impulse apart from other appetites. When Samuel Marsden, the clergyman, magistrate and landowner, condemned the immorality and wickedness of the colonists – as he often did – he certainly had in mind what we would now call sexual immorality. But he did not place it either above or outside a larger cluster of undesirable behaviours – drunkenness, blasphemy, idleness, theft, Sabbath desecration and radical politics – that he regarded as un-Christian and dangerous.[10] In any case, the authorities were in practice able to exercise only a limited influence on the sexual conduct of either convicts or free settlers in the early years. For one, they made only a desultory effort to replace popular acceptance of stable de facto relations as a kind of 'marriage' with a sterner state-imposed order.[11]

As in other parts of the Pacific in the age of enlightenment and discovery, Indigenous women aroused the curiosity and desire of European men far from home. Many early descriptions were blatantly erotic. Aboriginal men, meanwhile, seemed to want to protect the women from the presence of Europeans; yet they also, at times, appeared to be offering up their women as a kindness. Governor Arthur Phillip worried about conflict with the locals over sexual matters, and was especially concerned at the effects of liaisons between convicts and Aboriginal women. Some early racial conflict was a result of sexual relations of this kind; convicts incurred obligations and debts by accepting the sexual favours of Aboriginal women which they subsequently failed to meet. The appearance of light-skinned babies soon pointed to sex between colonisers and Indigenous women.[12] Mixed-race children were sometimes killed and one Aboriginal woman was spotted rubbing her too-white baby in some ashes, in a fruitless attempt to darken its skin.[13]

Many early authors of journals and diaries in the colonies were repulsed by Aboriginal sexual customs but they made no systematic effort to reform them. Commentators believed rape common in Aboriginal societies, and they seemed shocked at the regular resort of Aboriginal men to beating their wives.[14] Yet officials also remarked on the extent to which violence occurred between convict and emancipist settlers, frequently over sex. There was an uncomfortable affinity between the behaviour of the lower-class white and the Aborigine, one that contributed to the image of the convict as not fully civilised. David Collins commented of the gang-rape case with which this chapter began: 'They appeared to have cast off all the feelings of civilised humanity, adopting as closely as they could follow them the manners of the savage inhabitants of the country.'[15] But Collins's own adulterous behaviour – that 'Polygamist Governor' as one settler would indelicately remember him – raised awkward questions about the boundaries between the savage and the civilised.[16] After all, Aboriginal men's own polygamy was seen as a mark of their 'barbarism'. Similarly, the accusation that convict men were living off the immoral earnings of their 'wives' placed little daylight between native and convict forms of 'savagery', because Aboriginal men were known to dispose 'of the favours of their wives to the convict-servants for a slice of bread or a pipe of tobacco'.[17] A practice that for Aboriginal society was a form of hospitality and even a means of drawing the coloniser into relations of kinship, diplomacy and trade was, for the newcomers, indistinguishable from prostitution.[18] Among the settlers themselves, the much larger number of men than women from the outset meant that male opportunities for sex with a woman were limited. The total number of male convicts would eventually outnumber the women by more than six to one while the marines and, later, the soldiers of the NSW Corps were also mainly unaccompanied. Officials recognised the potential for disorder in these arrangements even before the First Fleet sailed, and they famously considered importing women from the Pacific Islands as mates for the marines in Australia's earliest scheme of sexual engineering.[19]

Officials, seamen and marines enjoyed an advantage over most convicts in forming stable relationships, having a higher status and more material goods to offer. From Norfolk Island in 1794, Lieutenant-Governor King reported regular complaints from convict and emancipist settlers 'of the ill-treatment they had received from the soldiers in seducing their wives'.[20] The colony's gentlemen, King among them, also often had convict mistresses, liaisons that sometimes began on the voyage out.[21] This kind of arrangement was in line with a contemporary acceptance in polite British society that married gentlemen would keep one or more mistresses, the latter often drawn from the lower orders.[22] David Collins, who had left a wife behind in England, fathered two children by a convict mistress in Sydney but his behaviour as Lieutenant-Governor of Van Diemen's Land was especially brazen. In Hobart, he had an open liaison with a woman married to a convict under his charge. Collins built a house for Hannah Power and her convict husband, Matthew – 'the contented cuckold', as John Pascoe Fawkner later called him – conveniently close to his own.[23] But Hannah lived in Collins's home. Eventually, he sent her away, her place being taken by a fifteen-year-old girl recently arrived from Norfolk Island, Margaret Eddington. She was less than one-third of Collins's age.[24]

Collins's behaviour, being both wildly indiscreet and openly hypocritical, was a source of turbulence. Yet scrutiny of his behaviour was informal, carried on through the intimacies of everyday personal contact. Judgments were delivered through the snub, the insult and the spread of gossip.[25] While these measures had their effects on local reputation, they could not as yet destroy the colonial career of a powerful ruler. Meanwhile, convicts and emancipists also enjoyed considerable freedom in their everyday lives. If a male convict's home was not quite his castle, so long as he (and his family, if he had one) did not behave in a blatantly disorderly manner, he was unlikely to experience much official interference in his domestic life.[26] Men in authority passed adverse judgment on the morals of convicts, especially women, but they did not closely scrutinise their sexual behaviour. For instance, neither sodomy nor bestiality charges came before the courts as a result of official surveillance or policing but rather from the complaints of passers-by, or those who were themselves attacked. It was members of the community, not the authorities, who were exercising supervision over male sexuality in these early years.[27] And even serious sexual crimes did not in the colony's early days arouse any wider concern about the nature of convict society itself.

In cases of child rape, it was frequently parents who brought cases to court. Convict society was rigidly hierarchical, providing convict and emancipist men with limited scope for the assertion of their power over others. Most lacked strong domestic attachments or opportunities for sexual release but they also enjoyed considerable personal freedom. Yet whereas in the 1830s the sexual dangers posed to children became a mark of the convict system's depravity and an argument for its abolition, sexual offences against the very young aroused no such panic earlier on. In 1789 a soldier who already had a reputation for assaulting children, Henry Wright, was found guilty of having raped an eight-year-old girl. Although he was sentenced to death, Collins recommended Wright for mercy. The Judge-Advocate's reasoning was that the man's offence 'did not seem to require an immediate example; the chastity of the female part of the settlement had never been so rigid, as to drive men to so desperate an act … beside the wretch in question there was not in the colony a man of any description who would have attempted it'.[28] That it was a soldier – and therefore an instrument of political authority – who committed the offence could potentially have raised uncomfortable questions about the lessons that sex-starved convict men might draw from his escape of the noose. But Collins treated the rape as an aberration.

The peculiar circumstances of a predominantly male penal society nonetheless increasingly influenced how many sexual offences were understood, both in the colonies and in Britain. 'I asked him if there was no woman in the Country', a witness testified having said to the accused in an 1812 bestiality case involving carnal knowledge of a dog.[29] In 1796 George Hyson, a labourer, also found himself accused of having had sex with a dog. Bestiality was a capital offence; Hyson was perhaps lucky that proving it was so difficult, for two witnesses were required.[30] He was instead found guilty of the lesser crime of intent, and sentenced to stand in the pillory three times.[31] James Reece was less fortunate. He was seen by two passers-by having sex with a sow; one of them was prepared to swear 'that he saw the prisoner withdraw his private parts from out of the body of the said sow and that his semen or nature flew from him upon the hinder parts'. The accused was found guilty and executed, and, in accordance with Leviticus XX:15 – 'if a man lie with a beast, he shall surely be put to death: and ye shall slay the beast' – the sow was also killed. It left behind a litter of eleven orphans who would necessarily be lost and the court recommended that the owner, a poor man who stood to sustain serious financial loss from the affair, should be compensated.[32]

In a society where people lived amid animals, that some turned to them for sex is perhaps not surprising.[33] On the face of it, such offences appear to have been regarded as particularly serious on account of their transgression of a 'natural order' separating people with souls from beasts without them.[34] Yet there might also have been more tolerance when such offences were committed by youths. In an 1819 Hobart case in which an older labourer was tried for buggering a mare, the defendant's age was considered sufficiently unusual to elicit expressions of disgust that 'a man of his years' would do such a thing.[35]

There were also cases involving what would in the twentieth century become known as 'homosexual offences'. Sodomy, like bestiality, was a hanging offence although, alternatively, men might be subjected to some combination of flogging, hard labour and a session in the pillory. In 1812 two men spent an hour in the pillory in the public market place in Sydney, where they were exposed to 'the indignation of the populace', police being required to intervene to prevent the throwing of 'stones and other hard substances'. Those convicted of 'abominable' offences were not popular heroes; these men's 'very sufferings were held in derision as they were themselves the objects of universal detestation and contempt'.[36]

Men's practice of sleeping in close proximity to one another could lead to trouble, especially when combined with heavy drinking.[37] James Cunningham and Caleb Wilson were sharing a bed one night late in 1813 in Parramatta. Cunningham testified that he was woken by Wilson, who had his face close to Cunningham's back, was holding his own genitals, and 'making a motion' as if to commit sodomy. Cunningham got out of bed and beat Wilson, who explained that 'he thought he was in bed with a woman'. Other witnesses backed up Wilson's claim of an abiding interest in women, testifying to his having been a widower and father of two, his respectable reputation, and his having pursued other women since his wife's death. Wilson was found not guilty.[38] Here, a sexual interest in women was offered as a defence against a sodomy charge, suggesting that it was considered unlikely that a 'normal' man – that is, one who had sex with women – would feel sexual desire for another man. In seventeenth-century England, ruling-class libertines who had sex with both women and boys, far from being held in contempt as effeminate, were seen to have an extreme virility. But the eighteenth century saw the development of a 'molly' culture in which men sometimes dressed and painted themselves as women, socialised in 'molly houses', adopted female names, and engaged in mock births and 'marriages' – the latter a euphemism for sex. The molly's appearance on the London scene strengthened the association of sodomy with effeminacy.[39] No evidence of a molly culture has been found in early Sydney but certain inns and theatres had acquired a reputation by the 1830s as places frequented by 'sodomites'.[40]

## Marriage and Sex

From around 1810 there were steps to regulate convict domestic life more rigorously. Especially after Commissioner John Bigge reported in the early 1820s and recommended more stringent punishment in the interests of private profit, convicts' freedom of movement was increasingly circumscribed. In many respects, both convict men and women were now set apart from the rest of society as a stigmatised caste; they had earlier rubbed shoulders and much else with free settlers in a less closely supervised community.[41] For men – and especially convict men with few skills and little or no capital – the chances of finding a wife remained slim. Perhaps as many as three-quarters of the males who arrived in the early colonial era would never marry, and most of those who missed out were convicts and emancipists.[42] Robert Crooke, a Van Diemen's Land clergyman writing in the 1840s, remarked that the prisoner 'was supposed to have no human passions, and although not permitted to marry, was if found out in any liaison liable to be flogged or sent to work on the roads in chains'.[43] Women, being in high demand, were far more likely to marry, and the majority of female convicts did so.[44] But where previously a female convict's marriage amounted to a grant of a ticket-of-leave, now the ability of both convict men and women to marry depended on good conduct and the approval of the Governor and their master. At a time when legal marriage was becoming a more widely accepted marker of respectability, for a convict, or anyone who wished to marry one, it was increasingly hemmed in with regulations and restrictions.[45]

Convicts resisted these impositions on their lives. Women who left their master's place without permission were frequently found in 'disorderly houses' (brothels), inns or sly grog shops, sometimes in bed with a man. Convict women smuggled their lovers into the houses where they worked but public parks and private gardens were also used for sex. Any farm overseer who valued his time would begin his search for an absent female servant in the men's huts. Some convicts enjoyed a casual liaison in a few hours snatched from their master's service, but others were courting in the expectation of marriage. Women knew they were in demand – that their sexuality was valued even as it was derided – and many female convicts used sex to make better lives for themselves. A convict woman who agreed to attach herself to a man was likely to be mindful of what property and prospects he brought with him, since she had the capacity to pick and choose. At their crudest, these arrangements can seem like a sexual barter barely distinguishable from prostitution, yet they make perfect sense in view of poor women's limited means of acquiring protection, property or status.[46]

Prostitution itself was also probably common enough in early colonial Australia, if not as common as many – invariably male – observers implied. Men in authority were in the habit of dismissing rebellious female convicts as whores, and they also tended to conflate prostitution with merely sharing the bed of a man to whom one was not married. Nonetheless, the conditions of early colonial life were conducive to a flourishing sex trade. Sydney and Hobart were port towns regularly visited by sailors; most male convicts were able to earn a little money once they had fulfilled their labour obligations and so could buy sex; and large numbers of civil and military officials were either unmarried or far from wives and families. The benefits of prostitution for these women were as obvious as for those who had entered into a de facto relationship or marriage to better themselves. Prostitutes could use their earnings to acquire goods such as clothing that not only made their lives more pleasant, but might also increase their allure – and future earning capacity.[47] But like wives and de facto partners, prostitutes risked a violent encounter with a man, and they could expect even less protection from the state than women with better claims to respectability.

The peculiar character of convict society also encouraged sex between male convicts and Aboriginal women and thereby contributed to a worsening of frontier violence. By the 1830s well-informed settlers were convinced that many 'outrages' carried out on both sides had their origins in the convicts' 'continually having connection with the black women'.[48] Lancelot Threlkeld, a missionary, commented that '[t]he *un*-matrimonial state of the thousands of male prisoners scattered throughout the country amidst females, though of another color, leads them by force, fraud or bribery to withdraw the Aboriginal women from their own proper mates, and disease, and death are the usual consequences of such proceedings'.[49] Even when they did not just abduct Aboriginal women, convicts had access to goods that gave them considerable bargaining power in these exchanges. Typically, if a travelling band of Aboriginal women encountered a group of convict workers, one or two women might visit the convicts to exchange sex and companionship for bread, potatoes or tobacco.[50] In 1837, having become aware of sexual exploitation of Aboriginal women in remote areas, Governor Bourke banned squatters and their men 'from forcibly detaining Aboriginal women'. Yet the provision did no more than make the whites 'a little more careful'.[51] The Australian Agricultural Company's assigned servants were similarly able to continue sexual relations with Aboriginal women, even after Governor Gipps in 1838 threatened to withdraw the company's convict labour if such liaisons were allowed to continue. But not all such relations were casual. James Bugg, a convict employed by the company in the Gloucester district of NSW, and Charlotte, an Aboriginal woman, formed a relationship in the 1830s that led to marriage and produced eight or more children. Their oldest child, Mary Ann, would later earn bushranging notoriety as Captain Thunderbolt's 'Lady' (or, less politely, 'Thunderbolt's gin').[52]

The sealers and whalers who formed isolated little republics along the southern Australian coast depended heavily on labour provided by Aboriginal women with whom they often formed stable relationships. Presided over by men wearing animal skins, these strange communities were like most of Aboriginal Australia in lying outside the effective rule of the British state. By 1820 some fifty men were living in Bass Strait, alongside roughly twice that many women taken from northern Van Diemen's Land. While sealers conducted coastal raids and used violence to gain control of black women, Aboriginal men were sometimes willing to exchange the temporary use of their wives' services for goods such as meat. In other instances, they traded women stolen from rivals in exchange for dogs, flour or muttonbird.[53]

Sex between whalers stationed along the South Australian coast and local Aboriginal women was also common in the 1830s, with occasionally violent consequences. In November 1834 whalers abducted five Aboriginal women from what is now the Port Lincoln district, taking them to nearby Boston Island. According to one eyewitness, the men shot two Aboriginal husbands of the women and then 'beat their brains out with clubs'. Some of the whalers involved in this attack were black, presumably Americans, including the notorious Jack Anderson who eventually assumed a de facto leadership of a ragtag band that lived by sealing and stealing in the extensive archipelago off Western Australia's King George Sound. Anderson usually had one or two Aboriginal women living with him, but also managed to secure a white lover when she was stranded in the islands as the victim of shipwreck.[54]

Abductions sometimes drew a violent response from Aboriginal men. 'Even now', reflected a contributor to a Perth newspaper in 1842 in reference to raids along King George Sound, 'in talking of these marauders, the natives describe them with symptoms of loathing and innate hatred'.[55] Sealers on Kangaroo Island near present-day Adelaide, like their counterparts elsewhere, abducted women from both mainland Australia and Van Diemen's Land. Among the local Kaurna people, the island's name, *Karta*, was the same as their word for female genitalia, a coinage that might have been both recent and derived from harsh experience of the sealers' ways.[56]

The overall effect of sex between whites and Aborigines was to undermine the cohesion and vitality of Aboriginal society. The traditional practice of older Indigenous men taking several, usually younger, brides while less mature men went without sometimes led to adultery and elopement. But the sexual competition now offered by white men further reduced the supply of marriageable women. In 1839 Threlkeld warned that if Aboriginal men from the Manilla River in the north-west came into his mission at Lake Macquarie accompanied by their wives, 'civil protection must be afforded by Government at this place, or, the women will be forcibly taken away by the tribes belonging to these parts, they being deficient of the Female Sex'.[57]

The sex imbalance among the settlers exaggerated a tendency that would have occurred in any case as a result of the sexual double standard governing the behaviour of men and women: legal marriage was overwhelmingly more important as the context for female sexual activity than for male. In the late 1820s, men on average married at twenty-nine, and women at twenty-three. At a time when marriage in one's early twenties had become the norm in Britain, and there were ever fewer people who never married at all, the colonial situation represented a sharp divergence from accustomed patterns at home, especially for men. Convict grooms, at thirty-two, were even older; they typically had to wait for eight years after arrival in the colony to marry, if they were indeed fortunate enough to find a willing partner. The wide age gap that often existed between husband and wife might have sometimes contributed to marital disharmony or infidelity,[58] but the more obvious and important phenomenon was the development of what James Belich has called a 'crew culture' among single men.[59] Women comprised just a quarter of the population in the early nineteenth century, and even these were concentrated in and around Sydney and Hobart.[60] Elsewhere, hard-living single males wandered the country, following opportunities for casual work as they arose, and arguably providing Australian masculinity with a complexion still recognisable today. Crew culture also developed in other settler societies, but in Australia it was called mateship.[61]

While nationalist writers later celebrated rugged colonial masculinity, from the 1820s British opponents of penal transportation gave increasing attention to the reprehensible character of a society based on both a preponderance of men and, even worse, on men who through their criminality had shown that they lacked moral restraint. In 1829 in *A Letter from Sydney* – actually written from Newgate prison in London where its author was serving three years for stealing a fifteen-year-old heiress – Edward Gibbon Wakefield proposed 'systematic colonisation'. Land in Australia would be sold at a price high enough to prevent the poor from buying it, for their labour would be required to work the land owned by the well-off. The proceeds would be used to pay for immigration of free labourers. Wakefield's aim was to replicate in Australia the

English class system, to create a normal society according to his lights. That meant an end to convict transportation but also the engineering of a proper sex ratio. The 'disproportion of the sexes', claimed Wakefield, was 'the greatest evil of all', for 'every female child in this colony, not defended by parents of some influence, is sure to be hunted by a dozen roaring lions, and … her destruction is almost inevitable'.[62]

After 1831 revenue raised from the sale of land was used to fund assisted immigration. In the early years, most of the money paid for single female immigrants, whose presence was supposed to mitigate the evils identified by Wakefield. The initial scheme to bring large numbers of single women to the colonies, however, aroused considerable controversy. Influential colonists did not want 'prostitutes' but moral and useful young women who would make good servants, wives and mothers. The central problem for the emigration commissioners, who oversaw the British end of the scheme, was how to find women who were suited to the life marked out for them in the colonies. An important qualification was chastity, and the commissioners accordingly refused to accept 'fallen women' for assisted passages. That automatically excluded pregnant single women, although some inevitably slipped through.[63] In 1834 Governor Richard Bourke, responding to evidence that on one voyage 'an almost unlimited intercourse existed between the seamen and a great number of the female passengers', demanded that greater caution be exercised in the choice of migrants.[64] The continuing association of single female immigration with prostitution led to the temporary abandonment of mass emigration of unaccompanied women in 1836, to be replaced by schemes that sought to balance an influx of unprotected women with emigration of women in family groups.[65] These changes did not prevent debauchery on the *Sir Charles Napier* during its 1842 voyage to Australia. There were well-founded allegations that the captain had selected a shipboard lover from among the female immigrants, and that much of the crew followed his bad example. The chief mate called the vessel 'a floating bawdy house'.[66] A more tragic set of events unfolded on the *Subraon* in 1848, when the captain and crew took 'servants' – and lovers – from among twelve Dublin orphan girls aboard. An inquiry later heard that the captain told a passenger who challenged his behaviour that 'if he [the captain] took a fancy to one or two of them, he could and would keep them in his cabin for six months, if the voyage continued so long'. He could 'f**k any woman in the ship' if he had the urge to do so, the captain was alleged to have boasted. He was forever pestering the girls for kisses – which he later explained as affectionate fatherly behaviour. This seems unlikely. Margaret Tuohy testified that she had decided to sleep on a table in order to avoid the rats that had been bothering her. When the captain heard, he told her that all she had to fear was 'the two legged rat, and that if I would accept a part of his bed, he would give it to me'. None of this would have come to the attention of the authorities if not for the first and third mates having taken lovers on board. The first mate, James Hill, slept with Dorcas Newman, 'a very interesting girl and a great favorite in the Institution from which she was sent'. Newman became pregnant during the voyage, although the doctor treated her for a fever. When questioned about his failure to detect her pregnancy, the response of the surgeon was remarkable for its cynical attempt to deploy the notion of virtuous female ignorance to defend his professional incompetence or worse:

> I never heard the slightest rumour among the single women, as to their impression that Dorcas Newman was pregnant, and am at a loss to conceive how they can be considered competent judges of a state of which every virtuous female is supposed to be in profound ignorance.

About two months after departure from Plymouth, Newman appears to have overcome her 'profound ignorance' and 'came down crying', telling a married female passenger that Hill had promised to marry her. She now received the bad news that Hill was already married. Newman soon miscarried and died; the baby might even have been aborted by someone on board, as the surgeon's instruments went missing for a time.[67] It was partly in response to such unusual, but notorious outbreaks of sexual disorder that regulation of the shipboard conduct of migrants became increasingly strict in the second half of the century, when around 100,000 single women made the journey.[68]

## Too Much Information?
The stricter regulation of convicts' domestic life was mirrored by increased state intervention in the erotic life of both prisoners and

officials, in the late 1810s and early 1820s. Convict sexuality became subject to closer surveillance, a shift that was part of a larger trend towards more systematic punishment.[69] Official expectations concerning the behaviour of their social betters also changed, partly on the grounds that those who governed Britain's empire needed to set an example to the ruled – both black and white – in sexual as in other matters of personal conduct. Yet in weaving the regulation of sexual morality so tightly into the fabric of penal society, the architects of this new order also provided some of the conditions for transportation's demise.

Christopher Bayly was right to call early NSW an 'imperial despotism in miniature', with its unfree labour, its state-sponsored land-owning class of civil and military officers and free settlers, its ruthless monopolist traders, its finely graded racial and social hierarchies, and its dictatorial governors. Yet this order was inherently unstable in an era of reform and revolution.[70] One impulse that contributed to its demise was a 'revolution' in the government's use of information. This involved the sensational exposure of 'social evil' to parliamentary and public view, often as a prelude to legislative reform. Sexual immorality was among the matters exposed through new techniques developed by the British state for gathering and presenting information. In particular, the evidence collected by parliamentary committees increasingly found its way into print.[71]

These developments also affected imperial rule. The vast intelligence gathered about the penal system made its way across an empire increasingly understood not as a collection of diverse and disparate colonies, but as an integrated unit run according to a uniform moral and administrative code by an elite with a shared sense of propriety.[72] In this climate of increasingly rapid communications, rumour, innuendo and scandal, no less than evidence resulting from more careful inquiry was able to gain the attention of elite opinion in Britain. Meanwhile, the more intense moral purpose that evangelicals and humanitarians brought to the business of governing in the 1830s meant that when scandal was in fact uncovered, the impulse to devise a 'respectable' remedy was stronger than before.[73]

A more efficient diffusion of information throughout the empire, combined with a sense that it was a 'body' in which the disease of one part affected the whole, created not only a new governing order but a new colonial sexual order along with it. For penal Australia, the results would be fatal. The convict system became subject to a degree of scrutiny it could not withstand. By the 1830s the sexual behaviour of convicts – especially men – had come to be seen by British elites as indicative of colonial society's character. Colonists themselves initially rejected the idea of convict sexual depravity as the visible manifestation of a deeper corruption of Antipodean society. By the 1840s, however, they were deploying similar arguments against convict transportation to Van Diemen's Land – transportation to NSW having ended in 1840 – to those which London-based radicals had been using for some years.[74] Aboriginal people, too, were by the 1830s being defined as British subjects,[75] and their sexual behaviour and treatment at the hands of settlers also now came under closer surveillance and regulation.

The changes that occurred in regulating the behaviour of convicts also affected those located higher up in the colony's hierarchy. The years after 1820 saw a clean-up in the conduct of officials, from the governor down, or at least a greater insistence on the appearance of regularity. Having seen off the dissolute Lieutenant-Governor Davey of Van Diemen's Land, Governor Lachlan Macquarie was deeply relieved when the amiable William Sorell and his respectable wife arrived in Sydney in 1817 on their way through to Hobart to replace him. Unfortunately for everyone concerned, it turned out that Mrs Sorell was back in London, and that the lady accompanying the new Lieutenant-Governor was actually a Mrs Kent. When this became known locally, Sorell's opponents began to write letters against him on grounds of his moral conduct. His principal enemy was a magistrate and wealthy businessman, Anthony Fenn Kemp. Kemp had business-related grievances against Sorell and despite having himself fathered a family with a convict woman without marrying her, he made sexual morality the issue: 'It is certainly lamentable to see the Highest Authority in the Island living in a public state of Concubinage; the evil example to the Rising Generation must be too apparent to your Lordship for me to expiate upon.'[76] Kemp related Sorell's immorality to his public role, and to the sexual conduct of those on whom the colony's future moral repute seemed likely to rest. How could an autocratic society be moral if its 'father' – the Governor[77] – had such irregular domestic arrangements, with Government House itself full of his bastards, and presided over by a prostitute passing as a respectable lady? Kemp's letters were not so forthright but he ensured that the message was taken, if not yet acted on.

Sorell was an effective and well-liked governor but, in light of Kemp's campaign, Commissioner Bigge had no choice but to investigate Sorell's domestic arrangements. He found that the main accusations against him were true. Bigge's principal concern, however, was less the immorality itself than the impossibility of its concealment, so that 'the moral feelings of the respectable portion of the Inhabitants have been much hurt by the example of the Lieutenant-Governor; while the worthless portion have found in it a pretext for their own open and repeated disregard of moral decency and domestic obligations'.[78] Sorell's removal followed. His successor, George Arthur, whose private life was unimpeachable, heralded a more austere and authoritarian form of rule.

If governors were needing to clean up their acts, there were similar things happening further down the ranks. John Oxley, the Surveyor-General and explorer, possibly saw the writing on the wall. Having taken a convict mistress on a voyage to Australia in 1812 and fathered children by her, he married a respectable woman in 1821.[79] Certain public officials, however, found themselves victims of the new order. In 1826 Robert Crawford, the chief clerk in the colonial secretary's office, found that many of his duties had been transferred to a new position and its occupant, that of assistant colonial secretary. Why? As Governor Darling explained to Whitehall, Crawford had been living with a woman married to another man. Darling had arranged for Crawford to be warned by the colonial secretary that he should end the arrangement, but he failed to take the hint. The woman's husband made another complaint, and the woman herself was now pregnant by Crawford. As Darling explained, 'it was not likely in my situation I should have shown that disregard to Morality, which his preferment would have evinced'.[80]

In the early 1830s a Sydney magistrate, E.A. Slade, was also dismissed for immorality. He was living with a woman who was not his wife – discreetly, according to his own testimony – but his dismissal at the hands of Governor Bourke came when he was accused of having brought a new female immigrant into his home for immoral purposes. Slade's explanation was that his lover had recently given birth, and needed assistance. Bourke probably saw the matter as an opportunity to rid himself of a magistrate belonging to a hostile faction but what is significant is that he was able to use alleged immorality as a reason for doing so.[81] Bourke's own domestic arrangements were as impeccable as Arthur's; his wife was a well-connected evangelical, and he was an Irish

Protestant of considerable piety. On the other hand, James Mudie, one of Bourke's harshest critics, believed that the Governor's son had fathered a child out of wedlock; an accusation that, if true, might help explain why the younger Bourke, his father's private secretary, returned to Britain in the mid-1830s.[82]

Even the crackdown on colonial officials' behaviour was insufficient to convince a growing chorus of critics in Britain and Australia that convict transportation could be made wholesome. Hostility to convict society among British critics now increasingly focused on its alleged encouragement of sexual depravity, especially among men. While sodomy along with bestiality was usually called 'unnatural crime', a vivid shorthand included terms such as 'vice', 'depravity', 'pollution' and 'contamination'. Witnesses before the British parliament's Select Committee on Transportation (or Molesworth Inquiry) in the late 1830s – most famously, the Catholic Vicar-General of NSW, William Ullathorne – drew attention to the prevalence of 'unnatural crimes', but this 'evidence' cannot be treated as an indication of the prevalence of sodomy among the prisoners. William Molesworth – an associate of Wakefield and radical critic of convict transportation – had handpicked and coached witnesses to ensure he got a result that would discredit convict society. The association between the colonies, convicts and sodomy received reinforcement in the 1840s, with further bad publicity about Van Diemen's Land and Norfolk Island. Opponents of transportation focused on men of proven bad character living in close proximity to one another, the hardened old convict thrown indiscriminately into the company of the unfortunate new chum or smooth-faced boy. The result, said critics, was sodomy on a grand scale.[83] Especially in Van Diemen's Land of the 1840s and early 1850s, anti-transportationists such as clergyman and journalist John West used homophobia as a potent weapon in the struggle for colonial reform.[84] As with the Molesworth Inquiry, much of the alleged depravity was invented by transportation's opponents. Nevertheless, moral panic about sodomy had a material effect on convict men's lives. Supervision of convict men was increasingly rigorous under the convict probation system of the 1840s, which concentrated convict men into gangs. The penal authorities even enlisted doctors to inspect the anuses of convict men while bunks were given side-walls and rooms were lit by lamps designed to burn all night. Ever larger inspection holes appeared in doors and guards wore slippers to surprise unsuspecting sodomites. Yet convicts resisted these encroachments on their freedom and dignity, and some continued to have sex with one another – much as they always had.[85]

By the 1830s sodomy was coming to stand for the unnaturalness of convict transportation as a system of punishment, which, in turn, called into question the moral legitimacy of empire. The attention that convict society's critics drew to sodomy was also part of a generalised dismissal of the colonies as places of loose sexual morality. Sodomy panic, however, was especially tied up with the threat it posed to the model of respectable family life becoming increasingly popular in the early Victorian era. The assembly of large numbers of men, supposedly engaged in sodomy, was as far from respectable domesticity as anyone then could imagine. Its distance from the desired model was dramatised by the alleged practice of sodomites adopting the roles of husband and wife, treating their relationship as a kind of marriage even to the extent of one partner adopting a female name. Here, as in London molly houses, there seemed to be a kind of carnivalesque parody of family life, and at a time when the connections between gender identity and sexual behaviour were becoming more rigidly defined.[86]

The effort to place the regulation of sex at the heart of the colonial order in the 1820s and 1830s had the unintended consequence of planting the seeds of convict society's demise. It was part of an imperial culture of inquiry that was unable to ignore the question of sexual morality and its relationship to government. By the time a new sexual order was emerging in the 1820s and 1830s, what moralists called the 'unspeakable' was actually being spoken about: in the courtroom, in the official inquiry, in the pages of the newspaper and periodical, in the street, hotel and the public meeting, and probably in the drawing room. In Britain itself, new patterns of law enforcement had resulted in a major rise in the number of homosexual offences coming to the courts in the first half of the nineteenth century. A legal language was needed to deal with this phenomenon. It was usually veiled, but the code would have been increasingly recognisable.[87] It is partly for this reason that although 'lesbian' sex among convicts did come to the attention of authorities in the same period, it did not assume anything like the same public significance as male 'homosexual' contact.[88] Even allowing for women being only a minority of the convict population, the lack of a legal language for 'lesbian' sex ensured that it received far less attention in the media and official inquiry. Yet even so, it disgusted authorities and a belief that he had treated the problem with insufficient seriousness contributed to the recall of Sir John Eardley-Wilmot as Lieutenant Governor of Van Diemen's Land in the 1840s. But there was no public scandal.[89] In the case of sodomy, however, an awareness of the 'unmentionable' and the 'unspeakable' became one of the ties that bound Britons together in an empire.[90] Both the convict system and the memory of it became casualties of this scandalous association with sexual disorder.[91]

# CHAPTER 2

# *The Victorian Scene*

## *Moral Disorder*

On Saturday 26 November 1864 Mary Frazer and John Hussell buried their child. The wake, held in Ballarat Street, Carlton, was a memorable affair. The mourners grieved deeply and drank heavily: so much so that, according to the Melbourne *Argus*, 'on going to bed, some of them were so far overcome with sorrow and drink as to mistake the houses and beds to which they retired'. Hussell became very drunk in his own home with a 27-year-old woman named Mary Challenger. Mary Frazer spent the night with her sister.

When Frazer returned home Sunday morning, she climbed in through a window and stepped on a woman's foot. It was Challenger's: she was fast asleep and lying with Hussell. Frazer called in their neighbour, Duncan Stephenson, who had lived for a decade with Challenger, so that he might see what his 'wife' was up to. Stephenson now threatened Challenger with a candlestick, but was dissuaded by Frazer from striking her. Challenger and Stephenson then 'went quietly home together', and '[a] general drink … took place amongst the neighbours'.

A little while later, the couple were heard quarrelling. Neighbours rushed in and found Challenger lying on the floor. Stephenson had, by his own admission, given her a 'kick which would prevent her from lying with another man': a doctor later coyly testified that it was a blow to the lower abdomen. Challenger was taken to hospital for treatment before being allowed to return home. But she deteriorated over the next few days and on Thursday was admitted to hospital, where she died.

Mary Challenger's parting words were that she had 'got it now, and only wondered that she had not got it long before'. The coroner's jury found Stephenson guilty of manslaughter and committed him for trial. He was later acquitted.

This tale from colonial Melbourne is a long way from conventional images of Victorian-era morality, yet also the kind of episode calculated to confirm middle-class prejudices about the lower orders' depravity. Indeed, the *Argus* found in the affair a strange mingling of 'the elements of dissipation, profligacy, brutality, and death'; and, as if to place a comfortable moral distance between its readership and the disreputable folk whose escapades it reported, suggested that Ballarat Street seemed 'a remarkable neighbourhood'.[1] But this is unlikely. There was nothing remarkable in working-class couples living together outside wedlock. There was nothing peculiar in heavy drinking among such people nor, one suspects, in their sometimes finding themselves in unfamiliar bedding. There was certainly nothing unusual about a man beating his wife.

Victoria came to the throne in 1837 and her name, in Australia as elsewhere, would become attached not only to an era but to a code of sexual morality. Victorianism has been seen as 'the paradigm of sexual hypocrisy', Victorian society as one that projected virtue while secretly flouting its own code of conduct.[2] Sex should not be spoken of, especially by women; unmarried women should not even know the facts of life. The reality was more complex: the high premium placed on female sexual modesty, for instance, was surely more likely to induce public chatter than silence about sex.[3] One could hardly seek to define rigid boundaries of morality, or call for the eradication of society's ills, without a public diagnosis and prescription; and colonial society, with its 'shameful' past and continuing imbalance of the sexes, seemed anything but healthy. In any case, the idea of a sexually repressed and hypocritical Victorian age is a product of the early twentieth century, when radical intellectuals began to use the era as a stalking horse to advance their own schemes for sexual freedom. Commentators during the Queen's reign itself looked on only the *early* Victorian era as an age of notable moral severity, seeing in the 'fast' 1860s an almost complete 'rebound from the extreme decorum and ascetic morality that marked the earlier years'.[4] At least so wrote the Victorian coroner and man-about-town Curtis Candler in 1867, but he was by no means alone in thinking so.[5]

The mid-century gold rushes contributed to the predominance of young, footloose men in Australia and to a broader impression of sexual disorder.[6] William Howitt, referring to the settlement in Victoria, criticised 'the rude, chaotic, and blackguard state of the lower society in this suddenly-thrown-together colony'.[7] Gold, said its critics, failed to attach the men to hearth and home, untying domestic bonds which, in a free and easy colonial society, were already fragile. Men rushed about in search of their fortune, while women and children huddled in disordered towns and cities without male protection.[8] Kate Browning, whose husband had departed for the NSW goldfields, was lonely and unhappy at having been left behind with her aunt in Sydney:

> I am afraid my darling husband that you will not do much at the diggings. I told you that you would have no luck having married a very unlucky person. If you make up your mind to stay at the diggings you must come for me for I have made up my mind if it please God to spare us both not to be long from you[.] [I]t is no use telling me to be happy when I keep fancying all sorts of things happening to you and I not with you[.] I would bear the cold dear if I was only with you[.] ... I am very lonely without you and ... I do not hear half often enough from you ...

She ended her plaintive letter with a pointed and hopeful postscript – 'I trust that there is no Gambling at playing cards' – but she was a fortunate woman if that was her husband's only vice.[9] John Buckley Castieau, a Melbourne prison governor whose carousing with prostitutes invariably led to guilt and self-loathing, described his own situation and, by implication, that of other young men during the gold rushes: 'Confined all day I gladly go out in the evening, but where am I to go to, no families know me, no friends but single men no amusements but theirs drinking & wenching.'[10]

### Ignoble Men?

The moral panic aroused by gold echoed long-standing worries about the kind of society being thrown together in the colonies. For large numbers of men in Victorian Australia, marriage to a white woman was out of the question; there simply were not enough to go around.

Liaisons with Aboriginal women, however, were readily formed, whether on a casual or ongoing basis. Some settler men took for granted the sexual availability of Indigenous women, and, from the point of view of lonely hut-keepers, shepherds, stockmen and their employers, they were a welcome compensation for the hardships of life on the fringes of empire.[11] For frontiersmen, the 'use' of Aboriginal women was no more likely to have prompted anguished self-examination than the appropriation of other parts of Mother Nature's bounty. The sexual appetite was as demanding as any other; if it were not satisfied in one way, it would find other – perhaps less wholesome – outlets.

White men saw Aboriginal women as among the spoils of victory in a country they had conquered and celebrated their lust in popular balladry. 'I can ride a hack and fuck a black', were the words of one bushman's song while another celebrated 'Black Alice so dusky and dark'.[12] An anonymous 'Shearer's Song' literally regards the female Aboriginal body as akin to a fresh piece of meat, there for the hungry shearer's taking:

> *Now, I ain't the sort of bloke that takes to fallen ladies;*
> *I'm just the kind wot speaks his mind and swears like bloody Hades.*
> *And when the shearin's done, down Southern roads I'm cuttin'*
> *To find me gin, who's tall and thin and pure as fresh-killed mutton.*[13]

For missionaries and protectors, however, the lust of the white rural workforce threatened the civilising and Christianising process.[14] At the Moravian mission of Ramahyuck in Victoria's Gippsland during the 1860s, Frederick Hagenauer prevented a marriage between a white labourer and a well-educated Aboriginal woman under his charge. Hagenauer had brought Bessy Flower over to Gippsland from a Western Australian mission to teach Christianity to local Aborigines, with a view to her eventually becoming the wife of a respectable Aboriginal convert. The budding romance with her white suitor threatened to upset this plan; so Hagenauer engineered her marriage to a 'half-caste', Donald Cameron, then living on Ebenezer mission in the Wimmera region in north-west Victoria. It was an unfortunate match; Cameron had an affair with another Aboriginal woman living on Ramahyuck. Both Bessy and Donald fell out of favour with white authorities, who enforced sexual proprieties among Aborigines in ways that would have been unthinkable in dealing with free settlers.[15]

There were good reasons to seek to protect Aboriginal women from white frontiersmen. Rapes and kidnappings of Aboriginal women were common and some of the colonists' behaviour notably sadistic. In 1867 Curtis Candler wrote in his journal of an acquaintance who 'used to put a stick of tobacco on the table in his hut and tell the black lubras they might take it, if they could'. The man's dogs would attack the women as they entered the hut, 'and his amusement was to lie on his sofa and watch them struggling for the tobacco against the terriers, when their rags would be torn off them by the dogs'.[16] Sexual maltreatment was a motive for many attacks by Aboriginal men on white settlers, the massacre of the Fraser family at Hornet Bank Station in central Queensland in 1857 being only the most famous example. In the early hours of 27 October a group of Aboriginal men made a surprise attack on the homestead, killed all but one of the males in the house, then raped, killed and mutilated Martha Fraser, a widow, and her two eldest daughters, aged nineteen and eleven. Eleven men, women and children lost their lives in the attack. But white men working for the Fraser family had earlier whipped and raped two young Aboriginal women, while other settlers were said to have allowed 'their black boys to rush the gins' – presumably a reference to notorious abuses perpetrated by native police. The Fraser lads themselves were said to have forcibly taken 'young maidens'.[17] Coming at the same time as Australian colonists were reading lurid accounts of massacre and rape during the Indian Revolt, Hornet Bank seemed to colonists no isolated incident but a local manifestation of the sexual danger that treacherous and lustful savages posed to white women and British civilisation everywhere.[18] For the time being at least, the idea that Aboriginal men lacked real virility (discussed below) gave way to fear of rape. One pastoralist later declared in parliament that for months after the massacre, he slept with a dagger under his pillow that he intended plunging into the hearts of his wife and children should they be faced with a fate similar to the Frasers'.[19]

Sexual relations between white colonists and Aboriginal women were not necessarily violent or exploitative. In some cases, Aboriginal women might have preferred white lovers, or used a liaison with a European to escape an undesired tribal marriage with a much older man. They, or their people, also gained material goods from the exchange.[20] Sexual relationships between white men and black women did sometimes receive approval in high places, so long as they occurred within Christian marriage. In WA, with its preponderance of single white men, settler men's marriages to Christian Aboriginal women gained endorsement in the 1840s as a means of building a more stable domestic order.[21] In South Australia from the late 1840s, the government sought to discourage licentious relations between white men and black women and to promote matrimony by making land available to the married couple. The land did not become the property of the European husband but was rather held in trust for the woman, to discourage the husband's desertion; in effect, he became economically dependent on his Aboriginal wife.[22] Colonial sexual engineers countenanced relationships across racial boundaries, but only where considerations of class and gender suggested the advantages of a match. Their expedients were designed to renovate the behaviour of disorderly working-class males, preserve Aboriginal women from prostitution and rescue 'civilised' black women from a 'slavery' enforced by 'savage' black men. There was no suggestion that a respectable middle-class man should consider marrying an Aboriginal woman, however well educated or conducted she might be. Nor, as we shall see below, was marriage between a black man and a white woman acceptable. The stereotype that rendered inter-racial marriage desirable in certain circumstances – the sexual savagery of the 'native' man – also placed marriage between a black man and white woman out of bounds.

It was a truth universally acknowledged that no white woman would consent to intercourse with an Aboriginal man. Yet there is a half-concealed history of sexual intimacy between Aboriginal men and white women; for example, a likely case of illegitimacy and infanticide in the Bega Valley, NSW, in 1864, the result of a liaison between the daughter of a pioneering settler, Margaret Tarlinton, and a 'half-caste' man, Dick Bolloway, working on her father's station. A witness claimed to have seen the mother burying her newborn child, and years later police did uncover bones that seemed to confirm the story. A court found Tarlinton not guilty 'without a stain on her character' but suspicions remain.[23] Near Yea in Victoria in 1861, Selina Johnson gave birth to a baby boy whose father was Davy Hunter, an Aboriginal employee of Selina's father. The child was the result not of a 'forced act on the black's part', a local official clarified, 'but mutual frequent connection between the two'. The incident attracted great local notoriety but, conveniently for the sake of appearances, the child did not survive. The determined Selina continued to insist that she would wed her Aboriginal lover when she turned twenty-one, while her distraught father offered his property to any white man who would marry his wayward daughter. Eventually, in 1864, Selina did what was expected of her and married a settler.[24]

Still, the fear that black men posed a serious sexual danger to white women was less intense than in most other settler societies. White women were, after all, few and far between on the Australian frontier, and there was a folk wisdom among the colonists emphasising Aboriginal men's lack of sexual vitality. Venereal disease (VD) spread rapidly among Aboriginal people and undermined the health of both men and women, probably inducing widespread infertility. Colonists under the impression it originated among the Aborigines called it the 'native' or 'black' pox.[25] The idea of declining virility sat well with the conviction that Indigenous society was fading away before a superior European civilisation. The most famous accounts of Aboriginal men's misbehaviour by early settlers pointed to the violence they practised against their own women, and their willingness to hand their wives over to white men in exchange for goods – none of which contributed much force to the idea that Indigenous men were ruled by a tyrannical lust.[26]

In any case, attacks by Aboriginal men on white women were rare and paled into insignificance compared with the number of white men's rapes of Aboriginal women. White women had much more to fear from the infidelity of husbands with Aboriginal women. Annie Baxter Dawbin kicked her first spouse out of the marital bed for good after she discovered him 'making a lubra his mistress' in an outbuilding of their pastoral property near Port Macquarie.[27] While Annie enjoyed some financial independence, most women had little choice but to tolerate a husband's dalliances. Divorce became possible in the second half of the nineteenth century but for a woman it was virtually impossible and a road to social disgrace and ostracism. Sexual jealousy must at times have been intense.[28]

When an Aboriginal man did assault a white woman, the vengeance of the colonists could be harsh. Rape was a capital offence in colonial Queensland until 1899, but men found guilty could have their sentences commuted to life. Juries usually recommended mercy when they found a white man guilty. Only one white man convicted of rape in Queensland between 1860 and 1900 was sent to the gallows, but ten Aboriginal men and three 'Kanakas' (Melanesians) lost their lives.[29]

Many colonists believed Aborigines would only be deterred from sexual attacks on white women if they understood that hanging was the likely punishment.[30] But in an 1897 Victorian case involving an Aboriginal man's rape of a white girl, the prosecution did not push for the death penalty because although the man had 'been brought up in a civilised community ... still he might have almost uncontrollable passions, inherent from a long line of savage ancestors'.[31] The widespread belief that no white woman would consent to sex with an Aboriginal man made it very easy to prove in court that a rape had actually occurred; defence lawyers could not convincingly argue that the victim had consented to sex. But it was exceedingly difficult to secure the conviction of a white man for raping an Aboriginal female, for such women were regarded as promiscuous and ever willing to barter their sexual favours.[32] To white settlers, Aboriginal men's willingness to offer sexual access to their own wives in exchange for desired goods and the women's apparent acquiescence in such arrangements were indicative of Indigenous society's overwhelming barbarity.[33]

### Chinese

By 1857 there were on the goldfields many thousands of Chinese men but only a handful of Chinese women. Most Chinese men could not afford to pay for their wives to come out and, in any case, families were hostile to wives' emigration, fearing that a married couple would not return to China.[34] A Victorian parliamentary select committee found that where Chinese had gone to other countries in large numbers, they intermarried with a local 'Asiatic' – although not necessarily Chinese – population. In Victoria, the Chinese men entering the country to dig for gold had no such opportunity, and so 'large masses of men congregate together on the various gold fields, producing, as a necessary consequence, great social evils, immorality and crime, and bringing about results highly detrimental to the habits of the rising generation'. Most were pagans, said the critics, 'addicted to vices of a greatly immoral character'.[35] This language was code for sodomy, easily recognisable to contemporaries from its use in earlier anti-transportation campaigns.

Indeed, it was sodomy rather than the prospect of interracial sex which panicked authorities at this time. Only a few Chinese had married white women. One case study of the central west of NSW found that brides were usually poor and young, and had often been domestic servants before marrying Chinese men. A few made the transition from 'housekeeper' – probably a euphemism for 'mistress' – to wife. Others had been involved in an unsuccessful marriage previously, or were widowed. Stable and – in some cases – large and apparently successful families resulted from these unions.[36]

In colonial discussion of Chinese sexual behaviour, child prostitution attracted unfavourable but less frenzied attention than sodomy.[37] Frederick Standish, the Chief Commissioner of Police in Victoria, claimed that Chinese men had 'a *penchant* for the young' while an 1868 report by the Reverend William Young, a missionary, called for legislation to prevent what the *Ballarat Star* had called 'a wholesale system of debauching, by Chinese, of girls of tender years'. 'The abnormal condition of the great mass of the Chinese people', Young said, 'must necessarily lead to great immorality'.[38] Unlike Standish, Young saw nothing in the Chinese 'race' or 'character' which disposed them to debauchery. Their immorality was a response to the peculiar and unnatural conditions into which they had been thrown by the lure of gold.

### Sex between Men

There were echoes here of arguments about male convicts, whose 'unnatural' crimes had also been explained as a response to the 'unnatural' circumstances in which they were placed. Indeed, the growing emphasis in the 1850s on Chinese sodomites may well have been a method of displacing the embarrassment that colonists continued to feel over the alleged prevalence of sodomy among male convicts. A rhetoric that had been notably successful in undermining the moral legitimacy of the penal system now translated readily from the chain gang to the Chinese mining camp and, rather like the efforts of the anti-transportationists, required precious little evidence of actual sodomy in order to stick.[39] Chinese gold mining, just like transportation, herded together large numbers of men whose previous conduct or racial characteristics pointed to grave and perhaps irredeemable defects of character. The convict and the Chinaman were both natural outsiders in a free and self-governing British community. Once they had been stereotyped as sodomites, neither conformed to the ideal of a real man as one who had sex with women, or the respectable man as confining sex to the marital bed. Neither had the qualities demanded of a citizen and subject: the capacity to rule over the domestic hearth with wisdom, self-control and firmness.

Surprisingly perhaps, witnesses before a NSW select committee on Chinese immigration in 1858 were virtually unanimous in denying that 'unnatural crimes' were common among the Chinese.[40] But as in the case of the occasional Aboriginal rapist whose reputed 'savagery' was invoked in extenuation of his crime, Chinese men's alleged partiality to sodomy could work in their favour. In 1853, when a Chinese man was found guilty of having committed an unnatural offence on a thirteen-year-old boy at Shoalhaven, the judge 'could not reconcile it with his conscience to sentence the prisoner to death … He had only recently arrived in this colony, and probably knew not the heinous nature of the offence'.[41]

In any case, it was impossible for either judges or juries to ignore the reality that white men also regularly came before the courts for unnatural crimes. In his 1958 book *The Australian Legend*, Russel Ward suggested that Aboriginal women helped prevent an outbreak of sodomy among the gum trees. Instead, a cult of mateship developed, which included the idea that the white bushman 'should have his own special "mate" with whom he shared money, goods, and even secret aspirations, and for whom, even when in the wrong, he was prepared to make almost any sacrifice'. For Ward, this close bond was possibly 'a sublimated homosexual relationship'.[42] More recently, historians of homosexuality have suggested that mateship might be the Australian male version of 'romantic friendship' – the nineteenth-century intense, emotionally charged relationships between men, and between women, without necessarily involving physical sex.[43] The 1880 death-cell letters of Captain Moonlite, the bushranger Andrew George Scott, suggest a close emotional attachment between him and his younger companion, Andrew Nesbit. Nesbit died in Scott's arms during a shoot-out with police; Moonlite subsequently wore a ring made out of Nesbit's hair, and asked to be buried with his companion. 'We were one in heart and soul, he died in my arms and I long to join him where there shall be no more parting.'[44] Historians have also pointed to the close emotional bonds between members of the Kelly Gang, notably Aaron Sherritt and the man who eventually shot him for his treachery, Joe Byrne. The historian John Molony believes that 'Aaron loved Joe with a love unbounded',

THE SEX LIVES OF AUSTRALIANS

while a contemporary observer declared the pair were 'more than a brother to each other'. Provoked by the taunts of Byrne's mother, Sherritt, who was by this time in the pay of the police, spat out, 'I'll kill him and before he's cold I'll fuck him'. The threat sealed Sherritt's fate; Byrne got in first.[45] Sidney J. Baker, the scholar of Australian English, believed the Kelly Gang to be 'a group of homosexuals'. But such a judgment seems an anachronism for an era, the 1870s, when rigid distinctions between the 'homosexual' and 'heterosexual' were yet to emerge.[46]

The complexities and ambiguities surrounding mateship and homosexuality are well illustrated by the friendship of Bernard O'Dowd, later a poet, and Ted Machefer, a boyhood friend who became a swagman.[47] Machefer was the son of a French wine merchant, and, in a cellar beneath a footpath in Ballarat, Ted and Bernard would help Ted's father bottle his wine, looking up the dresses of women as they walked over the grating.[48] Bernard congratulated himself on the memorable occasion in the mid-1880s when a young woman with 'an almost transparent white dress' and no drawers stood above the grating for a full five minutes. It 'was a very hot day', he recalled years later, and '[i]t was awfully rude to look, but she was delicious' with her 'thick black' pubic hair, 'the red of her pudendum' moist in the heat of the day, 'nude thighs … like temple columns' and 'buttocks and belly like a noble architrave'. Bernard admitted to having 'often raped her' in his 'dreams & imaginations'.[49] Yet this violent assertion of heterosexuality did not prevent O'Dowd from later telling his lover, Marie Pitt, that he had 'something of the woman-soul … [and] in my psychic experiences had often the woman-body too'.[50] There was an emerging understanding of homosexuality that attributed to 'inverts' a mixture of male and female characteristics and, as a result, a higher order of perception than 'normal' people. Since O'Dowd was familiar with this literature, his cultivation of sexual ambiguity was presumably deliberate.[51]

O'Dowd's 1888 diary certainly makes his affection for Machefer apparent: 'Letter from Ted. He is at Hay. I was awfully glad to get one as I was in a little suspense over him. I wish he would come to me; I long for him sometimes.'[52] At around this time, Bernard wrote Ted what can only be described as a love poem:

*Well, Ted, I sit down to address you*
*(Excuse my bad metres and rhymes)*

*With longings to see and caress you*
*With ardour and joy of old times.*[53]

If a poem such as this one had been written by a 21-year-old man to a female lover, one would assume a sexual interest existed between them.[54]

Yet actual sex between 'mates' in the bush was probably more common than historians of mateship have assumed.[55] The difficulty of proving penetration in sodomy cases meant that many offences recorded as 'indecent exposure' and 'indecent assault' would have involved sex between men, while prosecutors also found it easier to make a case for an attempt to commit an unnatural crime than prove sodomy. Offences that made it to court represent just a small fraction of such encounters on the frontier, where men lived in isolation, drank in binges, and shared beds. In short, 'unnatural crimes' were very difficult for the authorities to detect where two men colluded to commit them and had the wit to take reasonable precautions. Men in prison – even just briefly in a watch house for public drunkenness – were more liable to discovery, as were men and boys working on ships. Sodomy cases also arose from manly environments such as where navvies worked and camped in gangs, or men descended on pastoral stations for the annual shearing. In an environment where manhood was displayed through 'strong masculine labour', heavy drinking and other forms of hard living, men could have sex with other men without experiencing an overpowering sense of abnormality.[56] In 1882 near Wilcannia, 'a powerful middle aged' Irish shearer, John Ryan, was tried for having committed an 'offence ... of a very disgraceful character' on the station cook, Carl Anderson. Both men had been drinking at the races. Ryan, according to Anderson, had on three occasions during the night tried to sodomise him as the two men shared a sofa. Although the cook swore to the offence – claiming that Ryan's efforts to penetrate him had succeeded on one occasion – the Irishman was found not guilty. The two men were later seen drinking together; the celebrated mateship of the pastoral worker had clearly survived this ordeal.[57] In his 1990 novel *Fairyland*, set in Sydney during the 1930s, Sumner Locke Elliott was still invoking this tradition of the gay bushman. In a pub full of manly men, Seaton Daly, a homosexual, feels very much an outsider; but only until his eyes meet those of a rugged bushman leaning against a wall – 'the ultimate in manhood' – who winks at him, 'surreptitiously ... the wink ... as daring as nudity in the street, concupiscent and inviting'. It 'as good as said, come on over here a minute, cobber, and I'll give you the sweetest feel of your darling little arse'.[58]

In Britain and the United States, homosexuality was associated with the city;[59] by contrast, the sodomite's fabled Australian counterpart began as a convict and became an ignoble bushman. While the courts tried to protect women and children from male lust, sex between older men and youths was common enough.[60] William Chidley, the sex reformer, recalled in his *Confessions* having as a youth engaged in mutual masturbation with an older, effeminate man who was his boarding-school teacher.[61] Men also sometimes forced male youths to have sex with them. At Maryborough, Victoria, in 1868, Thomas Martin was sentenced to death for having sodomised Samuel Saxton, a thirteen-year-old boy. Formerly a seaman and miner, Martin now worked as a cook; Saxton did odd jobs around the mill where both he and the defendant were employed. One night in October 1867, Saxton went to his quarters, 'a little place under the cow shed in the yard'. His modest bed was an opossum rug, some calico, and a few bags sitting on some chaff. There, he found Martin, who gave him some small gifts. The boy undressed and went to bed but soon found Martin, dressed only in a shirt, lying on top of him:

… he got into my bed got on my back turned me round put his tool in my bottom it was stiff it passed up inside about two inches he was two or three minutes at this he then pulled it out put it between my legs some wet stuff came from it – he hurt me I did not cry out I was too frightened because he hurt me I had no other reason – he wiped off wet stuff from between my legs with a handkerchief –

There was some grease in a little tin match box in the room he rubbed it on his tool before he went to bed. [H]e wiped his tool after he wiped my legs –

Martin, who was married with three children, later told Saxton that he 'used to do this to boys aboard the Ship I gave them a shilling a time they never said anything about it'.

The boy told his employer, and the police were brought in. Interestingly, the policeman who made the arrest described Martin as 'a Steady man' who 'generally bore a good character up to the time of the Commission of the offence'. A Wesleyan minister who knew the defendant was also prepared to assert that Martin's 'former character has been good. He has not pursued a course of crime through successive years, so as to have become a hardened criminal'. He was 'an honest, industrious & well conducted man'. This pleading appears nonsensical in view of Saxton's claim that Martin had boasted of having paid boys for sex during his days as a sailor, but it seems to have worked; his sentence was commuted to fifteen years with hard labour.[62]

What the statements by the policeman and clergyman suggest is that there was no concept of a homosexual as a particular kind of person defined by his sexual behaviour; that would only come later. Instead, we have a married man of supposedly good character with three children who had erred by assaulting a boy on a spring evening. Both Queensland and WA, following England, abolished hanging for sodomy in 1865;[63] perhaps not coincidentally, these were the colonies where shortages of white women were most drastic. NSW retained the death penalty for almost another two decades (until 1883), and Victoria also kept it after 1864 'for sodomy of a person under fourteen years of age or of any person with violence and without their consent'.[64] This was unfortunate for Thomas Martin, as he would be convicted of sodomy again in 1887; this time, his victim was an eleven-year-old boy.[65]

Sex between men was not just a backblocks phenomenon: it would be peculiar if the massive emigration of young men to Australia to dig for gold in the middle of the nineteenth century did not see similar behaviour in the cities, towns and mining camps of eastern Australia. Large numbers of 'lone' males were thrown together in tents, hotels and boarding houses, remote from kin and with limited opportunities for sex with women.[66] As in the case of bush sodomy, most sex between men, when it was consensual and private, would have passed undetected by the law. Signs of the development of concepts of 'homosexuality' and the 'homosexual' are elusive but Walter J. Fogarty has suggested that they were emerging in NSW law between the 1860s and 1880s. Where the criminal law had not previously separated sodomy from 'unnatural offences' such as bestiality and buggery of a woman, by the 1880s it was defining a series of offences that implied a concept of homosexuality.[67]

### Sex between Women

Sexual contact between convict women came to official attention in the 1840s and, although not featuring in the public rhetoric of the anti-trans-portationists in the manner of sodomy, played a part in undermining the moral standing of the penal system in the eyes of Colonial Office officials and their political masters. There are also references to sex between women in nineteenth-century medical literature and pornography. Chidley referred in his memoirs to an incident in Melbourne, probably in the 1870s, in which a female 'invert' – 'handsome, talented and a great favourite with women' – was caught on top of another woman. Some years later, he encountered another such woman, a Miss Freudenberg, who was 'in the ballet'. 'I had seen young men escort her home after the theatre', recalled Chidley, 'but she would leave them indifferently and retire with her friend, eyeing her as a cat does a mouse'. A little later he caught his own de facto wife, Ada, in a bedroom with Freudenberg. 'Whether she was an invert or what they were doing with their clothes off I don't know', commented Chidley, for 'women will die rather than con-fess'.[68] Freudenberg, whom Chidley presents as predatory, seemed to leave her sexual conquests in a 'fit' – one wonders whether it was actually an orgasm. Ruth Ford plausibly suggests that despite the lack of public sources referring to sexual relations between women, there was likely an 'underworld' of male 'knowledge of "lesbian" sex which circulated through texts, images and bawdy club and pub talk'.[69]

There is also a tradition of 'passing' women; that is, of women who disguised themselves as men by dressing in male attire. We shall prob-ably never know why Flora Warburton, who was charged with being drunk and disorderly, appeared in the Melbourne City Court in July 1863 dressed in male clothing, 'a black suit and a cap'.[70] Nor shall we find out why, about a year before, by which time she was already said to be 'pretty well known to the police', she was found, drunk and 'on the street in an artillery-man's uniform'.[71] Joseph Furphy's 1903 novel *Such is Life* tells the story of a 'passing' woman, Nosey Alf, but he based his famous fictional work on the real case of Johanna Jorgensen. Jorgensen, who had a facial disfigurement after being kicked in the head by a horse, lived as a man, worked at labouring jobs, joined a volunteers' regiment and pursued women.[72]

Cross-dressing did not necessarily have sexual implications – such women sometimes declared that they had imitated men for a lark or adventure, or to get work for which women would not be considered. But in cases where the 'man-woman' had actually married a woman, it was more difficult to avoid the issue of sex. Were such situations a cover for same-sex relations between women? Lucy Chesser's study of the life and times of Edward De Lacy Evans is instructive on this point. Evans was born female and emigrated to Australia in 1856. Less than a year after her arrival, she was wearing male attire and had married a woman with whom she had shared a berth on the passage to the colonies. Passing herself off as a man for almost a quarter of a century, she married two other women during that time, a point that proved fascinating to the colonial press after the discovery at the Kew Asylum in Melbourne in 1879 that she was anatomically female. When it turned out that Evans was also reputedly the father of an eighteen-month-old child, it was as if the circus had come to town. It is unclear how many readers of the Bendigo *Advertiser* accepted the explanation of the current wife, Julia, that she did not know how she had become pregnant but assumed her husband must have smuggled a 'real man' into the family home to perform the deed. The Bendigo *Independent*, in attempting to explain why none of Evans's wives had exposed him, blamed it on 'nymphomania' – a sly, but rare and indirect allusion to sex between women.[73]

### Gold
Evans had been living in Bendigo, a gold town. The goldfields emerged as a site of panic about sexual immorality although, unsurprisingly, sex between women did not much figure. Rather, the dominant gold-fields image is of a rough, masculine community of independent diggers, largely free of gentle feminine influence. While this is an exaggeration, men did vastly outnumber women. According to the estimate of the Inspector of National Schools, A.B. Orlebar, the total Victorian goldfields population a couple of months before the Eureka uprising of 1854 was 'perhaps underrated at 88,000'. Of these, only 13,000 were adult women. Orlebar was no enthusiast for the society that gold had produced in the Victorian hinterland: 'The marriage bond is beginning to be thought a small matter, and many live together as man and wife without religious or civil sanction ... symptoms of moral disorganization in society already shew themselves.'[74] Howitt similarly claimed that Victoria had suffered 'the influx of adventurers'

who were 'extremely rude and vulgar'. 'To marry a stranger here', he declared, 'is a most hazardous affair; for many of these men have left wives at home ... numbers of them marry girls and go off to the diggings, and never are heard of again'.[75]

So, while there were plenty of opportunities for women to wed because they were in such short supply, there were also dangers in succumbing to the temptation, such as marrying a bigamist or being deserted. Many diggers, in any case, preferred the bachelor life, the casual encounter with a prostitute. 'I hear that lots of diggers get married almost every time they go down to Melbourne to spend their gold', Howitt declared; his remark is probably best treated as a euphemistic reference to the binges in which successful diggers engaged while visiting the metropolis.[76] In 1863 Annie Baxter Dawbin heard in Melbourne of a very beautiful young child who was 'raffled' by her mother at £20 a ticket and 'fell to the lot of a wealthy digger, who after taking her home, found to his cost that she was anything but the pure, pretty creature he had taken her for'. The story seems unlikely; but as a recollection of the disorderly recent past, it evokes the sense of sexual propriety having been cast aside.[77] Charles Thatcher, the colonial minstrel, produced a delightful satire on colonial courtship during the gold rushes. After two stanzas describing the supposedly staid customs of courtship 'at home', a sharp contrast is provided by colonial practice:

> But things are far different here,
>     The girls don't consult their relations,
> What's father or mother to them,
>     They follow their own inclinations;
> If you name the day here to a gal,
>     Don't think off her perch it will lick her,
> For nine out of ten will reply
>     *'Lor, Sammy, can't it be done quicker.'*[78]

Lord Robert Cecil, a future British prime minister who toured the Victorian goldfields in 1852, also experienced wry amusement when he encountered a digger 'walking arm in arm with a woman dressed in the most exaggerated finery, with a parasol of blue damask silk that would have seemed gorgeous in Hyde Park'. The woman was 'of Adelaide notoriety', and had 'been graciously condescending enough to be the better half of this unhappy digger for a few days, in order to rob him of his earnings'. Cecil learned from another digger who had been at Bendigo that a woman there 'had offered "to be his wife"' for one shilling and sixpence, a bargain basement price. 'These women', commented Cecil, were 'no rarities on the diggings'.[79]

Yet there were also signs well before the middle of the 1850s that the goldfields were assuming 'a more fixed and stationary aspect'.[80] And for all Orlebar's pessimism about the possibility of domesticating the gold-fields population, he also noticed that there was 'a tendency to give up so migratory a life'. Where once 'there was not one woman to twenty men', the proportion was now one to six, for the diggers were finding it both more economical and comfortable to have their wives with them.[81] His observations about the increasingly settled nature of life on the goldfields are supported by the testimony of other observers of gold-fields life from around this time. William Kelly noticed that women were much more in evidence on the Victorian than on the Californian goldfields, while a Bendigo digger referred in early 1855 to 'a visible improvement in society in very many respects'.[82]

### Love in a Hot Climate

It is usually in moments of disruption – the court case or the official inquiry – that we hear the common people speak of sex. The deep patterns of their behaviour and values otherwise remain elusive. But Benjamin Boyce, an English working-class migrant to SA, took premarital pregnancy for granted when writing to his parents in 1844, assuring them that 'i am gittingh a cumfortuble livingh and i is a doing very well my sun was born on the 22 of March 1843 and whe was married on the 15 of Semptember and is a livingh verry cumfortable together i think she will make me a very gud whife'.[83] For Boyce, there was no shame in marriage following the birth of a child. In May 1860, Annie Baxter Dawbin, now living on a property in Victoria's Western District, was waiting on a fence for her mail to be collected when her husband rode up to tell her that the postman had travelled another way because he had more pressing busi-ness: 'To tell a young man ... that he was to go to Woodford today, as the Minister had gone up there, and his Intended, a very pretty young girl whom he seduced.' 'There is more *honour* amongst the lower, than the higher class of society, in this respect', reflected Baxter Dawbin.[84]

One method that historians have used to explore working-class sexual behaviour is the study of premarital pregnancy rates. Their research suggests that notwithstanding considerable local variation, sex before marriage was very common in colonial Australia, with between a fifth and a half of brides pregnant at the time they wed. There were long-standing customs and traditions in Europe which saw sex as the natural and accepted outcome of a man and woman having made a commitment to marry one another (betrothal), and these continued to influence behaviour in Australia.[85] The custom was underpinned by a 'promise of marriage'; in fact, sex was likely seen as a kind of ratification of this promise, a deepening of a couple's relationship and an important step on the way to the making of a household and family.[86] As Alan Atkinson has elegantly summed up, when the bride went to the altar pregnant, 'the marriage ceremony was like a coronation. It was the celebration of something which had already begun'.[87]

These patterns were not the product of a free and easy colonial society but of long-standing British working-class customs transplanted to the Antipodes. So there is good reason to believe that when the likes of Dr James Beaney complained about the Australian climate intensifying 'sexual expression', and of the nearly unlimited 'freedom of intercourse between the sexes' removing the 'checks upon sexual extravagance' prevalent in more polished Europe, his diagnosis was faulty. Beaney was judging the sexual behaviour of the common people from the perspective of his class; he would have found a similarly alarming 'freedom of intercourse between the sexes' in mid-Victorian Britain.[88]

Fertility patterns provide other clues about the sexual lives of colonial Australians. In the mid-Victorian period a typical bride could expect to be in her early twenties; her husband was, on average, likely to be four or five years older.[89] In view of the double standard of morality which prescribed chastity for women while tolerating a sowing of wild oats for men, the greater youth of the typical bride and the larger degree of control that many families exercised over her behaviour, she was more likely than her husband to be a virgin on her wedding night. Indeed, she might have been rushed into early marriage to ensure a suitable match. As we have seen, there were vast numbers of unmarried and unskilled working-class males in colonial Australia, and the families of the middle class and the better-off working class are likely to have exercised considerable care to ensure that daughters married as well as possible.[90]

A woman who married in her early twenties would have borne, on average, a child every two years for the next twenty to twenty-five years, resulting in ten or twelve offspring, although not all are likely to have survived infancy. For such women, most of their sexual activity must have occurred while they were already pregnant or breastfeeding. Existing pregnancy was the most effective means of 'birth control' in mid-Victorian Australia. The arrival of a new baby is also likely to have hindered sexual activity between husbands and wives by making heavy demands on the time and energy of mothers, aided by taboos restricting sex during lactation. Almost all couples had their first child within a year or two of marriage, and, at best, they could look forward to only about a decade together at the end of their lives without children in the house. Consequently, most sexual activity occurred while they were sharing a home with their children.

The prevalence of large families meant that it was common to have eight people living in a house. Most houses being modest – and working-class homes especially so – married couples must have enjoyed little privacy. In 1860 Joseph Elliott, a printer, and his wife, Rebecca, shared their bedroom with two boys, one of them three, the other still a baby. Their five-year-old daughter slept in the sitting room of their modest four-roomed cottage in north Adelaide.[91] These were respectable and upwardly mobile working-class migrants on whose sleeping arrangements no one would have passed adverse moral judgment. Those further down in the colonial pecking order were less successful in avoiding the gaze of the censorious. A report in the *Australian Medical Journal* in 1857 described a 'a small two-roomed weatherboard cottage, the sleeping room as usual constructed so as to seal the inmates during repose in their own special atmosphere'. Four people slept in a single room, and two of these were children.[92] Certainly, among a large section of the working class, children inevitably grew up 'in the presence of sex'.[93] An 1862 Queensland contributor to the *Australian Medical Journal* declared that the eighteen-month sentence of imprisonment in a reformatory that had been recently inflicted on an eight-year-old boy as punishment for his sexual assault of a four-year-old girl would allow him to 'escape from a home which was alleged to have been of the loosest description, and probably the sphere in which his erotic ideas had been obtained'.[94] J.H. Palmer, a witness before the 1859–60 NSW Select Committee on the Condition of the Working Classes of the Metropolis, assured the committee that proper housing for the working classes would lead to a higher standard of sexual morality:

> The inability in consequence of the small space at command to secure the separation of the sexes, the sleeping of parents and children of both sexes in the same room, and the consequent observation by young children of all intercourse of domestic life, are all calculated to originate impure ideas and desires. The utter want of seclusion and constant association of girls and young women with the other sex can scarcely fail to destroy that natural modesty which is one of the chief ornaments of the female character. The outworks of female virtue once broken down, the utter destruction is comparatively easy, and this is facilitated by the natural excitement caused by a hot climate, and the almost if not actual contact with the opposite sex at night.[95]

Domestic privacy had become a critical marker of middle-class character, as the marital bed was removed from the prying eyes of servants, children and visitors. This ideal, in turn, spawned middle-class images of working-class sexual depravity, in the colonies and at 'home'.[96]

The idea that Australian youths were sexually precocious was widely accepted in the colonial period. Standish told an 1878 select committee that 'sexual intercourse commences at a much earlier period of life here than ... in most British countries'. He had no doubt that girls were generally 'deflowered' at about twelve or thirteen 'by boys about the same age ... or a few years older'.[97] Nevertheless, middle-class opinion also invested heavily in the idea of childhood sexual innocence. Beaney claimed that the child was, as a rule, 'entirely free from any knowledge of the sexual functions, or indeed of the existence of any sensation of pleasure in connection with them', at least so far as they were raised properly.[98] Theorists such as Beaney explained children's sexual knowledge and immoral behaviour as the result of their corruption by others. Sometimes, the explanation was genetic: one non-medical witness before the select committee did not permit a lack of specialist expertise to prevent him from commenting that 'the children of consumptive and scrofulous parents are known to be generally precocious', a point which helped explain 'the desire for sexual intercourse' among the Sydney children.[99] Beaney advised parents who desired 'that their children should be born with such sexual force as shall not overmaster them as they reach puberty' that they needed to 'exercise a judicious continence in their marital intercourse', as if an inclination to sexual excess could be transmitted from parents to offspring.[100] Even Havelock Ellis, a pioneering English sexologist who spent his youth in Australia, believed that the tendency of the eldest child in a family to be unduly sensual was a result of '[t]he warm love of the parents meeting in the first embrace' impressing 'itself on the offspring'.[101]

The idea that a hot climate made for sexual precocity was indebted to some long-standing British stereotypes concerning Italian amorousness. It was probably also a hangover from the traditional belief that the warmer the female body, the more closely a woman approached the kind of lust more commonly associated with male sexual aggression.[102] Yet while some attributed youthful sexual precociousness to a warm climate, others blamed 'the unwise latitude of the colonial home' and 'the absence of those checks which operate so admirably in English home life'.[103] Beaney repeated a complaint often heard in the sexual advice literature of the day when he blamed 'vicious servants' for teaching children to masturbate. The morality of Australian servants, he asserted, was 'of a very inferior order … infinitely lower than it is in the British Isles'. 'The bad practices of these girls must be stamped out', he said, 'if the children are to grow up in that virgin purity which we all expect in those tender years'.[104]

### Prostitution

Well-educated observers such as Beaney made sweeping claims about the depravity of the lower orders but we should not conflate their views with the reality of working-class life. Several witnesses before the 1859–60 select committee were rarely convincing when asked how they knew that particular groups of women they had observed were prostitutes. A medical practitioner, Isaac Aaron, claimed to have seen girls not more than ten years old working as prostitutes. When asked how he could be sure, he replied that '[t]here could be no doubt about it from their appearance and manner'.[105] A witness before the Victorian Select Committee on Contagious Diseases claimed that he could recognise a prostitute from her face. 'Everyone's occupation is stamped upon their features', he declared. The witness added that some prostitutes carried 'an innocent kind of look always after they have been years at it'; but still they could not deceive a trained eye such as his own.[106] For some observers, the mere presence of young girls on the streets or in parks was a sure indication they were harlots. The bailiff in the Sydney Domain was in no doubt that he had seen seventy prostitutes pass by in the course of an hour because of 'their language and the indecency of their behaviour – they pull each other about in an improper way, and their demeanour is indecent'.[107] The likelihood here, and in many similar statements from middle-class observers, is that any female conduct that breached an approved code of respectable behaviour was deemed the mark of a 'public woman'.[108] The elasticity of the term 'prostitute' was well illustrated by the Master of the Benevolent Asylum, S.W. Worthington, when he was asked if there were any such women in his institution:

> Prostitutes? Well, you must call them so in the strict sense of the term, though in many cases they are not what may be called common prostitutes on the town; but there are many young women with illegitimate children, who have been confined in the house.[109]

This last comment indicates that the term 'prostitute' was sometimes used in the more restricted sense, but attempts at enumeration inevitably run up against the problem of sources and definitions. Police estimates are unlikely to have included many women who engaged in 'clandestine' prostitution, often combining part-time prostitution with other occupations. The demand for the services of prostitutes fluctuated, an experience common to many other occupations in the colonial economy.[110]

Colonial authorities regarded prostitution as inevitable. Standish was only more brazen than most when he gave the cause of prostitution as '[t]he natural desire of men'.[111] As Police Commissioner, he kept a close eye on Melbourne's prostitutes, and mixed comfortably among the better class; this personal contact with the *demi-monde* proved useful when he took on the responsibility of pimping for the visiting Duke of Edinburgh in 1867.[112] In fact, prostitution was seen by many as beneficial to society, especially to one in which men outnumbered women. Not only would the whore help save men from sodomy, a shortage of prostitutes was likely to 'render virtuous women less safe' by encouraging sexual assault.[113] Hence South Australian parliamentarians could describe prostitutes as 'a benefit to society, as they might be in some instances a sort of safety-valve by which the crimes against children … were rendered more unfrequent than they otherwise would be'.[114] This perception of her social function meant that proving the rape of a prostitute was virtually impossible.[115]

Whether through marriage, or through prostitution, men were believed to have a right to sex with a woman. Although there was an unfortunate shortage of prospective marriage partners in the colonies, it was correctly assumed that there would always be 'fallen' women willing to cater to men's sexual drives. The dominant view was that women engaged in prostitution due to defects of character, 'strong passion', or an addiction to drink; but not because they had no alternative.[116] Australia's image as a workers' paradise reinforced this idea. Women, it was said, had alternatives to prostitution that were less readily available in the old world. Consequently, prostitutes exercised their own free will in choosing an ignoble, but necessary, profession, rather as the common hangman performed his distasteful duties by choice. The emergence of a Christian 'rescue' movement from the middle decades of the nineteenth century, including the construction of refuges and asylums for prostitutes who wished to repent, confirmed the conviction that prostitutes had only themselves to blame for having fallen into the moral gutter. These institutions also came to house single mothers and their children. From the point of view of the respectable, there was in any case little distinction between a woman who bore an illegitimate child and one who practised prostitution, for each had fallen.[117]

The colonial state concerned itself less with attempting to suppress prostitution and illegitimacy than with obscuring both from public view. The police used the highly versatile vagrancy laws against poor women in de facto relationships but more especially against prostitutes.[118] Yet authorities also became increasingly concerned with prostitution as a public health issue, since the commercial trade in sex was viewed as primarily responsible for the spread of VD. The hereditary nature of syphilis, in particular, was seen as a threat to the 'race'; gonorrhoea, by way of contrast, was sometimes regarded as just punishment for promiscuity, even if its effect on innocent wives undermined this argument.[119] Queensland and Tasmania followed Great Britain in introducing contagious diseases legislation that provided for the compulsory medical inspection of prostitutes.[120] In England, the measure was confined to garrison towns and aimed to provide a clean supply of women to the armed forces. In Queensland and Tasmania, the acts applied to the population more generally, although Tasmania only adopted the law in response to a threat from the Royal Navy to stop calling at Hobart unless its prostitutes were cleaned up for the benefit of British sailors.[121] Victoria also had legislation providing for compulsory inspection from the late 1870s but in the absence of any move to construct lock hospitals in which to incarcerate and cure the diseased, it remained a 'dead letter'.[122] There was discussion in other colonies of the possibility of contagious diseases legislation during the colonial period, but although bills were introduced from time to time, they bore no legislative fruit.

Prostitutes evidently found their clients among all sections of the male population. Machefer heard from 'a prostitute down on her luck' that married men were her most numerous clients, with bank clerks, doctors, lawyers and wealthy businessmen all prominent.[123] Witnesses before a 1878 Victorian inquiry indicated that it was perfectly normal behaviour, barely worth noticing, for 'respectable' and 'reputable' men to use prostitutes.[124] But different kinds of prostitutes catered to each part of the highly segmented market. Standish believed there were four types of establishment in Melbourne.[125] Firstly, there was the high-class brothel of the type he frequented. This was essentially a gentleman's club where wealthy and influential clients could mix with what amounted to a courtesan class left unmolested by police. Then there was 'the respectable receiving house', sometimes called a 'short-time house', where a woman could hire a room for a brief period to deal with a client. The house's owner or tenant – probably a woman – might act as a go-between, matching prostitutes with customers. The prostitute would not usually live on the premises and, in many cases, came into town from a suburban home two or three nights a week. Some shops were also 'fronts' for a brothel or house of assignation.[126] The third type Standish identified was the 'low accommodation-house', essentially a cheap boarding house doubling as a brothel. Publicans also rented out rooms, in some cases to street prostitutes by the half-hour, in others 'on an all-night basis' to a group of women informally attached to the hotel concerned. Hotels, moreover, were used as places where a client could meet a prostitute, who would take him to a brothel, private home, alley or park for sex.[127] Finally, there was 'the lowest style of brothel' – the mere hovel – found in certain back streets of every Australian city. Here, two, three or four prostitutes would ply their trade. Prostitution of this sort was tolerated by police; after all, what else would you expect in a slum? On the other hand, child prostitution, probably common mid-century,[128] became less so in later decades as the state came to strengthen its hand in protecting the young and vulnerable.

### Dirty Linen

By the mid-Victorian period, the ideal of respectability – associated with sobriety, thrift and the restriction of sex to the marital bed – was taking a powerful hold of sections of the working class.[129] Sexuality helped to define colonial society's sense of social order, but it was also constantly threatening to blur the line between the depraved and their supposed betters. No incident better illustrates this point than the Molesworth court case of 1864. Robert Molesworth, a Supreme Court judge, had become estranged from his wife, Henrietta, who was now suing him for maintenance. The judge, in turn, accused his wife of an adulterous relationship with Richard Ireland, barrister, politician and *bon vivant*. Although the jury would ultimately deem this charge unproven, they did find the relationship between Ireland and Henrietta 'was unduly familiar for a married woman'; and, more importantly, that Henrietta had given birth to an illegitimate child by another man while she was in England.[130]

Henrietta gave a remarkable performance in the witness box, achieving a degree of levity that both shocked and amused those present. The following exchange produced roaring laughter in the court:

> Mr Billing: In November, 1862, were you confined with a child.
> Mrs Molesworth: No; I distinctly deny it.
> Mr Billing: Were you confined of a child in October.
> Mrs Molesworth: Have two children in two months? What do you mean, Mr. Billing? No: I was not confined either in October or November.
> Mr Billing: But at the latter end of the year were you confined? In September or December?

MRS MOLESWORTH: What, another child in three months, is it? Let me see – a child in October, another in November, and another in December.[131]

If Henrietta's adultery aroused great interest in the court and out of it, that was nothing compared with the impact of Robert's conduct, most of it laid before the court by his own admission. He had listened at a keyhole. He had beaten Henrietta violently in the street outside their home, blackening her eyes and cutting her lip. He had had sex with her on two occasions after he had accused her of adultery. Sex had occurred in the parlour, breaking the rule that respectable married intercourse occurred only in the marital bed. Most sensationally, his wife accused him of having examined her for evidence of adultery. The judge denied this but he *had* at the very least examined a dress for stains, which were not found wanting.[132] One wit remarked that the judge had a new appointment: 'Inspector of Linen for Ireland'.[133]

The case was reported fully in the press. That the scandal had involved members of the colonial elite, including a senior judge and a former solicitor-general, was a particular problem for those who regarded themselves as the arbiters of colonial morality. The apparent nymphomania of Mrs Molesworth could only explain so much, although Annie Baxter Dawbin, who was living in the same boarding house as Mrs Molesworth in 1864, described her as 'much more of a prostitute than many who gain their bread by the sale of their poor bodies and souls'.[134]

Salvation, however, was at hand for those who needed to account for this strange affair: for neither the class of the transgressors, nor their colonial status, needed to be invoked. The Molesworths, after all, were Irish, as was Richard Ireland; and neither the *Age* nor the *Argus* overlooked the point. As the *Argus* commented,

There is something in the case … that is quite un-English, and with an odour about it such as only one nationality in the world could furnish. … where can we read anything to match this very Irish story?[135]

The *Age*, while commenting that 'Hibernian manners and customs will not account for this strange proceeding', nevertheless added:

It is right, perhaps, to make some allowance for the nationality of the principals in this affair. Some latitude, even in morals, must always be permitted to the inhabitants of that happy land where people and pigs huddle promiscuously. But even the license of that primitive and innocent state of society was exceeded.[136]

Not even Protestant religion, it seems, could save the Irish in these circumstances. Their sin was racial, not religious.

### *Lifting the Veil*

Respectable Victorian women were not supposed to appear in public as desiring, sexual beings.[137] At the same time, the cloak of the law gave legitimacy to the discussion of sexual matters, even while commentators complained about the public washing of dirty linen. It was the public aspect of the Molesworth case that some professed to find most disturbing. The press dealt more harshly with husband than wife because it regarded his parsimony as the reason why she had brought the case to court: he had done too little to keep the matter from public view. The *Age* wondered whether it had ever occurred to Molesworth that 'having lifted the veil from the abominations of his matrimonial state, he may have familiarised the minds of pure women with the obscenities of men, and decent men with the depravities of impure women'.[138]

Respectable folk designed rituals that allowed them to explore the erotic under cover of the quest for religious enlightenment, aesthetic enjoyment or useful knowledge. In the first category was the séance room, integral to the practice of the spiritualist movement, which could acquire a sexually charged atmosphere in the intense effort of believers to communicate with the dead. An account by James Curtis, a leading Ballarat spiritualist, of a local circle that met regularly between 1878 and the mid-1880s makes this apparent. Curtis recalled the appearance in a darkened room on one occasion of spirit lights, which rested on his 'naked skin' and on an approach to his hand 'became human fingers with soft and gentle touch'; in reaching his face they 'changed to lips with loving kisses'.[139]

The appreciation of art and culture could also contain an erotic edge; a visit to the opera or theatre usually involved more than one kind of performance. In the first place, there was what was happening on stage. Some moralists, in the finest Puritan tradition, found that in itself sufficiently objectionable. The evangelical preacher Henry Varley, admittedly one inclined to see lasciviousness in places where others did not, believed that 'the representations, dresses, actions, and postures, of half-naked women, covered with tight-fitting, flesh-coloured draw-ers, armlets ... are purposely designed to stimulate the sensual nature and lustful passions of the male spectators'.[140] Even a more sensible social purity campaigner, Dr Richard Arthur, advised that theatres were probably best avoided by young men struggling for sexual self-control.[141]

Yet the happenings on stage were the least of it. At the opera house and theatres in Melbourne, prostitutes assembled at the 'entrances to the stalls and in the vestibules'; so much so that the latter became known to racing enthusiasts as 'the saddling paddock'.[142] The journal-ist John Stanley James described the theatre vestibule as one 'of the chief marts of Melbourne prostitution'. Meanwhile 'dressed girls' loi-tered in front of the theatres each evening, exposing their moral contagion to a womanly virtue assumed to be teetering perpetually on a dangerous precipice: 'Virtue sees Sin in the stalls, clothed in rich gar-ments and sparkling with jewels; whilst she in the pit wears homespun.'[143] Castieau described the audience at a Melbourne entertainment venue as 'of a most villainous and Profligate character. Dirty gents, Jew Boys, Grey headed reprobates, and repulsive prostitutes'.[144]

The visual arts also worried moralists. H.B. Macartney, the Anglican Dean of Melbourne, refused to allow his daughters to travel to Melb-ourne via the Fitzroy Gardens after some nude statues appeared there.[145] And fifteen years later, in the controversy unleashed in Melbourne by the display in the National Gallery of Jules Lefebvre's nude *Chloe*, a correspondent with the *Argus* pointed out that there were 'at least three females to one male' among the visitors to the gallery, 'and all the pic-tures in the neighbourhood of this particular one have to be passed by, for no decent woman with her daughters would dare to stop in front of it'. He concluded that the picture was on display for the 'delectation' of men, 'and only those of vicious proclivities'.[146] The Victorian Coroner, Curtis Candler, reported the disappointment felt by men who attended a display 'expecting to see almost nude women'. The male and female figures, however, were thoroughly draped. One frustrated visitor complained that the whole thing 'was a swindle' and 'so decent' that the proprietor ought to be prosecuted 'for obtaining money under false pretences'.[147] Candler, meanwhile, reported that a customs official had hit on a formula for distinguishing porn from art: 'in art there is no hair'.[148] For the Victorians, the female nude functioned as a symbol of art's highest spiritual ideals but in pornography acted as a stimulus to base desire. As a marker of the boundary between art and obscenity, the moral and immoral, how the female body was presented was of overwhelming concern to those seeking to maintain propriety and combat lewdness.[149]

The controversy over anatomical museums also illustrates the complex eroticism of the Victorian era. From time to time in the colonial period, an individual claiming medical expertise would set up an anatomical museum and profess that its aim was to disseminate useful knowledge. The proprietors, who provided lectures to accompany the exhibits, only allowed men and women to visit on separate days. At best, these exhibits were a primitive form of sex education; at worst, a freak show in wax for the prurient. For instance, exhibit number 176 at the Anthropological Museum of Dr Jordan and Dr Beck was 'Virgin breasts. This model exhibits those rare beauties so peculiar to the female form, without which she would be despoiled of half her elegance and loveliness'. It is little wonder that this establishment found itself the subject of a vigorous press campaign, with the *Age* thundering that the proprietors 'accumulate models and casts of the filthiest kinds until the chief feature of the show was the horrible pathological distortions which the instincts of mankind have ever kept as secret as possible'. After an unsuccessful libel suit against that paper, Jordan and Beck closed their museum.[150]

It was women's eyes and ears that caused most concern, for in the Victorian respectable ideal they were supposedly ignorant of sex – or at least should pretend to be. According to Penny Russell, the Victorian obsession with the imposition of external restraints on women's sexuality, including the stress on fostering their ignorance of sex, shaded into a conviction among some men 'that it was ignorance alone which kept women chaste'.[151] At the very least, for the sake of social propriety, ladies – especially single ladies – were expected to feign sexual ignorance. When they did not, they inevitably raised the suspicion that their air of respectability or gentility was a mere charade. Some men were evidently excited by this possibility, for it hinted at sexual availability, even while most men expressed surprise or disgust at the breach of social decorum involved.

The 1860s diary of Curtis Candler contains many stories of apparently respectable women who know more than they should, and say things they should not. On one occasion, a conversation at the Melbourne Club turned to a story of a man with two penises that had appeared in a recent edition of the *Lancet*. 'There were a lot of young fellows present', Candler recorded, 'and the nature of the remarks may easily be imagined'. Yet what Candler thought most remarkable was a comment of 'R' who, after listening for a while, told Candler: "Mistress R was talking to me about this very thing this morning at breakfast. She told me she remembered a *precisely parallel case* when they were quartered at Malta.'" Candler evidently considered it surprising, or at least amusing, that a woman had apparent first-hand knowledge of these details.[152]

Well-bred women were not necessarily ignorant of sex, nor passionless in private. But in the language they used to communicate about sex, they would mainly have avoided specificity about anatomical matters. It was a language, Russell suggests, that would have been replete with 'significant glances, nods, and silences', yet 'fully comprehensible to those who spoke it', and well capable of transmitting gossip and scandal.[153] These women were setting themselves apart from the worldly working-class girl who used filthy language without compunction. But more subtly, they were also distinguishing themselves from the social climbers of the bourgeoisie by avoiding an excessive prudery.[154] Mrs Molesworth had overstepped the mark by a long way, and so presented herself as a fallen woman, unable to maintain the delicate balance on which a gentlewoman's status depended.

We encounter both genteel and fallen women in Candler's diary. He reported that when he first arrived in the colonies, he found the girls 'much faster' than those he had left behind at home. Candler recalled dancing with an unmarried woman in Hobart in the early 1850s; she began quoting from Thomas Moore's *Lalla Rookh*. On reaching the lines, 'Like a bride, full of blushes, when ling'ring to take / A last look of her mirror at night 'ere she goes!',[155] Candler recalled that 'she looked archly and stopped: then she said, "Now I wonder how Tom Moore knew what a bride would do under such circumstances"!'

But this euphemistic reference to sex is a far cry from the behaviour attributed to one Annie Macdonald, 'a really lovely Paphian [prostitute]', who appeared before the bench in Hobart for using indecent language. The magistrate asked what she had said but a coy policeman refused to repeat it. Macdonald helped him out:

> 'Oh!' she interrupted. 'I'll tell your worship what I said. I was walking along the street quietly, when this policeman stopped me, and asked me very rudely where I was going to? I told him to the Hungarian barbers. "What for?" said he, "Why to get my c– shampooed." – that's all I said.'[156]

Men were instrumental in defining the dominant codes of morality and behaviour for different varieties of womanhood. '[M]en, as a general rule, don't care about a bed-fellow with refined mind, so that her body is what they fancy', reflected Annie Baxter Dawbin.[157] But women such as Baxter Dawbin also drew boundaries around moral conduct by throwing their erring husbands out of the marriage bed. Eliza Clarke, wife of the wealthy squatter W.J.T. 'Big' Clarke, inflicted this penalty on her husband when she learned that he had impregnated her beautiful younger sister, Jane.[158] The Molesworths also maintained separate beds as their marriage fell apart.

Both Eliza Clarke and Annie Baxter Dawbin were able to exercise power over their husbands because of their privileged class and wealth. Baxter Dawbin threatened to return to England if her husband insisted on his conjugal rights while Clarke was a big spender even before her husband's infidelity with Jane came to light. When it did, she blamed her husband rather than her sister, insisted that he give Jane £3000 and a first-class ticket to England, and treated herself to some expensive retail therapy.[159] Mrs Molesworth's public disgrace was, to a great extent, a result of her financial dependence on her husband. The famous court case was an outcome of her effort to have him pay a higher proportion of his large judicial salary than he wished to surrender to a wife he believed to be adulterous.

There was also some recognition that normal women were capable of enjoying sex. Colonial medical opinion of the second half of the nineteenth century sometimes recognised women's capacity for sexual desire and pleasure without ever quite detaching it from the maternal impulse. Medical writers maintained a clear distinction between the normal male sexual appetite, which they presented as ravenous yet controllable, and normal female sexuality, assumed to be considerably less ardent. Dr Beaney's opinion was that '[t]here are thousands of women who would prefer to hold congress with their husbands once or twice in the month only, and who submit to more frequent intercourse out of a sense of duty or affection'.[160] He presented excessive sexual desire in women as a dangerous illness that, if it could not be cured by '[m]oral suasion', should be subjected to surgical treatment. 'Should the clitoris have been long subject to undue excitation, and exceed its proper proportions,' he declared, 'it can be reduced in size by excision, or be completely extirpated'.[161] Alexander Paterson, a Sydney doctor, agreed with Beaney that there were sharp differences between male and female sexual instincts:

> Many married men fancy that their wives expect and desire coitus with certain frequency, and exert themselves … to satisfy this self-imposed and imaginary duty to the prejudice of their health. They are not aware that women generally have very little sexual appetite compared with men.[162]

Paterson believed that women had a capacity for orgasm – and even that they 'derive from it as much, and in many cases infinitely more pleasure than the man' – but only when coitus was accompanied by 'other feelings' such as a love for one's husband and the 'desire to have children'. He understood sex as for pleasure as well as for procreation, but in the case of women, sexual desire could not exist independently of women's reproductive function. As he commented, 'Women allow themselves to become sexually excited during coitus for other reasons than that the coitus itself necessarily excites them'.[163] Similarly, Walter Balls-Headley, another Australian doctor, attributed young girls' love of dolls to the 'sexual instinct' found only in girls 'for the bringing up of the next generation'. This instinct, he claimed, had 'no reference to sexual appetite, which may develop subsequently as a cloak for propagation'. Whereas it was the sexual appetite – 'the desire of gratification in the act of union' – which was most pronounced in men, in women it was 'the natural, unreasoning impulse by which she is guided to the propagation of the race'. Maternity lay at the heart of the female sexual experience; women who did not marry and bear children were 'unsexualised'.[164]

A woman's orgasm, then, was assumed to have a different basis from a man's, but all of these doctors believed that women did experience a form of sexual pleasure. The idea that Victorian-era medical opinion presented women as sexually passionless is without foundation. In 1895 the Reverend F.B. Boyce had no doubt that women's sexual passions could be strong when he advised the octogenarian politician and old bull Henry Parkes why he should not marry the beautiful 23-year-old Julia Lynch:

> … we are all very human and the difference in age between yourself and Miss Julia can never be ignored. The question from a sexual standpoint must be considered. Her sexual instincts may be strong and in two or three years or less you may not be able to satisfy them. Is that likely to be happiness then? I know a case in which a man of 75 married a girl under 30 and the drain on his constitution was such that he died within three months: weakness then paralysis! … You understand and I need say no more … I earnestly ask you to reconsider the whole matter. A man must DISCIPLINE *himself sometimes.*[165]

Boyce's well-meant advice revealed not only his belief that a female sexual appetite could be strong, but that talk about sex between men was an accepted feature of colonial culture. Where women were expected to avoid the discussion of anatomy, there were no such strictures on men speaking among themselves. The habit, no doubt, began at school. The eleven-year-old victim in an 1887 sodomy case admitted under cross-examination that he knew 'of no decent boys in the school, we all tell each other dirty stories and talk about women & girls'.[166] Candler repeated a story about a boy of about twelve, who was sitting in the drawing room of a house with his young maiden aunt. When a male visitor asked the boy if he was thinking of marrying soon, the lad replied coolly: "'No, I fancy not. I dont think I shall marry at all: I mean to keep a wo–" – but here his aunt, blushing crimson, stopped his saucy mouth with her hand and checked all further revelations as to his future domestic arrangements.' The boy may have had a 'saucy mouth' but the spinster aunt quickly recognised the nature of the embarrassing scheme the boy was announcing.[167] Havelock Ellis, living in Grafton in the 1870s, recalled that his fellow male boarders told 'obscene stories of a monstrously crude and impossible type', utterly devoid of wit. 'No doubt my companions were more chaste in life than in speech', he reflected.[168] Curtis Candler, who, by way of contrast, moved in circles where wit if not chastity was abundant, recorded in his journal in October 1867 that Justice Redmond Barry had recently told him of a rape case in Ballarat 'in which the first offence was condoned by the lady and peace between them was ratified by a loving kiss, of an unusual kind, and where osculatino [kissing] is not generally performed; the ardent man, however, pushed his success too far, and on a repetition of the offence, the outraged one prosecuted him'.[169]

In the clubby atmosphere inhabited by ruling-class men, sexual gossip was a source of entertainment but their lives were also guided by the assumption that healthy men required regular sex. They frequented the better class of brothel and mixed freely with prostitutes. Men such as these shared pornography, kept mistresses and generally enjoyed the privileges that came with social status and a good income.[170] None of this is to suggest that we find among the male colonial elite a single code of sexual morality: there was variety in that quarter as elsewhere. Some kept mistresses and fathered children by them; some did not. Candler had four children by a woman named Laura Kennedy before marrying her, but he did not publicly acknowledge either his wife or children, nor did he let the relationship get in the way of a bachelor lifestyle.[171] His friend Redmond Barry remained unmarried while keeping a mistress, Louisa Barrow, and fathering a family by her.[172] Henry Parkes, the 'Father of Federation', was also the father of a family with a mistress, Eleanor Dixon, who despite being forty years younger became the second Lady Parkes after his first wife, Clarinda, died in 1888. Like Barry, Parkes managed to avoid scandal, although the affair was common knowledge and social propriety dictated that Government House be barred against Eleanor even after marriage.[173] The SA parliamentarian Charles Kingston was less fortunate. In 1886 he was named as the co-respondent in a divorce case, and although his adultery threatened to land him in disgrace, Kingston's vast talents and, perhaps, a colonial society actually more relaxed about such things than it could appear, meant his career was not ruined. Indeed, he later became a successful premier and, like Parkes, a Federation Father.[174]

A contrast with these men is provided by Sir William Stawell. An Anglo-Irishman like Barry, Stawell became an agnostic and 'took part in some of the more dissolute amusements of the era'.[175] On one occasion in 1848 Stawell was invited by his mother-in-law to listen to a sermon by the new Church of England Bishop of Melbourne, Charles Perry. Stawell replied, 'I am neither good enough nor bad enough to meet a Bishop, so I cannot go'. He must have changed his mind, however, because he did attend and Perry's sermon had a profound influence on him. Stawell soon returned to the faith in which he had been raised 'and became a devout Churchman'.[176] Barry is said to have 'kept alive memories of Stawell's early days in the Colony' which 'Stawell would have preferred forgotten'. Despite this history, in 1857 Stawell was appointed Chief Justice of Victoria in preference to Barry. Most clubmen were not tamed so readily but Stawell's experience is a reminder that, in sexual matters, human beings are something more than the playthings of powerful biological drives, compelling psychological forces or influential cultural mores. They are also the keepers of a conscience and it was the self-appointed task of evangelical churchmen such as Perry to remind them of it.

Stawell retained an Irishman's sense of humour. Candler noticed at a social function during Prince Alfred's visit to the colonies that whereas Perry 'looked grave' after the Prince's use of the word 'backside' on two occasions, the Chief Justice's 'eye was twinkling with fun'.[177]

## *Modernity*

In July 1875 an English youth of sixteen arrived in Sydney on the emigrant ship, the *Surrey*. He was officially the 'captain's clerk', for the skipper was the boy's father and the family had decided the lad should take a voyage to improve his health.[178] The young man remained in Australia, to pick up some colonial experience by working as a teacher. He was to spend the next three and a half years in NSW, including in two 'Half-time' bush schools at Sparkes Creek and Junction Creek, near Scone in the Hunter Valley.[179]

Over these years, the youth developed 'an affection', as he called it, 'for two women', one of them just ten years old, and he experienced emotional stresses – both sexual and religious – that are quintessentially 'Victorian' and seem unusual in an intelligent and sensitive young man only in that they were recorded with such disarming honesty.[180] After returning to England in 1879 he studied medicine for seven years but he would be no 'ordinary medical practitioner'.[181] Instead, he would be one of the most famous intellectuals in the world: Sigmund Freud would keep a photograph of him on his office wall.[182]

Henry Havelock Ellis would later reflect on that year he spent in the lonely bush at Sparkes Creek:

> I met no woman there, or man either, who meant anything to me, but I was to find there one who must mean more than any person: I found there myself. This year … was to be in all exterior relationships the loneliest, the most isolated, of my life. But it was also to be for my interior development the most fateful, the most decisive, of all my years.[183]

It was here, said Ellis, that he 'discovered the universe', himself, his art and his science.[184] Perhaps sexual modernism was *not* born in the shadows of Mount Tingaroo in 1878. But nobody would more powerfully influence understandings of sexuality in the period to be explored in the remainder of this book than the young, somewhat aloof schoolmaster who lived for a year in that lonely corner of the Australian bush.

# Chapter 3

# *A Pleasant Amusement?*

## Civilisation and Degeneration

By the last quarter of the nineteenth century, lovers of order and propriety rarely blamed the imbalance of the sexes for the depravity they
still saw all around them. In 1891 there remained many more white
men than women in Australia – 1,704,039 compared with 1,470,353 –
and males continued greatly to outnumber females in the backblocks.[1]
But in the cities, most young men no longer had any reason to expect
lifelong bachelordom.

Panic about sex took a new turn. Now, it was 'modern' social conditions that accounted for the unnatural sexual life of the people. While
not confined to Australia, the problem was especially pronounced in
the colonies because of their prosperity, democracy and egalitarianism.
Feminists blamed the failure of the state to control men's bestial sexual
drives; pronatalists – those who encouraged higher rates of reproduction – saw the selfishness of married women, their desire for pleasure
rather than procreation, as the main reason for Australia's ills.

Walter Balls-Headley, a Cambridge-educated physician and lecturer
at the University of Melbourne on midwifery and women's diseases,
knew that something was very wrong with modern civilisation in
Australia. In *The Evolution of the Diseases of Women* he condemned late
marriage, which he attributed to men's love of pleasure, comfort, socialism and strike action, and women's taste for tight-lacing and education.
There was no reason, he said, 'why the satisfaction of the sexual instinct
and the act of propagation should be deferred to such a late age of life'.

59

Neither animals nor natives delayed marriage and child-bearing so unnaturally, nor did they wear tight-fitting dresses. For Balls-Headley, women existed to bear children; men's role was to provide for them. Accordingly, educated women posed a racial problem:

> ... high mental culture is antagonistic to healthy sexual development and child-bearing ... These women, who are apt to be highly attractive by their refinement of feeling and appearance, are frequently devoid of sexual appetite of any kind ...

Educated women's distaste for child-bearing was producing social-climbing but frigid women; an argument which only made sense if women's sexuality was seen to derive from their will to be mothers.[2]

Balls-Headley was a distinguished professional with the status and privileges that such men enjoyed even in the dangerously over-civilised Antipodes. William James Chidley, by way of contrast, was a poor man who ultimately paid for his conviction that the sexual life of the people was unnatural by suffering public condemnation, criminal prosecution and confinement in an insane asylum. Chidley was born in Melbourne around 1860, the son of a toymaker involved in a 'free love' sect devoted to the teachings of the Swedish philosopher and seer Emanuel Swedenborg. Living mainly around Melbourne and Adelaide, the younger Chidley supported himself by producing drawings for medical texts of the very kind in which Balls-Headley reflected on the problems of modern humanity.[3]

From his wide reading and an active but guilt-ridden sex life, Chidley developed the theory that there was something profoundly wrong with the way in which modern people had sex. The introduction of an erect penis into a vagina, he said, was unnatural and produced shocks to both men and women that led to their physical and mental deterioration. As he explained in his 1911 pamphlet, *The Answer*, 'the crowbar has no place in physiology'.[4] Sex, claimed Chidley, should only occur in the spring, when the vagina would act as a vacuum and so draw the flaccid penis inside. Like Balls-Headley, Chidley based his views on observations of the animal kingdom; he was particularly impressed by the lessons offered by the sex life of horses.[5]

Although Chidley gained a following and found people willing to defend him from state persecution, he was also widely regarded as a crank. Yet he and Balls-Headley occupied some common intellectual territory; notably, a conviction that over-civilisation was producing racial degeneration. Where, however, the medical man saw a falling birthrate and women's improved social status as its clearest manifestation, Chidley blamed a social order based on an aggressive male sexuality. Balls-Headley's theories were largely consistent with a belief in a woman's role as a breeding machine, and were bolstered by his professional standing. Chidley's ideas challenged the patriarchal social order that Balls-Headley defended and were the work of a self-educated radical and freethinker. So Chidley died in poverty while Balls-Headley was showered with the usual sorts of rewards bestowed on successful men who parrot the prejudices of middle-class opinion.[6]

### Sex Wars

Balls-Headley and Chidley were each intervening in a public debate that revealed a society preoccupied with sex and reproduction and increasingly convinced that the future of humanity depended on how it organised them. It is not that a Victorian reticence was cast aside in favour of openness. Rather, participants in public debate now developed new ways of talking about sex. In doing so they drew on the emerging field of sexology, but it is far too simple to argue that science was displacing religion or morality. Modern understandings of sexuality in fact often developed out of an intense spirituality that refused to reduce erotic drives to biology. Sexual behaviour was now less likely to be seen as a response to environmental conditions, or some momentary stimulus or impulse. Sex was becoming central to the meaning of selfhood; it was at the core of character.

Two phenomena stand out as having done most to shape the sexual history of the period. One was the dramatic decline in the birthrate in the period after about 1870, which worried Balls-Headley. This trend caused a panic about the prospect of 'race suicide', but also contributed to a crisis in the middle class. It was suggested in the previous chapter that respectable women's adherence to a certain code of sexual behaviour became a critical marker of identity, thereby distinguishing them from the 'depraved' lower orders. But the widespread practice of birth control among apparently otherwise good and decent women from the better-off classes underlined for some middle-class men a sense of conventional morality's fragility. It suggested that new and insidious forms of sexual depravity were infesting the very people – 'respectable' women – who really ought to be the strictest guardians of propriety.

The judgments of such men about the drop in moral standards were confirmed by the connection they saw between the image of the 'New Woman' associated with the feminist movement, and the decline in the birthrate. Feminists discussed the 'sex question'; they advocated smaller families; they preached the evils of modern marriage; they argued in favour of improved educational opportunities for women; a few were even known to advocate contraception – it did not take much for a hostile judge to put all of this evidence together and hang the defendant. Feminists who blamed declining birthrates on the prevalence of VD among men seemed unconvincing in the face of such an overwhelming case for the prosecution.

The growing preference for small families would have been bad enough for the pronatalists but because it was accompanied by indications that some women were achieving this end through contraception rather than abstinence, the phenomenon raised profound questions about female sexuality. If sex was not essentially for reproduction, marriage seemed to become 'a mere sexual compact' and sex just a 'pleasant amusement'.[7] Moralists worried that women were having sex for pleasure, rather than out of a sense of duty to society or their overwhelming desire for motherhood. Moreover, if women could have sex without the natural consequence – pregnancy – their chastity would be sorely tested. T.P. Lucas, a doctor, addressed the Young Men's Christian Association to this effect in Melbourne in 1885. 'Nature is one', he declared,

> and laws apply generally to the whole animal kingdom. In accordance with this law woman at stated periods would be prepared for generation. And so she is. If, however, the fact were made known to her intelligence as it is to the lower animals, no woman could be virtuous; and humanity would sink into animalism, and collapse socially; and so the law is added to, and woman is specially defended when she is weakest.

This explanation portrayed female sexual morality as a very fragile thing indeed, suggesting that women had a sexual appetite that could not be reduced to the status of cover for maternal instinct.[8] If the fear of pregnancy and its corollary, female 'modesty and a fear of shame', constituted a 'special safeguard' designed by God to defend womanly virtue, contraception posed particular dangers to the moral order. Henry Varley, a fiery Protestant clergyman and social purity campaigner, believed that the 'disgusting doctrines' (regarding birth control) found in popular texts led to sexual excess, a danger to the morality and health of married couples.[9] The panic over Australia's declining birthrate was about the contested meaning of female sexuality. And it was about the fundamental purpose of sex.

The other major development of the period was the campaign to reform male sexuality, which forms the main subject of chapter 4. Marilyn Lake has claimed that, in the 1890s, there was a struggle for control of the national culture between men and women – a sex war – and that male sexual behaviour was an issue at the heart of this conflict. Writers in the famous Sydney *Bulletin*, she suggests, celebrated the wandering bushman in his freedom from domestic constraints, and so produced a political position she calls 'masculinism'. It upheld the right of men to enjoy various pleasures and freedoms without the interference of female busybodies, nosy parsons or a nanny state. Feminists, on the other hand, condemned the *Bulletin*'s idealisation of the nomadic bushman, and favoured a domesticated masculinity in which men assumed the responsibilities of a breadwinner while treating their wives with gentleness and respect.[10]

But what was the outcome of this sex war? Did it have a clear winner? Lake believes so, suggesting that it was not the vision of male freedom from domesticity but rather the feminist movement's ideal of a more self-controlled and chivalrous masculinity that emerged triumphant.[11] The victory of the domestic ideal, Lake argues, was manifested in Justice H.B. Higgins's *Harvester* judgment of 1907 and the concept of the family wage that it enshrined.[12] In his famous Arbitration Court ruling, Higgins assumed a male breadwinner who would provide for his family through wage labour; not one who would waste his family's income on prostitution, extra-marital sexual conquests or drinking and gambling. The family wage concept also registered the declining size of Australian families. Higgins allowed for three children; a basic wage founded on this assumption before the 1890s could hardly have been taken seriously.

Higgins's own experience of family life registered the shift towards smaller families that his most important intervention in Australian social policy recognised. The Higginses had only one child: a son, Mervyn, who was killed in World War I. Higgins's biographer reports that medical advice deemed his wife's health too precarious to bear another pregnancy, and that the couple possibly practised abstinence in order to avoid an unhappy outcome.[13] In their lives, the Higgins family embodied the trend towards smaller families, triggered by a preoccupation with women's health. Pregnancy was a peril in the nineteenth century, with death in childbirth a common danger to Australian women. This context was critical in conditioning women's experiences of, and attitudes to, sex. It meant, for instance, that most sex was haunted by the fear of pregnancy.[14] Yet the Higginses' experience also demonstrated the possibility that family limitation might lead to a grief-stricken, childless old-age in the unforeseen and unhappy circumstances of a cherished child's death. The sons of Australian families who fought and died in Gallipoli, Palestine and France in World War I mainly came from families in which the fertility of the mother had been deliberately and successfully restricted. This point might add a particular poignancy to the slaughter – as if it required more.

### A Little Knowledge

Between 1860 and 1900 Australia's birthrate declined dramatically. As we saw in chapter 2, in the mid-Victorian period large families were the rule. The downward trend appears to have begun in different parts of Australia at different times but was everywhere evident by the turn of the twentieth century. Where almost half of all Australian married women born in the period 1837–41 had, on average, eight or more children, only a quarter of those born in 1862–66 had so many.[15] The trend in smaller families was more apparent in the cities than in the country, and it reached the middle class slightly before the working class. Nevertheless, it eventually crossed lines of class, religion, birthplace and geographical location.[16]

Australian developments were part of a broader shift occurring in several countries in this period. For Australia it is especially important to consider what was happening in the British population from which such a large proportion of the Australian people was derived, particularly as it has been hypothesised that the British-born were the pioneers of the Australian birthrate decline.[17] These emigrants were leaving a country where there already was considerable momentum towards fertility control – birthrates fell steadily from around 1870 – and entering one where local factors were creating ideal conditions for a similar transition. In the second half of the nineteenth century, the fecundity of British-born women in Australia was lower than that of their native-born counterparts. One reason for this difference might have been that emigrants married later, but it is also possible that they were practising birth control in one form or another. It might be that men and women who are willing to endure the life change that follows from emigration are also more likely to embrace innovation in other aspects of their lives.[18] Or perhaps the culture of moderation in all things, including sex, was most advanced among an emigrant population accustomed to self-denial and preoccupied with respectability and self-improvement. Less frequent sex and *coitus interruptus* (withdrawal before ejaculation) will have significantly reduced colonial fertility rates, as has been argued occurred in nineteenth-century Britain.[19]

Birth control had been embedded in British working-class culture – in the form of folk knowledge and popular science – for generations. But these people primarily used 'pre-industrial' methods, such as abortion and withdrawal. Recent research suggests that periodic abstinence from sex within marriage might have been the most significant contributor to the decline of the birthrate in Britain during the Victorian and Edwardian eras.[20] At a time when respectability and chivalry were becoming influential and widespread ideals in British communities, and women were increasingly empowered to demand greater sexual consideration from their husbands, withdrawal and periodic abstinence were possibly more common within Australian marriages than many historians have assumed.[21] There was at least one author of Australian sex-advice texts of this time, a medical doctor, who warned that only in 'exceptional circumstances' was a wife 'justified in denying her husband sexual congress'.[22] Yet such advice would have been unnecessary unless it were recognised that many women were, in fact, refusing their husbands' sexual advances. If so, and if couples were also agreeing to reduce the frequency of sex, such restraint will have led to greater spacing of births and smaller completed families.[23] The overwhelmingly masculine late-nineteenth-century world that centred on the pub, the smoke night, the betting shop and the racetrack might have been, in part, a culture of mutual consolation among sexually 'hobbled' men. Men refused sex by the 'old lady', or placed on what they considered light rations, could always find consolation in mateship or perhaps even in the occasional liaison with a prostitute.

Both contemporary observers and historians have considered a wide range of factors in their attempt to explain how and why the Australian birthrate declined. Some have suggested that compulsory education, by reducing the scope for children to contribute their labour to farm and household management, also reduced the economic value of children to families. Declining religious feeling allegedly disposed couples to ignore the churches' moral injunctions.[24] The greater availability of effective contraception, including such innovations as the development of a technique for the vulcanisation of rubber in the 1840s – leading to more reliable condoms, caps and diaphragms – might have been a factor; yet, as discussed below, working-class people could not afford these items on a large scale. In any case, the main methods likely to have been used by the working classes – periodic abstinence, withdrawal and abortion – were all known to the masses well before the birthrate began to fall.[25] Others have pointed to the spread of contraceptive knowledge, especially after Justice William Windeyer's famous 1888 judgment *Ex Parte Collins*, which held that Annie Besant's tract *The Law of Population* was not obscene.[26] But Australian couples did not need Justice Windeyer or Annie Besant to enlighten them about traditional birth-control methods or, for that matter, the newer appliances on the market.

All the same, knowledge of contraception appears to have spread widely after 1880. An edition of American doctor Charles Knowlton's 1832 book *Fruits of Philosophy* was published by the rationalist H.K. Rusden in Melbourne in 1878. There were further editions in the 1880s and later, at least three produced by the leading secularist Joseph Symes, an advocate of *coitus interruptus*.[27] Besant's book was also widely available, especially after Windeyer's judgment. Advertisements in the press drew attention to booklets such as Stewart Warren's *The Wife's Guide and Friend*, produced in Melbourne by Saunders and Co., a text that came to the attention of the 1903–04 NSW Royal Commission on the Decline of the Birthrate. The company was subjected to an unsuccessful prosecution for obscenity in 1898 but the book went through several editions and must have brought contraceptive information to many women. It sought, among other things, to show 'Wives and Mothers how they may regulate the number of their family, and so avoid the manifold miseries of domestic poverty'. Indeed, in setting as its object 'the increase in domestic ease and comfort', it held up as desirable what the NSW royal commission would later condemn as immoral: the supposedly selfish desire of married women to avoid 'the interference with pleasure and comfort involved in child-bearing and child-rearing'.[28]

There were many such publications available by the end of the century. An advertisement in Sydney's *Truth* in 1895 under the heading 'Woman's Salvation' announced a treatise, 'free, sealed' and available by post from Professor Robert Herman of Collins Place in Melbourne, a 'French Specialist': 'The Wife's Welfare within her own control … This treatise will teach you more about prevention in ten minutes than all the years you've lived.'[29] *The Limitation of Offspring*, by Melbourne feminist and freethinker Brettena Smyth, similarly offered information about how couples could restrict the size of their families. Smyth, unlike her fellow freethinker Symes, condemned *coitus interruptus* as harmful to men:

> When emission occurs without the female organs it is always more incomplete and slower than when it occurs within, owing to the absence of the customary warmth and pressure of that peculiar influence which the organs of one sex exert over the other. A portion of the semen therefore remains undischarged at the time, and escapes slowly afterwards, thus giving rise to a weakness and irritation of the urethra and seminal parts, which in time become permanent and lay the foundation of involuntary looseness and final impotence.[30]

Medical opinion was divided on the effects of withdrawal. Dr Alexander Paterson, the author of a number of sex manuals, saw no harm in it,[31] but the doctors who appeared before the royal commission generally believed it dangerous. Ralph Worrall said that 'incompletion of the sexual act' was very common, but likely to lead to various ailments, including 'growths of the womb from chronic congestion'.[32] Another doctor dismissed *coitus interruptus* as 'the bad type of sexual abnormality'; he thought it produced worse ailments in men and women than mechanical and chemical contraceptives.[33] The idea that the regular injection of semen was necessary in preserving women's health was resilient. Dr W.J.S. McKay, probably correctly, believed withdrawal to be the most common form of prevention. Couples were eager to have a first child, he said, 'because if the woman does not have one child the man always considers it a reproach'. After a second child, however, they were likely to 'begin to adopt the plan of withdrawing', a habit that produced 'nerve troubles' in women.[34] This testimony about the popularity of withdrawal explicitly registered men's responsibility for contraception, which makes it all the more ironic that pronatalists blamed women and not men for the declining birthrate. *Coitus interruptus* could only have been practised successfully with a very high degree of self-control on the part of a husband. But it was women who were seen to be responsible for the future of the race, and, for pronatalists, it was their morality that birth control called into question.

### Abortion

McKay also believed abortion a common form of birth control, and those like Smyth and Paterson who advocated contraception presented it as a far preferable alternative to 'child murder'.[35] The idea that life began at conception became widespread within the middle class in the nineteenth century but many working-class people held to some version of an older idea 'that abortion was acceptable up until the time the soul entered the foetus ... forty days for boys and eighty for girls'.[36] There was testimony at the Royal Commission on the Decline of the Birthrate that these ideas died hard: one doctor remarked that 'the popular opinion seems to be that as long as the child has not quickened, as they call it, there is no moral offence'.[37] Another was asked whether he had found that women were more willing to raise the matter of abortion than earlier in his career. 'I am sure they do', he replied. 'To a medical man they do not scruple to talk about it; they do not see the moral wickedness of it.'[38]

The commission found a thriving trade in abortions, with nurses and midwives seen as major culprits, along with women advertising as fortune tellers. Female community networks and folk knowledge were essential, but, especially in large cities, there was a movement away from dependence on word-of-mouth information and towards thinly disguised advertisements. Men sometimes paid for a termination but there were instances of wives having multiple abortions without their husbands ever knowing anything of the matter.[39] Abortion was women's business in a way that contraception was not. Self-abortion, with drugs or implements such as knitting needles or syringes, was probably the most common means of getting rid of a foetus. It was also highly dangerous, with many women turning up at hospitals hideously infected and requiring urgent treatment.[40]

Until about World War I most abortionists were female.[41] Madam Harper of North Terrace, for instance, was a doctor's wife and well known on the Adelaide grapevine as an abortionist, while in the same city another abortionist, Madam Hillier, advertised her services as a herbalist.[42] In Sydney, Dr F. Mary Young of Redfern announced in the Sydney *Evening News* that she could be consulted on 'all Female Complaints'. But there was also in the major cities a large network of male 'quacks', 'irregular practitioners' and qualified doctors.[43] An insurance agent who testified at the NSW Legislative Council Select Committee Inquiry into Medicine and Surgery in 1887 claimed that abortions were available from a man named Willis, who practised under the name 'Dr Smith' in Macquarie Street. Willis vehemently denied this charge but if he was indeed innocent, his advertising must have caused confusion. It promised 'Ladies' with 'love and domestic troubles' that his treatment would remove 'all difficulties' and restore 'health'. It is possible, if unlikely, that he was telling the truth when he claimed that his advertising referred to VD. Another practitioner named Sheridan, who was found by the select committee to have signed several death certificates in the mid-1880s, was subsequently convicted and sentenced to fifteen years' imprisonment for having caused a woman's death through an illegal operation.[44]

The advertising columns of the popular press in the years around the turn of the century also suggest a thriving trade in abortifacients – concoctions to procure abortions – and information about how to make them. In 1895 women could write to H.A.D. Leon about 'Madam Hedburg's Famous American Female Remedy' which 'restores Regularity Without Medicine'.[45] If this did not work, there was always the possibility of a dose of 'Parisian Female Powders', which 'restore regularity and remove obstructions without fail'.[46] This trade deeply worried pronatalist fanatics such as Octavius Beale, whom the federal government indulged by allowing him to chair a Royal Commission on Secret Drugs, Cures and Foods, which reported on the huge trade in abortifacients in 1907. And while most attempts at abortion were made by the pregnant woman herself, there were at least a few genuinely qualified medical men prepared to carry out illegal operations.[47] L.L. Smith, a parliamentarian and doctor with a large and lucrative practice in Melbourne, was a reputed abortionist. He spent large sums of money advertising his practice, sold his own medicines, and provided consultations and prescriptions by post. His commercial and democratic approach to medicine was obnoxious to his profession but popular with ordinary folk. Smith also published a yearly *Medical Almanac* that gave advice on home remedies, wrote 'cheap pamphlets' about medical – including sexual – issues for public consumption, and even ran his own anatomical museum until it suffered the normal fate of such institutions, on the usual grounds of offence to public taste.[48]

Abortion and infanticide were important techniques of birth control in Australia. This was especially so for working-class folk who had limited access to expensive contraception, and for single women who had every motive to avoid the dire consequences of pregnancy.[49] Pregnant women usually placed themselves in the hands of midwives, nurses and fortune tellers. Middle-class people also procured abortions, but were more likely to turn to a qualified doctor.[50] It is likely that a significant number of doctors performed occasional operations for private patients in difficulty. Crimes of this kind were difficult to detect and the law was poorly enforced. There were few arrests, very few convictions and, on the rare occasions that judges did pass sentence, light punishments. A small number of women were executed for infanticide but there existed something close to a regime of state tolerance.

## Contraception

The widespread nature of abortion would help to explain why birth controllers such as Brettena Smyth were so careful to distinguish 'preventing' from 'destroying'. 'Before conception,' she claimed, 'no life exists to be destroyed'. Smyth was addressing a working-class audience; she faced not only the task of selling the virtues of contraception, but also of suppressing abortion. Her contraceptive of choice was the French *Pessaire Preventif*, a pessary she believed to be the most reliable

device available and 'the only article of the kind that can be used without the knowledge of the husband'.[51] This feature was especially
important to Smyth, a feminist who wanted to empower women by
increasing their control over their own fertility. There is some contemporary testimony that the demand for female contraceptives such as
pessaries was increasing at the same time as that for condoms, generally purchased by men, was in decline.[52] If accurate, this claim suggests
that women were playing a more active part in contraceptive practice.

A decision by the rubber company Dunlop to discontinue manufacturing condoms in 1905 is consistent with such a trend. The Ansell
family attributed this change of tack to the influence of company chairman Nicholas Fitzgerald, a prominent lay Catholic. Yet, if that story is
correct, perhaps it was the combination of pronatalist panic and declining profitability that prompted the decision. Eric Ansell, a London-born
employee of Dunlop's engineering section, famously bought the relevant machine and set it up in a small rented house in the inner Melbourne
suburb of Richmond. Ansell soon resigned from Dunlop and began
producing condoms in a small way. The trade does not seem to have
been terribly profitable at first, since Ansell also worked full-time for
another rubber company between 1912 and 1919. Condom manufacture
a century ago was labour intensive and a far cry from later highly mech-
anised processes that would help turn Ansell into one of Australian
manufacturing's most extraordinary success stories.[53] Indeed, despite
the pronatalist critics' stress on the massive scale of the trade, both the
manufacture and distribution of contraceptives before the 1930s were
carried out exclusively by small concerns. An advertisement in Smyth's
*Limitation of Offspring* reveals that she was selling from her North
Melbourne address a wide range of contraceptive devices, both male
and female, including pessaries, condoms, caps, sponges and syringes, a
trade supplemented by her publications and illustrated lectures on sex,
physiology and phrenology. The failure of qualified doctors to offer
advice on contraception helped to construct birth control as a branch of
popular 'science' and medical 'self-help', while also contributing to the
continuing atmosphere of mystery that surrounded the sexual functions.[54] Hence, birth control continued to be associated with fortune
telling, palmistry, phrenology and clairvoyance.[55]

The royal commission of 1903–04 nonetheless revealed a large trade in
contraceptives, in which word-of-mouth among informal neighbourhood

networks might have been more important than press advertising or pamphlet literature. With a wide range of devices on the market, women consulted with one another to separate the wheat from the chaff. *The Wife's Guide and Friend* reads like an extended catalogue for contraceptive devices sold by Saunders & Co.; the range of items must have been bewildering, especially to the inexperienced. Were 'Saunders' Soluble Quinine Tablets' really '[t]he simplest and best for the wife's use'? What about 'The "Sanitas" Sponge'? Was it 'a perfectly simple and reliable preventative'? Was it as good as Mrs Smyth's French contraption?

But men, too, must have wondered how their money would be best spent. Were men to believe in the efficacy of the 'Malthus Sheaf', constructed on the same principle as those 'so successfully used by the French peasantry'? These were made of either thin elastic or pink rubber and were available in three sizes – small, medium and large. One variety of condom was so strong that it could 'be used six or eight times', which is probably just as well; for at 7/6 a dozen, a single purchase would have accounted for well over a day's wages for most labourers. Perhaps gentlemen for whom economy was a consideration went for 'The New Permanent Malthus Sheaf', which could be 'used and re-used continually', although they needed to be careful to order the correct size from among the five available, 'as a sheaf of this kind if either too large or too small does not give satisfaction, and we cannot make any allowance for one that has been used'. There must have been a few anxious moments with the measuring tape.

The cost of contraceptives would have been prohibitive for many families, but especially for the working classes in the 'hungry nineties'. 'French Goods' for men were being advertised at six shillings a dozen in the Sydney press at this time, although Mrs Smyth was selling hers at the much higher prices of 10/6 and 15/6. Only the well-off could have afforded these sums. Pessaries in *The Wife's Guide and Friend* ranged from four shillings to 8/6; Smyth's best French female preventatives were 10/6 each – more than most skilled tradesmen earned in a day – although the English preventative, at the bottom of the range, was available for a more modest 5/6.[56] Even the better-off working class and the middle class must have been reluctant to lay out such sums, and it is easy to understand the continuing appeal of withdrawal.

The young and unmarried were nevertheless evidently gaining access to mass-produced contraceptives. John Hore, a Melbourne police officer, commented in 1909 that there was 'a deal of sexual immorality carried on that never comes to light, through the use of preventive measures, and I have seen evidence of such practices after social gatherings'. Calling for legislation to prevent manufacture and sale, he claimed to 'have seen the sheaf for the male organ and there is also one for use by the female'.[57] But an increase in the rate of premarital pregnancy and illegitimacy at the end of the century suggests that many single people were not using them, or doing so unsuccessfully.[58] Young courting couples were by this time taking advantage of increased opportunities for unchaperoned intimacy. The development of urban public transport networks in the 1870s and 1880s was a boon for those who wished to remove themselves from the prying eyes of family and neighbourhood. Parks, gardens and vacant lots, especially after dark, were common resorts for those who wanted a little privacy; but even the walk home from church could provide some with the opportunity for their first sexual encounter.[59] Easy intimacy between young lovers contributed to panic about seducers. Guardians of public virtue worried that girls were too ready to surrender their virginity: a man willing to debauch a woman before he married her was 'a lustful and dishonourable scoundrel' in spite of his ultimate intentions.[60] Perhaps a majority of courting couples agreed; a large minority, by their actions, showed they did not.

### Rising Women or Fallen Girls?

Neither knowledge of contraceptive technique nor the easy availability of appliances would lead to a lower birthrate without the will to restrict fertility. Some contraceptive devices could be used by men without knowledge on their wife's part, especially if they took Varley's advice and avoided unnecessarily exposing their bodies to one another 'by undress'.[61] Other contraceptives might have been used by women without the knowledge of their husbands. Yet it seems likely that couples were negotiating the size of their families by discussion, not the fiat of one partner or the other. A woman who had given birth to sixteen children claimed at the royal commission that limitation of family size was 'sometimes made a sort of agreement on marrying' – but presumably not in her case.[62]

The 'general relaxation of control over women' helps to account for the transition to lower fertility and the shift in sexual practices and values that it implied.[63] Divorce law reform, which gradually in the late nineteenth century provided the means by which women could, in extreme circumstances, end a marriage to an abusive or adulterous husband, was emblematic of this changing gender order. While few women actually sought divorces, the reform registered the sense that married women were something more than mere annexes to their husbands. By 1914 Australian women had the vote, were better educated than ever before and were entering a range of jobs and professions previously closed to them. Women who undertook paid employment before they married had seen something of the world outside the home and were perhaps less likely to regard obedience to their husbands as the foundation of modern marriage.[64]

The connection between paid work and women's enhanced status might help explain the sense of panic that centred on the factory girl in the late nineteenth century, for the mingling of the sexes on the workshop floor received a degree of censure that seems disproportionate to any real danger it posed to young women's chastity. Many critics focused on the mischief in which they became involved while walking home from the factory after dark; Melbourne policemen complained in 1909 that the poor lighting in most parks made them a haven for couples wishing to indulge in sex. A witness before the Victorian Select Committee on the Prevalence of Venereal Disease in 1878 painted an alarming picture of two sisters' downward spiral from factory floor, to dancing saloon, to sex in a garden on the way home.[65] Thirty years later a Victorian policeman, while recognising that the 'pittance' the factory girl received in wages helped account for her 'immorality', presented her lot in terms that also blamed inadequate parental discipline and an excess of female vanity:

> The factory girl is rather a queer one. Her life is a hard one & it is lived hard. In the majority of cases she is of poor uneducated parents & has been in many instances reared in an atmosphere of immorality & drunkenness ... They work eight hours a day & at night are free. Then they meet fellow workers both male & female & in many instances especially Saturday nights adjourn to the comic cafes & when 'the wine is in the wit is out' & so she suffers. Like her better class of sister she has an inordinate love of finery & will unostentatiously solicit prostitution to obtain it.[66]

It was said that 'amateur ladies' of this kind, young women who supplemented their meagre incomes by trading their sexual favours, were more dangerous than full-time prostitutes in spreading disease. One witness before the Victorian inquiry, a doctor, claimed to know of an instance of 'one machine-girl syphilizing six young men'. Factory girls' bodies were presented as pools of disease undermining the moral and physical health of the community.[67]

Those who worried over female immorality presented domestic service as a means by which the fallen woman could seek to rebuild her shattered moral virtue. Factory employment was less likely to be recommended for this purpose, although witnesses before the 1892 South Australian Shops and Factories Commission did point out that making shirts was preferable to prostitution.[68] Still, from the point of view of female chastity, the factory remained a sexually dangerous place in the middle-class imagination. A conversation on a Melbourne train in 1897 illustrates this moral ambiguity that surrounded factory employment. A free-trade advocate was reported to have said to Sam Mauger, a protectionist politician and hat manufacturer, that tariff protection debauched factory girls and led to immorality. Mauger replied that he was 'better acquainted with the lives of factory girls' than the speaker, and 'they are as moral and pure as shop girls, domestic servants or any other class in the community'. Mauger, of course, had a vested interest in the defence of the factory system but the critical point is that he found it necessary to defend their morality from a traducer as part of a larger defence of protectionism and manufacturing.[69]

## Shame

These changes in the status of women were disturbing to many male observers, for they suggested that women's horizons were not formed exclusively by marriage and motherhood. Perhaps women were not bound by their bodies after all. This idea also raised troubling questions about whether a woman could exercise sexual autonomy without degenerating into a 'whore'. In the second half of the nineteenth century, sexual morality – especially among women – had been used by social observers to define class difference. As noted in chapter 2, different codes of sexual morality distinguished the 'rough' and the 'respectable' working classes. Middle-class identity was also founded on ideals connected with sexuality, such as the innocence of children, the ignorance of single women, female reticence about sex and the necessity of marital sexual privacy.

The evidence presented to the NSW Royal Commission into the Decline of the Birthrate was troubling because it pointed to 'immorality' among those whose social identity was supposedly founded on their adherence to certain sexual norms. A doctor who appeared before the Commission, E.T. Thring, was certain that 'preventive practices go right through, excepting in the very lowest classes'.[70] In other words, the very social group that was most commonly associated in the bourgeois mind with sexual immorality, the poorest among the working classes, was the only one which did not, in his view, practise contraception. That did not necessarily make the brutish working class any more 'moral', for their sexual behaviour was understood as depraved in other respects; but it did call into question the morality of their social betters. Another witness, a chemist, made it equally clear that the demand for contraceptives crossed class boundaries, coming from 'gentlemen in garb and appearance', ladies, and the wives of working men.[71] Witnesses agreed that contraception was being practised by those who were well educated, well off and outwardly respectable.

Perhaps more disturbing than anything else to the royal commissioners was the sense that Victorian notions of female modesty had been thrown overboard. Whether genuinely or not, both witnesses and commissioners professed surprise at women's lack of shame in regard to contraception. A blushing woman signalled that she knew more than she should, yet at least showed that she possessed a sense of shame; but women were asking for contraceptives 'unblushingly'.[72] Where large families once allowed commentators to maintain the fiction that women engaged in sex because of their intense desire for maternity, by their words and deeds women now seemed to be saying that they had sex for pleasure rather than procreation.

The concept of sex for pleasure was a primary target of the commissioners. For instance, they showed great interest in whether or not particular chemists were selling condoms containing 'spikes' or 'ticklers'.[73] There was a trade in such items; an 1895 advertisement in Sydney *Truth* refers to the 'Latest London Sensation – Gents' Preventative and Novelty combined', which was available from a Flinders Street address in Melbourne.[74] But it was women's role in contraception that was most disturbing to the royal commissioners. A doctor, having told the commission that women seemed more willing to discuss contraception now than earlier in his practice, was asked whether they appeared to regard it as something to be ashamed of:

> All women who express a desire to limit their offspring do not, by any means, belong to the kind that are not ashamed to discuss it openly; still, a large proportion of women do tell me openly that they do not desire to have more children, and say they will not have more children … And they have asked me again and again to tell them the means of limiting offspring; and they repeatedly have asked me to get rid of the product of conception for them; and, finding that that cannot be done through me, they sometimes say that they know where it can be done. Ignorance, as well as perverseness, is at work.[75]

The royal commissioners, in fact, faced the problem that there had been a clear shift in both sexual practice and accompanying moral attitudes among a broad cross-section of society. The change is reflected in the medical texts produced in the 1870s and 1880s for popular consumption, such as those by Beaney and Paterson. Beaney, unlike feminists who advocated small families on the grounds that they helped preserve the health of mothers and enhanced the welfare of children, focused on men's motives and behaviour. Family limitation would reduce prostitution by encouraging young men to marry and start a family, instead of avoiding domestic respectability on the grounds that marriage inevitably brought with it 'uncontrolled procreation'. Nevertheless, he had little to say about how couples could avoid conception, except to suggest the use of 'cold water and other simples under medical direction', and advising, erroneously, that conception in most cases occurred during menstruation or soon after it.[76] Paterson, writing two decades later, was almost unique among Australian doctors in approving such devices as condoms, but he also proffered much the same advice as Beaney about women's 'safe period'.[77] Their injunctions, if followed, would have been a great boon to the birthrate, but the idea of a safe period allowed some doctors to enter the realm of birth control while retaining respectability. The association of mechanical or medicinal contraception with illicit sex, at a time when 'qualified' doctors were engaged in the business of placing as much daylight as possible between themselves and 'quacks', meant that the overwhelming majority could not give open support to mechanical birth control.[78]


### Sex and Motherhood

Two ideas were critical in the emergence of the conviction that, as Beaney put it, a married couple should be able to 'determine whether they shall have one or ten children, and at what periods they shall produce them'.[79] Firstly, because life began at conception, it was not immoral to practise contraception. This idea had taken hold among the middle classes. Secondly, although procreation was a reason for sexual relations, it was not their only, nor perhaps even their primary, purpose. A Methodist minister who appeared before the royal commission, W.W. Rutledge, was the only clergyman prepared to express these ideas at that inquiry,[80] but the testimony of a newsagent and father of thirteen (with ten children still living) provides a clear indication of the shift in values that was occurring in the last third of the century. Despite a series of leading questions from the royal commissioners intended to elicit testimony on the virtues of large families such as his own, 68-year-old John Calvin Hume would not play ball. He said it would have been better if his wife had only had six children, for he 'felt sorry to see her being oppressed with bearing and rearing children in the state that she was in'. He had taught his married son 'that it would be wise to limit his family … I feel that the power to limit the family should be in the hands of every man and woman'. The commissioners quickly brought the interview to a close, but the brief testimony of the humble and compassionate shopkeeper had provided a clearer insight into the decline of the birthrate than the combined testimony of various medical and clerical windbags.[81]

Activists in the emerging women's movement supported this preference for small families over large, for quality over quantity. Motherhood was to be voluntary instead of the result of mere 'animal passion' on the part of husbands. Only by curbing the powers of men within marriage would women have the freedom and vitality to produce the healthy children essential to the advancement of the race.[82] Bessie Harrison Lee, the Woman's Christian Temperance Union (WCTU) activist and suffrage campaigner, in her 1893 tract *Marriage and Heredity* advised husbands that if they could restrain their passions, rather than fathering 'too many fractious little inheritors of suffering', they 'would have noble, splendid boys, and handsome, vigorous girls'. She argued for sexual self-restraint in husbands and voluntary motherhood for wives; married couples were enjoined to avoid double beds in order to help them achieve an ideal marriage.[83] Other feminists, such as Vida Goldstein in Melbourne and Rose Scott in Sydney, similarly condemned the assumption that a woman's proper role was as sexual slave and breeding machine.[84] Louisa Lawson, the prominent feminist, in arguing for liberalisation of the divorce laws, asked whether there could be

> anything sacred in the bond which binds a good woman to a sot, felon, or brute? ... What sober, strong, cleanly man would submit to share his bed with another in the worst stage of drunkenness? But the confirmed sot, if he possesses enough command of his tottering limbs to bring him to his lawful wife's chamber, may then collapse in abandoned beastliness upon the floor or conjugal couch if he reaches it, and proceed to make the night hideous for her ... How often does the patient wife quietly steal from the chamber of horrors to seek shelter by the bed of her sleeping children ...[85]

Here was a grim view of marriage, but sufficiently plausible for Justice Windeyer to incorporate a similar set of images in his 1888 judgment in favour of the publication of Annie Besant's birth-control pamphlet.[86] Feminists did not oppose motherhood so much as sex on demand and compulsory maternity. As Sydney feminist Maybanke Wolstenholme put it, the mother 'alone should decide whether she will be a mother, she alone should possess her body'.[87] Female autonomy was in the interests of both women and society because 'the children born of unwilling mothers – the offspring of sexual gratification – can never become a noble people'.[88]

Some feminists were arguing for a voluntary motherhood that, whether through heredity, environment or some combination of both, would produce a superior race of beings. They linked these arguments to a need for a new and improved maternity, based on small rather than large families, and a renovated, more egalitarian marital relationship founded on love and mutual respect. The future of the race was at stake. Contraception, many feminists recognised, could contribute to small families but only at the cost of encouraging male sexual excess and thereby endangering women's autonomy and health. For Vida Goldstein, it was an understandable response by women to the prospect of 'unwanted, overworked motherhood', but also 'frequently a misnomer for a sex-indulgence that dares to call itself the expression of "love"'.[89] But not all were hostile. Smyth, as we have seen, was a firm supporter, arguing that women had a definite right to decide how many children they would have. Her intellectual roots were in a secularist movement that had also spawned Besant's birth-control activism, but at least one other feminist was also willing to countenance contraception. Catherine Helen Spence, in her utopian novel *A Week in the Future*, envisaged a society a century hence in which, through the use of contraception, it had become a disgrace to have more than three children – a beneficial change because 'children were much dearer to their parents when there were fewer of them'.[90]

In contrast with the feminists in whose company they frequently found themselves, male radicals and socialists more commonly advocated pronatalism and sexual freedom. It was orthodox socialism to reject the Malthusian idea that overpopulation led to social misery.[91] Socialists argued that class inequality, not overpopulation, was at the heart of the sex problem. As a corollary, to the limited extent that they explored birth control at all, socialists tended to reject it. The communist-anarchist J.A. Andrews went so far as to argue that preventatives produced 'cancerous or scrofulous and tuberculous disease' in women, and damaged men even more than masturbation. Although admitting that his own tastes inclined to celibacy, he declared it 'the duty of every reformer to beget as many children as the woman or women he consorts with may be naturally fitted to bear'. He would do the same as a 'duty to mankind' as soon as he had the means.[92] Andrews's friend the Melbourne radical Bernard O'Dowd also worried over the contribution of women's 'voluntary sterility' to race suicide.[93] In his 1897 poem 'Land of the "Terrible Rite"', O'Dowd speculated that the descent of Aboriginal society into barbarism was connected with its practice of the ritual of sub-incision, as performed on and by Aboriginal men.[94] Following some nineteenth-century authorities on Aboriginal sexual practices, O'Dowd believed sub-incision performed a contraceptive function. The self-destruction of the Aborigine might therefore presage a similarly tragic fate for a white Australia that through its own degraded social practices – such as birth control – was creating 'wifeless men' and childless women as mere 'outlets for his lust'.[95] O'Dowd's belief that European society in Australia might descend to the sexual savagery of the 'native' takes us back to fears that settlers had expressed in the very earliest years of the colonies.

## *Censorship*

Just as conventional morality demanded sexual ignorance of women and children, so the state established public rituals whereby it communicated an authorised version of public decency. These were publicly justified as an effort to protect the working classes – especially women and children – from the threat of depravity or corruption. Yet considered as public policy they sit oddly beside the vast number of column inches in the popular press devoted to salacious divorce cases, French goods and abortion remedies, which authorities left mainly untouched. For instance, on 3 June 1906 in Melbourne, T.G. Taylor and P.L. Harkin were arrested and charged with having distributed some sex advice literature written by Taylor's wife, Dr Rosamond Benham. Benham advocated Karezza, or practical continence: a form of sex in which through the power of thought a couple could supposedly avoid 'the final orgasm' in favour of an 'exchange of magnetism'.[96] On 15 June, in the Court of Petty Sessions, Taylor was sentenced to three months' imprisonment, while Harkin received one. Their convictions were later overturned by the Supreme Court, but the episode showed that the authorities were prepared to make an example of sex radicals who sought to bring unorthodox ideas before a working-class audience.[97]

William Chidley's persecution is better known. Chidley's enemies detected in his ideas the ravings of a dangerous lunatic. But they also worried that the ignorant and impressionable might take them seriously. In Melbourne in 1911, booksellers distributing his recently published pamphlet, *The Answer*, as well as Chidley himself, were prosecuted on the grounds that there were sections of the book 'which would tend to deprave and corrupt the morals of any person reading it'. The court ordered the destruction of copies seized by police.[98] In the following year the bearded and earnest-looking man, now dressed in a simple Grecian-style tunic and sandals, took his message to Sydney for the most famous phase of his career. Although regularly arrested and prosecuted – sometimes simply for wearing his unconventional tunic – the willingness of friends and supporters to pay his fines meant that police were unable to prevent the determined sex reformer from continuing his agitation. After a number of public lectures, police threatened to prosecute any owner of a hall who leased him their premises.

Yet Chidley still wandered the streets, carrying a bundle of his pamphlets which he offered to passers-by for a small fee. And he continued his lectures, now usually delivered in the Domain or the Botanic Gardens. In August 1912, having been further provoked by Chidley's plan for a lecture to 'Ladies Only', the authorities assembled a conga line of obliging doctors and arranged for him to be certified as insane and compulsorily detained in the Callan Park Hospital for the Insane. Popular agitation against this blatant abuse of the law soon led to his release but leading doctors continued to campaign for Chidley's incarceration, arguing that he was suffering from 'paranoia'. Late in 1912, the courts also imposed fines on several booksellers who stocked *The Answer*, although full suppression only came with a Supreme Court decision in 1914.

As authorities in Melbourne and Sydney acted against Chidley, a popular campaign in his defence gathered momentum. Socialists and radicals especially insisted on his right to free speech, although not all Chidley's supporters were of the left.[99] Archibald Strong, whose politics leaned towards the conservative end of the Melbourne's cultural liberalism, believed that treating either Chidley or his book as 'obscene' was 'a perfect absurdity'. Strong appeared in court to testify in Chidley's favour in 1911.[100] But support for Chidley's right to be heard did not, in most cases, amount to endorsement of his theories. While his condemnation of a thrusting male sexuality was appealing to some feminists, much pro-Chidley agitation was about defending the public discussion of sex, as well as opposing the use of the lunacy laws to silence a sincere enquirer after truth.

As revealed in the Chidley affair, booksellers who dealt in sex and birth-control literature were sometimes prosecuted. Beginning with Victoria in 1876, colonial governments passed obscenity acts, based on English legislation, giving police substantial powers to enter premises suspected of containing indecent literature in order to seize it and impose fines on the occupant and owners of the obscene material.[101]

Earlier legislation, such as the 1851 NSW *Vagrancy Act*, had included among the offences marking an individual as a 'rogue' and 'vagabond' the exposure of obscene material to public view; but the new legislation of the 1870s and 1880s significantly strengthened the hand of the state.[102] Meanwhile, Australian common law practice followed the precedent in the famous 1868 English case *R. v. Hicklin*, which prohibited publications that had a tendency to 'deprave and corrupt' those susceptible to 'immoral influences'. Windeyer's celebrated 1888 judgment was a victory for birth controllers, but it was not the last prosecution of a purveyor of such literature. Publications that dealt with sexual themes, whether a scurrilous newspaper or birth-control pamphlet, were vulnerable to action by the police or customs officials.

The first recorded seizure in Australia of indecent material by customs occurred in Launceston, in 1848, when some sailors had 'obscene Chinese paintings on glass valued at one shilling' taken from them and destroyed. Less than five years later, 'smugglers' suffered a more costly loss when fifty pounds' worth of obscene books, imported from New York, were grabbed by officers on the Melbourne wharves.[103] This incident is the first known seizure of indecent literature in the colonies, and so opened one of the great struggles over civil liberties in modern Australian history. Victorian customs officers were also responsible for the seizure, in 1887, of some of Emile Zola's novels and then, two years later, 'of 162 French novels' that had been imported by the Melbourne bookseller and freethinker E.W. Cole. In order to avoid prosecution, Cole allowed the government to destroy the books. A new era of censorship had dawned.[104] The main provocation for Victorian authorities to act against Melbourne booksellers was the prosecution, in London, of the publisher of Zola's novels in English translation; colonial developments were part of a broader imperial thrust to suppress impure literature.[105] In 1894 another Melbourne bookseller, Frederick White, was prosecuted for having in his possession a translation of *Ovid's Art of Love* which, according to a customs official, 'was calculated to induce impure thoughts in the minds of the young in both sexes'.[106]

Before long there were other cases, such as the 1901 prosecution of a Melbourne bookseller over English translations of Honoré de Balzac's *Droll Stories* and Charles Paul de Kock's *Monsieur Dupont*, books which had been publicly available in Melbourne for decades. In this case, the first to be prosecuted after Federation, the magistrate was sympathetic to the defendant but imposed a hefty £25 fine, which was nevertheless only a quarter of the penalty that he could have inflicted on the hapless bookseller.[107] But this case turned out to be atypical of the behaviour of the customs department in the early Commonwealth. Despite the perceived need to protect virginal Australia from the corruption of the old world – and especially the decadent French – the customs service 'was less rigorous in the prosecution of books for which literary merit could be claimed as a defence'.[108] This is indicative of the relative openness and fluidity of Antipodean culture in the Edwardian period compared with the later, interwar years. Nevertheless, the foundations of Australia's 'quarantined culture' were laid between 1880 and 1914.[109]

For a late-era Victorian or Edwardian, indecent matter was vulgar, erotic and immoral. That meant that if a work was likely to inflame sexual desire but nevertheless contained literary merit, the authorities were in some cases prepared to approve its availability – this saved them from having to advocate censorship of Shakespeare, Swift and Fielding.[110] In particular, there was a tendency to distinguish between books that could only be read by an educated elite whose morals and capacity for self-control were beyond reproach, and publications aimed at a wider, working-class audience. It helped the cause of literary freedom, naturally, if the text was in the foreign language, although foreignness certainly did not save 'French cards' from official attempts at suppression. Chidley, as a young man in the 1870s, acquired a packet that provided him no end of entertainment. These, he recalled, were photographic prints of wash drawings of 'naked and (worse) partially naked men and women in all sorts of lewd attitudes, of which coitus was the least filthy'. There were men licking women, women sucking men, women masturbating men, and women masturbating themselves and one another. Chidley found them so exciting that he claimed to have successfully performed oral sex on himself, a practice in which he engaged guiltily for some years afterwards.[111]

Postcards were instrumental in shifting pornography from words to pictures and in extending its reach well beyond the wealthy and literate who had been its traditional devotees. The cheapness and accessibility of pornographic cards were especially worrying to authorities because they made it all but inevitable that the lower orders, particularly women and children – all assumed incapable of exercising the kind of self-control characteristic of gentlemen – might get their hands on them.[112] So in

1904, with the help of an expert in the French language, customs officers successfully prosecuted an importer of cards from Paris, fining him £5. And in the years immediately before World War I, dirty postcards were among the targets of an Indecent Literature Committee formed in Melbourne. The authorities also suppressed novelty watches containing the image of an almost naked woman, while 1904 saw what was arguably Australia's first obscenity prosecution for moving pictures: that of a Melbourne man, later quashed on appeal, for exhibiting through a mutoscope – effectively a penny-in-a-slot peepshow machine.[113]

Norman Lindsay's emerging reputation as the *bête-noir* of Australian wowserdom also belongs to this Edwardian moment. Born in the Victorian gold town of Creswick, by the early years of the century Lindsay was in Sydney working for the *Bulletin* as a cartoonist. His *Pollice Verso* attracted adverse comment from the puritanical when exhibited in Sydney in 1904. It depicted a hillside crucifixion, with a group of naked men and women in the right foreground, apparently giving Christ's asceticism a derisive thumbs-down in favour of a world of hedonism and sensuality. A newspaper critic was unable to understand Lindsay's preference 'for depicting only the bestial types of humanity'. A further Lindsay painting which outraged the nation's moral guardians was *The Crucified Venus*, first shown in Sydney in 1912, which depicted a naked woman being nailed to a cross by a monk while a group of wowsers of various shades – including clerical – looks on. When it was shown in Melbourne, protests led to its temporary removal from the exhibition. While some accused Lindsay of blasphemy, it was his depiction of the voluptuous naked female body that earned him the greatest ire, and made him famous.[114] It was the obscenity of the body – and especially the female body – that underpinned nearly all sex censorship in Australia between the 1880s and the 1960s.[115]

## Conclusion

There was legislative activity in the early years of the twentieth century that aimed to reverse the decay of civilisation but governments were only prepared to go so far in their efforts to regulate morals. Police and courts trod warily in crimes related to sex and reproduction. After all, contraception, abortion and infanticide facilitated male sexual freedom. Pronatalism upheld masculine privilege and sought to tie women down to a life of breeding, but it also had the potential to limit men's liberties, both within marriage and out of it, by reducing access to contraceptives and opportunities for disposing of an unwanted foetus or child.

It is hardly surprising, then, that a patriarchal state would hesitate to stick its nose into such matters.[116] Laws regularly appeared on the statute books that could be used to clamp down on birth control, abortionists and peddlers of quack remedies. But it was one thing to legislate, another to prosecute, and still another to secure a conviction. Australian lawmakers diverged from those of Britain in their more stringent legislative treatment of both the advertising and sale of contraceptives. To a settler society increasingly preoccupied with threats to the purity and security of the nation, the task of promoting healthy, moral and reproductive sexual activity in the white population seemed especially pressing. Australia also had stronger traditions of protection and state activity with which to rationalise sexual engineering of this kind.[117] But birth controllers could, by using discreet wording, get around any obscenity law that parliament threw at them. And nobody could do anything about the informal networks that conveyed such information verbally.

Judith Allen suggests that the birthrate royal commission was 'characterised by draconian repression' of birth control, with 'the tightening of laws prohibiting the advertisement of contraceptives'. But the critical NSW legislation in this field was passed in 1900, before the royal commission sat.[118] It banned, as indecent, advertising concerned with 'any complaint or infirmity arising from or relating to sexual intercourse, or to nervous debility, or female irregularities, [or] which might reasonably be construed as relating to any illegal medical treatment or illegal operation'.[119] A 1908 amendment of the *Police Offences Act* tightened obscenity legislation by making successful prosecution of a retailer of obscene material easier, but the essentials had been laid out by 1901. Victorian amendments to the *Crimes Act* in 1891 had similarly included a ban on the display in public places of advertising concerned with syphilis, gonorrhoea, 'nervous debility', or any other complaint connected with 'sexual intercourse';[120] yet Charles Mackellar, president of the Royal Commission on the Decline of the Birthrate, believed that the sale of contraceptives was more open in Melbourne than Sydney.[121] His inquiry *was* followed by increasingly rigorous efforts by the Australian Customs Service to protect public morals by excluding contraceptives from the young Commonwealth – despite the apparent lack of legal authority to do so – and David Day goes so far as to suggest that Customs' efforts in this direction may have contributed 'in halting the drop in the Australian birth rate'.[122] This is unlikely. Customs officials could stop goods coming into Australia but they could not prevent the local manufacture of contraceptives, nor interfere with birth-control literature published in Australia. And no state authority could do anything about methods such as abstinence or withdrawal. Abortion and infanticide continued without undue interference by the authorities. While birthrates would, in the early years of the century, reach a plateau rather than continuing to fall, a sexual revolution had by this time already been accomplished.

# CHAPTER 4

# *The Foe within Ourselves*

## *Protection*

In the Federation era, 'protection' was the watchword in sexual matters, as in so many other aspects of Australian life. Yet where the male bread-winner was the object of much of the famous social legislation of the era, in sexuality the focus was protection of the young single female.[1] This effort met with only mixed success. Feminists such as Bessie Harrison Lee who wanted castration of hardened seducers, or Antoinette Sterling, who thought they should be 'taken away and hung', were never likely to get their way – although the Victorian parliament debated the castration of rapists in 1891.[2]

Young women's entry into industrial employment intensified fears of seduction and, partly for that reason, divided middle-class opinion. Women were a conveniently cheap source of labour in manufacturing but were also seen to belong naturally in the home – as servants, wives, mothers and daughters – where their virtue would be safe under respectable men's protection. Factory employment brought them into the company of men of their own class – on the factory floor, in the street and even in the parks and gardens of the metropolis, where factory girls and their larrikin paramours reputedly abandoned all propriety.[3]

Since the 1830s there had been global dissemination of the colonies' image as an Arcadian paradise, or at least one where the working man could raise a family in frugal comfort.[4] Australia was no replica of industrial Britain; rather, women would assume a place in their natural sphere, the home. Female industrial employment betrayed this domestic ideal, uprooting young women from their guardians and placing them in moral danger. Worse still, urbanisation and industrialisation were creating slums reminiscent of the worst in the old world, laying further temptations and threats in working-class women's path. Overcrowded housing caused factory girls to linger on the streets after work – and, in the bourgeois imagination, a working-class girl on *the street* was on the way to being on *the streets*.[5]

Cramped homes were also said to be breeding grounds for incest. The enactment of incest laws in the colonies from the mid-1870s was a response to this belief in the 'rough' working class's deviation from 'normal' sexuality and family life.[6] Previously, offenders could be charged with rape, indecent assault or carnal knowledge. The criminalisation of incest recognised that a father who debauched his daughter was exploiting his natural authority, or perhaps even unfairly taking advantage of a residual sense of 'ownership' of the women under his care.[7] Political democracy itself depended on the idea that all men were 'able to govern within their families'.[8] It was therefore imperative that those who proved themselves unable to do so be punished as deviants. Despite this widely held view, some fathers still regarded sexual access to their own daughters as a prerogative of paternal authority.

As noted in chapter 1, in the mid-nineteenth century the authorities had treated the physical separation of men and women on immigrant ships as essential in preserving sexual order. The preoccupation with the mixture of sexes in factories represented a continuation of these older ways of thinking. A Victorian official report recommended that '[w]herever possible there should be a division of the sexes over the age of sixteen' on the grounds that the

> present system of crowding men, women, and children into the same rooms cannot fail to be conducive of evil consequences, and … the system of promiscuous grouping leads to conversation and to the interchange of ideas that must serve to contaminate the minds of the young of both sexes.[9]

Social purity campaigners also had factory girls in their sights. The Reverend Charles Olden, in a lecture to the NSW Social Purity Society in 1885, claimed that 'girls hand themselves over from one paramour to another, if not with indifference, at least with the utmost ease'. He advocated not only separation of the sexes but the appointment of a matron to supervise factory girls, a proposal presumably inspired by practice on immigrant ships.[10] But there was also scepticism about the morally deleterious effects of the mingling of the sexes, whether in factories or on streets. A Port Melbourne police sergeant commented that while public reserves and gardens should be locked up at night, 'very little harm can come to a girl in the public streets where exercise and fresh atmosphere is necessary for Factory girls who are cooped up all day'.[11] Thomas Hawker, a SA union official, believed it desirable to prevent such contact in factories but added that if men were 'moral and good … there can be no harm in them working in the same room … there are some things in which you can go a little too far. As boys are better educated the evils will decrease'.[12] Here, the stress was on taming the sexual unruliness of young men. As one speaker remarked in a SA parliamentary debate, 'Some of the worst foes we had lived within ourselves, and it was against these foes that we must take action'.[13] Dangerous impulses – what Sydney feminist Rose Scott called 'the animal in man' – were to be controlled, and boys taught to avoid the slippery slope that led to corruption of bodies and souls.[14] It was not the outer world but the inner self – a *sexual* self – that had to be remade.

These assumptions were central to the campaigns of social purity reformers.[15] Organisations such as the Social Purity societies, the Society for the Promotion of Morality, the Young Men's Christian Association and the White Cross League preached a manly self-restraint that would protect both women and men from vice and disease. Their campaigns were influenced by similar efforts in Britain, including the famous series of articles by W.T. Stead in the *Pall Mall Gazette* in 1885 – 'The Maiden Tribute of Modern Babylon' – that drew attention, in sensational style, to the prostitution of young girls. Australian reformers did not slavishly follow metropolitan precedents in devising measures to protect girls from sexual exploitation but, like their British counterparts, they condemned the double standard of morality for men and women embedded in contagious diseases legislation.[16] In a lecture to the NSW Social Purity Society in 1882, Dr H.W. Jackson likened a proposal for a *Contagious Diseases Act* to the elimination of cattle plague 'by slaughtering heifers, while the young bulls were allowed to spread infection all over the country'.[17]

These reformers saw men's sexual behaviour as a threat to Australian women, with adolescent girls especially vulnerable. Quite apart from the enduring attractions of young female flesh, sex with a virgin or a 'clean' woman retained a place within folk culture as a cure for VD, and was an unambiguously pleasant alternative to mercury or permanganate of potash.[18] But the social purity movement's propaganda also tapped into concern about the sexual behaviour of the young – especially the young working class.[19] Legislators and police complained frequently about parents' failure to exercise adequate supervision. In 1885 SA parliamentarian Dr Edward Stirling blamed 'juvenile immorality' on 'the unfettered association which parents permitted young people of both sexes at all times and seasons'.[20] While Stirling was not specific as to the class of these parents, another contributor to the debate on the Protection of Young Persons Bill, Josiah Symon, declared that the 'children of the upper classes ... were kept under more control and had more amusements at home'.[21] But following British precedent, where the figure of the aristocratic rake had long featured in public debate over sexual morality, the social purity movement and sections of the press made a particular 'folk devil' of the upper-class seducer, expressing outrage that the 'honour of a poor man's daughter might be dragged in the dust in order that the sons of the wealthy might be spared from public obloquy'.[22]

Not all, however, agreed with this analysis. Symon claimed that sexual immorality 'among the lower classes was due, not to those above them in social status, but to those with whom they mixed every day'. Raising the spectre of incest, he claimed that the 'seeds of immorality were frequently sown' in overcrowded housing, where 'father, mother, grown children, and young children herded together'.[23] In these debates, incest signified the 'white' savagery of those lowest in the social hierarchy, rather as polygamy, child betrothal and the 'sale' of sex were still seen to mark 'black' savagery. Those who argued for the protection of women and girls on class grounds were therefore vulnerable to the reply that what they needed was not so much protection from casual seducers, as from the unrestrained lust of their own fathers. Here was truly 'class struggle' – although not one much noticed by labour historians.

## Handing on Useful Knowledge

Panic about masturbation, by contrast, crossed class boundaries and fed into fears of national and racial degeneration. Only gathering real momentum in Australia in the last third of the nineteenth century, fear of self-abuse was part of a larger concern with the so-called disease of spermatorrhoea, or loss of sperm – either involuntarily or as the result of self-abuse – to which both qualified and irregular practitioners attributed a variety of ailments.[24] But it was the act of masturbation which increasingly worried Australian doctors. A report in the *Australian Medical Journal* in 1860 described a case in which masturbation had produced 'excessive spinal irritation, debility, and indirectly death'.[25] Self-abuse was also connected with the social purity movement's campaigns because it was believed that once unleashed, male sexual drives could not readily be controlled; today's masturbator was tomorrow's rake.[26] As Dr Richard Arthur explained, the boy was truly 'a sexless being' – and he would stay that way until manhood if not for 'a constant turning of the attention to sex matters, and a pruriency of imagination'.[27]

Purity reformers were, ironically, sex education pioneers, arguing that parents needed to ensure their children went out into the world pure in mind and body but not ignorant of sex. Mothers, they said, had a particular responsibility to educate young children but at puberty either parent could instruct. When a lad was leaving school and heading out into a dangerous world, it was the father's job to tell him of the need for chivalry and the dangers of VD, while mothers were held responsible for enlightening their adolescent daughters 'about some of the deep secrets of their own bodies'. Religious instruction was not enough, nor should parents confine themselves to discussion of plants, kittens and chickens. If respectable mothers and fathers did not teach their children properly, the young and vulnerable would obtain their knowledge of sex from the 'criminal poor'. Sex education was an assertion of middle-class social power in the face of 'threats' to the innocence of children and the sanctity of family. Indecent conversation needed to be vigorously suppressed, while parents were to 'maintain a vigilant watchfulness' and consult a doctor if they suspected masturbation. On a hopeful note, Dr Arthur claimed that it was often caused by a local irritation, and that circumcision would sometimes be a successful remedy.[28]

It was one thing to talk about sex education, quite another to give it. A pamphlet produced by the Australasian White Cross League, a

Church of England purity organisation, designed for boys aged ten or older, did little beyond telling them that they should not talk about sex with other boys, that babies grew in mummy's tummy, and that they should refrain from playing with themselves – if not quite in so few words.[29] One Adelaide doctor told the 1912 SA Royal Commission into Education that sex education was 'a prurient matter to deal with. I think it would be better to leave it to nature. I am, perhaps, old-fashioned, but I think that the less things are ventilated the better'.[30] In 1903 a father objected to the short talks being given by the AWCL in Victorian schools, on the grounds that they interfered 'with the duty of parents in regard to their children'.[31]

While fear of incest centred on the working-class home, despite its reality among those of greater wealth and status, anti-masturbatory rhetoric focused more on the middle class, not least because thrift and restraint formed the foundation of its social identity. As Thomas W. Laqueur has pointed out, masturbation was 'the avatar of a seemingly impossible land of sexual plenty and unlimited freedom'.[32] Children, therefore, needed to be educated in the self-control expected of them in their adult lives. But there was a Serpent in the Garden: the growing gap between puberty and marriage. Puberty was occurring earlier in Britain from about the 1840s, probably as a result of changes in diet, and some believed that Australian children were achieving sexual maturity even younger. Meanwhile, young men – especially of the middle class – often delayed marriage as they built careers; some banks forbade their clerks from marrying at all until their salaries had reached a certain level.[33]

Delayed marriage stimulated fear of masturbation but is also likely to have increased the market for prostitution.[34] In the lurid imaginations of social purity reformers, a man's abuse of his own body was just a step along the road to the abuse of someone else's. So they suggested vigorous exercise and manly games, while also calling for early marriage as an antidote to the related problems of self-abuse and prostitution.[35] Yet no one seriously argued in favour of marriage at puberty, associated with 'savages' such as the Aborigines. So moral reformers, 'reputable' medical scientists and a large army of 'quacks' pedalling cures for 'youthful indiscretions' and 'nervous debility' combined to stoke panic.[36] Henry Varley claimed that self-pollution, as he called it, was 'sapping the vigour of our youthful and national life'. The retention of 'the seed' was for him 'a necessity of the highest moment to youth and manhood. The vigour of the nervous system is mainly dependent upon the seed, which may be fitly described as the sap of the whole man'. Self-abuse led to a 'want of moral force', 'simpering effeminacy' and 'lewd speech', all observable in modern youth.[37]

The views of the religious fanatic were echoed by those who stood to gain from panic over masturbation. Howard Freeman and Richard Wallace, a pair of quacks who ran a 'medical' institute in Sydney, also published *Rescued at Last: Being Clinical Experiences on Nervous and Private Diseases, by Sydney's Leading Specialists*. The most frequent cause of nervous debility, they said, was neither VD nor alcohol, 'but … the exit from the body of what may be truthfully termed the ESSENSE [sic] OF VITALITY, the SEED OF LIFE, the germ or active principle from which springs the human form divine'. Fortunately, for a £1 fee, the 'doctors' would send advice and medicine, and they also sold various electrical appliances and belts, at prices from £2/2 up to £6/6 (the latter about three weeks' wages for a well-paid labourer) designed to cure the impotence arising from self-abuse. Suddenly, 'the flabby, soft, and pallid penis, more like that of a delicate child than the organ of a full-grown man, renews its former healthy condition and accomplishes with natural energy the part for which it is intended'.

Freeman and Wallace claimed to be able to spot a masturbator at a glance, but an examination of the testicles was the clincher:

> … on examining his private parts, why they might have belonged to a man of seventy-five; thus the penis was small and very soft, moisture about the orifice, and the foreskin is attached to the glans penis as if it were glued. His testicles were unequal and very pendulous [that is, they] hang down a good deal, and the Scrotum or purse wrinkled, and felt as if a bag of worms was in my hands.

Among the other symptoms of the masturbator, they said, were a voracious appetite, especially for rich foods, and 'a peculiar gait'. In girls, masturbation led to arrested development including a flat chest, round shoulders, a head that constantly drooped forward, hollowness at the pit of the stomach, a crooked posture when seated, and a tendency to sleep on her left side when in bed. But for both men and women, it was the face that gave the game away.[38] Dr Bottrell, another charlatan,

numbered among the signs of self-abuse 'the hollow cheek, the droop-
ing form, the lack-lustre eye. The hands are either feverishly dry, or
else clammy with moisture. There is no animation in the gait of these
phantoms, and they start at the merest sound. They are shy and
reserved, especially in the society of women'.[39]

At a time when European doctors were moving away from the idea
that masturbation caused insanity and a wide range of other ills, medical hostility to self-abuse in Australia remained undiminished. The
high level of investment in reproductive sex in Australia was perhaps
one reason for this difference; another might have been the particular
strength of a culture of manly respectability and self-restraint in colonies with a powerful legacy of both the convict system and an
'uncivilised' frontier.[40] As a result, qualified doctors in Australia had
some difficulty differentiating their views from quacks.[41] Masturbation
was no more than abortion or VD a subject on which doctors tended to
dwell, but those few who did so sought to enhance their own professional credibility by condemning the self-interested exaggerations of
medical charlatans. Dr Alexander Paterson, in an 1889 pamphlet on
*Nervous Debility*, declared that the loss of semen was in itself no more
dangerous than the loss of saliva. In this respect, his approach departed
from Arthur's but was consistent with a developing emphasis in the
medical profession on the danger of 'nervous shock' caused by self-
abuse. Masturbation, according to this view, was harmful not because
it wasted sperm but because of the loss of 'nerve force', especially in
bodies that were still developing.[42] Self-abuse made the body 'more susceptible to disease'.[43] Paterson's suggested cures included electricity,
any healthy outdoor exercise except riding, avoidance of a 'second
sleep' after waking in the morning, and a preventative device attached
to the penis. Like Arthur, he recommended circumcision for hard
cases.[44] Cold baths and hard mattresses were frequently offered as
remedies.

First-hand accounts of how young people responded to anti-
masturbatory propaganda are rare. Percy Grainger, the musician, must
have been unusual in his joyful celebration of the 'bliss' of what, with
post-Victorian irony, he called 'self-help': 'What unique ecstasies! What
liberation! What protection from dangerous and exasperating diseases!
What independence from women and marriage!'[45] But Grainger, although
reflecting on his youth, was writing in 1945, by which time he was a man

of considerable sexual knowledge and experience, and attitudes to masturbation had changed. By way of contrast, in 1890, Ted Machefer, the
young swagman, told a friend that he intended to launch a public campaign against 'the nation-destroying practice of self-abuse' that was
'handed down from [p]arents to children'. 'I remember speaking to a
tart one time,' he added, 'and she told me that that very day she had
"jerked" a married man off'. It was therefore clear to him that the habit
had 'become permanent in the constitution of men'. He even suggested
installing a mechanical device on a child's penis to prevent masturbation. Ted's main worry was that he lacked 'reliable information' on
female masturbation, although he was certain that candles and carrots
were 'pressed into service'.[46]

Self-abuse could induce much guilt. William Chidley believed that
masturbation was shrinking his head and brain, damaging his sight,
and responsible for 'an ugly ridge or double crown' on the back of his
head 'where the hair would not lie but stuck up in a spout'. On one occasion when a mood of lust overcame him at school, he visited the toilet
but instead of masturbating slammed the seat on his penis, causing it to
blacken.[47] Most presumably did not resort to such measures. But there
were also probably very few who did not experience guilt and fear even
into married life where, considering the role of sexual restraint in
avoiding pregnancy, masturbation likely remained common. And in
contemporary medical opinion and folk wisdom, masturbation offered
a ready-made explanation for almost any medical – and especially sexual – problem you cared to name.

### Taming Men
Panic over the sexual precociousness of the young was also at the heart
of public debate about gang-rape. A series of such crimes in the late
nineteenth century crystallised concern about the morality of working-class men.[48] Was the convict taint still infecting the people's blood?
Or was the race degenerating, producing a weak-willed and immoral
people unable to distinguish right from wrong? Several hideous gang-
rapes in the 1880s fuelled panic over the 'larrikin', a young working-class
male seen as responsible for the brutality. The larrikin came to embody
a middle-class fear that the city was being taken over by its most bestial
form of humanity.[49] And while there was reassurance in the impression

that working-class girls of dubious character were their most likely victims, there must also have been a nagging fear among the respectable that their own daughters were endangered by these youths' reputedly unbridled sexual aggression.

Gang-rape accounted for a high proportion of all rape charges in the late nineteenth century. Jill Bavin-Mizzi's study of the rape trials in Victoria, Queensland and WA between 1880 and 1900 found that of 190 cases, 70 (or almost 37 per cent) were gang-rapes. Defendants were invariably young, and many attacks occurred in broad daylight, leading some historians to speculate that gang-rape might have been a larrikin rite of passage.[50] But as Simon Sleight has suggested, it is unlikely that most larrikins committed rape. Rather, larrikin subculture, with its stress on masculine aggression, made such assaults more likely by weakening moral barriers.[51]

In contrast with modern condemnation of gang-rape as un-Australian, especially when committed by 'Muslim' youths, the impression developed in the late nineteenth century that it was a distinctively Australian crime – indicative, as one judge put it, of 'a degraded state of morality here'.[52] The 1886 attack on sixteen-year-old Mary Jane Hicks, at Mount Rennie in Sydney, represented the climax of contemporary concern about sexual depravity in the rising generation. Outraged by a series of brutal gang-rapes that had recently come before his court, Justice Windeyer this time sentenced the young defendants to death. Five men had their sentences commuted to life, but four were hanged early in 1887 amid riotous protests. The popular press portrayed the young men as victims of grave injustice, and Hicks as a 'lying little street tramp'.[53] Good girls did not become rape victims; or at least those who were raped did not remain good girls, having 'their morals corrupted' so that 'they led other children in the paths of vice'.[54] A decade after the Mount Rennie case, the *Truth* was still campaigning on behalf of those it affectionately called the 'Mount Rennie boys', the men whose death sentences had been commuted. The trial, it said, had been conducted in the midst of a 'moral panic', while the woman these 'mere striplings' raped was a 'female fiend' and *'partially a consenting party'*.[55]

Much of this discussion assumed male sexuality to be particularly difficult, if not impossible, to control – a stream that, if dammed in one place, would break through elsewhere, in ways more destructive than if running a natural course. Rowland Rees, arch-enemy of moral purity campaigners, was the most vocal and unabashed proponent of this view of sexuality in the SA parliament. Rees believed that legislative attempts to suppress male sexual drives would make more prevalent a range of vices, including masturbation and rape. 'Every old schoolboy of the House', he said, would agree 'that in proportion as legislation of this kind was instituted there were increased secret sins over which thought and memory mourned'.[56] More subtle defenders of male privilege than Rees still assumed that a man possessed certain sexual rights that arose from his status or destiny as a husband and father. So, when it was proposed in a Victorian draft bill in 1878 that men believed to be suffering from VD should be subject to compulsory examination, there were objections that this course would undermine the rightful domestic authority of the father and husband. And when witnesses recognised the discriminatory character of legislation that imposed inspection on women and not men, they still declared that you could not 'go into a family and take the father of a family and punish him'.[57] But you could, apparently, go into a family and take the mother of a family and punish *her* – provided you had reason to believe she was a diseased prostitute.

Those who defended men's sexual rights pointed to the dangers that vicious and conniving women posed to boys and men. Girls, it was said, even when respectable, were during certain phases of their lives 'subject to some of the many curious phases which hysteria presented'. At such times, 'they were hardly responsible for what they said or did'; and it was not at all uncommon for girls to make unfounded accusations against innocent men.[58] If it was women's irrationality that was at fault in this instance, it was the 'new woman's' capacity for reason that worried another parliamentarian, who warned that educated women were more dangerous than the uneducated: 'It was impossible to say to what extent a designing and handsome woman might not ... take advantage of members of the male sex.'[59]

### Age of Consent

Whether rational or irrational, mature or childlike, a woman's word was not to be trusted – an attitude that also pervaded efforts to raise the age of consent. The main purpose of such legislation was to protect young girls from sexual exploitation and prevent them falling into prostitution. If girls married in their early twenties, the years between puberty and their coming of age were especially dangerous to female virtue. The aim of raising the age of consent was to protect young girls during some of these years in a way rape laws could not. A rape conviction required that a jury be convinced a woman had not consented to sex. If defence counsel could prove, on the basis of a woman's character, that she might have consented, a conviction was unlikely. But in a carnal knowledge case, consent was theoretically irrelevant. Provided a male had sex with an underage girl, he could be prosecuted. If a defendant claimed the woman had given consent, it made no difference to his guilt or innocence.[60]

In practice, juries found it impossible to ignore consent despite its formal legal irrelevance. One-third of defendants in carnal knowledge cases surveyed by Bavin-Mizzi in the 1880–1900 period raised consent as a defence, a pattern that would indicate a gulf between popular custom and the statutes being passed under the pressure of social purity activists. The problem was the ambiguity inherent in the idea of childhood: it was so bound up with sexual innocence that, if a girl who had reached puberty consented to sex, it was difficult for judges and juries to see her as a child needing protection.[61] Sergeant McGillicuddy, a Melbourne policeman, complained in 1909 that he had 'known Juries to bring in verdicts of not guilty against the strongest evidence, and after the Judge had summed up strongly against the accused, because the girl although under 16 was to all intents and purposes a woman in physique'.[62] In cases where the male was also young, judges imposed light sentences; and even social purity campaigners had their sights on the 'old sinners', not mere 'lads'. One SA parliamentarian suggested that boys under sixteen, instead of imprisonment, might be given 'a dozen strokes of the rod' in the backyard of the police station, while Queensland legislation actually provided that young offenders could be whipped and sent to an industrial or reformatory school.[63] A case at Bairnsdale in Victoria in 1911, however, suggested that where race was a consideration, the law could be more stringently applied. In this instance, a 21-year-old 'half-caste' man, Alfred Stephens, received three months' imprisonment after pleading guilty to sex with his fourteen-year-old Aboriginal girlfriend, Elsie Barrett. The authorities wanted to remove the young man from the district, and the age of consent laws furnished them with a convenient instrument to effect their purpose.[64]

In other circumstances, age of consent legislation recognised boys' lesser culpability. The 1891 Victorian amendment of the *Crimes Act* made the girl's age sixteen, and laid down that her consent to sex was no defence in carnal knowledge cases unless she 'be older than or of the same age as the defendant'.[65] Yet in an 1892 case in Collingwood, a twenty-year-old labourer, Alexander Hastings, charged with carnal knowledge of a fifteen-year-old girl, Ellen Berwick, was found not guilty and released. Hastings admitted that sex had taken place, but claimed that Berwick had given her consent. The girl's parents were primarily interested in whether Alexander intended marrying their daughter.[66] A similar case, in a Victorian country town, did not even make it to court. Denton Miller, a twenty-year-old painter, was charged with having had carnal knowledge of a girl under sixteen. The offence was due to come before the court at Stawell on 21 January 1907. Miller's lawyer wrote to an interested party:

> I think it not unlikely that owing to certain proceedings which I am instructed will take place today the prosecution will not be proceeded with. The proceedings I refer to are the marriage of Denton Miller and the young girl whom he is charged with having violated.

On 12 January 1907 Miller and Emma Brown, a pregnant sixteen-year-old domestic servant, were married.[67]

In the late nineteenth century, around a third of children born in wedlock had been conceived out of it. The overwhelming majority of births to mothers under twenty, and a slight majority of those to women in their early or mid-twenties, were either illegitimate or the fruit of sex before marriage. All of this suggested a high level of sexual activity among the unmarried young; there was little prospect that age of consent legislation could provide girls much protection once they reached puberty.[68]

Calls to raise the age of consent were part of a wider agenda of women's rights. Women's suffrage organisations emerged all over Australia in the 1880s, with sexuality very much in their sights. Apart from their interest in age of consent laws, they also opposed contagious diseases legislation and called for divorce law reform that would remove the double standard: in all colonies, a man could end a marriage if his wife committed adultery just once but a woman had to prove repeated adultery, adultery combined with cruelty or desertion, or an 'unnatural offence'. By the 1890s Victoria and NSW allowed women a divorce on grounds of desertion but the double standard remained, inherited from Britain. Where a woman needed to stray from the marital bed only once for her husband to be granted a divorce, the law permitted men more latitude.[69]

Women played a subordinate role in the social purity campaigns of the 1880s but from around 1890 they achieved greater prominence. They confronted the male bias they found in both courts and legislatures. In Victoria the WCTU complained of the light sentences handed out in carnal knowledge cases, as well as successfully opposing an 1893 proposal to exempt the accused from punishment if he believed the girl to be over sixteen.[70] Although the trend in the age of consent was upward – in Victoria, just before World War I, it reached as high as eighteen – qualifications and exemptions were added that reduced the law's effectiveness. Legislation often provided that if a male believed, and had cause to believe, a girl was older than she looked, he might be acquitted. Here was a particularly useful rider for defence barristers, who were also assisted by provisions excluding from protection a girl believed to be 'a common prostitute, or an associate of common prostitutes' or even – as in the case of the Victorian legislation of 1913 – one merely thought to have previously had consensual sex.[71] In this way, a victim's morality, physical maturity or associations became relevant – much as occurred when barristers wished to persuade jurors in rape trials that a woman had agreed to sex.

At the heart of the campaign to raise the age of consent was a belief that the man who first seduced a girl was responsible for her 'fall' into prostitution. As Arthur advised young men, 'there is always a first step to the very lowest depths of degradation' and today's 'bright and innocent girl', having once yielded to male lust, might 'be the painted, gin-sodden harlot of a few years hence, whose consumptive cough drowns her hoarse and despairing laughter'.[72] A woman was capable of sexual passion but because girls were naturally innocent, the seducer bore responsibility for arousing her desire. In this way, reformers used conventional Victorian ideas about sexuality – such as the double standard and idea of the sexually innocent girl – to argue that women needed more protection. Illicit sex had greater physical and moral consequences for them.[73]

*Crossing the Racial Line*

In the late nineteenth century, many colonists saw in Chinese men an alarming source of depravity. But whereas during the gold rushes the focus had been on sodomy, the image of the Asian seducer of young maidens now gained greater currency. Dangers to the racial purity of the nation, through either military invasion or immigration, were popularly presented in terms of a threat posed by the oriental rapist to the sleeping virgin. A Labor Party newspaper in Victoria in 1910 issued the following warning about the Chinese market gardener, who

> is invariably at the white man's door haggling garrulously with the white man's wife or daughter about the price of the daily cauli- flower. There is, not infrequently, a lecherous gleam in the wicked slant eyes of the yellow cabbage vendor on such occasions. He is then as cheeky as a cock sparrow, whose thoughts in spring have lightly turned to love …[74]

Chinese, said the Sydney *Bulletin*, brought 'vice and vegetables';[75] a member of the 1891 Royal Commission on Alleged Chinese Gambling and Immorality closely questioned a bemused doctor about whether housewives could catch syphilis after coming into contact with vege- tables purchased from a Chinese market gardener.[76] But one historian of north Queensland has suggested that many relationships between Chinese men and European women did in fact begin 'at the front door'. So, once we allow for the prevailing racism of the era, it is easy to under- stand how the Chinese hawker could be portrayed as a devious and even lecherous intruder threatening the domestic authority and sexual rights of white men.[77]

Anti-Asian campaigns grew more vocal, as ideas of a strict racial hierarchy crystallised alongside fears of white racial decline. In the 1901 federal parliamentary debate over the Immigration Restriction Bill, Prime Minister Edmund Barton quoted, at length, the best known Australian theorist of Aryan racial decline, Charles Pearson. In his 1893 book *National Life and Character*, Pearson forecast a time – possibly 'not far distant' – when the Aryan and Christian peoples would be 'elbowed' aside by 'the black and yellow races', who would even 'be admitted to inter-marriage' with European people.[78] Federal Labor Party Leader Chris Watson, in the same debate, also raised this spectre of 'racial contamination', which he linked to intermarriage: 'The question is whether we would desire that our sisters or our brothers should be married into any of these races to which we object.'[79] Another Labor parliamentarian, James Ronald, likened the mingling of superior and inferior races to the 'pure-minded, noble woman' who 'marries some degenerate debauchee, with the hope of reclaiming him; but the almost inevitable result is that the man drags her down to his level'.[80] It was natural for parliamentarians to reach for sexual imagery in warning of the dire consequences of racial threats because it was ultimately mis-cegenation – sexual relations across the racial divide – that most disturbed them. Objections based on arguments about economic com-petition might appeal to the head or hip-pocket, but references to sex – whether veiled or open – moved a deeper self. So James Page, a Queensland Labor man, was only expressing common feeling when he asked another parliamentarian how he 'would like to see a black man married to his daughter or to his sister'.[81]

The alleged sexual immorality of the Chinese was used to justify discrimination and exclusion. Yet white Australian critics were never quite sure whether the salient feature of Chinese male sexuality was potency or a lack of it. Where some accused Chinese men in Sydney of luring girls into their overcrowded boarding houses in order to 'make use of them in every way to gratify their lusts and desires',[82] others judged that widely circulated tales of debauchery were exaggerated:

> There are very few women in the Chinese camp? – Few. The Chinese have not such a large selection as the Europeans, and the conse-quence is that one woman is more frequently used. In fact I said to a woman one day, 'How is it that you take up with the Chinese? If you want to carry on this mode of life why do not you give up the Chinese?' 'Well,' she said, 'the fact of the matter is this, we can deal with half-a-dozen Chinamen without feeling any difficulty.' In fact they have not the vigor, that is what she wanted to convey to me.[83]

Chinese men were both 'feminised in the rhetoric' of the day but also presented as a 'threat to White womanhood' because, like women, they were said to be notably cunning.[84]

Not all the images of Chinese men were disparaging. A police super-intendent, F.A. Winch, told an inquiry that many of the white women to be found in Melbourne's Chinese Quarter, far from being prostitutes, were married to Chinese men, or at least in stable relationships with them: 'They live quietly and comfortably with their men ... I have often spoken to those girls, and they say those men are exceedingly kind to them.'[85] Yet it was not this evidence of respectability but the image of the Chinese sexual predator that passed into popular currency. In 1892 a Melbourne labour newspaper reported that when a deputation of women waited on the Trades Hall Council asking for assistance in starting a cooperative laundry, one woman related how her fourteen-year-old daughter 'had answered an advertisement for a nursegirl, the occupants of the house ... to which she applied being Chinese'. 'Now, surely,' commented the paper in a report headed 'Lechery and Leprosy', 'the police can take cognisance of this statement, and prevent the defilement of the young girls of our community by the almond-eyed procurer or his leprous associates'.[86] In this way the apparently innocent act of advertising for a female employee was transformed into attempted seduction. Similarly, a report in Sydney's *Truth* in 1896 warned parents against allowing their daughters to enter a Chinese grocery store. The writer claimed to have frequently seen girls of ten to fourteen in these shops, 'half over the counter, in close confab with the yellow shopman, her face flushed, and a look in her eyes that tells the tale of inward corruption, of prurient suggestion falling on ground only too receptive. *She is being initiated!*' It was 'a sickening thought' that many girls who escape the worst consequences of their youthful folly, and eventually marry white men, have been pawed over and robbed of their bloom by a leprous, clawey Chinaman'.[87] Chinese men had soiled an article properly belonging to the white man.

When the NSW Royal Commission on Alleged Chinese Gambling and Immorality sat in 1891, it was stalked by the image of the Chinese seducer. But the 1892 report was a measured document and the inquiry, which included respected Chinese businessman Quong Tart, refused to treat at face value the dubious claims concerning sexual debauchery. Referring to allegations of Chinese seduction of white maidens, the commission found 'no ground for suspicion that our alien population is now a danger to youthful virtue'. Some women in relationships with Chinese men openly ridiculed the idea that girls under the influence of opium were, against their will, being debauched by Chinese men. The commission found that sexual relations were common between Chinese men and European women but that many women were 'living as wives in all but name with the men whose homes they share'. These working-class women responded to the inquiry's assault on their privacy by attesting to the kindness with which they were treated by their Chinese partners. Factory workers, domestic servants, casual prostitutes, there was even a circus performer – their 'seduction' had by their own account invariably occurred in the arms of a European; they had only gravitated to the Chinese after their 'fall'. They saw themselves not merely as having taken up with a 'Chinaman', but as having gone over to the 'Chinese'. And only in this limited sense does the commission's exaggeration that 'European women living amongst the Chinese are the common property of many Chinamen' make any sense.[88]

Outside the big cities, the Chinese formed large camps in town centres, often on rented land beside a river. These settlements usually accommodated between 100 and 300 Chinese men, perhaps half-a-dozen or so European women married to the men, the very occasional married Chinese woman, and a retinue of 'prostitutes'; however, some of those whom the authorities counted as prostitutes might have been women living in a stable domestic relationships with Chinese men.[89] White women who lived with Chinese men sometimes suffered official persecution, being especially vulnerable to the operation of the almost endlessly elastic vagrancy statutes. In the eyes of many police, living with a Chinese man was enough to demonstrate that a woman was 'idle and disorderly', an equation that magistrates readily accepted. Unlike in parts of the US, marriage between Asians and Europeans was not outlawed in Australia, but Antipodean authorities had ample means of making life miserable for anyone who dared cross the racial line.[90]

The state's concern extended to Asian men's relationships with Aboriginal women. But there was a chasm between the racially pure nation being conjured by wise statesmen in distant Melbourne, and the reality of life in northern Australia, where Asians, Europeans and Indigenous people rubbed shoulders and much else. In these places, Pacific Islanders, Malays, Indonesians, Japanese, Filipinos and Chinese men entered into casual or ongoing sexual relations with Indigenous women. In one case that came to the attention of the WA Royal Commission on the Condition of the Natives in 1904, a magistrate refused to perform a marriage between a Malay and an Aboriginal woman but informed the couple that he had no objection to them living together.⁹¹ There was, in fact, no law to prevent casual sex, de facto coupling or legal marriage between Asians and Aboriginals in WA at this time. Critics of interracial sex feared for the nation's racial integrity, but in Australia's tropical north, little could be done.⁹²

Along the coast, Asian pearl shellers, lugger crews and *bêche-de-mer* (sea cucumber) fishermen conducted liaisons with Indigenous women, handing over liquor, clothes, flour, rice, tobacco and pipes to the women and their families for sex. Some contemporary observers called this exchange prostitution but it was in reality a continuation of a tradition stretching back hundreds of years, to when the first Macassans arrived on northern beaches to collect *bêche-de-mer*. The Aboriginal people they encountered had long ago accommodated these sojourners into their life cycles and traditions.⁹³ Indeed, a WA police constable testified to the elaborate and highly organised character of the exchange with Asian visitors, explaining that some Aboriginals came 'from the coast and others from inland. The coastal natives tell them what they can get from crews and they are attracted. Some natives come from 100 miles inland to trade with the crews about twice a year'.⁹⁴ And so long as the visitors, having partaken of local hospitality, handed these women back to their husbands, there was little trouble. But as traditional society disintegrated under the impact of European colonisation, Aboriginal control over such exchanges declined.⁹⁵

The WA Royal Commission had also found considerable evidence of sex between European men and Aboriginal women. '"Kombo"-ism is rife', reported the Commissioner, Walter Roth, and he recommended legislation to prevent the abuses being carried on.⁹⁶ Roth had heard testimony of women being abducted and held captive by European men in chains. In one instance, when a woman's Aboriginal husband followed in an effort to get her back, he was threatened with a gun.⁹⁷ A white drover from Wyndham told the commission that a magistrate had covered up a case in which a man had chained an Aboriginal woman to his tent because the perpetrator was his friend, while another stockman claimed that in the Fitzroy district each 'boss' had 'his own fancy woman' and his overseer was allowed to choose from eight or ten others.⁹⁸ The police sergeant at Broome testified that the owner of Thangoo Station was notorious for cohabiting with Aboriginal women, and had fathered several 'half-caste children'.⁹⁹ The authorities complained that they were powerless to deal with most cases, but some were complicit. A police constable at Isdell River, John Wilson, admitted not only that it was his usual practice to chain to a tree a 'gin' being brought in as a witness to cattle-spearing, but that trackers or assisting stockmen could probably rape the women with impunity since he took no precautions to prevent it.[100] Wilson might have known much more than he admitted. Two male Aboriginal witnesses, both prisoners in Wyndham Gaol, claimed to have seen this constable 'marry' plenty of 'gins'.[101]

This evidence echoed earlier claims made by J.B. Gribble, a Church of England missionary in the Gascoyne River area of WA, in his 1886 pamphlet *Dark Deeds in a Sunny Land*. On one particular station, reported Gribble,

> several native men declared aloud in the presence of their owner that a young native girl about 15 years of age was their master's wife. On hearing this unexpected bit of information the settler adroitly smuggled the girl out of sight and hearing, and I saw her no more. At the same station I was informed by a white overseer that in certain places the choicest bit of hospitality that could be tendered to a visitor was the finest-looking black girl.[102]

Gribble was persecuted by the Gascoyne community and WA establishment for this exposure, and unsuccessfully brought a libel suit against the *West Australian* when it called him a 'lying, canting humbug'. Yet at the trial, one of the leading pastoralists in the region admitted that he had 'sent the women off to the white men myself', with the probable consequence 'that the women will be used as the white man wishes'.[103]

White men went about the country with Aboriginal women in train, sometimes with the latter dressed as men or boys, a practice that would not only have reduced the embarrassment of the white man but also have deceived sexual competitors.[104] Some whites formed stable relationships and accepted the responsibilities to the woman's kin and their mixed-race children that this implied. But interracial sex disrupted traditional Aboriginal society. As a well-informed police constable from Halls Creek in WA remarked, each Aboriginal woman belonged to an Aboriginal man: was it any wonder that white men who took them away sometimes found themselves at the sharp end of a spear?[105]

Authorities animated by humanitarianism worried about the sexual degradation inflicted by whites and Asians on Aboriginal women. But the same authorities were also motivated by an intense desire for racial purity, and they sought to prevent the creation of a population of 'half-castes', 'quadroons' and 'octoroons' that would pollute the nation's bloodstream. Archibald Meston, who was to become Protector for the Southern District of Queensland, believed interracial marriages 'unfair to the woman and degrading to the man',[106] even while allowing that the white men concerned were 'far lower in the scale of humanity than any tribe of Australian savages'. He advocated the *absolute isolation* of Aboriginal people on reserves, where they could 'marry and beget children, and live happily, free from all contact with the white race'. If, on the other hand, marriageable women were sent into service among the white population, it was inevitable that they would fall into sexual 'intercourse with white men': 'We can hardly expect the emotions of the savage woman to be under more severe control than those of the white.' Moreover, said Meston, Aboriginal men were unlikely to enjoy 'enforced celibacy'.[107]

Governments moved to protect Indigenous women from sexual degradation and to solve the 'half-caste problem' by trying to isolate Aboriginal women from European and Asian men. Queensland's 1897 *Aboriginals Protection and Restriction of the Sale of Opium Act* is perhaps the best known attempt by Australian authorities to achieve these ends, and it was a precedent for similar 'protective' measures in other frontier societies, such as WA, SA and the NT, in the early years of the century. New laws sought to eliminate interracial sex but their effect, inevitably, was to harass those who formed stable relationships while leaving casual sex untouched.[108]

The situation in the earlier and more densely settled south-east was different, since the white majority there was so overwhelming in numbers and power. But at a time of rising panic about threats to racial purity, the half-caste 'menace' was, to some minds, deeply unsettling. In early twentieth-century NSW, growing white concern about the proliferation of people of 'mixed blood' intensified official efforts to remove children from their families and place them in institutions. While often couched in terms of protecting the vulnerable, child removal aimed to reduce the number of people identifying as Aboriginal.[109]

Meanwhile, in Victoria, parliament legislated in 1886 to encourage the absorption into the general population of Aboriginal people of mixed descent – by getting them off government rations and stations – while keeping 'full-bloods' and some categories of mixed-race people on reserves.[110] By the 1880s the idea had already taken hold among Victorian officials that mixed-race Aborigines could be biologically absorbed into the mainstream community – or bred out – through marriages between 'half-caste' women and white men. This ambition even extended to marriage between Aboriginal or mixed-race men and white women. Surprisingly perhaps, Victorian authorities appear not to have been much perturbed by this prospect, seeing in it an opportunity to get Aboriginal people off the public purse and even as evidence of the successful assimilation of Aboriginal men into the white community.[111] If, as ethnologists now reported, Aborigines were like Europeans descended from the Aryans of south Asia; or if, as another theory held, they were primitive Caucasians, it was all the easier to rationalise sex across racial lines. The history of humanity was being rewritten to show that Aborigines and Europeans, despite their very different places on the scale of civilisation, had common origins. Perhaps they also had a common future? Aboriginal skins might be black but they had a white racial core recoverable through the fruits of marriage with the European settler.[112] In practice, though, few opportunities arose for young Aboriginal women to acquire white husbands. Some, rather, found themselves removed from mission stations to the same rescue homes and reformatories that received 'fallen' white women.[113] To this limited extent, black and white did indeed have a common future.

Despite the Victorian legislation, a white woman who partnered an Aboriginal man could expect social censure and scandal, as when Ethel Gribble, the daughter of the missionary we have just encountered in the WA phase of his career, fell in love with an Aboriginal man, Fred Wondunna, on a Fraser Island mission run by her brother, Ernest. Ethel was browbeaten by her horrified brother into marrying a white man in order to avert social catastrophe, but she was soon left a widow by her sickly husband, became pregnant to Wondunna, with whom she resumed her relationship on another mission, and then married him in Sydney with Congregational rites after they failed to find an Anglican willing to do the job. Meanwhile, Ernest – a married man recently estranged from his wife – found solace in the arms of an Aboriginal woman raised on his mission. She would soon bear a child by him.[114] The pastoralists who incurred their father's wrath might have smiled wryly if they had learned of the younger Gribbles' dark deeds in sunny Queensland.

The late-nineteenth-century marriage of Jimmy and Ethel Governor was haunted by community censure, followed by a more rigorous condemnation of the white working-class woman once it ended in an infamous tragedy. After Governor, a man of mixed descent, along with his brother Joe and another man, Jack Underwood, went on an axe-wielding spree in northern NSW that would leave nine dead, there was considerable public interest in what kind of white woman would marry a man with such a black heart and skin. A contributing factor to Governor and his associates' massacring several members of his employer's family, the Mawbeys, and a schoolteacher who lived with them, was Jimmy's belief that the women taunted Ethel, their domestic, that 'any white woman who married a blackfellow was not fit to live'. Ethel later testified in court that while she had been forced to suffer many unkind remarks, the Mawbeys themselves had not said 'she ought to be shot'; but they had once expressed 'wonder that a nice looking girl like' her should have thrown 'herself away on a blackfellow'.[115]

The prurient might have been even more fascinated by Ethel if, like recent historians, they had noticed discrepancies in the evidence that suggest she might have actually witnessed the killings in the Mawbey family home. Apparently without any such prompting, one reporter professed to be 'astounded and horrified' by the 'depravity of her nature' while another was certain that she must be a fool because she was unable to see 'anything extraordinary in having married a blackfellow'. Yet Ethel, by her own account, was not the only white woman who had shown an interest in the industrious Jimmy as a potential husband, and she had regarded her marriage to him as a personal triumph.[116]

In every Australian colony or state, governments enjoyed wide powers over Aborigines, including their sexual behaviour. In Queensland the 1897 legislation and subsequent amendments to it protected white settlers' Aboriginal labour supply by creating a permit system but also allowed authorities to remove to a reserve women and children deemed to be in sexual danger. Protectors had the power to prevent marriage between a non-Aboriginal man and an Indigenous woman. The state's discretion could sometimes work in favour of those targeted by the legislation, and some applications of Asian men to marry Aboriginal women received sympathetic official treatment. In a few cases, white friends were willing to support Chinese men and Aboriginal women against efforts to keep them apart, while even police sometimes defended stable relationships between Chinese men and Indigenous women despite their illegality.[117] Racial purity was fine in theory, but humanitarianism, resistance and pragmatism sometimes subverted the sexual engineers' best laid plans. It was after all hard to overlook that Chinese men were providing protection to Aboriginal women vulnerable to sexual and other exploitation in a rough, frontier society. And there were also cases in which white men – Irish, Dutch and Germans in particular – defied official panic about miscegenation by marrying Aboriginal women.[118]

### Prostitution

In communities with large concentrations of men and few marriageable women, prostitution played a large part in the sexual economy. Australia was part of an international sex trade in the late nineteenth and early twentieth centuries, with Japanese prostitutes usually arriving via Hong Kong or Singapore. Their role was especially to service the multi-ethnic male communities in the Australian tropics, and brothels appeared in northern towns as well as on the booming Kalgoorlie goldfield in the 1890s. Since these establishments were usually orderly, they were relatively safe from prosecution, and Japanese prostitutes often gained local acceptance for their quiet provision of an 'essential' service. Their clients also had much for which to be thankful: the Japanese were well-trained, discreet, sober, clean and willing to provide charming company as well as an outlet for sexual release.[119] But the *Immigration Restriction Act* in 1901 made it impossible to replenish the brothels with fresh young talent. During parliamentary debate on that bill, one speaker had claimed that there was a northern town in which it had become an axiom that the leading citizens 'eat with the Chows and sleep with the Japs' while others expressed disgust that northern Australian prostitution was sometimes defended by local worthies as essential in protecting respectable white women from sexual assault.[120]

From the point of view of some of Australia's sexual engineers, these brothels performed a useful service in areas where there were large concentrations of 'coloured' workers. As the Queensland Commissioner of Police, W.E. Parry-Okeden, commented, '[t]he supply of Japanese women for the Kanaka demand is less revolting and degrading than would be the case were it met by white women'.[121] In other words, Japanese prostitutes prevented the most reviled form of miscegenation, that between a 'coloured' man and a white woman who, even if a prostitute, was still a degraded member of a superior race. Yet these prostitutes also served European clients, who may have been influenced by orientalist 'fantasies of submissive, silently obedient females'.[122] After 1901 foreign prostitutes were more likely to come from Europe – especially Italy and France. Nevertheless, the continuing prominence of 'foreigners' among both prostitutes and the 'bludgers' and 'pimps' who lived off their earnings allowed some observers to celebrate, as a point of contrast, the virtues of pure Australian womanhood and civilisation.[123]

In parts of Australia where men predominated, the impulse towards state toleration of prostitution was strongest. Elsewhere – notably in the south-east – the authorities were more equivocal, and the campaigns of the social purity movement more successful.[124] As in other areas of sexual behaviour, the state sought to influence prostitution, although the effects of such intervention were often very different from the intentions that motivated it. In NSW, changes to the law in 1908 made soliciting an offence and clamped down on those who knowingly rented out their premises for prostitution. Yet far from suppressing vice, these reforms helped reduce opportunities for the self-employed prostitute and small-time pimp, and so assisted the criminal underworld to take control. Increasingly, only organised crime could pay the large fines imposed for offences connected with prostitution, thereby encouraging women to place themselves under its protection.[125]

A similar process occurred in Melbourne. In the 1870s and 1880s police there had tolerated prostitution in the slums near Parliament House. After 1890, more severe legislation, changing patterns of policing and clearance of the city slums pushed prostitutes out of the city, and into decaying inner suburbs such as Carlton and Fitzroy. A member of Victoria's Criminal Investigation Branch informed the Chief Commissioner of Police in 1909 that:

> The prostitute nuisance is not so much in evidence now as it was twenty five or thirty years ago when a number of prominent hotels in the City were the rendezvous for the flash women from the City and Suburban brothels.

The flash brothels have disappeared from the City, and for some reason or other the physically fine type of women of that period have also disappeared.[126]

Nevertheless, police complained about the effects of dispersion on 'moral welfare' of the inner suburban residents, arguing that it had placed a bad example in front of young people.[127] The trade, as in Sydney, also passed into the arms of illegal liquor traders, cocaine dealers, thieves, race fixers and gamblers. The effect was not only to strengthen the links between prostitution and crime, but to segregate prostitutes in the 'rough' working-class suburbs of the inner city.[128] In WA, too, there was a move towards the segregation of prostitution in Kalgoorlie and Perth into clearly defined red-light districts which respectable folk could shun and police supervise. Kalgoorlie evolved a well-organised – if informal – 'containment' policy that involved police supervision and regulation, tolerance of brothels within an agreed area centred on Hay Street, and elaborate rules by which they were to be conducted. The women had to live on the premises and were forbidden from visiting town except to see a doctor or hairdresser. Socialising in the local hotels was strictly prohibited. The policy effectively sought to reduce the prostitute to the status of a commercially available sex object. This trend towards segregation paralleled similar developments in Aboriginal affairs that have already been noticed. 'Protection' was intended in both cases but where it was primarily the Aboriginal woman or girl who was to be guarded from harm in the case of the reserves, a red-light district would help protect the male client – and, by extension, his wife and offspring – from disease, and the rest of society from moral contagion. And well before 1915 when they acquired legislative authorisation to do so, WA police cooperated with magistrates to incarcerate and subject to medical inspection prostitutes believed to have VD.[129] Legislation passed in NSW in 1909 had also introduced a de facto contagious diseases act to that state, for it allowed authorities to place anyone serving a prison term in a lock hospital if also found with VD. The vagrancy laws, of course, were available to help police deal with cases where the suspected sufferer was not yet in prison.[130]

*Perversion and Inversion*

The transition to increasing state intervention in the sexual lives of the marginalised is also evident in approaches to male homosexuality. The famous 1885 'Labouchere Amendment' in England, also known as the 'Blackmailer's Charter', would have its colonial echoes. It had provided that:

> Any male person who, in public or private, commits, or is a party to the commission of, or procures or attempts to procure the commission by any male person of, any act of gross indecency with another male person, shall be guilty of a misdemeanor, and being convicted thereof shall be liable at the discretion of the court to be imprisoned for any term not exceeding two years, with or without hard labour. [131]

The amendment did not bring about the revolution in laws related to homosexuality that some historians have assumed, either in Britain or Australia, because the authorities were able to prosecute men who had sex with other men well before the mid-1880s even when unable to prove sodomy. [132] Nevertheless, following English precedent, sentences for sodomy – as for most crimes – were becoming less draconian, with the abolition of the death sentence in England in 1860, Victoria in 1864 (unless the offence was committed on a person under fourteen or 'with violence and without consent'), Queensland and WA in 1865, SA in 1876, NSW in 1883 and Tasmania in 1887. The trend in the late nineteenth century was towards the prosecution of more men, for less serious – and more easily proven – offences. [133] For instance, a charge of 'gross indecency' often meant that fellatio had been performed. [134] Moreover, in July 1887 Sydney police used the vagrancy law to charge two men 'in the habit of walking the streets at night, impersonating females, and having powder and pearl cream upon their faces'. It was the same measure commonly used to deal with prostitutes, which is unsurprising when it is considered that they had been allegedly 'jostling men in the streets' and using 'disgusting expressions'. [135] Perhaps police feared that unsuspecting men might be tricked into an 'unnatural offence', as had allegedly occurred in a notorious Melbourne case of female impersonation in 1863. [136] Police were increasingly active in patrolling well-known 'beats', such as parks and gardens, and they were more likely to set up a homosexual encounter in order to secure a conviction. In Queensland, a clause in the 1899 *Criminal Code*, based on the Labouchere Amendment, provided for a maximum of three years with hard labour for 'indecent practices between males' in public or private: it became 'the most deployed charge' against men engaged in sex with other men in the first half of the twentieth century.[137] In 1892 WA also embraced the Labouchere formula, but Victoria did not do so until after World War I.[138]

An increasing intensity of policing might have contributed towards the end of the nineteenth century to the development of a male homosexual subculture and identity, a group of men more or less recognisable to one another through their body language, gestures, dress code and presence in certain urban spaces.[139] But cause and effect are not easy to untangle here, since police were presumably also responding to the emergence of homosexual beats. Australia's largest cities had certainly developed the kind of 'urban bachelor subculture' that seems to have been a necessary condition for the emergence of a 'gay world'.[140] There is some evidence that men who did engage in sex with other men now sometimes saw themselves as a type, not simply as ordinary men who had performed an extraordinary – or 'unnatural' – sexual act. In an 1895 case in WA, one such man had declared, 'I can't help it, it's a disease. I prefer a man or a boy any time to a woman'.[141] Well-publicised English scandals involving homosexual activity are likely to have raised awareness.

The Oscar Wilde case has been treated as a landmark in the modern western history of male homosexuality.[142] In 1895 the Irish playwright, poet, essayist and wit became the most famous victim of the Labouchere Amendment; according to the Sydney *Truth*, in a column that contained the suggestive subheading 'The Arsenal of Aestheticism', he had 'been adjudicated by the Court to be something lower than the beasts of the field; a creature for whose peculiar offending in Australia the lash would be the punishment'.[143] David Marr has suggested that the Australian response to Wilde's fall was gentler – or at least more pragmatic – than London's. While his shows in the West End were quickly closed down, in Melbourne the Australian talent for improvisation ensured that his name was merely removed from the playbills for *An Ideal Husband* and the show allowed to go on. Moreover, *The Importance of Being Earnest* opened in the second month of Wilde's imprisonment.[144] Yet the

*Age* was hardly being generous when it described Wilde as 'that curious species of human monster, a man entirely without conscience', and it treated his fall as the result of his bad character, perverted aesthetic doctrine and morbid philosophy: 'Everything about the man tended to abnormality – itself a species of insanity, at least in the sense that all vice is insane.' Wilde's case, it said, was not one in which 'a noble nature' had collapsed 'under the stress of temptation', for there was no nobility there: it was just unfortunate that the penal code did not allow the community to place such a man under permanent restraint.[145] Leaving aside the moral outrage, the *Age*'s response to Wilde's conviction gestured uncertainly towards new ways of understanding sex between men. His behaviour was considered an abnormality, even as evidence of insanity, an idea that would gain considerable currency in twentieth-century understandings of homosexuality. Nevertheless, the *Age* was unable to go too far down this path – hence its qualification that 'all vice is insane' – for such an admission would have undermined the notion that Wilde deserved severe punishment.

The Wilde case brought sex between men – or, at least, between men and male youths – to greater public notice. In an 1895 Sydney case brought against a clerk accused of indecently assaulting two Sydney paperboys, cross-examination of the lads elicited that they knew all about the Wilde case: they said Oscar Wilde meant 'Poof' or 'Joey', the latter apparently slang for a man who sexually molested boys. Here, the worlds of the press, courtroom and street came together to define a certain type of sexual act and being. 'I am not a man of that kind', the accused replied when questioned about whether he had kissed and fondled the boys. But of what *kind* was he? Possibly not 'homosexual', for the intergenerational character of these relations, as in the Wilde case itself, may well have remained critical in how they were understood, ridiculed and condemned.[146] Lisa Featherstone has added that Australian doctors showed little interest in sodomy around the turn of the century and that, unlike in Europe, there was little effort to link the prevalence of sodomy to social degeneration. While the reasons for this neglect are not entirely clear, Featherstone offers the association of sodomy with the convict legacy and the romanticisation of male 'mateship' as possible explanations. Both made homosexuality a difficult issue for doctors to broach.[147] Yet an equally salient reason for the failure to connect homosexuality with social and moral decay might have been the long-standing Antipodean association of sodomy with the bush. In Europe, homosexuality was far more closely associated with the development of city life, which was in turn connected with social degeneration and moral corruption. In Australia, where the the bushman's reputed attraction to sodomy had long been an intriguing underside to the myth of his nobility, these connections were culturally unavailable.

All the same, there was apparently a developing awareness within the social purity movement of the dangers of same-sex attraction. A booklet written by an English clergyman but reissued by the AWCL, while extolling the value of spinsterhood, also warned women to '[b]eware of the creeping in of an exclusive affection for any man or woman. Even the love of a woman to woman may become too exclusive, too passionate, too engrossing'.[148] Here, the dangers of sexual intimacy between women are treated euphemistically but also as one variety of unhealthy exclusiveness, something that might just as readily occur between a man and a woman. Homosexual love between women has not yet acquired a specialness that would mark it off from the 'normal', if sometimes morally hazardous, sexual attraction between a healthy man and woman.

Romantic female friendships might have been less common in Australia than in Britain or the US because of the comparative rarity of wealthy gentlewomen.[149] Nonetheless, well-educated professional women were gaining a foothold in the Australian workforce by the late nineteenth century at the same time as a more balanced sex ratio emerged; all of which made alternatives to marriage for women appear more feasible. Indeed, late-nineteenth-century Victoria experienced something novel in the demographic history of the colonies: an excess of marriageable women.[150] But in any case, at least for girls and young women, romantic female friendship was regarded as compatible with marriage. The idea that a young woman would experience 'crushes' with others of the same class and sex had widespread acceptance as a middle-class rite of passage, a stage through which normal girls would pass on their way to marriage and motherhood.[151] In 1901 an Adelaide newspaper published a utopian short story of life in 1950 by 'Irven', whose real name was Jean McKenzie. The protagonists, Rosamunde and Faith, are both twenty-five years old and feeling the urge for motherhood, which by the mid-twentieth century has been organised along appropriately eugenic principles. Yet the young women – in words spoken by Rosamunde to her 'more than sister' Faith – had 'found utter fulness in each other's love'. The two of them spend much of the story staring longingly into each other's eyes and end up in a passionate embrace after Rosamunde receives a marriage proposal from her beau that will allow her to achieve 'the crowning glory of her life-long effort to be – Woman'.[152] The story suggests none-too-subtly that while Rosamunde and Faith can only develop into true women through motherhood, the passionate love of one woman for another is both noble and consistent with a woman's racial mission to reproduce well. But in Henry Handel Richardson's 1910 novel *The Getting of Wisdom* it is the 'extravagance' of Laura's love for an older schoolfriend, Evelyn, that marks her as different from other girls her age, and suggests that we are witnessing something other than a normal adolescent experience.[153] Richardson based the story on her own experience of such a relationship at Presbyterian Ladies' College in Melbourne.

The new science of sexology spawned a sexualised understanding of such relationships that made it harder to avoid recognition of the elements of sexual pleasure and desire in passionate female friendship. Sexology is usually seen as having originated in mid-nineteenth-century Germany with writers such as Richard von Krafft-Ebing and Karl Heinrich Ulrichs, but there is also a related British tradition that can be traced through William Acton, Havelock Ellis, Edward Carpenter, Marie Stopes and Norman Haire, an Australian doctor (whose career will be explored in later chapters). But even when pursued by qualified doctors, sexology occupied a lowly status in the British medical profession. Especially before Acton and Ellis gave it a modicum of respectability, an interest in sex on the part of a medical man was seen to come 'perilously close to stigmatized quackery'.[154] Sexual science tended to be the work of those who were, in some way, outsiders, and their main object of study was the sexual outsider. It might, for example, be neither entirely coincidental nor insignificant that of two of the most famous figures in twentieth-century British sexology, one – Haire – was Australian-born and -educated and the other, Ellis, spent a critical four years of his early life in NSW as a teacher (see chapter 2). To be colonial, even if you were white, was to be something other than a natural insider in an imperial culture centred on London. And to be a homosexual like Haire, or a urolagnist (one sexually stimulated by watching a woman urinate) such as Ellis, was to be sexually

marginal in a culture that looked on heterosexual intercourse for procreation within lifelong marriage as the norm.

Much early British and continental sexology was, in fact, concerned
with abnormal or marginalised sexualities such as these and, as a result
of work such as Krafft-Ebing's 1886 *Psychopathia Sexualis* and Ellis's
*Sexual Inversion* (published in 1897 although temporarily banned in
England), a new scientific vocabulary became available for describing
them. Ellis, for instance, argued that male 'inverts' often approached 'the
feminine type, either in psychic disposition or physical constitution, or
both' and that the female 'invert' was frequently a mannish or boyish
woman (more often, he believed, than male inverts were 'feminine').[155]
While seeing homosexuality as abnormal – a 'congenital anomaly' – he
nevertheless steered away from suggesting it was a disease that could
be 'cured' by showing that it 'had always and everywhere existed' and
'was frequently associated with intellectual and artistic distinction'.[156]
Sexology might have been limiting in the way it eroticised and classified
identities, relationships and behaviour outside the heterosexual mainstream, yet it also opened up new possibilities for men and women whose
sexuality was conventionally regarded as an abomination.

Even the strange sadomasochistic enthusiasms of Percy Grainger,
the expatriate Australian composer, folklorist and concert pianist, had
their place in sexology. According to his own account, Grainger's 'highest sexual delight' was

> to whip a beloved woman's body. Her screams, her struggles to
> evade the whip, the marks of the whip arising on her body, all give
> me a feeling of male power & exultation that swells my love &
> devotion towards my sweetheart a hundredfold & makes our love-
> life more intense & impulsive.[157]

As a teenager, one of Grainger's sex-fantasies 'was of sticking 2 fishhooks, slung on 4 pulleys, one into each of a woman's breasts, & then
pulley-raise the fishhooks till the weight of the woman's body caused
the fishhooks to rip thru the breast-flesh'.[158] When touring, Grainger
invariably took a selection of whips along with him, and he usually had
to wash his own shirts rather than having them laundered commercially because they were covered in blood.[159] By the early years of the
century, there was a growing awareness among some well-educated

Australians of sexological research on some of the lesser known 'perversions' such as flagellism.[160] 'For a few years Grainger's awareness of his own sexual inclinations caused him considerable worry', his biographer has recorded, but a visit to Amsterdam bestowed 'lasting peace of mind'. Here, he found a veritable cornucopia of pornography and sexology.[161] One shop even specialised in books concerned with his own sexual preferences.[162] His relief is palpable in a letter written to his beloved mother in 1908 after reading a sexological work of Iwan Bloch: 'He deals at great length with queer sexual instincts that I luckily suffer delightedly from & labels them all healthy & even desirable & dangerless. I knew so.'[163] Later, he would admit in an unpublished memoir that his sexual nature was 'low and nasty', but not 'perverse or unnatural'.[164]

In the hands of such a man, sexology appears to justify the kinds of criticisms that some feminist historians have levelled at it; notably that it helped legitimise an aggressive male sexuality. Yet this was never the whole story. Much, of course, depended on which sexologist you were reading, and perhaps even more on what you did with it. Edward Carpenter, an English sexologist writing around the turn of the century, declared that between men and women was an 'intermediate sex', called an 'Urning'. Carpenter believed himself to be an 'Urning', and so shared their special mission of 'social and heroic work, and in the generation – not of bodily children – but of those children of the mind, the philosophical conceptions and ideals which transform our lives and those of society'.[165] His was a positive message, and must have been a great reassurance to isolated men and women attracted to the same sex. Whether or not Carpenter was a direct influence on him, there are later echoes of this understanding in the writings of Patrick White, the Nobel Prize–winning Australian novelist (1912–90). White saw the homosexual 'as part woman and part man', a sexual 'ambivalence' that provided him with 'insights into human nature, denied ... to those who are unequivocally male or female'.[166]

A rare piece of evidence concerning Carpenter's impact – and the crystallisation of a new sexual identity – has survived in the form of a letter written to him by a Brisbane woman, Winifred M., in 1914. Winifred had just read Carpenter's book, *The Intermediate Sex*, which made 'a tremendous impression' on her:

I belong to this class of people myself [Urnings, or members of the intermediate sex], though not to a very marked degree, in fact I had not realised it until I read the chapter called 'The Intermediate Sex' in 'Love's Coming of Age' ... I have always been much attached to my own sex, and though by no means a man-hater, have always preferred women as companions and friends ... Now this used to worry me a good deal, as I always felt myself apart from normal people, and never suspected the explanation. Since reading your book it has been a tremendous relief to find that there are so many others in the same position, and more especially that you think it is a sign of evolution towards higher things.

Winifred informed Carpenter that although she championed women's rights, she often felt 'quite apart from them, almost as if they were of a different sex from myself'. The female form had always appeared 'much more beautiful' to her than the male, and although she was not herself 'at all masculine in appearance or manners', she had warm friendships with women and was 'rather fond of small demonstrations and caresses'. In this way, Winifred both identified with the 'masculine' – she seemed to see the world through men's eyes – and yet resisted it by emphasising her feminine appearance and manners.[167]

A major theme in the historical writing on Australian lesbian sexuality is the coexistence of diverse kinds of relationships among women, as well as of the variety of ways in which contemporaries understood behaviour that from a twenty-first-century perspective is usually seen to have obvious sexual connotations. Cross-dressing, especially by women, is a case in point. When it came to public notice in 1906 that a man living in Melbourne and calling himself Bill Edwards was actually a woman born as Marion, there was coyness about the sexual implications of his marriage a few years before. It soon came to light, moreover, that Edwards, quite the Lothario, had engaged in other sexual conquests and had many female admirers attracted to his gentlemanly manners. Indeed, he seemed almost to epitomise the kind of chivalrous man beloved of social purity reformers and feminists. Yet none of these revelations gave rise to open discussion of lesbianism, a term which itself was not yet in use in Australia. Nor was the term 'lesbian' applied to Harry Crawford (Eugenia Falleni), the twice-married 'Man-Woman Murderer', who attracted great notoriety at the time of the 1920 trial for the murder of his first wife. Instead, Crawford's behaviour was understood primarily as that of a fraud – a woman passing herself off as a man as many had done before – or a freak, a 'man-woman'. However, the prosecution's argument that a dildo found among the defendant's belongings was evidence of sexual deviance, and the efforts of Crawford's barrister in cross-examination to raise 'inversion' as part of the case for the defence were indications of a moving frontier of sexuality.[168]

## Conclusion

The period after 1875 saw the threads between sexual behaviour and national destiny being bound more securely than ever. In the mid-nineteenth century, prostitution was 'sinful', but rarely treated as a danger to the race. VD had been common earlier in the nineteenth century, but it was only in the last third of the century that it came to be seen as a serious national menace requiring stringent state, medical and moral intervention. Reformist doctors now pointed to the inadequacy of current medical facilities – for many voluntary hospitals refused to accept VD patients – and they called on governments to set up lock hospitals.[169] Masturbation had long been regarded as the cause of this or that illness, but it was only in the late nineteenth century that it was presented as a reason for declining national vigour. Gang-rape and sexual precocity in the young did not originate in the 1880s; but it was then that they came to be linked to national character and racial degeneracy. Interracial sex and the production of mixed-race children had long been a characteristic of colonial life but, under the impact of 'scientific' racism, these sexual acts sometimes acquired new and more pejorative meanings. Yet, paradoxically, the emergence of a mixed-race population in the south-east was seen as an opportunity to eliminate blackness from the national bloodstream. What both perspectives had in common, however, was a sense that sexual engineering was a necessary form of race-building. Homosexual acts by the end of the nineteenth century were coming to be understood not simply as unnatural offences committed by morally weak individuals as a result of temptation being thrown in their way, but as arising from men's very fibre. The activities of social and political movements, changes in the law, innovations in policing, new medical understandings, and shifting media representations were combining in complex ways to create new possibilities for sexual identity and expression while gradually closing off others. By the time of World War I, the stage had been set for the sexual saturation of Australian culture.

CHAPTER 5

# Tabbies, Amateurs and the Cream
# of Australian Manhood

### Violation

Australia went to war in 1914 because Britain was at war. Great Britain itself was at war for various reasons, but a factor that carried weight with the otherwise doubtful was the German violation of Belgian sovereignty. More importantly for the mobilisation of popular opinion, Imperial Germany's treatment of Belgium was brutal, and included the slaughter of over 5000 civilians. But before the end of the year, the real cruelty of German soldiers had been magnified into a collection of lurid fantasies masquerading as news from the front. Throughout the English-speaking world, stories of German atrocities, many of a sado-sexual nature, featured prominently in war coverage: a seventeen-year-old girl 'violated by an officer before her mother's eyes'; the 'married woman forced to strip herself naked and parade for nearly an hour before the troops'; '[t]hree young girls and their mother attacked in their beds at night, mutilated, and defaced'; women and children sexually assaulted, doused in petrol and set alight; others raped and then disembowelled – all calculated to show the 'bestiality of the German invaders'.[1]

Stories of girls being 'ravished' before helpless parents were especially common. The Australian politician and social reformer Dr Richard Arthur claimed that the German army had reverted to the 'sexual bestiality of the ape and the cave man'.[2] Germany was seen to pose a direct threat to the sanctity of the bourgeois home, including the authority of its male protector; many atrocity stories emphasised the middle-class status of the female victims, that they came from 'good families'.[3] It is ironic that some feminists who had been involved in the age-of-consent campaigns came to oppose the war, since their prewar agitation contributed to the success of the propaganda about 'poor little Belgium'. After all, they had for years saturated the public with stories of sexual violation that dramatised the threat that male sexual violence posed to innocent women and children. Moreover, fears of sexual violation by Asians that had featured in labour movement propaganda and the popular press before the war were now projected on to the 'Hun'. One 1918 film that attracted the censors' notice, *Satan in Sydney*, actually managed to combine the Germanic and Oriental threats: a German choirmaster seduces an Australian country girl and then uses an opium den to encourage some soldiers to desert.[4]

Meanwhile, feminist and social purity campaigners' powerful injunctions to male chivalry were put to work for the war effort. In his attempt to recruit men in the Victorian Western District town of Koroit in 1916, the Victorian Premier, Alexander Peacock, asked rhetorically '[w]hat man would not risk his life if his wife or sister' had been subjected to the kind of treatment the Germans had meted out to the women of Belgium, 'where the nuns and sisters had been dragged out of their holy places and treated in a way that was worse than death to them?'[5] But it was not only dyed-in-the-wool loyalists who deployed images of foreign sexual threat, vulnerable white femininity and Australian male gallantry. 'If you are in favour of sending all our fighting men to Europe', declared one piece of anti-conscriptionist propaganda, 'do you realise you are in favour of leaving your mothers, wives and children to the mercy of any coloured or enemy race that might attack Australia?'[6]

## Mates

By way of contrast, those who 'shirked' military duty were presented as sissies or mummies' boys, an equation that tapped into a growing concern about male effeminacy.[7] In 1916 the Melbourne *Truth* drew attention to 'a knot of effeminate youths' in the habit of loitering near the Town Hall. One who stood out from the rest was usually wearing knickerbockers and a panama hat but a 'squeaky' or 'boyish' voice was, for *Truth*, most easily recognisable as a badge signifying male sexual 'inversion'.[8] The same paper was soon complaining about the city's 'queans and similar noxious bipeds', who in its view warranted more police attention than the 'harlots' who were being uselessly harassed by the law.[9] In the same year, a pathologist in the Victorian Lunacy Department, W.A.T. Lind, warned of the danger posed to Australian youths by the 'pervert who makes a practice of frequenting public baths to try and secure a victim for his degraded appetite. The sins of Sodom and Gomorrah are his'.[10] The bronzed Anzac was implicated in this effort to fan the flames of moral panic, for *Truth* professed to be concerned about 'the number of soldiers, who, more or less boozed, are led to participate in shockingly indecent orgies' near the corner of Swanston and Lonsdale streets. A policeman described the male defendant in one indecency case as 'one of those' who 'attracted soldiers' to this part of the city.[11]

Historians from Charles Bean onwards have recognised the intensity of the bonds that connected the men of the Australian Imperial Force (AIF) in the face of battle; Albert Facey, a Gallipoli veteran, recalled that '[a] sort of love' developed between them.[12] But diggers contrasted the martial and sexual prowess of the Anzac with what they saw as the effeminacy and weakness of the British officer class, and a popular Australian army song even extended the label of 'poofter' to Australians 'fighting' the war from AIF Headquarters in Horseferry Road.[13] The idea, however that an army of over 300,000 men with limited opportunities for sex with women could have been free of homosexual activity is ridiculous. Elioth Gruner, the painter, confessed to Norman Lindsay in 1918 that he had been deeply worried about joining the army because of his attraction to other men, and we can be certain that others belonging to the emerging homosexual subcultures in Australia's larger cities enlisted.[14] Perhaps a few even 'discovered' their sexuality among the cream of Australian manhood. Peter Stanley has found a few examples of homosexual offences committed by Australian soldiers during World War I but he also suggests the likelihood that there were considerably more instances than have survived in the official record. Homosexual behaviour, when discovered, was possibly dealt with quietly and informally, so as not to draw attention to its embarrassing presence.[15]

### Sex and the Anzacs

The 'official' Anzac legend, in its celebration of the manly Australian soldier of World War I, is ironically a rather asexual thing. A legend created for the consumption of an entire nation may well be able to incorporate a strain of larrikinism, but it could hardly be expected to celebrate sexual incontinence – and the Anzac legend did not. On the other hand, sexual ribaldry and misbehaviour *were* part of a digger culture that can be seen as a more down-to-earth – even rough working-class – version of Australian military manhood.[16]

Middle-class or respectable working-class soldiers certainly found little to admire in the conduct of some of their fellows. Percy Bird, the son of a Presbyterian boilermaker from Melbourne, was disgusted with their bawdy humour. He recalled a joke about masturbation: 'Where we were sleeping and that, somebody would yell out, "The old squire's been foully murdered." And of course, they'd all [say] "What? Again?" This seemed to be one of the little jokes. Poor joke I thought it was.'[17] Cecil Hemsley, a 22-year-old private educated at St Peter's College in Adelaide, also felt a pace or two apart from most of his fellows, and for similar reasons. After attending Holy Communion while shipboard in August 1916, he reflected in his diary that 'when one is far away from home and amidst those whose thoughts are often anything but religious, the resolution and increased strength of purpose with which one is inspired becomes a real source of spiritual strength, and one feels greatly strengthened to stand against that which is evil'. Once he had arrived in England, Hemsley regularly attended the Young Men's Christian Association's huts, provided to keep men from temptation, but when he returned to camp he would again be confronted with drunken men. 'I have never, not even in my camp life heard such a flood of immoral, filthy talk and blasphemy', he reflected. It was difficult for such a young man to work out a way of relating satisfactorily to his rough comrades: 'To attempt to stand aloof … as a superior individual, or to take offence at everything with which I do not agree would be sheer folly. It would only serve to alienate those whom I wish to see rise to better things, and would make my own life miserable without serving any good purpose.'[18]

For the likes of Hemsley, the YMCA provided a place for the performance of a respectable masculinity.[19] On Sunday 8 October 1916, he attended a meeting in 'the quiet room of the camp Y.M.C.A.' and joined the Soldiers' Christian Fellowship Society. 'A Society of this nature', he explained, 'with the opportunities which its meetings provide for quiet talks on religious matters as affecting the soldier's life is very useful and helpful to all who have any desire to live a clean, honorable life'.[20] A young officer, country solicitor Clive Hunter, was amazed at the prostitution in Cairo, but like Hemsley found consolation in his own respectability:

> I did not know there was so much immorality in the world and the sight lowers one's estimation of woman fifty per cent and in spite of the knowledge that so many have fallen a prey to these brutes and in spite of the warning we have had the streets are full of thousands of soldiers who keep these brutes, it is too awful for words, and once more I earnestly thank God that my Father and Mother are so good and that I have a name that is something to keep up.[21]

One would expect just such a letter from a young middle-class man writing to his parents but there is no reason to doubt his sincerity, nor his sense of alienation. His impressions are confirmed by Graham Butler, a doctor who would later write the *Official History of the Australian Army Medical Services*. In a letter to his wife late in 1914, he contrasted some German prisoners that his ship had picked up from the sinking of the *Emden* – 'awfully decent chaps' – with the Australians, who were 'filthy ... in their language their habits & their persons ... The language is very foul often'. On New Year's Day, 1915, he was thinking of 'our little house & the sweet peas and roses', which he could only contrast with the 'very masculine & rude sort of life here. The conversation – language – thoughts &c are crude & elementary & are mostly of fighting & women and the work'.[22]

The conduct of the Australians in Egypt became notorious, especially after a controversial despatch, widely published in the Australian press, written by Bean as official war correspondent. It drew attention in guarded terms to VD and rowdy behaviour among a small fraction of the troops in Egypt. Bean wrote the piece at the instigation of Major General William Bridges, who had decided to send the worst troublemakers and venereal cases back to Australia as an example to the rest, but it was on the messenger that the anger of many Australian troops and their supporters fell.[23] Bean's problem was that his despatch had created an unpalatable picture of the Australian soldier – of an immoral and diseased wastrel. Yet even Bean, writing for his diary at this time, managed to convince himself that most of the infected were 'old soldiers, many of them not born in Australia at all'.[24] The riots among the brothels of Cairo – the so-called First and Second Battles of the Wazza (the city's brothel district) in April and July 1915 – nonetheless underlined the problem of rowdy behaviour.[25]

### *Venereal Disease and Prostitution*

One cause of the first of these riots was that Australian troops were angry at having 'got a dose off a woman', and so decided to settle a score or two before they left Egypt for Gallipoli.[26] Some of the men whose heroic deeds were said to be responsible for the 'birth of the nation' on the first day of that doomed campaign were infected with VD at the time – a reality that has been studiously avoided in most subsequent discussion. In September 1915 the *Medical Journal of Australia* reported that of 492 Australian VD cases in the Abbassia Barracks at Cairo, '190 were among the brave Australian boys who performed deeds of unexampled bravery at Anzac Cove on April 25, 1915'. Lieutenant Colonel John Nash, who was in charge of the hospital, had expressed 'his wholehearted admiration for these men, in spite of the fact that they were at the time detained under his care for the results of their folly'. Here was a valiant effort to reconcile the rough and the respectable images of the Australian soldier abroad.[27]

Butler later called VD the medical service's 'most difficult problem in the war'.[28] By 1917, 144 in every 1000 Australian soldiers had VD, compared with just over 134 for the New Zealanders and 34 for the entire British army.[29] A major reason for these great disparities is that, unlike the British, when the Antipodeans went on leave they were not returning home. Between 1915 and 1918, excluding readmissions and relapses, almost 44,000 members of the AIF were admitted to hospital with VD.[30] Some authorities in the latter years of the war went so far as to claim that men were going out of their way to become infected – to take a break from the front line, for instance – and they 'really consider it a joke altogether and laugh and rag one another about it'.[31]

Many Australian recruits brought the disease into the army with them from their civilian life; men found to be suffering from VD in the Australian camps in 1914 were thrown out. But on arrival in Egypt, there were immediate signs of an increase in the number of venereal cases as men threw themselves into Cairo's fleshpots. Butler recalled 'a startling outburst' within the first fortnight, and reported to his wife, 'Much, or most, of [the men's] debauchery among women is done when they are drunk'.[32] There was little that could be done to prevent the thirsty, the randy, the adventurous or just the plain delinquent from visiting the bars and brothels if they were sufficiently determined. As one soldier commented, despite the worthy efforts of a battalion of Territorials who were engaged in police duties in Cairo, 'it would take 10,000 or more to control things properly'.[33] The Australians had piles of money, plenty of leave and often little compunction about slipping away from camp without permission in order to sample the city's delights.

It is easy enough to understand the allure of Cairo to citizen soldiers who had spent several weeks on a ship and were now subject to the inconveniences of military discipline and the discomforts of camp life. There was also the traditional sexual allure of the orient which, with its cornucopian image of the harem, provided Australian men with the materials for many a sweet fantasy about life in the brothels and bars of Cairo.[34] For some, war service provided an opportunity for what we would now call sex tourism.[35] Men who came from a society which was doing its best to conceal its sexual vice, by suppressing soliciting or confining its prostitutes to orderly establishments in red-light districts, were suddenly confronted in Cairo with a veritable sexual bazaar, in which prostitution was on parade and available to all able to pay for it.

It was this openness that impressed itself most firmly on the Australian soldier-tourist. Hunter told his parents that the women 'hang over the balconies and stand at the street doors and walk about the alley ways practically stark naked and call out and even catch passers-by. Street after street contains nothing but houses full of these filthy low brutes'.[36] In Australia, any number of laws concerned with vagrancy or public decency would have given these ladies short shrift, but the prostitutes' brazenness led Australian soldiers to come up with ridiculously exaggerated figures for the number working in Cairo. There were, in reality, 660 'native' prostitutes registered in the city in early 1915, and slightly fewer Europeans, although many more in the latter category were likely to have been unregistered.[37] All the same, Hunter was clearly exaggerating when he claimed that there were 38,000 licensed prostitutes of all nationalities in Cairo, while Lieutenant Arthur

Mountain's similar figure of 35,000 is hardly less far-fetched.[38] These estimates are, on the one hand, a testament to the openness and ubiquity of prostitution; on the other, they show the extent to which Cairo was epitomised, for Australian observers, by its public women's depravity. Military authorities tried to reinforce this association. Sapper Harold Grant, a married man, reported that on the twenty-second day at sea on the voyage to Egypt in 1917, the ship's doctor had lectured on 'the evils of Egypt', which were to be avoided, 'as the effects of disease contracted there are terrible and the fine well-dressed women are so deceptive'.[39]

Many believed they had evidence of those 'evils' in the unsightly sores that now disfigured their genitals. In the four months before the Gallipoli landing, 2000 Australian men were struck down with VD.[40] Mountain, a clerk from Geraldton, could only marvel at 'the damned foolishness some men calling themselves "white" get up to'. He reported that while some had managed to avoid VD after paying a mere five piastres (about a shilling) for sex, others gained a very nasty dose after forking out 100 or 200. 'The only safe course', he believed, was 'to leave all these women alone, white and colored alike'.[41] But an already dangerous situation was made worse because the influx of thousands of troops had driven up prices in the licensed (and probably safer) brothels, and so prompted men to seek sex with women operating less openly.[42] The army, for its part, had few remedies at its disposal. Medical officers sometimes gave informal instruction to the troops but apart from stern warnings and 'the individual efforts of enthusiasts, little was done'.[43] For prevention, beside the threat of punishment the authorities relied on moral suasion and counter-attractions, such as those provided by the Red Cross and YMCA. But in the year after February 1915, 5924 cases of VD among Australian troops received treatment, and 1344 men suffering from the ailment were returned to Australia.[44]

At this stage, the authorities treated venereal cases as outcasts. Their pay was cut off, a punishment that was especially severe because it also resulted in the stoppage of allotments to dependents in Australia. The result was that a soldier's folks at home would learn of his infection. Venereal cases were sometimes made to wear a white ribbon on their right arm, kept under armed guard and subjected to humiliating isolation.[45] A revealing sign of this stigma is the flurry that occurred in official circles when an army major alleged that military authorities proposed returning the body of Major General Bridges, who was killed at Gallipoli, to Australia in the same ship as VD cases.[46]

By 1916 the army had adopted a more humane approach. The old stigma remained, pay was still withheld and the Australian Dermatological Hospital regarded with disdain by military authorities. Yet, influenced by the famous safe-sex campaigns of the New Zealander Ettie Rout, authorities now gave troops access to prophylactic kits – known as 'dreadnoughts' after the famous battleships – and condoms went on sale, a practice authorities managed to keep out of the glare of publicity back home. Orderlies received proper training, doctors were given the opportunity to study the latest developments in venereology, and blue-light depots were set up, allowing men to gain discreet if uncomfortable treatment soon after infection. These initiatives naturally assumed that Australian men would indeed have intercourse while on leave, and they stand in sharp contrast to the lack of such provision for non-white troops of the empire; for no countenance could be given to sex between a 'coloured' man and even a working-class white woman. The handful of Aboriginal men in the AIF could in the circumstances be quietly overlooked.[47]

Medical authorities delivered their message about how to preserve good health within a moral framework. They lectured Australian men on the virtues of continence, rejecting the idea that indulgence in sex was essential to the health of the human male, and advising soldiers to 'avoid unhealthy literature, obscene pictures, sexual conversation', prostitutes and too much drink: 'The finest and healthiest man is he who is master of his passions, not their slave.'[48] The efforts of medical authorities were supplemented by the work of chaplains and voluntary organisations such as the AWCL, which gained permission to distribute literature on troopships, and in recruiting depots and camps.[49] The 'medical' had not detached itself from the 'moral'. From 1917 Australian men hospitalised for VD were banned from taking leave for a year afterwards and although by early in the following year infected men were no longer losing all of their pay, they were still being denied 2/6 per day out of their usual six-shilling allotment. But the tendency to subordinate all other considerations to the cause of victory strengthened the doctors' hand against those who advocated a 'Christian' approach.

## In Action

After Cairo – in Bean's judgment, the 'home of all that is filthy and beastly' – Gallipoli was a monastery.[50] Hunter told his parents that although the food kept the body strong, 'the flame of lust completely dies out and leaves the mind so much more healthy'.[51] This seems like wishful thinking from a respectable young man still reeling from the behaviour of the men in Egypt. As Joanna Bourke has shown, the battlefield could also be an arena for sexual fantasy and 'although the act of killing another person in battle may invoke a wave of nauseous distress, it may also incite intense feelings of pleasure'. For at least some combatants, argues Bourke, killing is a sexual turn-on, and they gain excitement, joy and satisfaction from an experience more commonly associated with fear, anxiety and pain.[52] Her point seems well illustrated in the unmistakably sexual imagery contained in the letter of an Anzac fighting in the Gallipoli campaign: 'Up the hill … we swarm … the lust to kill is on us, we see red. Into one trench, out of it, and into another. Oh! the bloody gorgeousness of feeling your bayonet go into soft yielding flesh.'[53]

In this phase of Australia's war, the only circumstances in which a soldier could experience female company was if he became a casualty. Throughout the war, apart from Australian civilian volunteers in London, nurses were the only Australian women whom the men encountered in significant numbers. Even then, just 2550 Australian nurses served overseas.[54] With only single women eligible, the danger of sexual contact between nurses and soldiers was well appreciated by authorities and actively discouraged. Every sex-starved, homesick or just lonely young man knew that beneath the grey and shapeless uniform was a female body; that it was usually unavailable probably only increased the allure.[55] Most Australian soldiers could only fantasise. After all, nurses were usually middle class, whereas the AIF was overwhelmingly a working-class army. And the overall number of nurses was small compared with the vast numbers making up the mass armies of the British Empire. But not all of the men missed out. The wounded Australian soldier Joe Maxwell, after an operation, 'awoke to look into the eyes of a goddess' – actually a Canadian nurse – 'and in a couple of days' he was 'wildly in love with this beautiful creature'.[56] Another Australian soldier, Eric Evans, had a guilty love affair – for he had a girlfriend at home – with a Welsh nurse whom he met while in hospital in England.[57] No matter how motherly or sisterly their bedside manner in the wards – or how assiduous the moral surveillance of matron – flirtation, fantasy and romance were inevitable.

### On Leave

The chance to escape from fear, anxiety and pain – if ever so briefly – was one reason why leave was so popular with the Anzacs. 'The leave pass', remarked Australian officer George Mitchell, 'is a passport to ten days of heaven'.[58] For the men who endured the horrors of the Western Front, heaven was usually London, but it was occasionally Paris or Amiens.[59] In his 1937 war memoir, *Backs to the Wall*, Mitchell describes one period of leave in London. On arriving at Victoria Station, he observed Tommies being greeted by loved ones. It is easy to imagine this sight having accentuated the loneliness of the Anzac far from home but for Mitchell it initially provides a sense of 'absolute freedom. Not one tie, not one relation, not one friend in the whole of the land of England who cared whether I came or went, lived or died. Not even a dog to wag its tail at my passing'. The diggers, he said, were 'a race apart', rather like a Roman Legion sent for years to a far-off land, 'alien to the new land and old, sure only of themselves'. Already, his 'absolute freedom' seems to have acquired an ambiguity. Mitchell 'swaggered down the Strand with an air that inferred [sic], "make way for an Aussie on leave"'. Soon, he was enjoying 'approving side glances'. 'Plenty of time to pick and choose', he told himself, before approaching two pretty girls in a restaurant. They are very receptive to his initial advances, and even more receptive to his lavish entertainment of them. These were gold diggers, and he quotes a popular piece of doggerel among the diggers:

> Here's to the girl in high-heeled shoes,
> Who eats your food and drinks your booze,
> And then goes home to sleep with mother,
> Stingy———

By the end of his account, an ambiguous freedom has been transformed into loneliness. 'To fill our need for companionship, hordes of harpies competed', he reflected. 'But those whose friendships we should have valued, we could seldom meet.'[60]

Many diggers, however, had much success with English women, or 'tabbies', as the men called them (the term was also applied to female Australians).[61] For one thing, the Australians were well paid. A young digger recalled that the war had instilled 'a dare-devil spirit' in some English girls, while 'the lure of cash' drew to the Australians 'the street girls, the lounge girls, the café girls, and the romantic thrill-loving English girls in the first exhilaration of their new-found freedom'.[62] As one young Australian soldier, Larry Anthony, told his parents in a letter home: 'The English girls are not half as modest as they would have you believe, they practically throw themselves at one. The cocked hat fetches them … we are the only troops that wear them.'[63] But there was also 'an added glamour about the Australians' who had come so far, as volunteers, to help Mother England.

A Victorian on leave in Bristol with a mate told his brother in a letter that they 'were not long in meeting with a couple of nice young ladies, that were coming out of the factory after their day work'. Having agreed to meet them in the evening, they wandered around 'and all told … had at least five different ones to meet, so it will give you an idea, of how they take to the Australians in Bristol, and of course as we were out for a good time we made the best of things, and in case one lot did not turn up, we could meet some other, and all different times, so you see we had it all readied up, before hand'. Like the military commander John Monash, these young men believed that every engagement required careful preparation, but the first girls turned up on cue. An enjoyable evening at the cinema was had by all: 'Really they were two very nice ones, and so before we left them we were right Oh.' These hospitable young women showed the Australians some of the countryside, and introduced them to their families. Unfortunately, the munition girls had to work the next day, but the diggers met another two ladies – both married – 'just by the wink of an eye'. They invited the men out for tea, but the unstoppable Aussies had already made other arrangements. Having taken the original girls out for tea, they asked them to the theatre, 'but [the girls] reckoned it would be much better up on the perham downs. So of course that wasn't easy to take right into our hands for we could have a better time their [sic] than in the theatre. So you bet we did enjoy ourselves'. But his joy in the company of the factory girls appears to have been wrestling with his Australian nationalism and loyalty to his girl at home: 'So in my mind I would vote for the English girl, but all the same I would not give mine in Australia for any of them, and for God sake. Keep this quiet … but Oh God, I had a great time.'[64]

At the time this man was frolicking with the munition girls, George Lancelot Allnutt Thirkell, a dark-haired and handsome junior officer from Hobart, was moving in very different circles – aristocratic and royal. Wounded on Gallipoli, 'Thirk' spent a part of his recuperation period at Glamis Castle in Scotland, the home of the Earl of Strathmore and his wife, Lady Strathmore. There he met Lady Elizabeth Bowes-Lyon, their daughter, then seventeen and a great admirer of men in uniform; she would eventually marry the future King George VI. The Strathmores invited the charming, feckless Thirk to spend his future periods of leave with them. This relationship presumably provided him with an entrée into the world of upper-class Britain.[65]

Stationed on Salisbury Plain in 1917, Thirk's immediate designs centred on Hinda, apparently the daughter of a European Countess. For a man from a downwardly mobile family living in an untidy suburban house where yesterday's *Mercury* was today's dunny paper, Thirk was doing rather well.[66] When they met in London one Sunday afternoon in 1917, the couple thoughtfully 'rang to see if mother was out but mother answered, so that was that! no tea party. we had tea in the Kensington Gardens, & a taxi drive home?!–!' – those peculiar punctuation marks at the end of the sentence might imply that the taxi served more than one purpose. A couple of days later, at afternoon tea with mother and daughter, Hinda 'was looking very sweet & flirtatious' while on one occasion a few weeks later, when the Countess was out for the afternoon, Thirkell recorded in his diary that 'Hinda was left alone to – my tender care'. In mid-July, it was a morning in the park with his girl, who was looking 'very swish in a champagne parachute dress, big hat & pink knickers'.[67] In the following year, the easygoing Thirk would marry a divorcee from a distinguished political, literary, artistic and intellectual family – the novelist Angela Thirkell. It was one of those hasty wartime marriages of a hopelessly ill-matched couple that was always doomed.

There was, then, no shortage of opportunities for sexual encounters in either France or England. Private Hemsley, perhaps still recovering from the shock of exposure to the immorality of the men in his camp, was soon confronted by an even greater darkness in London, where he 'obtained first-hand proof of the social evil'. He had heard much about 'the dark side of London by night', but the reality was worse than his expectations. In one bar, '[g]audily dressed women of the immoral class were drinking with soldiers, two of them Maori half-castes, in just the same manner as one sees in "cabaret" scenes at the cinema'. To a young, respectable Australian, the breaking of the racial taboo was especially disturbing, not least in happening at the heart of empire.[68] Soon, dominion representatives were applying pressure to British authorities to protect these 'innocents' abroad from the designs of local women. The most tangible result was notorious regulation 40D, introduced early in 1918, which stated that 'no woman who is suffering from venereal disease shall have intercourse with any member of HM Forces, or solicit or invite any member to have intercourse with her'. In this way, authorities sought to stem the flow of disease and moral decay at what they understood as its ultimate source: the conduct of 'bad' women.[69]

France also offered opportunities for sex. Paris was especially well endowed in this regard, with its hundreds of brothels, and thousands of streetwalkers and 'joy-girls' – the latter stylishly attired young women who offered soldiers brief companionship and sex in exchange for gifts and an evening out.[70] As Sergeant Cyril Lawrence commented of those he saw, 'Surely they were only made to tempt man, these women'.[71] Australians, notorious for their poor discipline, frequently went absent without leave to sample the delights on offer in cafés, bars and brothels. France's famous tolerated houses were used by allied troops and even, on occasion, inspected by Australian medical authorities.[72] A little less blatantly, the *estaminets* (little cafés) found in virtually every French village not only allowed soldiers to purchase a hearty meal of sausages and eggs and a glass or eight of 'plonk', but also gave them a chance to mix with local women. Some *estaminets* actually doubled as unlicensed brothels where an Australian soldier could buy sex for the equivalent of about a day's pay. More expensive and luxurious establishments catered to officers.[73]

In respectable premises the absence of male 'protectors' might have encouraged some Anzacs to get ideas above their station. Harold Williams, a junior Australian officer, recalled a visit to an *estaminet* where service was provided 'by madame and two buxom wenches, Jeanne and Marie. Each one of us must have asked the two ma'mselles about the prospects of spending the night with them. They did not destroy all hope for us, but fixed the appointment for *après la guerre*'.

Yet what might have seemed to some of his readers, even in the 1930s, as oafishness, was explained by the old digger as ordinary soldierly behaviour of a kind with which the mademoiselles in question would have been thoroughly familiar:

> … they knew that it was as natural for a soldier to ask an attractive ma'mselle for permission to sleep with her as it is in civilian life to talk about the weather. I really believe that if an attractive French girl working to quench the thirst of soldiers in war-time did not have the proposition put to her with every fresh drink that she served, she would hurry upstairs and critically examine herself in the looking-glass to learn what was wrong in her appearance.[74]

In his memoir *Hell's Bells and Mademoiselles* Joe Maxwell claimed that young French girls were accustomed to such matters being discussed in their presence with a frankness that would have been unacceptable to their counterparts in Australia.[75] Yet if Clive Hunter is to be believed, men were capable of controlling themselves when confronted with French womanhood. He, four other officers and 250 men were quartered on a farm where there were six girls – aged from twenty-five to eight – and their two young brothers but no father or mother. It could have been disastrous but Hunter reported that the men were 'absolutely trusted, and are looked to as kind of natural guardians … I have not known any man to use an insulting word or do a wrong act. I am well satisfied that the way to get the real good out of the Australian is not by orders, but by putting him on his honour'. The men 'created a splendid impression'.[76]

Especially in England, however, the Australians soon acquired a reputation for sexual misbehaviour and even bigamy, which attracted sensational press coverage.[77] Throughout the war, there were Australian soldiers who committed rape – including gang-rape – and other forms of sexual assault.[78] Albert Jones, an Australian corporal, reported in May 1917 at the end of a spell in London that Australians now had 'a rotten name and a decent girl don't like to be seen with an Australian soldier'.[79] In South African cities such as Cape Town and Durban, too, where troops bound for Europe went ashore, Australians were by early 1917 being shunned by white residents on account of their country-men's previous misbehaviour. Cape Town girls reputedly felt unsafe 'to be about after dark' while the Australians were in town. One visiting digger recorded in his diary that the diggers' 'doings' there and in Durban were 'too disgusting to mention'. In 1919 rumours of rape by Australians in Colombo, another port of call, reached the same man as he made his way home to Sydney.[80]

Many young men under the sway of religious and family influence remained chaste or mainly so; others knew a chance for a sexual adventure when they saw one. Eric Evans, who admitted having been sorely tempted from time to time, explained the impulses of these men with admirable clarity: 'Men who are perhaps to be killed in a very short space of time are hardly to be expected to control any sexual desires.'[81] Another Australian, George Mitchell, having just completed a training course in France, jumped the rattler to Boulogne with a New Zealander. There, while the companions sheltered from the rain, they noticed 'two charming damsels' arranging a shop window. 'All the time', he recalled, 'I could sense the bar that middle-class French girls keep to guard their reputation against foreign soldiery'. Offered a cognac by the girls, Mitchell insisted that it would be undignified for an officer to be seen drinking in a shop. After long and eloquent pleading on his part, the girls 'with a great show of reluctance' ushered the two men out the back:

> That was a different world altogether. It was a long time before we remembered to drink our cognac … Louise clung to me as we were about to go, demanding my stick and gloves as hostage to ensure our return.

During a later period of leave in Paris, Mitchell 'fell out of one affair into another, with such rapidity that the whole period seemed in retrospect a tangled kaleidoscope of happenings'. Just after the war has ended, he hears a piano being played in a home. A woman, presumably the mother of the pianist, invites him in for coffee. A pretty French girl continues playing. Mitchell returns for another visit but refuses invitations for a third. The war is over. A new life has begun, and a pretty French girl would be a heavy harness.[82] Similarly, Joe Maxwell provides a rather coy account of his affair with the lovely Germaine but nevertheless has her expire on the second-last page of his memoirs with a case of the 'pneumonic influenza'. In his tale, Germaine has served her purpose: 'It is good to reflect that when Mars erupted, and Europe was befogged by clouds of grey, there were thousands of little Germaines and Maries who brought so many hours of sunshine to the lads who shared so many of the risks and fortunes of war together.'[83] Maxwell, a Victoria Cross winner, had evidently enjoyed to the full his Germaines and Maries, and perhaps also their counterparts in Egypt and England; his service record reveals that he had managed to acquire at least one dose of VD along the way.[84] But the sexual encounter with French women is also, for him, something that needs to be left behind – rather as tourism ceases to be tourism if it becomes everyday life.

## The Women Left Behind

Sixty per cent of the men who left Australia to fight in the war were under twenty-six years old; the absence of so many young men overseas reduced marital opportunities for women.[85] In response, Marion Piddington, the feminist and sex reformer, went so far as to initiate a movement for celibate motherhood. Artificial insemination would allow single women to bear children without either a husband or the stigma of unmarried motherhood. These women, she said (under the pen-name 'Lois') in a 1916 pamphlet, would devote themselves to 'the sacred task of the replenishment of the race'.[86] 'Dr Henry Waterman Swan' (probably a pseudonym for the gynaecologist Dr Ralph Worrall)[87] also emphasised the eugenic purposes of celibate motherhood, in a pamphlet published in 1918. Modern warfare, he said, had brought about 'a process of "reversed selection"' in which 'the healthy, the vigorous, and the patriotic' perished while the future race was created by rejected volunteers and the least patriotic. Celibate motherhood for the supposedly 'superfluous' women produced by the war would permit patriotic women with well-developed maternal instincts to help fill Australia's vast open spaces 'without dishonour'. 'It is not every woman who is fitted to be a wife or mother', declared the author, 'but there are more women fitted to be mothers than wives ... the maternal instinct is a much earlier development than the sexual appetite'.

Swan also called for laboratories to be built in every large town, where artificial insemination could be carried on. Any healthy woman would be permitted access to the sperm bank, and she would be safeguarded from scandal by a certificate that would have equal value to a marriage licence. Strict medical monitoring of the quality of the semen would lead to improvements in the race, while the 'mental attitude' of mothers prepared to participate in such a program would ensure 'mental strength and independence' in the children. The introduction of celibate motherhood would, in his view, transform marriage, since a woman would now be able to perform her racial function without having to find a husband.[88] The idea, unsurprisingly, did not take off, but the campaign for celibate motherhood reflected a fear of racial decline that was not confined to radicals such as Piddington. When she laid her scheme before Sigmund Freud in 1921, he was characteristically polite but poured cold water on the scheme's 'tendency to sex-repression which will do more for the extinction of the race than war and pestilence combined'. He was also worried about the impact of too much 'motherly tenderness' on the fatherless children 'begotten in this way'.[89]

Reports of marriages in England must nonetheless have bitten hard on the sensibilities of young women raised to dream of romance, marriage and motherhood. Some British, French and Belgian brides received a cold reception when they arrived in Australia. In the end about 18,000 wives, fiancées and children would return with the men of the AIF.[90] The government had proposed legislation to allow marriage by proxy, as a means of assisting the pregnant woman whose boyfriend or fiancé was out of the country, and possibly also to reduce the incidence of marriage between Australian men and British women. But there was fierce opposition, especially from the churches, who argued that it would lead to hasty marriages. The diggers' press also aired claims that designing women would use the legislation to trick Anzacs into marriage, in order to get their hands on the soldiers' pay-packets or pensions.[91]

## Venereal Disease at Home

These accusations reflected increasing anxiety about the sexual morality of young Australian women. 'Total war' demands the efficient organisation of civilian populations as much as of the military, and the authorities moved to ensure that sexually immoral women were not permitted to reduce the efficiency of the war effort by infecting soldiers. Old contagious diseases legislation of the kind passed in Queensland, Tasmania and Victoria had targeted the professional prostitute, but World War I was marked by growing concern with the activities of the 'amateur', or sexually promiscuous – usually working-class – young woman. It was widely believed such women were now more ready than ever to surrender their bodies, whether for selfish or patriotic reasons, and that the war had loosened sexual morality.[92]

The authorities' treatment of male VD sufferers in the armed forces became more humane as the war went on, with incarceration behind barbed wire under armed guard at places such as Langwarrin in Victoria being replaced by a gentler regime based on moral reform and medical care. Nevertheless, it was these men's status as soldiers that allowed authorities to incarcerate them at all. Civilian women were subjected to increasingly rigorous and coercive control via new legislation which, in several states beginning with WA, instituted compulsory notification and treatment of VD from late 1915 onwards. While the new measures formally applied to both civilian men and women, in practice it was women – especially young working-class women – whose lives were subjected to greater surveillance and control. Yet the war was not solely responsible. The rising age of consent over the previous several decades had given the state's effort to suppress transgressive sexual behaviour among young women increasing legitimacy. Australian feminism's emphasis on protection and sexual danger, whatever its effect on men's behaviour, helped curtail the sexual freedom of young women.[93] In a book published in 1918, Everitt Atkinson, the Commissioner of Public Health in WA, and William J. Dakin, Professor of Biology at the University in that state, warned about the low chances of producing healthy bodies and contented minds

> if our young girls, mothers of the race to be, are to have their constitutions broken, perhaps ruined, through ignorance of precocious sexual activity. One has only to walk around our large towns at the present day to be struck with the laxity of parents. Young girls, 'flappers' of from 13 or 14 upwards, can apparently go out and spend the evening as they will.[94]

It was clearly working-class girls who were seen to be in the greatest danger, for Atkinson and Dakin believed that 'children of the poorer classes' and those attending large state schools in the towns required sex instruction earlier 'than children … sheltered in the homes of the well-to-do' attending 'small private schools'.[95]

While actual preventative measures remained few and far between, state authorities did take seriously their duty to reform the characters of young people who had departed from the path of virtue. In wartime Melbourne, it was common for women under the age of seventeen to be committed to a reformatory if they were found to have sexually misbehaved. About one-fifth of the ninety-nine cases examined in one study involved girls being picked up by authorities for hanging around in the streets with soldiers or sailors – a reflection of the fear that 'amateurs' were infecting young men with VD, but also of the desire to reform these working-class girls so as to fit them for maternity.[96]

At the same time, there was growing awareness of the dangers VD posed to all classes of women – and, by implication, to the future race – because of the possibility of infected men passing it on to their wives. Ralph Worrall affirmed before a parliamentary inquiry in 1916 that infection was common among married women of the 'better class' who caught it from their husbands.[97] Yet some doctors admitted that when they detected VD in married women, they refrained from telling them, even to the extent of trying 'to make them think otherwise'. Their justification was a desire to preserve the happiness of 'a fairly decent home' that 'would be broken up in a day' if it became known that a husband had infected his wife. One doctor thought that the woman should be informed if she was suffering from such an affliction but that it was her husband's duty, not her medical attendant's, to break the news. Another reported that because a married woman was unlikely to infect anyone else, only her husband needed to be considered. As startling as this kind of testimony might seem today, these doctors were only defending a conventionally patriarchal model of the family that assumed a husband's inalienable right of access to the female body, whether in the marital bed or the brothel.[98] His wife's health was, at best, a secondary consideration, and her rights as a 'citizen' – including any right she might claim to be free of VD – were qualified by her husband's superior sexual rights. Some men still regarded VD as 'a woman's disease', and even an indication of effeminacy. It was seen as 'inherent in the woman and they get it from her'.[99] Featherstone, however, has argued that by the time of World War I, VD was increasingly being 'constructed as masculine in origin'; that is, men more than women were understood as its source, thereby reflecting the growing concern with male sexual behaviour from the late nineteenth century.[100]

The trend towards surveillance and compulsion did not go uncontested. Feminist organisations criticised the new legislation, arguing that it both pandered to men's animal instincts and violated the liberties of women. They pointed out that although the measures seemed to apply equally to infected men and women, their 'chief victims' would be 'wage-earning girls and women'. It was therefore 'sex and class legislation of a most pernicious kind' because vagrancy laws were to be used primarily against prostitutes and working-class girls, who would then be forced into treatment against their will. Feminists instead advocated education, which would instil chivalry in males and chastity in females, as well as giving poor women greater economic independence and an alternative to prostitution. Their position, however, was an increasingly isolated one, and even feminists within the labour movement were unwilling to endorse a purely voluntary approach to VD.[101]

### Sex Education
Despite the growing medical ascendancy, there was also recognition within the state and among doctors of the need for sex education with a moral dimension, a trend that feminists and social purity campaigners welcomed. 'We are not inclined to the belief that this expedient [sex education] will stamp out prostitution or eradicate venereal disease', said a *Medical Journal of Australia* editorial in 1915:

> But there is little doubt that cautious and correct information at a suitable time and under auspicious conditions, will effect a saving of individuals from the dangers of both ignorant action and careless exposure to risk of infection ... [I]n a number of instances the child may be induced to adopt a clean attitude of mind and a healthy conception of sex functions.[102]

As we shall see in chapter 6, some women who combined their feminism with eugenics, birth control and sex education were able to influence public debate in the interwar years. By contrast, purely voluntarist approaches to VD along the lines promoted by some feminists during the war were never likely to win favour. In a climate of fear about diseased amateurs and soldiers, low birthrates, racial decline and threats – real and imagined – from Asians, Bolsheviks, Germans and Irish, VD became a metaphor for a more general national insecurity. Low birthrates were blamed on VD; syphilis was seen as having entered

Australia from Asia; VD was lowering racial efficiency: these connections helped ensure that in a climate of growing state power over a whole range of areas, voluntary approaches could not prevail. More generally, the viewpoint that refused to treat sexual pleasure as a centrally important aspect of the marriage relation possibly helped to discredit feminist approaches generally. It would lead to the alienation of most feminists from some influential movements and values in Australian politics and culture in the decades that followed the war.[103] Yet the construction of sex as a national problem, a process in which feminists and purity campaigners had been instrumental, also provided a new climate for efforts to educate the public about it.

Well before the war ended, some Australians had detected in their society a revolt against 'Victorianism'. It had become part of the recognised ritual in any public discussion of sex for the speaker holding the floor to bemoan the 'prudery' of the Victorian period, 'which was offensive to the truth and harmful to the race', while celebrating the greater honesty and openness with which such matters could now be treated in these enlightened times.[104] Perhaps every generation tends to congratulate itself on its own wisdom and common sense in contrast with the last – even a generation involved in the most destructive war the world had ever known – but this one gave the alleged false modesty of the Victorian era very rough handling indeed. Havelock Ellis, Edward Carpenter, George Bernard Shaw, H.G. Wells and Sigmund Freud appeared the great prophets of the age, for they treated sex with a candour that was a standing rebuke to Victorian reticence and hypocrisy. Even when it was acknowledged that there had been movement towards greater freedom of discussion *before* the war, few doubted that mass slaughter contributed massively to a shift in western civilisation's understanding of the meaning of sex.

Yet it was far from clear how, or even if, society was going to accommodate these momentous changes. If sex was so important – if it had such powerful potential for either creativity or disruption – how should the state regulate it? Few doubted that the 'sex problem' was also a 'national' and 'racial' problem, and that it was a proper field for public debate and state action. But the responsibilities of government, doctors, teachers, the churches and parents seemed far from clear-cut in the chaotic wartime and immediate postwar world. Many now favoured some form of sex education for the young, but there was little agreement over how it should be done, what should be taught, who should carry out the teaching, when in the life of the child it should begin, or at what age children should receive particular kinds of instruction. A few enthusiasts argued vehemently in favour of state primary schools providing classroom teaching: since so many parents were unable to give appropriate sex education to their offspring, teachers needed to be more involved in providing instruction in 'sex hygiene and moral questions'. Yet the very same advocates were advising teachers to tell children that 'the baby grew in a little nest within the mother, and close to her heart'. If asked who placed the baby there, or who made the nest, it was sufficient to answer that God had done so.[105] Advocates of sex education also sometimes warned that while diagrams might be employed to explain the functioning of the sexual organs, it was 'not advisable', and on no account should realistic pictures be used.[106] Here, 'Victorian' prudery refused to allow scientific rationalism an unqualified victory; but many proponents of sex education, even in the medical profession, were in any case deeply sceptical of the need for physiological instruction of children when it was really moral guidance that was required.[107] Some argued that it was more important to teach sexual morality, with its focus on right conduct and good citizenship, than scientific technicalities.

Dr Arthur and the AWCL were the most vocal and energetic proponents of sex education in schools. In 1916 the AWCL gained permission to have a lecturer address children in SA and Tasmanian schools, and some 'trial' classes were also carried out in Queensland early in 1917. But the Labor government of that state eventually set itself against school sex education, pointing out that it had little parental support.[108] Some private headmasters in NSW had allowed R.W.H. Bligh, the AWCL lecturer, to speak in their schools, although the AWCL's critics argued that sex education did not lend itself to traditional classroom teaching and would only encourage children in dirty discussion.[109] Sex education, they said, should only occur on an individual level, which would provide an appropriately private and confidential environment, leaving children with the 'feeling that they must not discuss the subject afterward'.[110] Indeed, to the extent that one can talk about 'public opinion' in a field that interested mainly a small minority of often noisy people, there was a strong belief that sex education was properly the parents' task, and one for which teachers were poorly equipped. But it was equally hard to make the case that parents raised in unenlightened times were fit to carry out such an important national duty. Clearly, they too needed to be educated, and groups such as the AWCL accordingly conducted lectures for parents on sexual morality.

Still, some remained doubtful that it was required at all, at least outside the family circle. The Catholic Church was insistent that responsibility for such matters lay with parents while even H. Tasman Lovell, a psychologist, saw no real danger in ignorance:

> Personally, I thrill at the thought of an innocent child; and I delight to meet, as I have done, men and women who remained ignorant of these things until well into their adult years ... I believe in purity; I believe further that it is a possible state; and, finally, I believe that the purity of innocence has been for many people their greatest safeguard.[111]

C.J. Prescott, a private school headmaster, thought that 'our traditional idea of reserve and abstention of speech on these matters, combined with reverence, carries with it a moral weight which is not borne by mere physiological explanations'.[112] The influence of Victorian prudery was certainly evident in the 1916 comment of R.H. Roe, the Inspector-General of Schools in Queensland, that he 'felt sometimes uncomfortable in hearing a lady teacher discoursing upon pistils, ovaries and germ development'.[113] While this climate prevailed, nothing dramatic in the field of sex education was likely to occur.

The debate about sex education was largely shaped by an understanding of sex as dangerous, a field full of snares for the morally untutored. In this respect, the continuities between the late Victorian era and the wartime period are striking. The pathologist W.A.T. Lind, in his paper at a 1916 WEA conference on sex education, depended on well-established ideas about moral contagion when he emphasised the capacity of a single '"bad" boy' to corrupt a whole school or neighbourhood by teaching the other boys 'all the sexual stories and sexual acts that he knows'. Much of Lind's paper focused on the dangers of masturbation in a manner hardly distinguishable from the Victorian era. For instance, he warned against the alarmism and exaggerations of 'quacks', while still treating masturbation as pathological: 'Every youth suspected of the practice should be sent for medical inspection.'[114] Other speakers agreed. Zoë Benjamin, a lecturer at the Sydney Kindergarten Training College, thought it 'a good plan to make the older child feel that the habit is a sign of illness, which will lead to a lack of strength when he is older'. Her phraseology here is revealing, suggesting an uncertainty about whether masturbation was truly 'a sign of illness', or whether instead such warnings were merely a convenient tactic. Nevertheless, she appears not to have doubted that masturbation needed to be taken seriously, for her other suggested treatments, apart from reasoning with the child, included a 'harmless but unpleasant medicine', 'occasional bathing of the parts with cold water' and, if these measures failed, 'a slight operation in the case of both boys and girls'.[115] The principal of the Melbourne Teachers' Training College seemed more certain about the effects of masturbation, advising that teenage boys should be told how the blood needed semen 'to build up muscle, bone, and brain, and how without it there can be no physical strength, and no power to think and plan. The semen has therefore to be conserved at whatever cost. It is one of the most precious of all possessions'.[116]

If the keynote here was continuity with the Victorian-era ideal of self-restraint, there were also indications of changing attitudes at the WEA conference. It is true that Lind embraced a 'Victorian' under-standing of the differences between male and female sexuality, contrasting the active sexual instinct of men with the natural passivity of women: 'In girls who have not had the sexual desire aroused, the "libido" lies dormant, and remains so unless accidentally excited, or is activated by the normal caresses of a lover or husband.' A sign of a changing understanding of female sexuality, however, was the adverse reaction that this comment provoked in several members of Lind's audience. Angela Booth, for example, a prominent campaigner against VD, asserted that 'the sex impulse gives the same pleasure to the girl as to the boy, but ... the inhibition cultivated in woman has prevented the excesses you find more generally in the male than in the female young'. Dr Grace Boelcke agreed with Booth that '[t]he sex impulse of the girl is a very strong part of her character'.[117] Prostitutes had tradi-tionally been seen as victims of their own abnormal sex instincts – their 'strong passion' – and the perverted morality that went with it. By extending this same image to an ever-growing circle of working-class women, bourgeois social commentators were now clearing the way for a recognition of sexual desire as a normal female experience, not a defect. In the interwar years, the circle would widen again, this time to incorporate the increasingly bourgeois image of the 'flapper'.

## *Chidley*

By the time of World War I, William Chidley's campaign for sex reform was reaching its final, tragic stage. Patrick White, then a very young child in Sydney, recalled Chidley 'dressed in his white tunic' and looking 'jaunty enough as he passed along the street followed by a laughing, jeering mob'.[118] But arbiters of public morality had long ago judged his opinions unfit for public consideration. Society, they believed, should not hear his crackpot theory that the answer to its ills was sex in the spring between a woman – her vagina acting as a vacuum in response to the joys of the season and the attractions of her lover – and a man whose flaccid penis would be drawn inside her during their divine union.

Yet the NSW Labor government did not know what to do with its Chidley problem, for he was now a figure attracting considerable public sympathy. While its inclination was to keep him in an insane asylum, his supporters remained vocal in condemnation of coercion. In August 1916 Chidley had been released on certain conditions, these being that he 'not address persons, and particularly women, by circular asking them to grant him interviews, in order that he might explain his theory to them'. He was also banned from holding meetings in public parks, nor could he sell his little book on the streets. But Chidley was soon addressing crowds in the Domain and, according to the Chief Secretary, George Black:

> there was no feature of sexual intercourse on which he did not expatiate in order to prove that his theory was the only one that should be followed by the human race. He stated that if that theory had been adopted there would have been no war, the conclusion which I drew from that remark being that there would have been no Germans.[119]

So Chidley found himself back in an asylum. In October 1916, as the country tore itself apart over conscription, some of his supporters came up with an apparently ingenious solution. Would the government pay for a passage either to the US or Canada? The Chief Secretary's department ran the idea by the Premier, William Holman, but when the US Consul was consulted, he replied that his government would regard any such initiative as 'an unneighbourly act'. The government let an otherwise attractive proposal drop but not before giving serious consideration to the Canadian alternative. Even the Governor was brought in to consider this most important matter of state.[120] But they need not have worried, for Chidley was nearing the end. In September 1916 he had doused himself with kerosene and set himself alight while at Darlinghurst Gaol. The fire was extinguished, but so too now was his fighting spirit. Chidley died on 21 December 1916 of heart disease. The government medical officer added that he believed 'the diseased blood vessels were due to syphilis', a claim subsequently denied by Chidley supporters, including some dissident members of the medical profession.[121]

For all his excesses, Chidley must be considered seriously in any account of the coming of sexual modernity to Australia. Havelock Ellis – to whom Chidley had written in 1899 asking him to 'write to me and be my friend' – believed him to be 'one of the most original and remarkable figures that has ever appeared in Australia'.[122] Edward Carpenter, the British sex reformer and socialist, was also willing to engage with Chidley's theories, although he thought his Australian correspondent tended to 'ride the sex question to death'. Chidley's belief that his scheme would some day save the world 'from all its misery, disease, crime, and ugliness' implied a sexual determinism that even sexologists such as Carpenter and Ellis could not accept.[123]

But Chidley is important for other reasons than his ability to attract the notice and even respect of famous men. There was his stress on sexual equality between men and women, on women's capacity for initiative and desire, and on their right to joy in intercourse. As Chidley told Ellis in 1899:

> The womb and vagina of a beautiful and healthy woman, believe me, is a living, vital, moving organ, sensitive to a look, a word, a thought, or a hand on the waist: but as we have coition now, a woman and her womb might as well be dead.

In the current unnatural mode of coition, he added, 'some people – especially women … always suffer: their married lives are one long suffering'.[124] In his attention to women's rights to sexual pleasure, Chidley was a true feminist and radical whose views look forward to

Marie Stopes, Germaine Greer and women's liberation. His notion of the cyclicity of female sexual desire and emphasis on the necessity of a divinely ordained affinity between men and women in sexual relations resemble the famous British sexologist Marie Stopes's position in her 1918 sex manual *Married Love*. And like Stopes, he was not writing for an audience of 'experts', even if he desperately sought – and, when he achieved it, flaunted – their approval. Instead, he placed his ideas before common people. Much hostility to Chidley among doctors and the judiciary arose from his status as a layman addressing a popular audience on matters that the medical profession regarded as its prerogative, and which they saw as dangerous if unleashed on the 'mob'.[125]

Chidley placed sex at the centre of life. It was for him the principal source of individual misery and social degeneration but also the way to human happiness. A few hardy followers would carry the substance of his teachings into the 1920s, but it was less in this sense than in the status he gave to sexual joy as the key to the gates of heaven on earth that his main significance lies. In this respect, Chidley and *The Answer* still speak to our own times.

# CHAPTER 6

# *Fast Times*

## Return

The heroes' return was a matter of apprehension. Would men who had experienced the horrors of modern warfare settle into 'normal' domestic life? Would they pass on to women venereal diseases picked up in Cairo, Amiens and London? Would a 'racial' battle won on the Western Front and in Palestine be lost in the marital beds of Australia? Many diggers must have looked on return with as much apprehension as joy. Some believed sexually disloyal women had betrayed them. The sense of entitlement nurtured by a voluntary system of recruitment extended beyond claims to employment and welfare. Even mild-mannered Bert Facey, when a prospective employer was trying to cheat him, asked whether the man was 'one of those cold-footed bastards that stayed home to take advantage of the enlisted man's wife or girlfriend for your own filthy lust!'[1]

Soldiers feared and sometimes experienced genital mutilation, facial disfigurement, the loss of one or more limbs, and spinal injuries. Any of these legacies was likely to have a profound and lasting impact on a man's sexual destiny. Bodies and minds were damaged in ways that contributed to sexual dysfunction.[2] Many diggers, far from displaying strutting self-confidence, were coming home broken men.

## Male Homosexuality

Indeed, by producing broken men at the same time as it idealised the body and character of the Anzac warrior, the war helped transform the intellectual terrain of male sexuality. Paul Dane, a Belfast-born Melbourne Freudian working at the Caulfield Repatriation Hospital in Melbourne, identified strongly with sexual modernity when he attributed the postwar mental problems of many of his digger patients to homosexuality. In a *Medical Journal of Australia* article published in 1925, Dane claimed that for some of these returned men, the problem lay in 'the death or mutilation of a loved comrade' rather than any 'actual trauma to themselves'. Others, despite massive sexual temptation during military service, were in denial, while a few had been traumatised by having 'witnessed homosexuality', or associating 'with either alleged or actual homosexual situations whilst on service'.[3] Dane implied a link between homosexuality and mental deficiency, a view echoed in other medical opinions between the wars. A 1919 editorial in the *MJA* not only drew attention to 'the prevalence of homosexuality among the dwellers in our large cities', but asserted that such activities were commonly associated with mental degeneracy. Perverts' victims were 'almost always weak-minded individuals' who 'inevitably become perverts themselves'. 'It is imperative', it added, 'for the moral safety of every young person in the Commonwealth that means shall be taken to recognize every case of moronity in the earliest detectable stage and to segregate every individual whose power of distinguishing right from wrong is defective'.[4] A 1927 article by W.A.T. Lind on 'The Sex Instinct and its Disorders' also linked sexual perversion to 'the moron class of mental defective', as well as 'the lazy sensuous temperament'. As a consequence, 'perversions are met with mainly in those cities where the moral tone is degenerate'. While every city in the world, he said, had 'its quota of the vicious and the sexual perverts', it was in such places as 'Port Said and the cities of the Levant' that one found fellatio, cunnilingus, sodomy and bestiality openly advertised. Lind's presentation of sexual perversions as foreign, and their most repulsive manifestations as oriental, echoed a more general xenophobia of the interwar years. But the association of homosexuality with the corruption of urban life was, in Australia, a rather novel departure, and one suggesting the growing influence of contemporary European social thought about sexuality on local intellectuals.[5]

Among these influences was the work of Sigmund Freud. It has sometimes been suggested that western medical opinion between the wars was moving away from the idea of the male homosexual as a 'feminine' man and embracing the Freudian concept of inversion. For Freud, 'the most complete mental masculinity' could be 'combined with inversion'. Homosexual men *might* be physically and psychically effeminate but this was no longer necessarily the case.[6] Nor was any particular sexual act the mark of a male (or female) invert. The sexual instinct, for Freud, was in its origins independent of the object to which it was directed. In these circumstances, 'the nature and importance of the sexual object itself' was a secondary matter, and the choice of a person of one's own sex as the object of desire a simple variation rather than a reflection of some deeper – and wildly aberrant – sexual instinct. Freud favoured the idea of a continuum with 'numerous intermediate examples of every type',[7] a notion seemingly recycled – if in a crude and simplified form – in a 1924 article by Adelaide doctor J.V. McAree. He claimed that it was possible for the skilled observer to detect 'the peculiar walk of a passive sodomite', but if that failed a man's manner of dress was a sure method 'of diagnosing his inversion'. As he went on to explain:

> Just as one may have all stages of physical inversion from a hybrid to a man who has merely a tenor voice, so in the mental order of things people are born whose psychic structure varies from complete sexual inversion to a mere single characteristic of the opposite sex.

Masculinity and femininity here comprised fixed and polarised physical and mental qualities manifested, in varying combinations, in the 'wrong' sex to produce either severe or mild 'inversion'.[8]

The challenges that interwar Australia posed to 'normal' masculinity would help explain the continuing popular association of homosexuality with male effeminacy. For the middle class, the rise of white-collar employment raised questions about whether the sedentary life of the pen-pusher sapped male virility and produced nervous disorder.[9] For the working class, persistently high unemployment and the Great Depression undermined two ways in which a man could prove that he was a true man: by performing hard manual labour and playing the part of family breadwinner. For men of all classes, heterosexuality became more significant as a way of demonstrating real manhood as other opportunities for the performance of masculinity receded.[10]

The association between homosexuality and the disorder of modern urban life, previously somewhat weak in Australia, strengthened notably in this period. Just after the war, the Melbourne *Truth* drew attention to a case involving a couple of 'human freaks ... who, though dressed in men's clothing, had the most effeminate looks and manners';[11] while on 9 April 1921 it complained that 'one of the most regrettable signs of modern life' was that 'as the feminine sex advances, the male sex shows signs of degeneracy':

> At a recent supper and dance party given by a well known bachelor of this city there was a great gathering of these creatures ['the intermediate sex'], who are spoken of by men about town as 'the Cissies'. They were there in all their glory of carmined lips, powdered faces, painted eyes, and long marcelle waved hair. The 'sisterhood' affect the 'brush back' to such an extent that no man can wear such hair now without being suspected.[12]

This report needs to be treated with caution, for the very same party seems to have occurred in Sydney and Brisbane, having also been reported in those cities' editions of *Truth*![13] Nevertheless, the preoccupation with male effeminacy is unmistakable. *Truth* warned parents to take precautions against their lads 'being decoyed into company where their instincts may be perverted so that they cease to be healthy-minded and wholesomely masculine, but develop "female minds in male bodies"'.[14] Similarly, in a 1933 physical culture manual, *The Book of Life*, effeminacy was recognised as 'a growing menace', although naturally one that was worse in foreign parts:

> So prevalent is becoming this cult of effeminacy that certain large European and American cities have recognised rendezvous where these men may meet and associate. In some of their restaurants these habitues dress entirely as women with such effect that a stranger might accidentally drop in and believe himself in a cafe reserved for the fair sex ... In the big cities of Australia they are also becoming more and more numerous. One is able to see them on all sides, easily recognisable for their habit of referring to each other as 'she', for their quiet, decorous, almost feminine voices, and for their rather effeminate style of dress and of dressing their hair.[15]

The terms used in everyday parlance for such men – poofters (an Australian coinage), fairies, sissies, queens – emphasised effeminacy.[16] 'Camp' subcultures that associated male homosexuality with theatricality, flamboyance, humour and the subversion of gender norms had emerged in the larger Australian cities by the interwar years.[17] (The word 'camp' itself acquired a specifically Australian usage in that until it was superseded by 'gay' in the 1970s, it meant simply 'homosexual man'.)[18] But even Sydney and Melbourne were too small and provincial to support the queer life of a London or New York.[19] In these global cities, a man might discreetly enjoy 'exhilarating sexual encounters' along with the romantic coupling that many homosexuals now craved; and all without any danger of running into Aunt Mabel or Cousin Geoff. It is no wonder that homosexual Australian writers such as Martin Boyd, Patrick White, Sumner Locke Elliott and Russell Braddon expatriated themselves. In Elliott's autobiographical novel *Fairyland*, Rat Ratcliffe enjoins young Seaton Daly – modelled on Elliott himself, who left for New York in 1948 – to just think 'of the Statue of Liberty and that *thing* she's brandishing, the biggest phallus on earth, my dear'.[20]

The Australian gay world was less lively. Although police harassment meant that men could not easily meet one another in public places, some hotels gained reputations as places where men might socialise and pick up other men for sex. A few churches, too, provided a haven for male homosexuals, while the larger cities had a private party scene.[21] In Adelaide, a remarkable establishment called Paul Carlile, which made artificial flowers and fashionable lampshades (and hence became popularly known as the Lampshade Shop), was a well-known meeting place for that city's homosexuals. Its owner, Bert Hines (or 'Big Bertha' as he was known), was recalled by a younger man as 'outrageous' and 'like Edna Everage'.[22] Middle-class homosexual men were most commonly able to take advantage of this kind of opportunity to meet, in private or semi-private places.

'Beats', however, were also important to male homosexual sociability. Every major city had its own homosexual geography.[23] The erotically charged Archibald Fountain in Sydney's Hyde Park, with its classically muscular and nude men, became a well-known homosexual pick-up after its construction in 1932, while the public baths at beachside St Kilda in Melbourne were serving this function by the time of World War I.[24] Certain public toilets were also important as meeting places for homosexual men in the major Australian cities. Although they provided anonymity and an excellent chance for men to size each other up at the urinal, they raised the risk of a bashing and had the unfortunate effect of connecting sex between men with sordidness. As before the war, particular boarding houses were also known as places where sex was to be had, as were certain parks and streets. The areas adjacent to the banks of the major rivers such as the Yarra in Melbourne, the Torrens in Adelaide and the conveniently serpentine Brisbane River were all well-known beats by the interwar period. From Sydney during the Depression, there were police complaints that a 'growing community of sex perverts' – many of them in female attire – were accosting unemployed men sleeping rough in the Domain, offering them food or money in return for sex. When rebuffed, it was reported, some attacked 'the man who, though down and out, is still honourable'.[25]

A climate of illegality ensured that homosexuality impinged on the public consciousness mainly as criminality or tragedy.[26] Catherine S., a working-class Sydney girl, recalled that her knowledge of homosexuality came initially from 'a homosexual murder' that received wide publicity in the press, although as a young adult she had mundane social contact with homosexual men.[27] Frank M., a miner, remembered what must have been a common enough attitude to homosexuality: 'We thought ... it was, well let me put it bluntly, we thought it was unnatural.'[28] Regular reportage of men picked up by police in lavatories and parks was supplemented by the occasional high-profile case, such as that of the wealthy SA Labor politician, philanthropist and publican, Bert Edwards, found guilty of an unnatural offence with a seventeen-year-old male employee in a 1931 trial in Adelaide.[29] While sensational reportage of court cases stigmatised homosexuals, it also had the unintended (and positive) effect of informing lonely homosexual men that they were not unique in their longings.

The unfavourable legal situation meant that the establishment of a homosexual household was difficult – more so than for lesbians – but more powerful still as a barrier was the social pressure in favour of heterosexual coupling, marriage and family formation. There are indications, however, that some Australian men did have sex with other men before fulfilling conventional social expectations – and that some continued to incorporate sex with men into an outwardly respectable family life.[30] Roderic Anderson, a young middle-class man who would lead an active homosexual life in the air force during World War II, believed that working-class youths were especially prone to such behaviour: 'Ordinary street-wise boys didn't have the inhibitions and qualms about having sex with other males that my sheltered upbringing had given me. They regarded it as a natural game and playfully groped each other and admired each other's erections.'[31]

By the 1930s the influence of authors such as Edward Carpenter, Havelock Ellis, Magnus Hirschfeld and Sigmund Freud made it possible for sex reformers and radicals to present male homosexuality in a more positive light than did either the popular press or the mainstream medical profession. Robert Vivian Storer, a Sydney doctor, argued in *A Survey of Sexual Life in Adolescence and Marriage* that although it was difficult to persuade 'many that homosexuality is an endowment rather than a vice', the 'homosexually inclined' were 'persons of taste, refinement, and sensibility'. They should be left alone to follow nature's dictates.[32] While Storer's ideas seem indebted to the likes of Ellis and Carpenter, the Freudian understanding of homosexuality as arrested development found considerable support among doctors.[33] One authority suggested that 'the pleasure of holding motions in the rectum, so often indulged in by children', had sometimes resulted in children growing up to become 'sodomists'.[34]

### Desiring Women

The growing recognition of women as sexually desiring probably made it easier to name lesbianism. Ruth Ford has found that the term 'lesbian' was used in the Melbourne *Truth* as early as 1920 in connection with an action for the restitution of marital rights brought by a returned soldier against his wife, who had left him for a woman. In this way, lesbianism became visible at a moment when male sexual prerogatives were being challenged.[35] In this respect and others, the emergence of lesbian sexuality has a very different history from male homosexuality. For instance, where the appropriation of public space was important in the emergence of a male homosexual identity, there is no evidence of beat activity among lesbian women. Women were likely to have felt threatened in the kinds of places men used for this purpose and, in any case, the quick and anonymous sexual release associated with beat activity might have been unappealing to most females.[36] Many of the older traditions of stable and loving relationships between women – notably 'passing women' and 'passionate friendship' (discussed in chapter 2) – were sufficiently entrenched to survive the sexualisation of Australian culture in the early decades of the twentieth century.[37]

The case of Aileen Palmer underlines the complexities of lesbian love in the interwar years. The daughter of the writers Vance and Nettie Palmer, Aileen was a gifted linguist who took out a first-class honours degree in French and German at the University of Melbourne in 1934 before spending time in a medical unit attached to the International Brigades during the Spanish Civil War.[38] At the university, Aileen was part of a small group of women that called itself 'the mob'. The relationships between them included both emotional and physical intimacy. In her diary for 1932, Aileen described a 'mob' party:

> Jo began to stroke my hair and gripped my shoulder with her sensitive supple fingers. I was as happy as I have ever been – and happier because this love will last and could have no jealousy and bitterness in it.[39]

Aileen had become aware of contemporary sexological writing on female same-sex love; yet she and her friends appear to have eschewed its unsatisfying scientific vocabulary in favour of one of their own making. Sally Newman has suggested that while this code acted as a way of concealing lesbian desire and its physical expression at a time when they were socially unacceptable, its use also indicated the lack of an established and satisfactory lexicon for the expression of same-sex desire by these young educated women.[40]

Yet Edith Young, a friend of the Palmers (and a flatmate of Aileen in London in 1939), was influenced by contemporary sexology and psychoanalysis in her attempt to make sense of Aileen's sexuality in a letter written to Vance in 1948 – the year Aileen had her first mental breakdown. Young, who was presumably unaware of Aileen's university experiences, believed that she had formed 'strong emotional attachments to women' as a reaction to a bad experience with a man in Spain. She claimed to 'know of two girls who were, what one might term, "in love with" Aileen … The extent of these attachments to her own sex I cannot pretend to know, nor how much they meant to Aileen'. Young continued:

My own feeling is, that for some reason or other, a deep seated unconscious reason, she early made an emotional transference from the feminine to the masculine role – Cutting her hair like a youth's, dressing in slacks in preference to skirts, cultivating an independent boyish attitude to other women – all seem to point to this.[41]

In understanding Aileen's mannishness as a disorder, Young's thinking was in line with contemporary sexological understanding of same-sex desire among women. At the same time, like most sexologists, she was unable to detach this desire from certain types of gender performance: Aileen appeared not only to have entered a world in which women loved women, but to have become man-like as a reaction to her bad experience of (normal) heterosexual relations.

The disruptive potential of female sexual desire sometimes focused on women who loved women, but much more frequently on the decidedly heterosexual flapper. In the late nineteenth century, the term meant 'a very young harlot' and even into the 1920s the association with sexual trade remained. Having appeared in the Australian popular press before the war, she had come to embody a wider recognition of female sexual desire as normal, rather than pathological or deviant.[42] New identities were becoming available to Australian women in the 1920s with the development of cinema, photography, and mass-circulation illustrated magazines and newspapers.[43] The 'amateur' of World War I and beforehand had been a working-class girl and, like her female convict ancestors, associated with danger and disease. Yet even while the flapper's early association with VD dissolved, she continued to stand in the shadow of the prostitute because she allegedly exchanged her sexual favours for gifts.[44] Increasingly, however, she was assumed to enjoy social advantages over the erring factory girl or domestic servant. If she worked, it was in an office which became a thoroughly sexualised workplace in interwar popular culture. But whether at work or play, the flapper was associated with youthful glamour.[45] A new generation of feminists between the wars responded by condemning this eroticisation of femininity. Like their mothers of the suffrage generation, they were committed to women's protection. The flapper, however, courted male attention and hinted at female sexual emancipation.[46]

Most importantly, the flapper was young. Popular magazines laboured this point, even to the extent of portraying the flapper as child-like.[47]

In 'The Waiting', a short story published in the *Australian Woman's Mirror* in 1924, Ellinor Wynne and Peter Strange are childhood friends, seemingly destined for the altar. But Peter, who is lower on the social scale than his companion, has his way to make in the world and is studying law. Ellinor waits patiently, and 'with a dull sense of heartache' she loyally sends packing a very gallant and eligible young man, Ralph Manners. Peter eventually graduates with honours and visits Ellinor, now in her thirties, to receive her congratulations. She believes he is about to propose marriage: '"I say, Nell." Her heart leapt; then, "I can see a silver thread among your raven locks, old girl."' Peter has previously expressed his distaste for flappers – their only use, he tells Ellinor, is that '[t]hey make queens of women like you'. To his horror, a member of the species is working as a typist at the firm he has joined: 'A typical young thing who had brought flapping to a fine art, whose boneless body seemed to collapse in the middle when she sat down, whose ingenue shoes had ankle-straps, but whose eyes held the wisdom of Cleopatra.' Ellinor advises Peter not to be so 'narrow-minded'. He takes her advice to heart – and marries the flapper.[48]

For all the cultural force of the new iconography, older identities, rituals and practices did not disappear before an all-conquering sexual modernity. In rural Australia of the 1930s, traditional patterns of family-supervised courtship sat comfortably beside newer, more informal modes of social intercourse between young men and women, a combination evident in the ritual of the local dance. Young people understood the ways in which skill at dancing and, in women, an appearance that men found physically attractive, 'could be cultivated to distinct social advantage'.[49] Yet the dance was a ritual marked by restraint, self-control, suppressed sexual urges, and, at most, a casual flirtation. If a boy was interested in a girl, he might secure the last dance with her and ask to see her home, possibly even snatch a kiss with her at the door. There was a general reticence about sex, and few opportunities for sexual activity. These patterns also occurred in many urban contexts, such as among those whose lives still moved within the orbit of the churches.[50] In general, there were strong threads of continuity with an older culture that sought to subject sex to the dignified disciplines of self-restraint and procreation within marriage. The new freedoms said to be enjoyed by young single women were heavily qualified by the dangers of disease, violence, pregnancy and disgrace.

## Aboriginal Sex

The meaning of singleness changed if you were Aboriginal.[51] The 'modern girl' was white.[52] She might spend time in business while young, but was ultimately expected to find fulfilment in matrimony. Aboriginal women, having limited opportunities either for marriage or participation in the market as consumers, were enjoined to seek their destiny in manual labour. This is not to suggest that Aboriginal women were immune to the new visual culture. Aboriginal domestic servants in interwar Queensland 'spoke glowingly of the dresses they could now afford to buy'. One woman, June Bond, watched 'the "older girls" return to the mission clad in beautiful clothes, and looked forward to the time that she could "dress up" in and afford such lavish outfits'.[53] Yet even the most progressive white feminist reformers saw chaste industriousness as the best option for Indigenous women. The undesirable alternatives were prostitution to white frontiersmen or sexual bondage within traditional Indigenous society.[54] Feminists campaigned for the extension of 'loving protection' to Aboriginal women. At a time when some Australian feminists were beginning to nurture doubts about the women's movement's traditional preoccupation with state 'protection' of white women – would it really make them free? – feminist efforts on behalf of Indigenous women never departed from the assumption that stringent laws were needed if they were to be liberated from sexual exploitation by both white and black men.[55]

While governments did act to afford Aboriginal women greater protection from sexual abuse, they were hampered by the ascendancy of the pastoral economy, prevailing assumptions about men's natural behaviour, and prejudices concerning Aboriginal women's sexuality. In 1934 the WA government appointed H.D. Moseley, a Perth magistrate, to head a Royal Commission into 'the condition and treatment of Aborigines'. He concluded that unless the 'half-caste' children around town camps were educated and employed they would become a 'positive menace to the community: the men useless and vicious, and the women a tribe of harlots'.[56] In 1936 the WA parliament debated a bill that embodied some of Moseley's recommendations. It was intended, among other things, to alleviate the 'half-caste problem' and stiffen penalties for white men who had sexual relations with Aboriginal women. Sex figured prominently in this debate. W.H. Kitson, the Chief Secretary who introduced the bill on behalf of the Labor government, remarked that WA's 'aboriginal problem' was 'purely a sex problem'.[57] Kitson proposed a £50 fine or a minimum of six months' imprisonment for men who had sex with Aboriginal women, but these penalties were opposed as too harsh by a group of parliamentarians protective of the pastoral interest. Leslie Craig led the charge for lighter penalties, and rather whimsically told the story of a boundary rider visiting 'a windmill with a 20,000 gallon tank, seeing there a sylph-like figure rising from the water, with no clothes on and receiving an invitation to join her in the tank'. Who could blame such an unfortunate fellow if he gave in to temptation? Then there were the men 'who, on returning to their camps, have found young lubras under their blankets'. The 'native girl', he reminded his fellow parliamentarians, was 'a child of nature, and her character is not sufficiently strong to withstand the urge of nature'.[58]

While no other member was able to provide so vivid an image of the awful temptations to which white stockmen were subjected, the injustice of interfering with men's natural sexual function was a major theme among the bill's opponents.[59] John Nicholson was worried about the young man who might 'start life' in a 'way-back centre' and 'give way to nothing less than the simplest impulse of nature'.[60] Nicholson opposed the white man who lived in a long-term relationship with an Aboriginal woman – he should be properly punished – but the case of a casual liaison was 'different'. His was a particularly brazen defence of the bush worker's right to the use of the female Aboriginal body, but also of the folk belief that a man had only really 'fallen' if he was in love with an Aboriginal woman.[61] Vernon Hamersley seemed more concerned with the needs of employers when he referred to 'the difficulty of getting white men to go' into the 'back country', and the severe strain on those who did. This argument sounded awfully like an embarrassing suggestion that access to 'gins' was being used by pastoralists as an inducement to attract workers to their stations, but Hamersley denied that he meant anything of the sort; merely that 'back country' folk were tested more severely than their city cousins.[62] There was certainly no denying that city men rarely experienced the discomfort and inconvenience of finding 'lubras' in their bedclothes when they returned from a day's work in a Perth office or on the Fremantle wharves. J.J. Holmes, another pastoralist, referred to the additional complication that some of the 'half-caste' women were 'absolutely white', while there were some white women who spent their time lying about on beaches with few clothes on 'doing their best to make themselves like half-castes'. Would a young man charged with having had sexual relations with a 'coloured girl' be able to defend himself by declaring that he thought she was white?[63]

Parliamentary and public debate also registered the growing alarm in Australia's white community about the 'half-caste problem'. Whereas the number of 'full-bloods' seemed in continual decline, the 'half-caste' population was increasing – 'breeding like rabbits', as one sensitive soul put it – a phenomenon that raised awkward questions about the future of White Australia.[64] Cecil Cook, the Chief Protector in the Northern Territory, was worried that in his part of the world, a fast-breeding black population might eventually drive out the whites and menace Australia's security. One solution that gained a measure of official support between the wars was 'biological absorption' of the 'half-caste' population into the white community. Women of mixed blood would be prevented from marrying full-bloods but encouraged to wed whites, presumably from the working class. By judicious state-controlled breeding, the Aboriginal veins would be absorbed into the national bloodstream, and the dark shades of 'native' skin overcome by the overpowering whiteness of British Australia. The idea was based on the belief that because the Aboriginal was a primitive Caucasian, there would be no throw backs: that is, white women would be spared the nasty surprise of giving birth to a black baby two or three generations down the track.[65]

The policy of breeding out the colour was driven by sexual engineers such as A.O. Neville, the Chief Protector in WA, and Cook, his NT counterpart.[66] It has been suggested that in NSW the Aborigines Protection Board even deliberately exposed Aboriginal women in domestic service to the sexual abuse of white men with the aim of breeding out the colour and ultimately 'eradicating the Aboriginal population'.[67] But in Queensland, the Chief Protector, A.W. Bleakley, opposed official encouragement of miscegenation on the grounds that 'it was highly unlikely that many whites would be willing to marry crossbreeds, no matter what the inducement', and the few who agreed to do so 'would probably be of a low type'. His state, he explained at a 1937 national conference of native administrators, had for a quarter of a century given every encouragement to the 'marriage of crossbreed aboriginals amongst their own race'.[68] Yet despite the penalties for sex between the races in Queensland, there is abundant evidence of its occurrence, including between white bosses and Aboriginal servants.

As one woman recalled, 'From my experience all the masters wanted to do was to jump into bed with you'.[69] Meanwhile, in the SA outback, white bushmen combined marginal pastoral activity with the collection of dingo scalps, for which the government paid a bounty. In these isolated areas, the white men formed sexual relationships with Aboriginal women and could buy scalps collected from local Indigenous people, selling them on to the government at a profit. The growing hostility of official and humanitarian opinion, however, led to legislation banning interracial sex. But in cases where long-standing relationships existed, the authorities were pragmatically willing to encourage marriage rather than prosecuting.[70] In general, the lives of Aboriginal people were subject to a range of interventions that sought to control how they deployed their sexuality. Here too was a story of continuity with the Victorian and Edwardian era, rather than of radical interwar transformation.

### Sexology, Sex Education and Eugenics
For white women romance, pleasure and freedom were held up as both desirable and attainable. Sex advice literature, popular Freudianism and consumer culture combined to redefine woman as an essentially sexual being who achieved an ideal womanhood in beauty and glamour. Sex manuals taught that sex was for the mutual pleasure of a monogamous couple, a view most famously promoted in British author Marie Stopes's 1918 bestseller *Married Love*.[71] Sexual compatibility between a husband and wife formed the foundation of a successful marriage, with mutual orgasm the holy grail of every married couple – not, as medical opinion once held, because it was necessary for impregnation – but to preserve a happy and fulfilling relationship.[72] The manuals gave couples explicit information about how they might develop a mutually pleasurable technique but it was men who were seen as requiring firmest guidance in the art of pleasuring their wives.[73]

Sex manuals sometimes attracted the censor's wrath but were nevertheless widely distributed in Australia. In 1924 a Sydney bookseller reported that chemists were constantly sending to his shop young men about to marry so that they might acquire a copy of *Married Love*, while the eugenicist, sex reformer and feminist Marion Piddington claimed in 1926 that Stopes's book was 'selling widely' and 'girls save up & pay off weekly to get it'. She also reported 'clothes lines of "Married Love" draped from end to end of the stalls in stations & wharves'.[74] A woman employed by a prominent Sydney rationalist recalled that he thoughtfully left copies of Stopes's books lying around the office when his young employee married.[75] While Leigh Summers is right to point to the antifeminist implications of some ideas in Australian sexology, it is harder to agree completely with her conclusion that it offered 'neither understanding nor liberation to women readers'.[76] Much depended on which sexologist you were reading; even more, perhaps, on what readers did in their own lives with the ideas gained from sexological texts.

The career of Marion Piddington reveals one way in which Stopes's ideas were disseminated in Australia.[77] While Piddington was not diverted by *Married Love* from her own campaign for artificial insemination of unmarried women (see chapter 5), she informed Stopes in March 1919 that since reading her book she longed 'more than ever to see the sacred Institution of marriage holding its assured position as a bulwark of ... our nation'.[78] Piddington also sent Stopes a copy of Chidley's *The Answer* and tried to persuade her to endorse that reformer's teachings. As she told Stopes, '[t]here are many waiting for your opinion of the Chidley pamphlets[.] I am deeply convinced of the truth of his discovery. I believe that the too early sex awakening is caused by erection & that every child should be told that erection should not take place in the process of natural functions'. She had raised her own son according to Chidley's philosophy. When she noticed him, as a five-year-old, with an erection, she gently advised him, 'The little organ should not get stiff darling'. As a result, she claimed, he had been 'spared the suffering and excitement of desire'.[79]

Piddington, like most proponents of sex education at this time, assumed that mothers had the key role to play in educating their young in the mysteries of sex.[80] That was the main theme of Piddington's 1926 book *Tell Them! Or the Second State of Mothercraft*, which presented sex education as an essential part of a mother's duty to produce healthy racial specimens.[81] Having informed Stopes that her own book was about to appear, Piddington learned that her correspondent was engaged in a study of the same subject. She replied deferentially: 'My book will not be needed. If I had known you were writing on the same subject I would not have printed mine.'[82] The Antipodean, it seemed, could be an acolyte and populariser, an agent for a British firm; she could not gain serious consideration of her ideas at the heart of empire.

BLACK-EYED SUE, and SWEET POLL of PLYMOUTH,
*Taking leave of their Lovers who are going to Botany Bay.*

'Black-Eyed Sue, and Sweet Pol of Plymouth, Taking leave of their Lovers who are going to Botany Bay', 1792. The association of working-class women with dissolute behaviour and sexual excess is clear. (National Library of Australia, nla.pic-an5577509)

'E-Migration or a Flight Of Fair Game' by Alfred Ducôte, 1832. The speech bubbles on the left, from apparently envious British workhouse women, say 'I'd be a butterfly' and 'Varmint'. Those on the right, from the men of Van Diemen's Land, say 'I spies mine' and 'I sees a prime un, get ready Clargyman.' Single female migrants were intended to help rectify the shortage of marriageable women in the colonies. Ducôte satirises the expectation that they will bring a softening feminine touch. (National Library of Australia, nla.pic-an6589648)

'Sly Grog Shop at Hanging Rock Diggings'. A lively group of gold miners with their female companions, black and white. (National Library of Australia, nla.pic-an8003926)

SLY GROG SHOP AT HANGING ROCK DIGGINGS.

'Wake, Australia! Wake!' Australia, a sleeping virgin, is in dire peril from a cunning Chinese invader. Her left hand seems strategically placed as if to emphasise the specifically sexual nature of the threat. *Boomerang* (Brisbane), 11 February 1888, p. 1. (National Library of Australia)

'Piebald Possibilities – A Little Australian Christmas Family Party of the Future' by Livingston Hopkins. Here was White Australia's nightmare: miscegenation leading to a racially impure population. *Bulletin*, 13 December 1902, p. 25. (National Library of Australia)

William Chidley on Tour. (Mitchell Library, State Library of NSW, PXA 1276)

*The Crucified Venus* by Norman Lindsay, 1912. *The Pen Drawings of Norman Lindsay*, Angus & Robertson, Sydney, 1918. (National Library of Australia)

Soldiers and Egyptian civilians in front of fire-damaged buildings in the Cairo quarter known as the Haret el Wasser in April 1915. Australian soldiers, who had recently rioted in the red-light district, called the area 'The Wazza'. (Australian War Memorial C00184)

Rexona Advertisement, 1926. Between the wars, advertisers regularly reminded Australian women that they needed to make themselves sexually attractive to men. Soap, a powerful weapon in the fight against body odour, would help them. *Australian Woman's Mirror*, 14 December 1926, p. 29. (National Library of Australia)

MRS. A. B. PIDDINGTON

Marion Piddington, sex educator
and eugenicist, by Frank Dunne.
*Smith's Weekly*, 16 January 1932, p. 16.
(National Library of Australia)

Norman Haire (left), with colleagues Magnus Hirschfeld, J.H. Leunbach, Antonin Tryb and Josef
Weisskopf at the 1932 World League for Sexual Reform Congress in Brno, Czechoslovakia.
(Rare Books & Special Collections, University of Sydney Library)

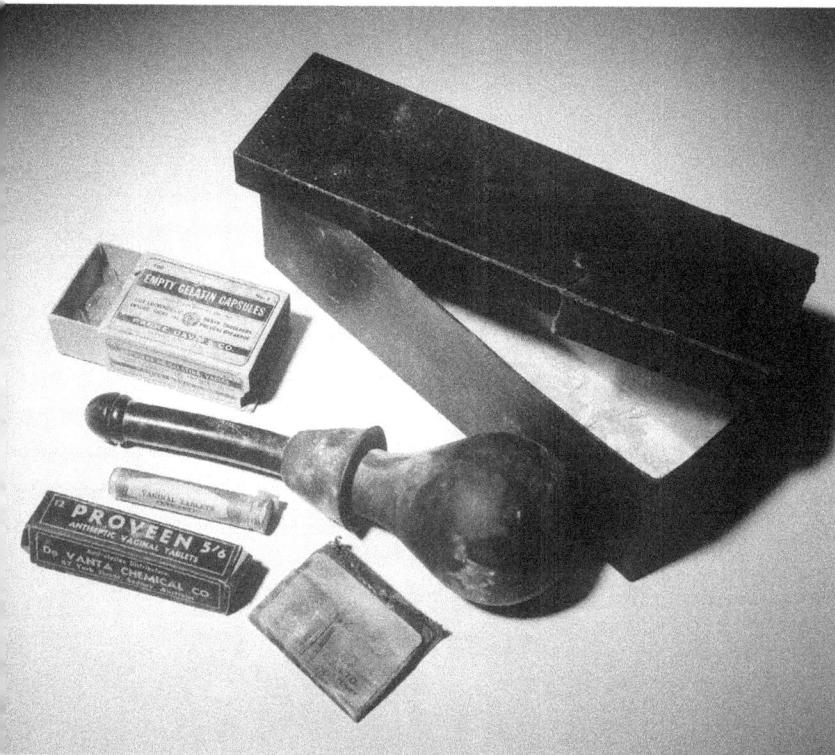

The contents of a box of contraceptives, owned by a Hurstville (Sydney) woman who married in the late 1920s. Kept away from her children on the top shelf of a wardrobe, they were discovered after her death in the 1990s. Photographer: Penelope Clay. (Powerhouse Museum, Sydney)

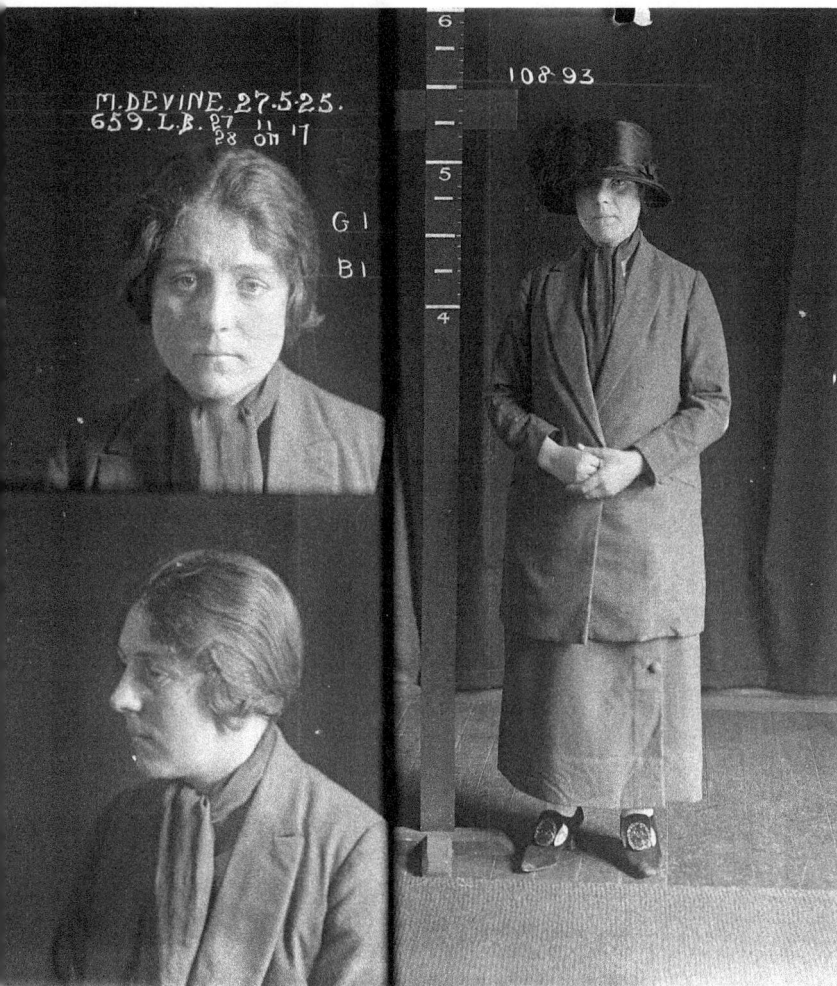

Left: The artists' balls typify the image of the 1920s as an era of pleasure and freedom but they also aroused moral panic. Picture by Stan Cross, 1929. (Stan Cross Archive of Cartoons and Drawings, 1912–1974, National Library of Australia, nla.pic-vn4306130)

Above: The infamous madam, Tilly Devine, in a brush with the law. She had slashed a man's face with a razor in a barber's shop and received a two-year sentence. (Matilda Devine, criminal record number 659LB, 27 May 1925. State Reformatory for Women, Long Bay, NSW. New South Wales Police Forensic Photography Archive, Justice & Police Museum, Historic Houses Trust DES_FP07_0226_002a)

A World War II meeting of Australian wives and fiancées of American servicemen.
(Australian War Memorial: 042776)

A crowd outside the Paramount Theatre in Bundaberg, Queensland, in the 1950s. The sex hygiene film the *Secrets of Life* was being screened; the salacious appeal can hardly be missed. (John Oxley Library, State Library of Queensland, 64547)

Mug shot of transvestites Neville McQuade (aged eighteen) and Lewis Keith Stanley (aged nineteen), North Sydney Police Station, early June 1942. McQuade, at least, was soon in trouble again: see chapter 7. (New South Wales Police Forensic Photography Archive, Justice & Police Museum, Historic Houses Trust DES_COS074)

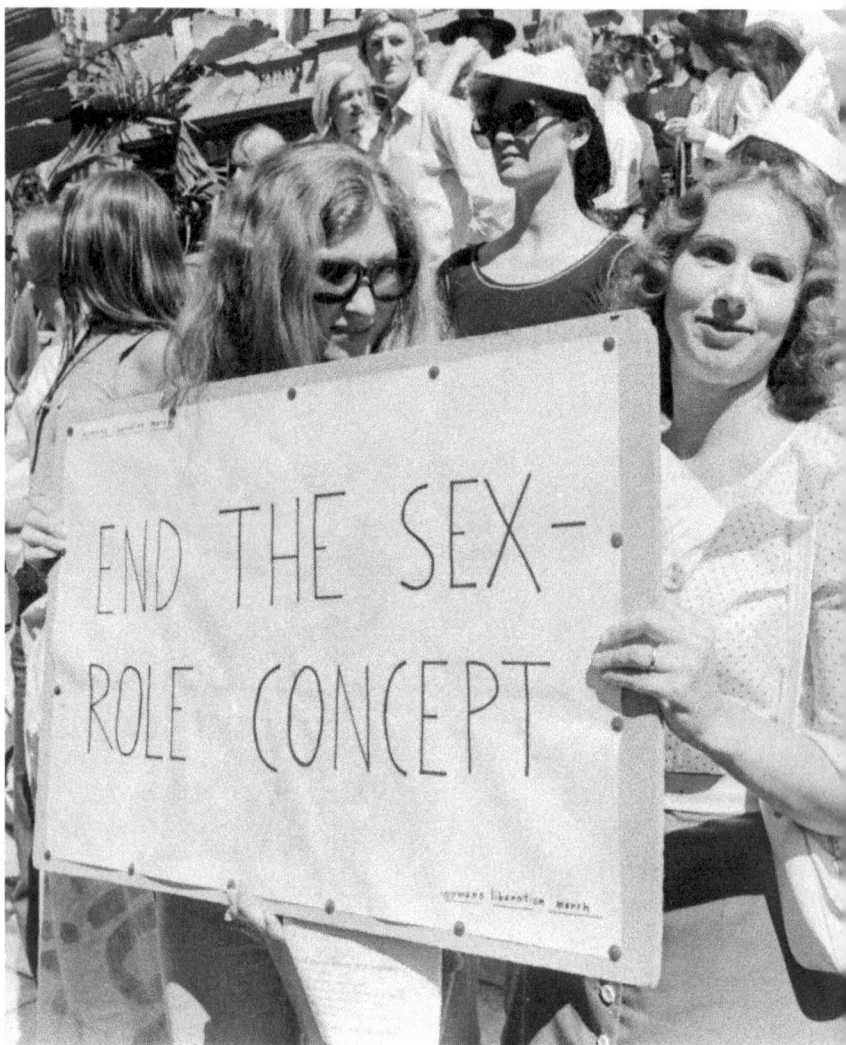

Sydney women's liberation march, 11 March 1972. Photographer: Berry. (*Sydney Morning Herald*, Fairfax Syndication)

Sex workers in Hay Street, Kalgoorlie, 1988. Photographer: Robin Smith. (National Library of Australia, nla.pic-vn4231257)

Dennis Altman (centre) and Craig Johnston (right), gay demonstration, Sydney, 1981. Photographer: William Yang. (National Library of Australia, nla.pic-vn3097668)

Same-sex marriage emerged as a new frontier in the struggle for gay and lesbian rights in the 1990s. This cartoon by Judy Horacek is from 1999. (© Copyright Judy Horacek, www.horacek. com.au, National Library of Australia, nla.pic-vn3293867)

Yet this is not quite so; for one Australian did manage to establish a reputation in Britain and Europe between the wars. Norman Haire was born Norman Zions in Sydney in 1892, the son of a Jewish emigrant from Poland and his London-born wife. After graduating from Sydney University, he developed an interest in gynaecology and travelled to Britain in 1920. He now became 'Norman Haire': his father's original surname had been Zajac, Polish for 'hare'.[83]

Haire set himself up as a pioneering sexologist on Harley Street. Overweight and egotistical, Haire's Jewishness, homosexuality and Antipodean birth secured his status as an outsider. Yet he was also successful in wielding his medical authority as a weapon in forging a reputation for himself and a respectability for sexology. Haire acquired an uneasy English mentor in the kindly, generous and reclusive Ellis, and an important continental supporter in Hirschfeld, the German sexologist. He joined the British Society for the Study of Sex Psychology soon after his arrival in London and, in 1929, with Dora Russell (the wife of Bertrand, the philosopher) organised the London Congress of the World League for Sexual Reform. Formed by Hirschfeld in 1928, the League aimed to bring greater enlightenment to sexuality. Although its program was originally Hirschfeld's creation, Haire redrafted it for an English audience. Among its points were reforms covering marriage and divorce, women's rights, birth control, eugenics, compassion for 'inverts', non-interference of the law in sexual relations between consenting adults, and the decriminalisation of 'sexual aberrations', which at the time included homosexuality, cross-dressing and whipping. Greater freedom of sexual relations outside marriage would reduce prostitution and VD, and bestow rights to children born outside wedlock. Better sex education should be made available, especially for the young. At the 1929 Congress, Haire deliberately played down homosexuality. His work contributed to the shift in sexual science away from an absorption in 'abnormal' sexual behaviour and towards an interest in 'all aspects of sexual life'.[84]

Debate about sexuality in Australia itself was less lively but by the 1930s and 1940s, sexology and Freudianism were encouraging closer attention to sexual questions and their relationship to individual and social development. Not that there was a lack of local resistance to such ideas. In 1936 W.A. Osborne, the professor of physiology at Melbourne University, dismissed psychoanalysis as 'of oriental origin', with 'its emphasis on sex' being 'out of place in a Nordic community like Australia'. But in the same city the bohemian doctor Reg Ellery was by this time blending Marxism and psychoanalytic theory in an innovative attempt to explain the nature of modern sexual problems. Ellery accepted that male sexuality was naturally aggressive and centred on the penis but, in a more romantic formulation, he saw women's as essentially passive, diffused through the body as a whole, and in need of arousal in the skilful hands of a man. Coitus, for Ellery, was fundamentally 'a sadomasochistic act' – with the men sadists and the women masochists.[85] The more radical approach to sex reform was also taken up in Sydney by George Southern, the author of a self-published booklet in 1934, *Making Morality Modern*. Southern tried to commence an Australian branch of the World League for Sex Reform but he was also preoccupied with defending his particular penchant for sadomasochism, if in guarded terms:[86] 'That love should be expected to manifest itself only in "tenderness" and never in violence ... is indisputably unhealthy.' The normal male, he said, desired to hunt, and the normal female to be hunted; man's 'instinctive desire' to slap the female buttocks should be classed not as a 'perversion', but along 'with such preliminaries as chasing, fighting, wrestling, biting, kissing, and fondling, all of which are but variations of the one theme: the eagerness of the male and the reluctance of the female'.[87]

Southern was more hostile to masturbation, and in this he was by no means yet swimming against the tide of more authoritative opinion: the interwar years witnessed the persistence of opposition to masturbation and the conviction that it was producing racial decay. Some historians have detected a growing emphasis on its adverse psychological consequences, as opposed to the earlier stress on physical manifestations.[88] The 1935 *Guide to Virile Manhood*, produced by the Father and Son Welfare Movement and the League of Youth and Honor, provided detailed advice to boys about keeping their penises clean, and warned against 'over-handling', 'a stupid childish act ... those who do it, find that they cannot concentrate on their lessons or any work they may have to do'. Boys might, however, have felt reassured that it did not cause 'insanity' or 'consumption ... If the boy drops it he will be quite all right'.[89] Here was the hint of a less alarmist approach but sex educators were not yet prepared to sever the connection between avoidance of masturbation and personal and national efficiency. That would have undermined some deeply entrenched ideas about the importance of self-restraint which, in an interwar context of economic depression, seemed more salient than ever. Some sex educators and medical practitioners went so far as to advocate male and female circumcision in order to cure the 'precocious' young masturbator.[90] It is unlikely, moreover, that Haire found much support for the opinion, expressed in 1927 and condemned by Piddington, that 'moderate auto-erotic activity in the child is harmless in itself'. He sought to empty masturbation of its association with sexual guilt, which could lead to 'mental anguish and even physical disorder', while at the same time acknowledging that it was so inferior to 'normal sexual activity in its capacity for giving pleasure' that a mature adult would only practise it in the absence of the more satisfying alternative.[91]

Haire's ideas registered the influence of the Freudian revolution. Masturbation had become a stage through which children would pass on their way to sexual maturity: to master the urge to masturbate was to become fully adult, and fully civilised.[92] But another radical sexologist whom we encountered earlier in this chapter, Storer, took the argument further by specifically condemning solo masturbation because of its anti-social character, while endorsing mutual masturbation, even between youths of the same sex. It is easy enough to see why Haire became rich and famous and Storer landed in gaol for sexual offences committed with much younger men.[93]

Public debate about sex in Australia stressed dangers and pitfalls and gave less attention to sex as a source of pleasure. In the years between the outbreak of war and the Depression, the problems of preventing VD or dealing with violent sex 'maniacs' who lurked in dark alleys accounted for a large amount of public discussion of the 'sex problem'. As a result, sexuality remained powerfully connected in the popular imagination with illness, crime and disorder. Yet for some sex radicals, healthy sexual relations were connected with the quest for bodily health and race improvement; there is a strong thread of continuity between the late-nineteenth-century alliance of sex reform with race-building, and the eugenic preoccupations of the interwar years.

Eugenics was a movement concerned with enhancing 'the racial fitness of populations' and it had some currency among the kinds of middle-class progressives advocating sex education.[94] Where pronatalists were concerned primarily with the *quantity* of populations, and bemoaned low birthrates, eugenicists were more worried about the overall *quality*. In particular, they claimed that the working classes and feeble-minded – that is, the racially unfit – were reproducing at a greater rate than the middle class, with the result that the quality of the population was declining. A few reformers, such as Marion Piddington, advocated the sterilisation or segregation of 'unmarried fathers and mothers' found to be 'mentally deficient'.[95] But Norman Haire went further. For him, eugenics was providing a scientific basis for sexual morality. Even the prostitute, argued Haire in 1927, did less damage to society than a wife who bore 'a family of physically or mentally defective children'. Contraception and abortion could be used to prevent the unfit from reproducing but where they failed, infanticide was the answer; it is chilling to read Haire's suggestion that 'defective babies' be examined by a board of medical experts who would decide whether the infant lived or died. Meanwhile, 'sexually abnormal' people who infringed the 'sexual rights' of others should be subjected to '*preventive* treatment, whether by medical means, by segregation, or in the last resort by painless death'. One wonders whether Haire saw the irony when he found himself assisting Jewish sexologists forced to flee Hitler's Germany.[96]

Sex education was important in this context because the racially fit had to be encouraged to do their duty by producing healthy children, and the unfit – in the absence of compulsory sterilisation – discouraged from reproducing at all. At the same time, the field of sex education lay open to the efforts of voluntary bodies such as the Young Men's Christian Association, the Young Women's Christian Association, the Women's Christian Temperance Union, the Mothers' Union, the AWCL, the Workers' Educational Association, Marion Piddington's Institute of Family Relations, the Racial Hygiene Association of NSW, the Victorian Society for Sex Education, the Eugenics Society of Victoria, the Father and Son Welfare Movement and the New Education Fellowship. They had much work to do, but in the virtual absence of sex education from schools, finding an audience was no mere formality. The YWCA took its message of sexual purity to young female workers in factories,[97] while the AWCL, for a time, managed to gain the SA Education Department's approval for school visits. Yet girls were excluded from these talks and Catholic opinion, in SA and elsewhere, remained resolutely opposed to sex instruction. Lessons delivered to large groups of young boys, said the sceptics, were likely to arouse a dangerous curiosity about sex before they had 'the comprehension and will-power' to understand and apply such knowledge properly.[98] In Queensland, the Department of Public Instruction refused to allow school sex education. At most, the department's nurses sometimes made tactful reference to the subject of sex to girls about to leave school, a practice also followed by the chief medical officer for the older boys.[99] But even in universities, sex education was too hot to handle. Just after World War I, the Professorial Board of Melbourne University forbade the undergraduate Public Questions Society from organising a lecture on sex education because it would be 'undesirable' in front of 'a mixed audience'.[100]

Those who sought to educate young people about sex in any case faced the difficult task of finding a language in which to do so. A correspondent with a women's magazine in 1927 recommended the children's stories written by the New Zealand author Edith Howes, but acknowledged that there were few authors prepared to 'advocate the teaching of the part the human father plays'. While it was admirable that little Twin and Win in Howes's 1916 book *The Cradle Ship* were able to dismiss Granny's claim that babies were found under gooseberry bushes, it is doubtful whether their tour of Babyland – for all its charming plant, animal and even human stories – would have made them much the wiser. Certainly, the Mothers' Union was prepared to recommend the book but another magazine correspondent claimed that 'most parents' regarded *The Cradle Ship* as unsuitable for children because it spoiled 'their innocence'. When teaching in the country, she had once lent the book to some older girls and read it to others in a sewing class, only to find an indignant school committee threatening to complain to the education department.[101]

Some organisations with avowedly eugenicist intentions also entered the field of sex education, often supplementing their activities with advice about family planning and even the provision of contraceptive devices. The Racial Hygiene Association (RHA) was formed in 1926 with the aims of promoting sex education, campaigning against VD and educating the community in eugenics. It even received a government subsidy that reached £500 a year by 1929–30 – courtesy of the Minister for Health, Dr Richard Arthur, that old warrior in the social purity cause. Lilian Goodisson, the RHA's energetic secretary, took the RHA's mission of sex education to girls in private schools but the

Country Party education minister, David Drummond, refused access
to their state counterparts for fear of upsetting the Catholics.[102]

The RHA entered especially turbulent waters when it considered
setting up a birth-control clinic. While some objections were raised
during a June 1931 debate within the organisation – with one member
declaring it would 'give our organisation a bad name' – others pointed
out that contraception was now being 'practised everywhere'. One
member pointedly remarked that although she had been 'against it'
once, there were now 'so many degenerates & mentally deficient people'
that 'such measures were necessary'. Goodisson, a nurse and strong
supporter of birth control, tactfully tried to move the debate to the
means by which contraception would be achieved, asserting that birth
control was 'now quite general' and that 'the best article or preparation
should be used'.[103] The RHA drew on a strong connection with reformist doctors to give its cause greater legitimacy. By the 1930s, in the face
of widespread use of birth control and a growing consciousness of the
dangers of repeated pregnancy to women's health, the Australian medical profession was softening in its attitude to contraception.

The RHA decided to go ahead with plans for a clinic, which was
established in Martin Place, Sydney, in 1933. It fitted women with the
evocatively named 'racia' cap, actually a variety of diaphragm.[104] Like
many middle-class birth controllers in this era in both Britain and the
US, the RHA favoured a clean, clinical and female method of birth control that would not interfere with the kind of erotic life being extolled
in the sex manuals. Stopes, the author of the most successful of them,
advocated a cervical cap; Haire, her Australian-born rival, a vaginal
diaphragm. The promotion of newfangled devices of this kind aimed to
displace often male-centred techniques, and especially withdrawal,
now widely condemned for its alleged ineffectiveness and psychological
damage to couples. Yet along with condoms, which were becoming
available in latex by the 1930s,[105] withdrawal continued to occupy an
important place in Australian sexual practice between the wars. A survey
of married women carried out in Melbourne in the early 1970s found
that withdrawal (31 per cent), condoms (21 per cent) and the rhythm
method (12 per cent) accounted for almost two-thirds of those practising some form of birth control between 1935 and 1939. As at the turn of
the century, men probably shouldered a large share of the responsibility
for birth control.[106]

In 1935 the RHA treated 677 women in its clinic, and another 239 by correspondence; an impressive record, but no contraceptive revolution. The association went out of its way to emphasise that it provided contraception only to married women and opposed abortion – another traditional and resilient method of birth control whose eradication middle-class reformers desired (see below).[107] Although this might have mollified Anglican opinion – the 1930 Lambeth Conference had agreed that birth control should not be condemned 'under certain circumstances' – it did nothing to discourage Catholic criticism. The (Protestant) Council of Churches also attacked the clinic.[108] As RHA member Ruby Rich later recalled, 'We were regarded probably by some as being very subversive. Oh no, we weren't loved, we weren't liked, and I suppose by very many we weren't respected'.[109]

In 1939 the Eugenics Society of Victoria also aroused 'a storm of protest' when it decided to establish a birth-control clinic to service the 'slums' of inner-suburban Carlton, Fitzroy and Collingwood – with contraceptive instruction 'to be given not only for medical, but also for eugenic and economic reasons'. After divisions emerged within the organisation, the proposal was abandoned. Nevertheless, a few Eugenics Society members led by its secretary, Dr Victor Wallace, persisted with the plan, which eventually came to fruition early in 1941 when the Social Hygiene Society Clinic was quietly established in Collins Street. The timing was unfortunate for although the venture enjoyed early success, it was forced to close in September 1942 when wartime rubber shortages undermined its supply of pessaries. Nevertheless, even before this controversy Melbourne had three birth control clinics that were unobtrusively going about their business. The first to be established, the Mothers' Welfare Clinic, opened late in 1934 at the Melbourne District Nursing Society and was discreetly associated with the Royal Women's Hospital. Meanwhile, Wallace opened another significant front in the medical conquest of birth control when he began performing vasectomies in 1936.[110]

Marion Piddington's Institute of Family Relations (IFR), in Phillip Street, Sydney, emerged in 1931 as a rival to the RHA. Piddington probably gained her small room, courtesy of the Lang Labor government, by emphasising the IFR's desire to eradicate promiscuity and VD.[111] According to its publicity, the IFR also supplied 'the latest and most reliable methods of contraception for the wife's use … The wife can learn to place her contraceptive soon after marriage'. This was a sponge that had been developed by Stopes, and which Piddington supplied in Australia as a virtual franchise, but the IFR also distributed sheaves and jelly that could be used either alone, or in conjunction with the sponge. Indeed, it was suggested in the publicity that, after the initial outlay, a wife would be able to 'make her own contraceptives', and Piddington clearly intended that the device could be used without a husband's knowledge. The IFR provided counsel by letter or interview for five shillings, evening classes for parents and teachers (for a shilling), threepenny evening sessions for boys and girls, as well as classes conducted for groups in the suburbs.[112] Piddington also disseminated her 'new objective method' of sex education through the popular press and conducted meetings with groups ranging from the Feminist Club to the Council of Jewish Women.[113] By early 1928, she estimated her audience as 400–500 people a week; this missionary endeavour took her to places such as Grafton, on the NSW north coast, and the mining town of Broken Hill in the red interior. On her own estimate, during 1928 alone she conducted 270 classes involving 8000 people.[114]

The popularity of Piddington's talks – and of Stopes's books – is not difficult to explain. Many Australian men and women who came to adulthood in the 1920s and 1930s knew little about sex beyond what they had managed to pick up from conversations with friends and siblings, the yellow press and graffiti encountered in public toilets where one could find 'puzzling drawings of genitalia looking like half apples, or sausages with round lumps of mashed potato, like the ones you got in Coles Cafeteria'.[115] Clearly, many children acquired a sexual knowledge of sorts from their fellows. Jim Comerford, later a union leader, learned about sex from the other men as a fourteen-year-old working in a Hunter Valley coal mine. Asked if he had 'shot the bishop yet' (masturbated), he replied that he was 'saving it all for the pope' – but actually hadn't the faintest idea what his comrades were on about. A man who taught him how to drive the winch during the afternoon shift threw in for good measure an exhibition of masturbation, but it was with a friend that he used to talk about such matters and 'swap the knowledge' they were acquiring: 'He told me that one of his wheelers told him how much he enjoyed having sex with his wife in the chair, that she'd straddle him, you know with her breasts against his mouth.'[116]

Jim was employed in a workplace dominated by proletarian men but for many young Australians, particularly girls, it was quite possible to reach adulthood and marriage with little knowledge of sex at all.[117] Ivy T., a Maitland girl, recalled that she 'didn't know one little thing about it! If that was mentioned in the home I can remember Mum saying – "Oh you go outside dear now" you know and we didn't know a thing. It was never mentioned'. She eventually learned the basics from a book her older married sister gave her when she was about fourteen or fifteen.[118] A butcher's daughter from rural WA recalled: 'When I was first married, I didn't know what sex was all about. Me mother knew I was expectin' a baby, but she never told me anything.' She went on to have seventeen children.[119] There are stories from the middle decades of the twentieth century of married women and mothers – one with eight children – who had never seen their husbands naked.[120]

### Sexual Disorder

These men and women grew up in a culture in which sex was something shameful yet unavoidable because it was increasingly under public – and often sensational – notice. Australia in the postwar period was haunted by the sense of a world gone awry. Moral panic between the wars about violent crime – fostered by the popular press – included a preoccupation with sexual predators. The 1921 rape and murder of a twelve-year-old girl in Melbourne – in the so-called Gun Alley case – created a popular sensation that led to the hanging of an innocent man for the crime.[121] Angst about the loose morality of the times also focused on the 'Artists' Balls'. The Sydney *Truth*'s front-page report of the 1924 ball, a fancy-dress 'do' with a children's theme held at the Sydney Town Hall, would have left few readers in doubt that something was deeply wrong with jazz-age Australia. It described a drunken orgy, in which semi-naked men and women cavorted on the dance floor, and fondled one another in the basement, toilets, corridors and balconies. The behaviour of some girls, reported *Truth*, 'would have brought a blush to the cheek of a Magdalen'. One parliamentarian worried over 'the presence of a notorious type of effeminate male' at the 1924 ball, men who dressed 'in female attire'.[122] Yet the Melbourne *Truth*'s report on the 1925 Artists' Ball in St Kilda ('Like 1870 inside and 1970 outside!'), while drawing attention to the presence of hairy-legged men in female dress, seemed more concerned about a girl 'with brightly rouged lips' whose thin, tight-fitting costume 'showed her seventeen-year-old body to improper advantage'. She 'should have been soundly spanked and sent home to bed': one suspects, from his porno-graphic prose, that the journalist concerned would not have found the task an onerous one.[123]

In 'modern times', social and sexual disorder seemed to go together, a connection made in an academic paper that appeared in the *Medical Journal of Australia* in 1934. 'Modern social life', it asserted, increased 'the possibilities of the derangement of genital organs of women'. In particular, the author blamed music based 'on the native melodies of the most salacious race in the … world' and 'dancing' with its origins in 'the savage ritual of tropical tribes'. But there were also influences that could not so easily be blamed on the fashionable influence of 'savages': 'scanty and suggestive' sporting costumes, young people's independence and lack of restraint, and the 'tumbling authority and prestige' of major social institutions – all had 'increased sexual stimu-lation' and discouraged a shouldering of 'responsibilities to the species'.[124] The thoughtful John Springthorpe, a Melbourne doctor, recognised social benefits in the greater openness and honesty about sex in the 1920s but thought it 'incredible that every girl who shows her bosom & limbs knows and thinks of its sexual effects'. Yet he concluded sadly that 'many must'.[125]

### The Depression and Birth Control

Some commentators continued to condemn birth control on moral grounds and associated it with this decadence. A writer in the *West Australian* in 1934 acknowledged that the matter was one for the con-sciences of married couples, but added that 'it will be a bad day for any country when the knowledge and use of contraceptives become gen-eral. Under cover of helping a comparatively small number of difficult cases … we are in danger of making vice easy'.[126] In 1939 the WA Minister for Health turned down a request from the Labor Party Metropolitan Council for the establishment of free birth-control clin-ics in Perth and Fremantle Hospitals. He was worried that they would be used by 'those who, for selfish reasons, do not want children'.[127] Just as in the early years of the century, contraception's potential for trans-forming the essential meaning of sex – from procreation to recreation – troubled the pronatalist conscience.

More likely, in straitened circumstances, couples had simply delayed having children, for Australian births reached an all-time low in 1934. Some men had no choice but to take leave of the marital bed as they went bush in search of work, while in other cases marriages were repeatedly postponed. Contraception must have made long engagements at least tolerable for such couples. The decline in 'illegitimate' births, along with that in the marital birthrate, points to a growing control over fertility.[128] Abstinence played a part in this process – some men 'retired' to the back room or veranda[129] – but to the main early twentieth-century contraceptive methods, such as the condom, pessary, douching, less frequent sex, withdrawal and abortion, were now increasingly added diaphragms, caps, jellies and spermicides. Word-of-mouth remained important in spreading contraceptive information but it was now supplemented by lectures, pamphlets and – for a small minority – clinics.[130]

Abortion made a substantial contribution to birth control in the 1920s and 1930s, not least because no contraceptive method except complete abstinence could avoid the occasional 'accident'. Officially, and even after the 1938 *Bourne* case had given British doctors a limited protection where they judged the life of a pregnant woman in danger, the medical profession remained hostile. Doctors between the wars campaigned for stern official measures against nurses and midwives who carried out abortions, and in NSW at least, authorities responded with prosecution rates that were double those of the late nineteenth century.[131] Abortion, like contraception, was being slowly pulled into the orbit of the medical profession. In Melbourne the basements of a Collins Street hotel and a Flinders Lane private hospital were used, with the latter reportedly 'patronised by all the senior consultants of Collins Street'. A press commentator remarked in 1940 that abortion was 'such a common practice in Victoria that fashionable abortionists have as many as 40 cases to deal with in a weekend … Abortion has become prevalent among the well-to-do and the socially respectable more than among others'.[132] Norman Haire knew of half-a-dozen Sydney doctors in the 1940s 'whose practice seemed to consist of nothing but abortions' and the same number who carried out a very large number annually. But there were many more who performed the occasional abortion for their own patients while turning others down.[133] By 1940, medical abortion had achieved considerable toleration at the hands of police, sometimes the result of collusion and corruption, but also because it was notoriously difficult to secure a conviction.

A matter that had very often been treated as women's business now came increasingly under male control. Not only were doctors more likely to be performing an abortion but husbands and lovers now 'often arranged the operation, paid the bills, stayed for the duration, and desperately sought medical assistance' when complications occurred.[134] However, a self-induced abortion remained the only option for many women in rural areas. And at fifty guineas a time in Melbourne in the mid-1930s – fifteen times the basic weekly wage – the cost of medical intervention was prohibitive for most.[135] The usual solution for a working-class woman was still self-abortion or the backyarder, often a midwife or 'nurse'. Yet authorities also cracked down on their activities in the late 1920s and early 1930s.[136]

Perhaps this trend encouraged self-abortion. Those treated for post-abortion infections at the Royal Women's Hospital in Melbourne in the 1930s were usually married women who had tried aborting themselves with the same kind of syringe that was commonly used for douching after sex.[137] An unqualified abortionist's services could be secured in Melbourne in the mid-1930s for about twenty guineas,[138] but a cheaper service was available from some female abortionists.[139] The occasional kindly doctor performed abortions for working-class patients cheaply or even for free. Horror stories concerning backyarders and desperate women with knitting needles have featured prominently in stories of this era, yet many women were able to secure a successful abortion without medical help.[140] It was still, however, a dangerous business. Women continued to lose their lives in horrifying circumstances from infection.

### Censorship

While some blamed 'the pagan outlook of many women' for abortion, professional and amateur worriers found plenty of other fertile fields.[141] Women's and religious groups condemned the depiction of erotic themes in films. In 1921 Dr Springthorpe worried about films that 'appealed to the sex instinct with every form of suggestion' including 'semi nudity', 'bedroom situations, & the "all but" in every direction'. He was unable to understand how 'nice girls can frequent such shows in mixed company … the finer feelings of restraint & modesty are

obliterated'.[142] In 1934 Arthur A. Lyons, a Perth Methodist, complained
that American films were wrecking 'the moral fibre of the people'.[143]
There were particular concerns among such critics about the impact of
immoral films on the impressionable minds of children, while the
Women's Citizens' League condemned 'abhorrent kissing scenes', at a
time when the kiss had come to be recognised as a critical marker of
heterosexual love. Even 'social hygiene' films, which dealt with themes
such as VD, abortion, seduction and the international sex trade, were
subjected to censorship campaigns by moral guardians and sometimes
cut or even banned outright by censors. There were suspicions that such
movies simply pandered to the prurient.[144]

Censors kept a close idea on the relatively new medium of cinema,
being especially worried by the preponderance of women and children
among audiences. The Commonwealth Censors explained in their 1925
report that they always removed from films 'assaults on women', 'indecent and vulgar attitudes', '"first-night-of-marriage" scenes', 'prostitution',
'the advocacy of free love', 'scenes of child-birth', 'and scenes in brothels'.[145] In the following year, they complained that '[t]he most damaging
indictment' that might be brought against contemporary cinema was not
that it was 'immoral', but that it was 'vulgar':

> Why should it be necessary so often to film women in the act of
> undressing or engaged in the toilet? What end is attained by sitting
> all the actors in a drama down to dinner in bathing costumes? …
> [W]hy should the climax of so many films be an attack on an unpro-
> tected and innocent woman? Certainly in good drama no one will
> rule out as a legitimate theme the ravages of sexual passion, but we
> are speaking now of films which merely depict in a succession of
> loose scenes the luring of a woman on board a yacht, or to a lonely
> hut, so that a man may do as he likes with her. We will continue to
> eliminate these scenes on moral and artistic grounds … [W]e shall
> not in any circumstances pass a scene where the man spills soup or
> wine on a woman's clothes, so as to compel her to undress … All
> honeymoon scenes will be also eliminated, if it is apparent that the
> motive behind them is not a genuinely artistic or dramatic one.[146]

In their 1927 report, the Commonwealth authorities complained not
only of the tendency in American films for characters to be 'shown

without their nether garments', but about certain European films which had to be banned 'because standards of morality and conduct on the Continent often differ considerably from those in vogue in English speaking countries'.[147] Yet in 1929 Cresswell O'Reilly, a Methodist lay-preacher who had become Chief Censor earlier in the year, complained even about British films, which with increasing frequency depicted 'the hero and heroine spending the night together, sometimes after only a few hours acquaintance'.[148]

Film censorship was tightened in the second half of the 1920s, a trend that coincided with a new wave of book suppression. In 1923 the federal government banned a cheap edition of Boccaccio's *Decameron*, on the back of which appeared contraceptive advertisements, while Stopes's book on birth control, *Wise Parenthood*, was also briefly prohibited.[149] The customs department kept a close watch on birth control and sexologi-cal literature generally, at a time of continuing concern about declining birthrates. Thousands of titles were suppressed.[150] Customs applied a remarkably broad test of indecency – its officers were to be guided by 'what is usually considered unobjectionable in the household of the ordi-nary self-respecting citizen' – and state police were also becoming more active against local publications.[151] In a sweep of western literature that spanned centuries, the *Decameron*, the sex manual *Aristotle's Masterpiece* and the works of Marie Stopes were among 700 volumes seized by Sydney detectives from a Martin Place bookshop in early 1930.[152]

Norman Lindsay, through both art and writing, extended his revolt against 'Victorian' mores into the 1920s.[153] But his voluptuous nudes were arguably now closer in their ethos to a mass culture he despised than their creator would have cared to admit. As in much interwar adver-tising, Lindsay's women were self-consciously fashioning and displaying their bodies for the visual pleasure of an audience assumed to be male and heterosexual. Women were not to be intellectual, political or cul-tured – 'over-dressed shadows of a sociological problem' – but should 'return to our embrace naked and lovely, offering their plump hands with long tapering fingers, and their white breasts to our devout kisses'.[154] It is hardly surprising that some feminists were troubled by Lindsay's art. And as the poet A.D. Hope pointed out, although there were images in Lindsay's art of lovemaking between women – a common male hetero-sexual fantasy – he failed to show 'the slightest interest in the ... love of the male for the male'.[155] Lindsay saw in this latter aberration an asceticism that was life-denying. His pose as the eternal rebel against conventional morality had less plausibility in an era that produced Katharine Susannah Prichard's *Coonardoo*, Eleanor Dark's *Prelude to Christopher* and Xavier Herbert's *Capricornia* – all Australian novels exploring the complexities of (hetero)sexual experience with a subtlety that had no place in Lindsay's apparently endless procession of large-bosomed sirens and leering satyrs.

Changes in the censorship regime in the second half of the 1930s did bring some liberalisation in its wake but church groups campaigned to ban American comics and penny dreadfuls. In 1938 the Victorian parliament heard the devoutly Catholic parliamentarian Bert Cremean condemn the trade in these publications:

> Honorable members who have been abroad know of, and probably have been confronted by, dirty niggers who sell dirty postcards at Port Said and other places on the voyage to the Old Country. During the last two or three years in particular, there has developed in the City of Melbourne ... a dirty type of bookseller who is engaged in disseminating dirty literature, which ... has a very harmful effect, particularly on the youthful section of the community.

Cremean's orientalisation of the 'threat' was consistent with the established Australian habit of racialising sexual depravity, but it was now updated to speak to the experience of Australians who had acquired first-hand knowledge of Egypt as soldiers or tourists, and the many more who had been exposed to the popular stereotypes of the 'Gyppo'. Cremean saw the 'dirty' books and magazines as increasing promiscuity, masturbation ('secret vice') and prostitution, and called on the government to deal sternly with booksellers.[156] Meanwhile, the federal customs minister, Tommy White, complained that 'in the enormous output of Great Britain there are unfortunately some of the worst examples of obscene and indecent writing, printed, perhaps, for export'. As in the case of film, even the British product was a threat to Antipodean morals.[157]

## Prostitution

Prostitution was also sometimes understood as a foreign blot on the country, as Australia's place in 'the obnoxious traffic' of sex workers received increasing attention. As we have seen, foreign prostitutes had once been seen as performing a useful role in servicing foreign workers. Now that the latter were a declining presence, the government sought to remove Australia from the international sex trade.[158] As in the case of their campaign to protect Indigenous women, feminists worked through international organisations in pressing the federal government to cooperate with the League of Nations in ending this so-called white slave traffic. Nevertheless, they also argued for rehabilitation of the women involved, and worried over a tendency to coerce – and deport – the prostitutes themselves. The Australian government did, in fact, use its famous fifty-word dictation test, originally introduced to keep out non-white immigrants, to deport prostitutes and exclude those whose morals were questionable.[159]

There was a strand of medical opinion deeply influenced by eugenics that associated prostitution with 'feeble-mindedness and mental deficiency' and called for the 'permanent segregation' of those exhibiting these hereditary strains.[160] In practice, through vagrancy laws which were tightened in NSW in 1929 – when it became an offence to consort with a criminal – state authorities had great discretion at their disposal in dealing with prostitution.[161] In Sydney, this was the era of the famous criminal rivalry between Kate Leigh and Tilly Devine. Kate was a girl from Dubbo who made a life for herself as a prostitute among the crooks of Sydney; Tilly, a London prostitute who married an Australian soldier, 'Big' Jim Devine, while he was in England. Jim pimped for his emigrant wife in Sydney in the early 1920s; they reputedly charged an impressive ten shillings a time and 'always collected', using a large Cadillac to solicit, service clients and, when troubled by police, make a getaway.[162] But both Leigh and Devine would find the profession of madam far more profitable than prostitution. Each took advantage of a law that made it illegal for a man, but not a woman, to live off immoral earnings and with acumen, charisma and ruthlessness combined a highly profitable commerce in cocaine, sly grog and sex. Each accumulated a large fortune and a long police record.[163]

Leigh and Devine used their considerable resources to mobilise gangs to protect them from the other, and from potential rivals – with guns, knives, fists or razor blades, as required. These operators also had the resources to pay off corrupt police, protect their employees from violent or welshing clients, and pay bail and fines when their girls went to court. The prostitutes naturally had to surrender a substantial portion of their earnings to the madams. Devine, who reputedly had between twenty and thirty brothels in the 1930s, took as much as 50 per cent, and prostitutes commonly accepted part-payment in cocaine.[164] Opportunities for freelancing were limited.[165] The 1929 consorting law, however, loosened the power of criminal gangs – it provided stiff penalties for anyone caught associating with reputed or convicted criminals – while the Depression saw some women enter or re-enter prostitution outside the control of criminal gangs to make ends meet in desperate times.[166]

Despite the limited opportunities for self-employment, this was paradoxically also an era in which certain individual prostitutes achieved celebrity status. In Sydney's inner-city Woolloomooloo, King's Cross and Darlinghurst, gangsters fought over the favours of beautiful women such as posh, blue-eyed Nellie Cameron and 'Pretty' Dulcie Markham, 'a tall, slim, striking blonde'.[167] At the peak of her reputation, Markham was said to be charging two pounds a time (of which she would have kept perhaps half), in an era when a domestic servant earned between one and two pounds *a week*.[168] Another woman able to command the best prices was Anne Brennan, who progressed from juvenile delinquency to street prostitution (as 'German Annie' – her mother was German-born) to courtesan. A woman of legendary beauty, vivacity and intelligence, Anne frequented the same Sydney bohemian circles as her father, the poet Christopher Brennan. Having been undressed by a generation of young Sydney writers and artists in the 1920s – much more frequently in their minds than in actuality – Anne died of consumption in 1929.[169]

Women such as Markham, Cameron, Brennan and other lesser known but classy and attractive prostitutes operated in expensively furnished houses, catered to wealthy businessmen and professionals, and charged top prices. A few operated independently of the criminal syndicates, servicing carefully selected men in the manner of modern call girls.[170] Less glamorous women, and premises to match, were available for lower middle-class and working-class men – here sex was about a pound in the mid-1920s – while older prostitutes catered to those able or prepared to pay just a few shillings. There was also a fourth category of brothel, about which we know very little. In 1933 a woman named Josephine Naughton was mentioned in the NSW Criminal Register as the keeper of a 'brothel, and is known among the

criminal classes as "the queen of the bitches," as she keeps rooms especially for the use of male sex perverts'.[171]

Nowhere else in Australia did the world of organised crime and
prostitution become so entwined as in Sydney. In Melbourne the trends
towards one-woman brothels (which were lawful) and relocation of
the trade from the city to the inner suburbs continued, with beachside
St Kilda also emerging as a significant locale. Criminals were sometimes involved, if nowhere near as ubiquitous as in Sydney, while
police corruption appears to have been less common.[172] But not everybody swallowed the story that the man found by licensing police in a
Fitzroy brothel in 1925 bearing Police Badge 80 – that issued to the Chief
Commissioner of Police, Thomas Blamey – was really an unknown person who had mysteriously come into possession of his medal. One
anonymous sceptic told the Victorian Premier that 'not even an imbecile
would be deceived'.[173]

Queensland continued its system of tolerated brothels, including
police registration and regular compulsory health checks of prostitutes,
while similar arrangements evolved informally in Perth and Kalgoorlie.
Adelaide saw relatively little prostitution, with stiff legislation in SA
probably encouraging prostitutes to take their business elsewhere.[174]

### Conclusion

Many Australians were haunted between the wars by a sense that their
society was out of joint. Some blamed a war that had been fought for
freedom but seemed to have produced only licence. Male homosexuals
were persecuted and prosecuted but, partly as a result, might have
achieved a stronger sense of group identity. Labels designed to present
sexual desire between women as deviant contributed to an emerging
lesbian identity. Capitalist modernity and consumer culture seemed
impervious to national boundaries and were spectacularly successful
in reshaping sexual cultures. Yet interwar governments, egged on by
sections of the medical profession, the churches and the feminist movement, appeared more determined than ever to protect the Australian
citizenry from 'foreign' sexual perversion. Internally, the whiteness of
the nation had to be preserved from the 'half-caste' menace but influential individuals argued that controlled breeding between white men and
mixed-race women was the way to achieve it. The young single woman

was offered a sip of freedom; but if she drank a draught, she was seen to have joined the ranks of whoredom. Whoredom, meanwhile, in the eyes of those whose judgment had been formed by older codes of moral conduct, seemed harder than ever to distinguish from a womanhood not yet 'fallen'. Prostitutes were supposedly 'morons' yet glamorised as celebrities. But perhaps the greatest paradox of all was that a sexual modernity widely touted as the antidote to Victorian hypocrisy and prudery created new labels, categories and prescriptions threatening a more subtle form of slavery.

# Chapter 7

# *War and Peace*

### Before the Revolution
Historians sometimes divide the period between World War II and the 1960s into two phases. The war and postwar years are seen as times of rapid and far-reaching change, which are then followed by the over-whelming moral and political conservatism of the Menzies era. In the history of sex, the 1950s slip into an interregnum between the relative openness of the war years and the sixties 'sexual revolution'. This chapter will treat the period in a more unified way, stressing mid-century continuity. Images of the asexual fifties as a kind of ersatz Victorian era will be treated as simplistic and exaggerated.[1]

### Sex in the Services
At first, it all looked much like 1914. An expeditionary force again went off to the Middle East and similar problems with VD emerged as in World War I. The military authorities' efforts to deal with it this time, however, were better organised and less punitive, and infection rates were lower.[2] The army supervised brothels and provided men with condoms and ointments. Blue-light depots were set up at camps while all units had to provide a prophylactic ablution centre. Medical officers delivered lectures on the dangers of infection – standing orders required a talk within ten days of a recruit's arrival in camp – and the army's education journal, *Salt*, carried frank advice about VD.[3] It has sometimes been hinted that these improvements, as well as the availability of

sulphonamides and later penicillin, increased the amount of sexual activity in and around the armed forces. Yet more than half the respondents to a 1980s survey 'had little or no extra-marital sex while in the army'.[4] Sex was a topic for much contemplation and discussion – but less action. In the Pacific theatre especially, busyness and isolation were major barriers and infection rates accordingly low. Disgust and racial contempt might also have acted as deterrents: one soldier recalled wishing that 'the New Guinea women would turn white and not smell'.[5] In a postwar novel, when a soldier arrives in New Guinea he is advised that if he runs into any local women, he will 'need a scrubbing brush and a piece of soap'. When the new hand replies that 'all cats are grey in the dark', he is put right: 'These sheilas aren't. Not if you can smell they aren't.'[6] But infection occurred among troops serving in Borneo who admitted to 'contact with Indonesian, Chinese or half-caste girls of good appearance'.[7]

Australians who fell into the hands of Japanese were more concerned with food than sex; malnutrition, overwork and fear undermined the libido. Finding themselves unable to achieve erection as captivity wore on, some prisoners worried that they had become permanently impotent.[8] Nonetheless, a warrant officer later recalled that 'certain couples were known to be going to particular spots and indulging in homosexuality'. Some blamed this behaviour on prisoners' rice diet.[9] But one doctor more plausibly claimed after the war that 'sexual perversion was rare' among the men, which he attributed partly to '[t]he absence of stimulus, external and internal, physical and mental … The diet was certainly not exciting'.[10] A brutal captivity nonetheless helped make adjustment to postwar life especially difficult for many. One female patient of Melbourne's Dr Victor Wallace was probably not alone in finding her husband 'a nervy ex-POW'. Although this couple had sex once or twice a week, she was dissatisfied, describing her spouse as 'most unappreciative'.[11] Sleep disturbed by vivid nightmares and even vomiting cannot have made for easy relationships.[12]

In occupied Japan, an Allied non-fraternisation policy did not prevent sexual activity between the conquerors and the conquered. Sex and plenty of it in the land of a hated and now humiliated enemy seemed a just reward for victory. As with conquering armies in other times and places, some men raped while the behaviour of many more prefigured the antics of randy rock stars, as they worked their way through an apparently limitless supply of young women. As one young Australian British Commonwealth Occupation Force (BCOF) man later put it, 'The Japanese pussy got us all in the long run'. Poverty and desolation unleashed thousands of women and girls willing to exchange access to their bodies for modest comforts. Although officially banned, prostitution was rife and the port city of Kure, where most of the Australians were based, had it in abundance. Unsurprisingly, VD emerged as a large and embarrassing problem. At one time, Australian troops comprised about a quarter of the BCOF total yet almost three-quarters of infections. But Australian men and Japanese women also formed stable and, as it turned out, lasting relationships. Once the authorities relented in their determination to keep them out, about 650 Japanese war brides made a new life with their ex-BCOF husbands in White Australia.[13]

### The Yanks Arrive

The Pacific War is often recalled as a disruptive episode in which neo-Victorian sexual mores and Depression-era restraint gave way to freedom, even licence. US servicemen began arriving from late 1941, and their presence has been seen as a strong ingredient in wartime sexual disorder.[14] Stimulated by a massive American presence, the commercial sex trade entered its most lucrative era.[15] One Sydney prostitute recalled that she 'moved straight from a depression into a time of money ... The Yanks were here and they were good with money, buy you anything you wanted'.[16] US military police cooperated closely with brothel owners to ensure orderly provision while cities attracted a camp following of hostesses, escorts, streetwalkers and brothel workers.[17] Brisbane, which housed General Douglas MacArthur's headquarters, had about twenty brothels but other Queensland towns also saw increased activity. In Townsville the showground became a makeshift red-light district, with prostitutes working out of tents.[18] New clubs appeared in the eastern cities, with both grog and sex for sale.[19]

In popular memory, the Americans' arrival is sometimes recalled as a 'powerful aphrodisiac'.[20] Some feminist history has reinforced this impression, emphasising the opportunities for female sexual experimentation and adventure the American presence provided. Women recalled the era as 'the best time of their lives', a chance for 'a little experience'.[21] Others stress the dangers posed and costs borne by Australian women, such as the growing danger of sexual assault or worse.²² In Melbourne in May 1942 panic occurred when, within a few weeks, three women were brutally strangled during the city's eerie nightly 'brownout'. It was soon rumoured that a US serviceman was the culprit – and so it proved. Eddie Leonski – a troubled GI from New York – was arrested, tried and executed by US authorities. The Leonski affair lent authority to one stereotype of the American soldier: that of the sex-crazed maniac.²³ Yet a young Brisbane girl recalled that she and a friend wandered at night around New Farm Park, 'a favourite mating spot for American soldiers' and that '[i]t was quite safe to do that in Brisbane then'.²⁴

At a time when women were rapidly entering new occupations, they were also receiving mixed messages. They should do their bit, which might require long hours in a factory or office, arduous duties in the women's branches of the armed forces, or devoted volunteering; yet these new roles were seen to place them in sexual danger. There was encouragement for 'our girls' to make the Americans welcome; yet the same women were treacherous if relations became too intimate. The character Guinea in Dymphna Cusack and Florence James's novel, *Come in Spinner*, was probably not alone in being made 'sick' by 'the way the Aussies came back and squealed about the Yanks getting off with their girls. You'd think they were a lot of monks themselves'.²⁵ Australian women found themselves accused of being 'Gold-digging harpies' and 'Lounge Lizzies', while critics of 'dating' said it turned women into prostitutes who bartered access to their bodies for gifts.²⁶

When American and Australian men came into direct competition in the sexual marketplace, the former possessed several clear advantages. At a time when there was a thriving black market, they had considerably more spending power – the pay of an American private was comparable with that of an Australian captain. Meanwhile, 'Darwinian' sexual selection in this wartime survival of the fittest was reputedly helped along by the Americans' attractive uniforms, with their 'superbly tailored beige-pinks, olive drabs and light khakis'.²⁷ The baggy khaki uniforms of the AIF seemed unattractive in comparison. If the smart appearance and reputed good manners of the American soldier could not turn Joe Schmo into Clark Gable, it at least made it a little easier, after a drink or five, to maintain the fantasy.²⁸

Above all, the manipulative GI threatened to usurp a status seen as rightly belonging to a new generation of Australian warriors. The

Americans are sometimes seen to have brought to Australia a style of masculinity that challenged local customs and values. Where the typical Australian male was not known for his conventionally romantic ways, the Americans reputedly wooed their girls. They were charmers who brought you and your mum flowers, your father cigarettes, your younger sister chocolates and your baby brother a model plane. Everyone was 'sir' and 'ma'am'. But to some Australian men, it could appear hypocritical because everyone knew all they were really after was a good fuck before heading north. And when combined with an unhealthy preoccupation with grooming and dress, the Yankee visitors could seem unmanly. For the stereotypical Anzac, true manliness was displayed in loyalty to your comrades on the battlefield, not in cloying behaviour towards women. The bond between a man and a woman could never be as close as that between mates.[29]

Visiting African-American troops also received a surprisingly cordial reception from many of the daughters of White Australia. In early 1944 the Sydney *Truth* complained of 'half-drunken, dishevelled women and girls, sharing drink from bottles with negroes, and submitting to their caresses in doorways, laneways and back streets'.[30] More than one white American visitor expressed revulsion at Antipodeans' failure to observe racial niceties as understood in Montgomery or Chicago. In the end, about fifty black Americans took white Australian brides back to the US after the war.[31] Perhaps, under wartime pressures, taboos about sex across racial boundaries – and especially between black men and white women – were breaking down. The new flexibility did not yet extend beyond the exotic sojourner to the more familiar black Australian, but there was wartime excitement in remote WA where 'female half-castes' were said to be 'soldier mad'. There were also reports of sex between black American soldiers and Aboriginal women.[32]

### Victory Girls

Wartime sexual disorder also included rising rates of illegitimacy and VD, which combined to fuel renewed panic over the 'amateur' or 'good time girl'. Labelled 'racial dynamite', these women were blamed for the spread of disease.[33] One commentator quoted a medical authority to the effect that '[o]ur greatest danger is in the young woman susceptible to the box of chocolates and the soft word'.[34] There was now less concern about the professional prostitute than supposedly more lethal 'amateur sources'.[35]

In 1942 the federal government introduced the *National Security (Venereal Diseases and Contraceptives) Regulations*, which allowed each state's chief health officer to compel anyone suspected of carrying VD to undergo medical examination and detention.[36] While they theoretically applied to men as well as women, '[i]n practice these powers came to be utilized for the control of promiscuous girls and women', primarily in Queensland and WA.[37] A report prepared by a Queensland Committee of Inquiry Regarding Sexual Offences blamed the increase in the rate of female infection on 'promiscuous intercourse by women who were not under any economic stress' and 'the deterioration of moral standards and ... rejection by a large portion of the community of any moral basis for conduct and ... any duty of self-control or self-discipline in sexual relations'.[38] But there were remedies at hand for young women seen as over-burdened by vanity and under-endowed with sense. In an eerie echo of a punishment meted out to female convicts, Dr John Cooper Booth, the NSW Director of Social Hygiene, suggested that girls treated twice for VD should have their heads shaved.[39]

The impression of a loosening of sexual morality finds some reflection in the statistics. The official number of female venereal cases among Queensland women increased from 220 in 1941–42 to 1117 in 1942–43. Meanwhile, the proportion of children born outside wedlock rose from well under 5 per cent in 1940 to a peak of just over 7 in 1944.[40] But the national picture seems rather less alarming. The proportion of women of child-bearing age having babies outside of marriage rose from just over six per thousand in the late 1930s to around ten per thousand by the war's end. Yet by far the largest increase occurred *not* among reckless girls, but more mature females in their twenties and early thirties, women whose marriage opportunities had been most seriously disrupted by hostilities.[41]

## Sexual Education and Citizenship

The *Medical Journal of Australia* called in October 1942 'for the treatment of young men and women as reasonable and healthy-minded individuals, who will be the more likely to respond if they can be made to feel that they are in some measure responsible for one another'.⁴² A year later, it advised that although education in sexual continence was needed, it should not be implied 'that those who, having made the attempt, find that they are unable to maintain complete continence are weak in character or even to be held blameworthy'.⁴³ This amounted to an extraordinary recognition of the claims of sexual desire, irrespective of social convention and orthodox morality. Scientific knowledge, properly disseminated and applied to sex, had a role in producing the good citizen. It was not, said the author of a sex-education booklet, 'a question of being sufficiently strong to resist so-called temptation, but of having that knowledge which will reduce the possibility of consequences to a minimum'. Education was the answer to the problem of 'sexual mal-adjustment', for it would develop 'an appreciation of the individual's place and responsibility as a member of the community'.⁴⁴

As part of this quest to create a new and better citizen, organisations such as the New Education Fellowship and the WEA added lectures on sex education to their programs.⁴⁵ But these were exercises in adult education; sex education for schoolchildren remained more controversial. This duty was still seen to lie primarily with parents. The school should play only a supportive role and 'in no circumstances should it be treated as a subject of mass or class instruction' because of the varied sexual knowledge and maturity of the children, as well as 'the emotional aspect of the matter'.⁴⁶ Or so thought the Queensland Committee of Inquiry into Sexual Offences in 1944. Yet in a departure from the 'Victorian' stress on natural childhood innocence, some doctors, psychologists and educators – influenced by psychoanalysis – were beginning to cast the child as 'sexual' from birth. Childhood sexuality was now an impulse to 'be harnessed to form a healthy personality'.⁴⁷ Lotte Fink, the Freudian educator, argued that sexual knowledge should be imparted before puberty, when it could 'be taken in without emotional reactions'.⁴⁸

Publications aimed at children themselves, however, remained apparently obsessed with the mating habits of plants and animals. So *The Guide through Girlhood* in 1945 celebrated the 'wonderful method by which a father and a mother may have children' – while avoiding explanation of what sex actually involved – and then went on to warn that 'it is very wrong for those who are not married to one another to act in this way'. Girls should not talk to boys they did not know, who 'might ask you to go away with them either for a walk or in a car, or offer you money or chocolates in order to do you a very great wrong'. And in extenuation of her own coyness, the author added that 'the reason we do not talk much about the private parts of our bodies is not that they are *impure*, but that they are *sacred*'.[49]

Such reticence was connected with a continuing fear of female sexual desire. In a book with the misleading title *Plain Words*, aimed at an adult market, W.J. Thomas defined the clitoris as 'a small organ' that was 'highly sensitive to stimulation' and played 'a most important part in sexual relations'. But he offered no further explanation of its functions or operation, a silence that possibly reflected disagreement among sex experts about whether clitoral orgasms were to be encouraged or condemned.[50] Even for the liberal-minded, female sexuality could be dark and dangerous. The nymphomaniac had been a disturbing figure for Dr James Beaney in mid-nineteenth-century Melbourne, but she was hardly less so for Dr Victor Wallace, practising in the same city a century later. Wallace worried about the oversexed wife who had 'rapid, strong orgasms', especially in cases where the husband was not so 'strongly sexed'. Such a mismatch was likely to result in extramarital sex on the wife's part. To avert this disaster, Wallace suggested hypnotism, exposure of the ovaries to X-rays, removal of the ovaries or clitoris and, if all else failed, institutionalisation for her own and others' protection.[51]

### The Return of Norman Haire

A striking and original wartime example of 'public pedagogy' in the field of sex occurred in the pages of the popular weekly magazine, *Woman*. Between its covers, most weeks from early 1942 and into the early 1950s (despite its author having returned to Britain in 1946), the remarkable 'Dr Wykeham Terriss'[52] produced a column in which 'A Doctor Looks at Life' – in fact, mostly at sex. The doctor, as it happens, was Norman Haire, who had returned to Sydney at the outbreak of the war to resume his career in medicine, sexology and public stirring.

Soon, it became hard to avoid Haire. When not in his Macquarie Street rooms treating the afflicted, he was in the lecture hall or on the airwaves, declaiming his brand of sexual modernity. Even when his vast bulk was not physically present, and his mellifluous actor's voice out of earshot, he was possibly being excoriated from the floor of the parliament, condemned from the pulpit, or maligned in the newspapers as a corrupter of public morals. Besieged by churchmen and God-fearing politicians, Haire came to believe that Catholics in the postal service were intercepting his mail. He was a walking public controversy, a censorship scandal waiting to happen.[53]

But the censor never struck – a point that, in itself, says a great deal about the climate of greater openness that war engendered. In his column, Haire explored an extraordinary array of subjects, from female frigidity and male impotence through to VD, sex education, masturbation, prostitution, contraception and abortion. But like so much sex talk of the war years, Haire's goal went well beyond the diffusion of useful knowledge. His interest was in creating a new kind of citizen.[54] While a wartime opponent would later recall him as 'the first bright harbinger in Australia of the permissive age',[55] he condemned 'promiscuity' and even 'physical familiarities' (petting) – on the grounds that either could lead to VD – and argued instead for early marriage.[56] Haire advocated contraception, but opposed its use for 'purely selfish reasons', which was 'against the interests of the community'.[57] Haire remained loyal to an older understanding of sexuality as an adjunct of race-building.

But there was a rough sexual egalitarianism at the heart of his vision. For Haire, women as well as men had sexual needs, and intercourse should never occur unless both partners wanted it.[58] While he believed the average woman more difficult to arouse than a man, she had a right to sexual satisfaction – and it was a husband's duty to help her get it.[59] Sex was seen as an arena of negotiation, not a duty to be performed by a wife really more interested in making babies.[60] But Haire was also preoccupied with the fragility of male self-esteem, worrying that a husband whose wife refused his advances was likely to have his 'masculine pride' wounded. There was nothing abnormal, he said, about a husband wanting sex three or four times a week: such a woman should 'regard herself as fortunate that her husband still finds her so sexually attractive'.[61]

### Masturbation

Haire's editor at *Woman* resisted his efforts to write about masturbation but the doctor nevertheless found an opportunity to argue that '[t]he ill-effects ... commonly attributed to these practices are really due, not to the habit itself, but to worrying about it'.[62] The main problems with masturbation were its association with guilt, and its potential for undermining 'mature sexual activity'.[63]

Haire might have been a sex radical, but on this subject his views were swimming with the (Freudian) tide of medical opinion. Indeed, one medical authority in the mid-1940s went so far as to suggest that it was the ignorant and emotionally unbalanced mother worrying over it, rather than the masturbating child, who truly required advice and treatment.[64] And even the relatively conservative sex-education literature of the Father and Son Welfare Movement now sought to reassure youths that '[t]he physical effects of masturbation moderately practised may not be very marked'. In an admittedly unfortunate turn of phrase, the youth was warned not to allow himself to become distressed by masturbation, but to 'face up to it quietly and reasonably, and it will tend to lose its grip on his life'.

Masturbation was presented here as an anti-social and immature habit to be overcome in the development of a normal (hetero)sexuality. Full sexual development involved the permanent and mutually satisfying union between a man and a woman, with 'normal' sex at its centre. Other forms of sexual release were at best deficient, signifying an arrested sexual development. But the Father and Son Movement, being grounded in Christian morality, went further than the sexologists in its concern that masturbation produced 'an atmosphere of unworthiness and regret' around something that 'God meant to be good and wholesome'. There was also a traditional ideal of bourgeois masculinity at the heart of the advice that 'the self-discipline used in facing and overcoming ... masturbation is of very real value in the general development of character'. Here, a 'Victorian' stress on the role of self-restraint in forming character had managed to survive the arrival of the atomic age.[65]

### Birth Control and Population Panic

The spectre of Japanese invasion intensified fears that Australia was under-populated. The same 1942 regulation that dealt with VD also prohibited advertisements for birth-control products. The health minister, E.J. Holloway, defended the measure on the grounds that Australia's birthrate 'was now considerably below that of the Axis Powers'.[66] Modern wars needed to be fought in the nation's bedrooms as well as

African deserts and New Guinea jungles. Fears of invasion went hand in hand with panic about those undermining the nation from within, 'old women from the neighbourhood' whose bad advice to young mothers made them 'the best fifth columnists for wrecking family life and the Australian birth rate'. So claimed one doctor who reported that when confronted with women over thirty-five requesting an abortion, he tried persuading them that pregnancy 'would keep them young and make them appear young to the outside world'.[67] Pronatalists looked back fondly to a golden age when women's reproductive lives were in closer touch with nature, an era before artificial roles and demands had increased their independence at the expense of their femininity.

Women's duty to populate Australia still went largely unquestioned. Nevertheless, a widely discussed interim report produced by the National Health and Medical Research Council in 1944 on the decline of the birthrate, based on 1400 letters received from Australian women, registered significant changes in attitudes to women's rights since the early twentieth century. Its authors shared the widespread panic about declining birthrates, agreeing that 'the future of Australia and of the Australian people depends upon the individual decision as to child-bearing of each Australian woman'. Yet they specifically rejected the findings of the NSW Royal Commission of 1903–04 that women's selfishness was the heart of the problem, and argued instead 'that better facilities, services and financial inducements' were needed. Women's use of birth control came from 'a sense of insecurity under circumstances that were neither unworthy nor unduly selfish'. The report also trod carefully around contraception, and did not recommend additional restrictions on its availability. Women should perform their maternal duty, yet their willingness and ability to do so was now seen as dependent on the state's moulding of conducive 'psychical and environmental' conditions. But there were some significant continuities with the past, too. The 1944 report, rather like pronatalist propaganda of the early twentieth century, was unforthcoming about men's role in contraception. The particular responsibility of women for reproduction, and its prevention, was simply assumed.[68]

Even if women's right to birth control had increasing acceptance by the 1940s, the nation hosted just two specialised clinics and contraceptives were more expensive than in Britain.[69] Withdrawal was still widely practised and rubber shortages meant that many types of contraceptive were hard to come by. Some politicians in any case called for stronger government action to suppress both their manufacture and advertisement, while one correspondent in the Sydney *Daily Telegraph* wondered whether Australia's soldiers had 'fought and died in vain for a race of abortionists, intent on wiping themselves out just as surely as the Jap would have done had he landed in Australia'.[70] Catholic commentators seemed especially unhampered in their condemnation of birth control and those who practised it. For Colin Clark, a Catholic economist and public servant in Queensland, contraception involved 'acts which were filthy, vicious and disgusting', constituting 'one of the worst forms of sexual immorality'.[71] 'It is useless', claimed a Melbourne Jesuit priest, 'to win the war against a foreign enemy if the nation is to die by a cancer within'. Young men and women, stimulated by the advertising industry, had become addicted to the easy life. A major problem was 'the steady propaganda of a diffused sensuality which relaxes the old tough fibres and undermines the virility by which nations live and thrive'.[72] It was the old enemy, pleasure, that needed to be conquered if the extinction of the race were to be averted.

The unreliability of contraception, however, ensured abortion's continuing presence in the reproductive lives of Australian women. Haire said that it 'flourished to a surprising and alarming extent', which he blamed on the greater difficulty of access to contraception, compared with Britain.[73] Wallace, meanwhile, estimated there was probably about one abortion for every two full-term confinements. One of his own patients told him that she was eager to use a reliable contraceptive 'because I don't want to have any more illegal operations done. I nearly died after the last one. The expense and the risk are too great'.[74]

Better-off women were still most likely to be able to pay for medical abortions, while the poor resorted to the cheaper backyarders or aborted themselves. Amy, from Melbourne's western suburbs, remembered using a bewildering variety of contraceptive techniques in the 1940s: condoms bought from door-to-door salesmen; do-it-yourself pessaries made of quinine and coconut butter; washing soda, hot gin and half a cup of mustard in a bath ('It nearly burned the skin off your bum'); a sponge soaked in Lifebuoy soap; vinegar and cold water injected into the vagina with a syringe ('My insides must be made of leather'). Her bathroom was a veritable birth-control laboratory. Unfortunately, her efforts at contraception failed and, speaking of the birth of her son, Amy remarked: 'I reckon he would have broken through the iron curtain.' For her next pregnancy she turned to a backyard abortionist about whom she had heard 'on the grapevine'. It cost her £10, which her husband borrowed. Two years later, she required another abortion, after which she went back to 'syringing and swallowing everything again'. Eventually, she heard about 'the coil', perhaps a Gräfenberg ring, 'and I never got pregnant no more'.

For women such as Amy, sex was hard work. 'When you read about sex now and you hear about it on the radio it sounds like a luscious piece of cake', she reflected, when interviewed in the 1980s. The 'grapevine' to which she referred – essentially women's neighbourhood networks – continued to disseminate information of variable quality. It was through such chat about 'babies, pregnancies and what-have-you' that Sarah, a British migrant living in Newcastle in the 1950s, learned about 'slippery elm bark' (her source of information was 'this little woman up the street'). Bought in sheets from a chemist or from 'women who would sell it', it would then need to be cut into the right shape and placed in the vagina to induce an abortion. Other women used catheters or syringes. Some did themselves great damage; others were damaged by abortionists. Penicillin would drastically reduce the risk of death from a post-abortion infection but the whole business could still be a painful, frightening and traumatic experience.[75]

In Sydney and Melbourne especially, the abortion industry was becoming dominated by doctors, better organised and more deeply entangled in the murky world of syndicated crime and police corruption. Yet abortion was also woven into the everyday lives of women and local communities, including among new migrants who developed their own networks and arrangements.[76] For Australian women of the mid-twentieth century, the fear of unwanted pregnancy remained a central reference point in their lives. Yet the meaning of marriage was also being redefined by mass culture, sexology and contraceptive practice.[77] Some women saw in reliable contraception a means of improving the quality of their erotic lives and thereby strengthening their marriages, arguing that the alternative of continual child-bearing sowed the seeds of sexual frustration and marital discord. At the time of the war, two-thirds of those employing artificial methods relied on condoms, jellies or spermicides, but by the end of the 1950s, one-third were using diaphragms. These were predominantly Australian-born couples, who were twice as likely as immigrants to be using such methods. There were also local variations. The Gräfenberg ring, an early intra-uterine device (IUD), was particularly popular in Melbourne due to the preferences of locally trained doctors.[78] Although they sometimes induced bleeding, these rings were reliable and could be used without a husband being any the wiser. Significant religious differences in contraceptive practice continued in the 1950s. Many Catholics sought to use the rhythm method – or 'Vatican Roulette', as it was colloquially known – which was now approved by their church.

### Managing Marriage

By mid-century, marriage was seen as a fragile institution requiring modern expertise, the latest technologies, and Christian moral guidance if couples were to achieve 'adjustment'.[79] The war itself had contributed powerfully to the sense of traditional marital relations being under siege. A hasty wartime marriage could later seem like a fit of temporary insanity. Yet even for those wed before the war, long periods of separation raised issues of fidelity that might be handled with much or little fuss, or with a nagging sense of doubt on either or both sides. One Melbourne woman was deeply hurt when, having agreed to marry her Air Force boyfriend after the war, he announced that he had had sex with another woman. They had been together since she was seventeen.[80] The hero's return might be a 'marvellous reunion' in which couples once again became accustomed to the enjoyment of each other's bodies and minds; or a sad disappointment serving only to remind each that it had been a long war and the world had changed. Men will have returned anxious about their sexual performance and prospects. Dreams of bliss nurtured in the deserts of the Middle East, the jungles of South-East Asia or behind barbed wire in POW camps, and by women who waited patiently for the lover's return, could either find fulfilment or be exposed as dangerous fantasy when confronted with the banal daily challenges of a married life shadowed by war.[81]

As if these were not in themselves sufficient barriers to happiness, housing was also in desperately short supply, so that many young couples were forced to live temporarily with other family members. Newcomers faced even greater difficulty. British migrants were dismayed to find that husbands and wives were expected to live in separate quarters on the ships that brought them to Australia. And when they arrived they faced a similar lack of privacy in the hostels that were their temporary homes, a problem that made marital intimacy a matter of great delicacy and potential embarrassment.[82] Non-British migrants generally fared even worse, with husbands being segregated from wives in reception and training centres. Private moments were stolen by quiet late-night visits between husband and wife, and by using blankets as makeshift partitions. When 'breadwinners' accepted jobs as part of their two-year contract with the Australian government, 'dependents' would be shunted off to live on their own or with children in distant holding centres. In this manner, newcomers were forced to accept a degree of interference in their private lives that would, by the postwar era, have been considered intolerable by most 'old' Australians.[83] Or at least by 'old' white Australians; the sexual lives of many Aboriginal people remained hemmed in by onerous restrictions.[84] Aborigines and their supporters increasingly demanded the right to marry whom they chose, rather than being forced to follow the diktats of racial theorists, author-itarian officials and an assortment other busybodies.

Divorce rates soared after the war, from an average of 23.3 per 10,000 between 1936 and 1944 to 43.2 from 1945 to 1949. They peaked at 8803 (over 50 per 10,000) in 1947. But the divorce rate was merely the tip of a large iceberg of marital unhappiness. Many more couples were trapped in unsatisfying marriages than availed themselves of the divorce laws, which still compelled one or the other partner to demonstrate the existence of a matrimonial offence, usually adultery. Psychologists mean-while claimed that sexual disharmony in a married couple produced maladjusted children, leading to a potentially damaging cycle.

There was also a postwar marriage boom. Both single men and women were marrying ever younger: the average groom was twenty-five, and his bride only twenty-two, by the mid-1960s. While marriage had become virtually synonymous with full and responsible citizenship, there was also growing acceptance that it depended 'on autonomous, self-monitoring individuals and their self-discipline'. Sexual compati-bility and mutual pleasure were essential to a successful union, but they required careful management by both partners, helped by experts. Modern scientific knowledge would be critical, yet the trend towards secularism was tempered by the prominence of a Christian framework

in much marriage guidance counselling. The number of divorces, however, remained relatively high, with the total in 1953 again exceeding
8000. The nation's first uniform divorce law, introduced at the end of the
1950s, allowed for the easier dissolution of marriage, for it controver-
sially included a provision permitting divorce after five years' separation.
The Catholic Labor parliamentarian Arthur Calwell saw this as the road
to moral perdition, refusing to give 'smelly, secular sanctification to
barnyard morality'.[85]

Decades of marriage manuals, from Stopes through to the popular
guide of the 1940s and 1950s, Hannah M. and Abraham Stone's *A Marriage
Manual: A Practical Guide-Book to Sex and Marriage*, had helped to
reshape understandings of the place of sexuality in marriage. Dr Wallace
sometimes recommended the Stones' work to his Melbourne patients.
They came to him with a wide range of sexual problems but his patient
notes indicate that many now believed a satisfying sexual life both possible and essential to marital harmony. Couples, and especially women,
were increasingly likely to recognise sexual fulfilment as a means of
deepening the love between a husband and wife. Many of Wallace's
patients had read sexology or sex manuals, and were willing to experiment with different forms of contraception and a variety of sexual
positions and techniques. Their expectations of what sex could deliver
had been accordingly raised. As one woman put it, 'I have had a nice
feeling but not the wonderful thrill that other women seem to have'.

Women frequently consulted Wallace on their lack of interest or
enjoyment in sex, or their inability to have orgasms. Men worried over
their sexual performance and their lack of interest in women, and
sought treatment for impotence and premature ejaculation. Wallace
had male patients in their sixties who hoped he might have a cure for
their loss of sexual potency, but younger men and women complained
that they were simply too tired for sex. He also heard the occasional sad
story of a marriage that had never been consummated because of some
sexual dysfunction, and many of appalling ignorance on the part of
married couples. Some told Wallace that they had been raised to think
of sex as 'dirty' or 'animal'. One married woman apparently believed
kissing breasts 'rude' while a man in his early twenties claimed to have
been traumatised when a woman tried tongue-kissing him. Some
women, in particular, still experienced a strong sense of shame even in
marital sex while others complained that their husbands shunned

foreplay as 'a waste of time' and 'silly', with unfortunate consequences for their own level of pleasure. Lillian Roxon, later a member of the bohemian Sydney 'Push', was only slightly exaggerating when she recalled that 'anything outside intercourse in the conventional, or missionary, position' was called 'the fancy stuff'. 'Australians disliked fancy stuff in bed', she said, 'and thought it unmanly.'[86]

Wallace had some happy patients. There is a touching 1950 letter from a woman who had consulted him about a sexual problem. The doctor had suggested psychoanalysis as a possibility, but added that it was expensive and not guaranteed to work, so he suggested that she should

> persevere ... having intercourse only when feeling like it and work for the orgasm myself, which I did and with the help of my husband, who was very patient, actually achieved it!! I could hardly believe it had happened – after ten years marriage and having been trying for at least two of those years.
>
> I now get results every time, average about five or six times per month (two or three days before period and two or three days after).
>
> I seem to have no hope of achieving the orgasm if my husband is on top, but have no difficulty at all if I am on top and do most of the work, my husband being fairly still, it sometimes takes longer than others, but I am always confident of a result and it comes, not only once, but I can repeat it several times (that when ~~'father'~~ my husband can last the distance).

This woman's decision to cross out 'father' and replace it with 'my husband' seems a striking confirmation of how marriage was being eroticised, and sexual compatibility replacing reproduction as its most fundamental basis. Yet there was a heavy investment in heterosexual sex, perhaps at the expense of other possibilities. Wallace's diagnosis of a woman who was only able to bring about an orgasm by clitoral stimulation was 'Failure to achieve orgasm normally'.[87]

Male identity was also being sexualised; earlier images associated with the noble bushman, hardy pioneer, or domestic suburbanite were notably asexual, or, at best, concerned with periodic sexual release.[88] But men were now seen to have a responsibility to woo their wives and provide them with sexual pleasure. The active role that sexologists assumed men would occupy in heterosexual intercourse necessarily gave them additional responsibility.[89] The 'frigid wife' was certainly considered a problem but it is notable that even *Man* magazine was urging its (male) readers to lift their sexual game: 'Men should realise that *they* may be the culprits in the tragic murder of many happy marriages.'[90]

## Sexual Repression?

This stress on sexual performance belies the 1950s' image for prudery and repression, if not asexuality. The two great Australian 'sex scandals' of the era – the Orr and Goossens affairs – both occurred in 1956, and each has been used to underline the era's reputation as sexually repressive. The Orr case concerned the accusation that Sydney Sparkes Orr, Professor of Philosophy at the University of Tasmania, had seduced Suzanne Kemp, an undergraduate. Orr had recently played a leading part in a public campaign for the reform of the university administration, which led to suspicions that he had been framed by the conservative local establishment. Orr denied the seduction accusation and, while receiving a beating in his own home from Suzanne's father, accused the timber merchant of having sexually abused his own daughter. He added for good measure that Suzanne was both mentally disturbed and immoral, having had sex with seven or more men.[91] Despite his denials, two university committees investigated and upheld complaints against him. Orr offered to resign, but the university dismissed him instead – thereby sparking a bitter controversy that divided Hobart's little society, and the even smaller Australian academic community, for a generation. Orr supporters were divided among themselves. Some argued that even if Orr *had* slept with his student, it was not grounds for dismissal; others, that sleeping with a student was indeed a sackable offence, but that Orr had been framed by unscrupulous enemies.[92]

The other major scandal of 1956 centred on Sir Eugene Goossens, the composer and conductor. The London-born son of a Belgian father and English mother – both musicians – Goossens was already a major figure in international music when he arrived after the war to take up the prestigious positions of conductor of the Sydney Symphony Orchestra and director of the conservatorium.[93] He was a great success in both roles; from his combined appointments, he earned a larger salary than the Prime Minister and had almost as high a profile.[94] But when the recently knighted Goossens arrived at Mascot Airport in Sydney on 9 March 1956 after a lengthy overseas absence, he was immediately whisked away by customs officials for an interview with the vice squad. It had been investigating Goossens for six months, having uncovered an association between the conductor and Rosaleen (Rosie) Norton, the 'Witch of Kings Cross'. The ABC offices, where Goossens was based, were not far from the home of Norton and her lover, the poet Gavin Greenlees, a converted laundry in a run-down terrace house. Goossens, who had interests in occult religion, was a regular visitor and participant in their magical rites, having become associated with the pair while working on his oratorio, *The Apocalypse*. Police managed to acquire a collection of letters Goossens had written to Norton, which they believed would support a charge against him of 'scandalous conduct'. But the conductor was overseas, so the vice squad arranged for him to be trailed in London, where he was spotted buying large volumes of pornography.[95]

When he arrived back in Sydney, officials found in his luggage over 1000 photographs, three books on sexual themes, some film, a quantity of incense and some rubber masks.[96] He was also confronted by detectives with copies of his letters to Norton, and admitted to having engaged in various 'sex perversions' with her, including having 'placed my tongue in her sexual organ and ... moving it until I stimulated her'. Norton herself was bisexual, with a penchant for oral sex with male homosexuals and lesbians, as well as sadomasochism. Her art had been the subject of several obscenity prosecutions, and she achieved notoriety for a series of photographs showing her and Greenlees engaged in various 'perversions', including anal sex.

Goossens was charged under the *Customs Act* with having attempted to import various indecent works and articles.[97] The media coverage was sensational; stories of satanic rituals and sex orgies circulated widely. Something very rotten was festering in the city's darkest corners, and it was convenient that the source of the corruption happened to be one of those cultured, 'up-themselves' European types, fortunately caught in the act of trying to defile innocent Australia with the vile scrapings of decadent Europe – or at least decadent Soho. Well over 800 of the photographs were supposedly obscene, and Goossens was fined the maximum amount of £100. But it could have been worse, for the Minister for Justice, Reg Downing, instructed the police commissioner to take no further action, an order which gave rise to accusations of conspiracy and cover-up.[98] Claims from Goossens' barrister that his client had been the victim of a blackmailer, and that there would be further revelations in due course, have naturally fuelled suspicions.[99] Goossens, meanwhile, resigned his positions and left the country, never to return.

Both the Orr and Goossens affairs have been understood as emblematic of the era; individuals were punished for transgressions that, in a more sexually enlightened time, might have been tolerated or even celebrated. Neither case was so simple, but both point to the existence of sexual practices and subcultures that complicate our image of the 'asexual' fifties.[100] For instance, notwithstanding the obstacles encountered by Goossens, foreign pornographic films *did* enter Australia during the middle decades of the century. There had been a boom in their availability during the war, which provided a more or less captive market both in the Australian services and among American visitors. After the war, halls and clubs were used by informally assembled all-male audiences for the screening of blue movies. In a nation where so much of the social lives of men and women remained highly segregated, such activities were an extension of the male tribal rituals of football, racing and the six o'clock swill.[101]

The era also saw a brief revival of sex hygiene films, sometimes accompanied by a personal appearance from a supposedly eminent expert – in one case, really a local magician. Here, those who wished to view porn could conveniently pass themselves off as responsible citizens consulting a reputable authority about the *Secrets of Life* – to give the title of one popular film. Meanwhile, European films that managed to get past the censor provided university students, intellectuals, migrants – and a few selectively attentive spectators who fit none of these categories – with the chance to sample fare more risqué than anything emanating from Hollywood or Ealing.[102]

In the largest cities, some of the intellectuals who attended such films preached and practised sexual freedom and flouted what they saw as the dominant 'wowserism' of their time. The Melbourne 'Drift' was less ideological than the better known Sydney 'Push', a group of libertarians and anarchists influenced by Freud, Wilhelm Reich and the teaching of John Anderson, the controversial Professor of Philosophy at the University of Sydney.[103] Push members colonised certain city pubs and engaged in heavy drinking, lots of sex and much discussion of how to create a truly free society. It was generally agreed that this noble cause of freedom required many orgasms, and the respective merits of the vaginal and clitoral varieties formed a common subject of earnest conversation. Sexual freedom was the foundation of all other liberties; fucking was an act of rebellion against authoritarianism. The Push was indeed radical in its message that both men and women were desiring beings with a need for sexual expression, and it was accepted in Push circles that women could and should initiate sexual encounters.

Nevertheless, in practice the Push was still sexist: sexual freedom had radically different implications for men and women.[104] As one Push woman recalled, 'Free love was free, in that men didn't have to pay, or even take a girl out, or buy her a beer; for a few of them, it was a new and loveless way of exploiting women'.[105] Judy Ogilvie, in a Push memoir, has commented on its sexual inequality:

> In the early days, a woman had sufficient prestige in the Push if she were attached to one of the really big men, but the failure rate among relationships was appallingly high and when a relationship broke down, unless the woman could form another very quickly, if she continued to hang around the Push she was likely to go from one man to another and get a bad reputation for being indiscriminate, or become increasingly marginalised until she dropped off the edge altogether. Freedom in sexual relationships was only theoretical in the Push, in practice the leaders acted as censors over everyone's sexual behaviour, and, since the worst crime of all was secrecy, their control was probably greater in practice than in many other social groups. Whom you slept with was of overwhelming importance. As they grew older, life in the Push became harder for women, their position in the group more tenuous … The men in the Push, on the other hand, tended to remain there, mateship enduring as a stronger bond than sexual attraction. They stayed together, growing older, while the women were continually being replaced by younger ones.[106]

Not only was there a de facto 'hierarchy of fucks'[107] among the Push men, from which the women derived status; the 'frigid woman' and 'penis envy' were more commonly discussed problems than the impotent or sexually inept man. One Push woman recalled that 'The Push were hopeless sexually … The missionary position was the only one you could get into ... With these sort of fucks, I never had an orgasm'.[108] Push men also refused to take responsibility for contraception. Abortions were common and treated as a casual inconvenience – at least by the men, who funded them by sending round the hat.

Germaine Greer was at different times a member of both the Drift and the Push; her career was a 'bridge' between the bohemian sexual radicalism of the 1950s and the 'sexual revolution' of the 1960s and 1970s. Beginning as an undergraduate at the University of Melbourne in 1956, she had her first abortion at the end of her second year. As the former convent girl lost her Catholic faith, she moved from heavy petting to the loss of her virginity to an active sex life.[109] At a time when ladies didn't say such things, she would come into the university cafeteria boasting of her conquest of the night before. But Greer was also raped and bashed at university: sexual violence featured prominently on the agenda of the 1970s feminist movement in which Greer would achieve prominence.

### Young People

Greer's 'progress' would have well and truly exceeded even the worst fears of those who worried over the loose sexual morals of the young in the 1950s. *Just Friends?*, a booklet issued by the Father and Son Welfare Movement, advised 'that apart from a firm, definite friendship which has marriage in view, love play or petting must be considered both inadvisable and wrong'.[110] The move by such a conservative organisation towards an implicit acceptance of erotic contact short of sex – so long as it occurred in the context of courtship rather than the casual date – represents a redrafting of the moral code whose significance should not be underestimated. Moral panic instead focused sharply on working-class youth, often in the guise of the 'bodgie' and 'widgie'. Bodgies wore the zoot or drape suit, which was baggy in the knees but pegged at the waist and cuffs, and their hair was long and slicked back, with a dovetail hanging over at the front – and all at a time when 'real men' wore short back and sides. Widgies wore dark gabardine skirts, flat heels and short-sleeved or sleeveless tops.[111] Both emerged in the 1950s as the latest in a long line of young 'folk devils' stretching back to the larrikin and larrikin girl.[112] And rising rates of pre-marital pregnancy and illegitimate births in the 1950s and the 1960s helped fuel concern about juvenile sexual conduct.

Young women who 'got into trouble' experienced strong pressure to give up their babies for adoption and most did so. One result of the rise of romantic love and its bedfellow, modern sexology, was that those who proffered advice to pregnant single women were now less likely to suggest a hasty wedding. In the modern age, there was nothing to be gained from a marriage between incompatible partners. Instead, relinquishing a baby had become an alternative and preferred means of recovering respectability and social esteem. Informed Australian opinion followed the US rather than Britain; in the latter, there was a continuing stress on the importance of the bond between a natural mother and her child. But in Australia, babies were removed from their mothers at birth. In theory, both mother and child could assume a new and better identity; the former as a more responsible and reputable woman, the latter as a cherished member of a happy family. Perhaps this belief that human beings could start anew and remake themselves was especially appealing in a settler society such as Australia (and the US); the similarities with the rhetoric accompanying the contemporaneous immigration program are notable. But the abrupt separation of mothers from their babies had painful consequences. The intense grief experienced by many mothers received little attention. Nor would many children's natural curiosity about their origins be satisfied by the shroud of secrecy with which governments covered the adoption process. [113]

Women who endured this experience were left in no doubt that they were paying a necessary price for their sexual misbehaviour. Australians of the 1950s were bombarded with stories of depravity among the young, often with a strong sexual theme. [114] The new category of 'teenager' was entering common currency, an identity inhabiting a time between childhood and adulthood in which young people had access to money and leisure in a rapidly expanding consumer culture. This was all deeply unsettling to many of an older generation who had endured the privations of war and depression, and saw bodgies and widgies as symptoms of moral decay or social sickness. In *The Bodgie: A Study in Abnormal Psychology*, A.E. Manning called bodgies and widgies 'social boils on the body of a tense and emotional society'. [115] A January 1958 article in the Sydney *Truth* seemed to confirm this conclusion. Headed 'Bodgies in Sex Orgies', it reported on a recent Newcastle case in which a group of teenagers, after a session of drinking and dancing, had gone to a local park to play spin the bottle. 'When all of the girls and boys were partnered', *Truth* reported, 'a vile sex orgy' ensued.[116] Manning, in his investigation, found among his bodgie and widgie interviewees a tendency to treat sex as a simple 'biological and meaningless satisfaction of a primitive urge stimulated, not by personal attractions, but by excitements and tensions'.[117]

There were strong continuities here with the late nineteenth-century panic about larrikins, as there were in the remarks of a judge in a 1957 Sydney trial. While describing the young defendants in the case before him as having 'the morals of barnyard animals', he added that young men now needed protection from girls.[118] The image of the young female temptress, prominent in colonial age-of-consent debates, was clearly resilient. A judge in another 1950s case went so far as to advise a man charged with having indecently assaulted a teenage girl when she had acted provocatively towards him that he ought to 'have smacked her bottom'.[119]

Bodgies and widgies were more thoroughly sexualised in media and social commentary than either the larrikins or larrikin girls before them. The tastes of both in music and dancing departed from the restraint associated with the country or suburban dance discussed in chapter 6, extending now to the improvised steps associated with the American innovations of jitterbug and jive. Like the rock'n'roll music that was becoming the most powerful emblem of youth culture, these dance styles suggested a loosening of sexual morals and contributed to panic about young people's sexual behaviour. Visiting journalist Malcolm Muggeridge, reporting in 1959 on an evening spent with the bodgies of Melbourne, claimed that in the dance hall the 'tang of adolescent sex was in the air'.[120] Yet as Jon Stratton has suggested more recently, the world of the bodgie and widgie also continued a tradition of working-class cultural forms, tastes and conduct that had long drawn the hostility of their social betters.[121]

While the bodgie did not become associated with gang-rape in the way the larrikin had, the accusation of sexual deviancy still loomed large. Muggeridge claimed that one of the Melbourne bodgies he encountered complained that the reason he had acquired a carnal knowledge conviction was his misfortune that the girl concerned had been able to recall his name – but not those of the fifteen others with whom she had sex. Indeed, there were frequent allegations that bodgies and widgies engaged in 'orgies', while a February 1951 article in *Truth* criticised their 'subnormal habits' and 'outlandish styles' of dress: 'from their ranks graduate degenerates, perverts and criminals'. Not all such people would turn into 'killers' and 'homosexuals', it reassured readers, but the 'seeds' were 'there'.[122] Manning similarly claimed to have found homosexuality, exhibitionism, sadism and masochism among the Australian bodgies and widgies.[123]

This association of bodgies and widgies with sexual perversion was in line with the common understanding of homosexuality in particular as a symptom of arrested development. For this reason, argued one medical authority, a person should not be 'diagnosed' as a homosexual before the age of twenty-five: 'Should we not regard the adult homo-sexual as a person who has never grown up, an escapist from life, who, while refusing the responsibilities and sacrifices of parenthood, seeks a substitute gratification?'[124]

*Jump in my Car*
Motorcycles, cars and speed all featured in media stories about sexually wayward youth. Among homosexual men, mass car ownership made it easier to 'do the beats', allowing men to cruise some distance from their own homes.[125] More famously, cars facilitated heterosexual activity. One young woman, who was then Hazel Masterson but later and better known as Hazel Hawke, the wife of a prime minister – recalled of the early 1950s that 'the car' – in this case, her father's car – 'was one of the few private places we had to share thoughts, and bodies'.[126] The rise in car ownership among the young, especially men, coincided with, and probably contributed to, an increase in the number of ex-nuptial births.[127] It was also common in press reports of sex cases involving the young for a 'jaunt' in a car to appear prominently, as in a 1952 case when the male accused had approached a young woman by driving 'up to her in the street in his sports car'.[128] What young woman could possibly resist? Certainly not the 'shapely brunette teenager' who was '"picked up" in a car' by three or four young men and a couple of girls, driven at eighty-five miles an hour 'burning it along the Mad Mile' on what she took to be a 'joy-ride', taken to a park and then sexually assaulted.[129] And if Orr's accusers were correct, impulsive *older* men were also taking the opportunities for sexual adventure being offered

by the car, because that was mainly where he was alleged to have taken advantage of Suzanne Kemp.[130]

Manufacturers aggressively used sex in their marketing campaigns for cars; a canny strategy, because a survey of Sydney male youths found that their three main topics of conversation were 'sports', 'mechanical things' and 'sex'.[131] But there was a reminder of the dark underside of sex-saturated consumerism in 1967 when the director of the Melbourne Spinal Injuries Centre criticised manufacturers' promotion of the modern car as a sex symbol, emphasising 'speed, potency and sex'.[132]

Parents worried over what their children were doing with and in cars. It was reported in 1958 that mums and dads in one Sydney suburb on the North Shore had chartered a bus so that their children's trips to Palm Beach would occur under the watchful eye of the driver: 'There would be no fleet of family cars to give one of the drivers a chance to work off his exhilaration in reckless speed; no chance for couples to stray off to a private lovers' lane or bar.'[133] The appearance of drive-in cinemas in Australia from the mid-1950s would also provide opportunities for youthful sexual adventure, although they were mainly promoted as respectable family entertainment in the early years.[134]

*Censorship*
Another manifestation of contemporary concern about youth and sex was censorship. There were high-profile cases of literary censorship across the 1940s and 1950s: the period began with the reimposition of a ban on James Joyce's *Ulysses* in 1941 and ended with action against D.H. Lawrence's *Lady Chatterley's Lover*. In between, Lawson Glassop's *We Were the Rats*, Robert Close's *Love Me Sailor* and Vladimir Nabokov's *Lolita* all incurred the authorities' wrath. The Melbourne *Love Me Sailor* trials focused on Robert Close's frank treatment of the elemental sexual drives – and language – of a rigger crew; not even the author's use of 'rutting' throughout the text in preference to 'fucking' could save him. Close was sentenced in 1946 to a three-month term of imprisonment, although as the result of an appeal he would only serve a few days.[135]

Much more energy and angst were devoted to publications for children. Between 1953 and 1955, five states enacted laws intended to widen their control over undesirable publications. This legislation was concerned mainly with comics and penny dreadfuls. Courts were to take account of the audience likely to be exposed to the works, as well as their tendency to deprave or corrupt.[136] In Queensland, the parliament set up a Literature Board of Review authorised to prohibit works that unduly emphasised 'sex, horror, crime, cruelty or violence'. It banned certain illustrated romance stories, apparently having found objectionable their 'portrayal of passionate embraces and … the suggestion … that happiness in … marriage was in some way proportionate to the *corpus* or *quantum* of such embracing'. The ban was upheld in the Supreme Court of Queensland and overturned in the High Court.[137] A wide range of groups, from the Communist Party to the Catholic Church, was active in protecting the morals of the young from the effects of comics and 'trashy' fiction.[138]

### New Australians

In the most influential accounts of postwar Australian history, migrants from continental Europe are usually seen to have endured some privation and prejudice but to have fitted well into a society in need of their labour and fearful of the 'Yellow Peril'. That they were also sometimes a source of sexual fascination and moral panic is largely forgotten. Josie Arnold, who grew up in the increasingly Italian Melbourne suburb of Northcote, commented that the 'unashamed sexuality' of 'New Australian' men made them 'very attractive to girls and very suspect to their parents'.[139] Meanwhile, in the hostels that housed recent migrants, there were simmering tensions between British and Italian men with sexual rivalry at their heart.[140]

Mass migration influenced Australian sexual history in other, quieter ways. National groups brought with them their own traditions of birth control. Mechanical and chemical contraception was used mainly by the Australian-born and migrants from Northern and Western Europe. Condoms, more widely available in Britain than Australia, were predictably popular among immigrants from the United Kingdom. Withdrawal – known colloquially as 'getting off at Redfern Station' (that is, the stop before Central in Sydney) – had declined in significance among British-Australians but its overall importance was maintained by its popularity among southern European migrants. Douching, which had for decades been a significant form of contraception in Australia, was similarly falling into desuetude except among the Greek-born and Eastern Europeans.[141]

Sensational media coverage of the 1950s continued the tradition of emphasising the foreignness of prostitutes and those who lived off them. As a magistrate told a Maltese man found guilty of living off the earnings of prostitutes in March 1956, 'I'd be glad to see you return to Europe and stay there'.[142] A vice case in the following year involved a Redfern woman who kept '"good-time-girls"' in her place 'for the entertainment of lovelorn New Australians'.[143] *Truth*, also in 1957, reported the story of an Italian migrant who had procured two young women for work as prostitutes in the migrant camps on the Snowy River scheme.[144]

The rough, masculine and largely New Australian communities on the massive hydro-electric project recalled the conditions of the colonial frontier. Women were outnumbered ten to one in the towns while the camps were essentially without permanent female residents at all. Although some prostitutes worked alone, more commonly entrepreneurs would bring a few women into camp in a caravan on the Thursday of a pay week. The men paid two pounds for a visit at a time when they were earning twenty-five times that amount each week. The queues soon resembled in length those seen outside brothels during the war, as hundreds of men chatted amiably in the tongues and accents of many lands and waited for their turn with the lovely visitors.[145]

Prostitution declined after the war as a result of reduced demand, and stories about New Australian pimps, randy migrants and cashed-up prostitutes contributed to an impression that those who engaged in commercial sex were outside the pale of citizenship. There was also a substantial, if still little known, trade in male prostitution. In the larger cities, men bought sex from street boys or transvestites.[146] But whereas public perception of this kind of activity shaded into a more general contempt for homosexuality, female prostitution was presented as an undesirable practice sustained by women on the game through choice or mental weakness rather than economic necessity. If clients were noticed at all, they were seen as men who went to prostitutes because they were unable to get a woman the 'normal' way. In particular, 'lonely and woman hungry' migrants were believed to comprise a large proportion of the industry's postwar clientele.[147]

Some commentators also linked the 'rapid influx' into Australia 'of not always the most desirable kinds of immigrants' – and the resultant 'inequality in the numbers of the sexes' – to a rise in sex crime. 'Many streets', said A.E. Manning, were 'no longer safe for women and girls'.[148] Here was another reprise of a nineteenth-century theme; the sexual danger posed when large numbers of men could not find marriage partners. As if to confirm these fears, in 1958 a Melbourne judge complained of the number of cases coming before him of 'Greeks and other Southern European nationalities – interfering with women in crowds and acting in some indecent manner':

> These people have to learn that that sort of conduct will not be tolerated in this community. I do not think our women in Australia should be subjected to the danger of such happenings … One wonders whether there is some tendency among these people that they do this sort of thing.

When the defence barrister remarked that Australians had committed similar offences, the judge replied:

> No. The cases which have come before me have almost invariably been of Southern Europeans. I have never struck a case yet, as far as I can remember, of people of Australian or British nationality on such a charge.[149]

### Male Homosexuality

Even British migrants – by far the largest group – could be seen as a danger to normal sexuality. A 1958 *Truth* report headed 'Shock Rise in Perversion' drew attention to a 66 per cent increase in arrests for homosexual offences in NSW – from 286 in 1954 to 475 in 1957 – and claimed that a police investigation had shown that the 'State's huge perversion' had drawn 'many recruits from England, where, in some circles, homosexuality almost amounts to one of the social graces'.[150] Australians had been raised on images of English effeminacy. More recently, there had been various scandals concerning aristocrats and spies, as well as the publicity attached to the Wolfenden Report, which had recommended the decriminalisation of homosexual acts between consenting adults in private. From the US in 1948 the Kinsey Report had revealed sex between men to be much more common than usually imagined, but it received little attention in Australia.[151]

World War II had increased the visibility and vibrancy of 'camp' Australia.[152] There were, of course, homosexual men in the Australian armed forces, despite the inability of the Victorian RSL President, Bruce Ruxton, to 'remember one single poofter in World War II'.[153] As a member of the air force in the latter years of the war – stationed in Australia, the Dutch East Indies or Borneo – young Roderic Anderson enjoyed a rich homosexual life among his comrades. If his account is accurate, when the men were not having sex with one another, they spent much of their time frolicking naked and comparing erections.[154] Drag acts were also popular with troops,[155] but men whose penchant for donning female attire could not be construed as a contribution to patriotic entertainment were subjected to the long arm of the law. When a police constable found a nineteen-year-old labourer, Neville Ernest McQuade, and a 25-year-old salesman, Alfred John Crockett, cavorting in the street early on New Year's Day in 1944, he was unwilling to put it down to normal revelry of the festive season. McQuade was notorious for his habit of dressing in female clothing. Indeed, his life's ambition was to be a female impersonator, and McQuade's striptease dances were already much admired by his friends. McQuade, it turned out, was already under the treatment of the ubiquitous Norman Haire, who appeared in court to give evidence. Characteristically, Haire put McQuade's transvestism down to heredity and alcoholism, and recommended that he be bound over to abstain from strong drink. The magistrate agreed, fining McQuade £3 and placing him on a twelve-month good behaviour bond. Crockett was fined £2.[156]

The social atmosphere in the armed forces was outwardly heterosexual and homophobic. As Mick Reynolds, the narrator in Lawson Glassop's *The Rats in New Guinea*, remarked: 'That was one thing you feared – having a queen in your section.'[157] Displaying pin-up girls in various states of undress, sharing the pornography in which there was a thriving wartime trade, and boasting about one's exploits with women could contribute to male bonding. Yet despite the sexual ribaldry that marked the conversation of soldiers among their own, doctors found that 'the average Australian soldier will not readily discuss his sexual difficulties, except after considerable contact with his physician'.[158] And while exuding a contempt for 'poofters', 'queens' and 'pansies', attending cabaret shows that featured cross-dressing male performers could strengthen homosocial bonding, so long as the boundary between audience and entertainer was carefully maintained. Yet such rituals also acted as means of exclusion. A wartime study of psychotic ex-servicemen commented that quiet, introverted youths, often from the country, soon became 'the butt … of veiled or open accusations of homosexuality generally intended as a joke, but taken by the patients at face value. Men in the herd are cruel, and fall upon this type of individual as the pack falls on the wounded wolf'.[159]

Still, one homosexual serviceman recalled that when he entered the army he was worried how he would cope with the situation and determined to 'be very "butch" and straight'. But he found plenty of 'camps' in camp. By his account, those whose homosexuality was most obvious were mocked as 'poofters' and quickly discharged, but this only made the others more careful.[160] This was how Sumner Locke Elliott's fictional Seaton Daly – who like Elliott himself spent most of his time as a soldier in the outback – managed to survive; by developing 'a slouching male walk like a wrestler leaving the ring in triumph. Only his deep blue eyes occasionally registered a cry for help'. Yet Seaton – and apparently Elliott, too – found the comradeship of army life a blessing; 'the acceptance of him by "mates" and the continuous serenity of their peculiar brotherhood made it a singular appeasement'.[161]

Homosexual American servicemen, for their part, boosted the visibility of emerging male homosexual subcultures in the major cities; it was not only Australian women who were attracted to the glamour of the visitors.[162] A Brisbane youth recalled that, if you evaded the front desk, you could walk fully clothed into the showers of the YMCA while the Yanks were naked: 'Two shillings and six pence was the going rate for a head job.'[163] On Melbourne's 'Chicken Run', a stretch of St Kilda Road between Princes Bridge and the Shrine of Remembrance, men in uniform, well fuelled with grog, cruised the night looking for sex with other men.[164] In the turbulence of war men turned temporarily to sex with other men but more sustained relationships also developed.[165]

While experiences of this kind have led one historian to call the wartime period the 'end to unknowing', the 1950s were a less comfortable period to be a male homosexual in Australia.[166] Some of the intensity with which Australian authorities persecuted homosexuals in the 1950s may well have had its roots in the greater sexual fluidity that the war had called into being. Sexual norms were seen to require postwar reconstruction after the 'abnormal' erotic impulses unleashed by wartime disorder. Although the coupling of the 'pink' and 'red' menaces that was so powerful in the US did not occur to the same extent in Australia, the Cold War climate is critical in any exploration of attitudes to homosexuality in this era. Masculinity needed to be hard and heterosexual if the west were not to succumb to the communist threat.[167] For Colin Delaney, the NSW Commissioner of Police, homosexuals were 'the greatest social menace' facing the country.[168] There were over 3000 convictions for homosexual offences in Australia's superior courts between 1945 and 1960, and many more in the lower courts, where individuals often pleaded guilty in order to avoid publicity.[169] The NSW parliament legislated new homosexual offences; punishments were stiffened; police increased their harassment; and offenders were segregated within the prison system. A special unit was set up within the Victorian Police to deal with homosexuality; it comprised one-third of the vice squad.[170]

Paradoxically, repression might have increased the visibility of male homosexuality.[171] Court cases such as that centred on the prosecution of the so-called Yellow Sox Gang in 1952, for all the press hyperbole and sensationalism they attracted, also revealed to casual readers the existence of homosexual men in their communities. In this instance, members of a 'society of perverts' based in Newcastle were (inaccurately) rumoured to have recognised one another by wearing yellow socks bought from a member of their group. After several police arrests, all the defendants pleaded guilty, most received suspended sentences, but four were imprisoned.[172] The fifties was also an era in which minders of the comedian Graham Kennedy at GTV Channel 9 in Melbourne worried over his 'little effeminate hand gestures' and ensured that he was seen around town with attractive women. 'It was all to give Graham a good-old hetero image', recalled comedy writer Hugh Stuckey.[173] The notoriously homophobic station owner, Frank Packer, reckoned he could spot 'one' mile off and would have liked to sack him. But Packer's love of profits was greater than his hatred of homosexuals; Kennedy was the station's biggest star.[174]

Aberrant forms of sexual behaviour had to be punished, cured and suppressed because they were seen to endanger the heterosexual norm. Yet this very point underlines the extent to which Freudianism

The Sex Lives of Australians

and sexology had recast understandings of sex. On the one hand, sex-education literature for adolescents could assert:

> ... whereas we can always have many close friends of the same sex, our opposite sex friendships will in the end probably lead to a life-long partnership of marriage with *one* person, however little we may have marriage in view just now. All our thinking, and actions, are affected by it, and our emotions are more deeply stirred than they ever will be by a friend of the same sex.[175]

This position could only be maintained by defining homosexuality as a wrong sexual turn; yet it was seen as a danger to which anyone could be prone if raised incorrectly, or lacking willpower:

> In the community to-day are many unhappy men and women who have developed this preference for their own sex and are involved in experiences of a homosexual nature. They have misdirected the drive of sex and cannot know the joy of marriage, home and family life that should be the happy and satisfying lot of all who handle their life wisely. The great majority of people who are troubled in this regard were not born with this interest in their own sex. They have acquired it, perhaps due to factors in their early upbringing. By a lad giving way to sex practices with a member of his own sex he may cause these tendencies to develop and become fixed habits in his life.[176]

The final statement assumed a fragile male heterosexuality. Unless young men were trained in wise conduct from an early age, they could easily give way to sexual perversion.

### Lesbianism

Female sexual impulses were also seen to need direction. The war had removed large numbers of young women from parents' supervision, thrown them together in the armed forces and in factories, replaced their frocks with uniforms, and presented them with duties that seemed unwomanly. Public reassurance was needed, and given, that the army woman would retain her feminine charm, that barrack life had not

218

undermined her sexual attractiveness, that she had not been ruined for her future role in the nation's bedrooms. Once again, it was the female body itself on which these fears were inscribed. Not only did wartime propaganda emphasise that 'many have been improved by the severities of uniform', it also stressed that servicewomen received a 'standardised physical training, not of the hard muscle-building type, but designed to improve deportment and figure'. Any man who met such a woman would 'find her neither unduly masculine or a harpy', but rather 'as attractively feminine as any other Australian girl'. There was naturally a danger in this insistence on the sexiness of the average army girl that she would be seen as available to every man who came along. So it was also claimed in an army publication that most women looked forward to marrying, that many were preparing their glory boxes, that half of those questioned were wearing engagement rings. In short, they were a chaste or at least monogamous lot; neither military nor nation had claimed for themselves what rightly belonged to all men – and especially the returned man.[177]

Nor had other women been allowed to usurp men's rights. During the war military authorities tried to ensure that sexual relationships would not develop between servicewomen by splitting up particular friends, policing physical contact and discouraging relationships seen as unnaturally close – all arguably in a manner that would have been unacceptable among Australian soldiers bred on the culture of mate-ship and trained to see it as a military asset. No official action was taken to rid the services of lesbianism, perhaps through fear of bad publicity and the danger to recruitment.

Sexual relations did occur among women in the services, and Ruth Ford has suggested that the attention authorities gave to its dangers contributed to the formation of a lesbian identity. Where lesbianism was an indistinct presence in female military circles during the war, rising official recognition in the postwar era led to both greater surveil-lance in the armed forces and clearer subcultural formation.[178] All the same, we still know very little about lesbian life at this time. There were lesbian subcultures between the 1940s and the 1960s in the larger cities, centred on the army, certain sporting organisations, motorcycle and car clubs, and the more traditional havens for camp activity such as the theatre, music and art. Noel Tovey, a young Aboriginal man who was beginning to make a career for himself in Melbourne's musical theatre, recalled a bohemian world in which arty types, intellectuals fond of debating existentialism, aspiring actors, prostitutes, 'drag queens and their boyfriends' and lesbians wearing 'masculine clothes and Elvis Presley hair dos' called each other 'darling' at parties and in the few establishments where their presence was tolerated or welcomed.[179] But in her investigation of Melbourne lesbianism in this era, Lucy Chesser found no specifically lesbian venues before the late 1960s. Lesbians gravitated to a peripatetic coffee shop run by a lesbian named Val, while a few hotels also attracted a Saturday afternoon butch-femme clientele – lesbian couples in which one partner adopted an ultra-feminine style while the other wore men's clothing and short hair – when the regulars were at the football or races. There was plenty of what we would recognise as lesbian coupling, yet only a limited sense of community.[180] By contrast, a recent study of London in the same era has shown that a small number of bars and clubs had emerged by the 1950s as unmistakably lesbian venues, even if, as in Melbourne, there was some sharing of territory with male homosexuals, immigrants, criminals and prostitutes.[181]

But the silence about lesbianism was coming to an end. By the late 1950s and early 1960s, some sex-advice literature designed for the young was warning that when friendships between women verged 'on the sexual', they could lead to later problems in adjusting 'to the other sex in social life, courtship and marriage'. In some cases, 'disturbed girls or women' became 'too deeply attracted to a member of their own sex in a physical way', which led to 'mutual masturbation or other sex contact'. These practices were dangerous because they turned the sex tide the wrong way.[182] Solo masturbation by girls was dangerous because it might make the girl selfish in relations with her husband in the future, when her 'sex drive should be directed toward him'. Mutual masturbation, however, led to homosexuality. The common factor, of course, was the perceived threat to heterosexuality and marriage.[183]

### Even the Christians
It would be hard to imagine a figure more evocative of the 1950s' reputed conservatism than Dr Billy Graham, the American evangelist. In 1959 Graham visited Australia and was greeted by massive throngs everywhere. During just the first nine days of the Sydney leg of his crusade, over 290,000 people came out to see him. But the Galilean was not, apparently, the only thing on Graham's mind when he addressed 'a

record weekday crowd of 33,000' at the Sydney Showground; for, along with the message that they should decide for Christ and live 'a full home life' with his Father, they would also have heard Graham tell Australian women 'that they should not dress like Sabrina'.

Sabrina was a well-known actress and model of the period, a blonde-headed and large-busted British 'response' to Jayne Mansfield. What is truly interesting about Graham's speech, however, is the value he attached to married women making 'themselves as attractive as possible to their husbands', without painting 'themselves like a Jezebel'. Among the foundations of a happy marriage was the 'wife who made an effort to look attractive'.[184]

That a conservative Protestant clergyman such as Graham could put matters in this way is telling evidence of the eroticisation of marriage. The two decades before the pill came to Australia witnessed changes without which the 'sexual revolution' would have been unthinkable. This new sexualisation – stimulated by shifting medical discourses, sex research, and the imperialism of consumer culture – was a precondition for the revolution to come. At the same time, the emergence of an often sensationalist media coverage of sexual issues paved the way for increasingly explicit public representations of sex in the 1960s and 1970s. Heavily sexualised images of the young featured in the popular media and even, ironically, in respectable sex-advice literature, so that it was impossible to miss the message that responsible citizenship involved both sexual self-control and the capacity to engage responsibly and ethically in erotic relationships. While 'responsible' and 'ethical' usually implied heterosexual relations within marriage, rising rates of extra-nuptial pregnancy and illegitimacy and the large number of prosecutions for homosexual offences suggest that many were acting outside the bounds of traditional Christian morality. They might have been encouraged by a developing sense of the fragility of marriage itself, a bond seen to require careful nurturing by husband and wife under the guidance of moral and scientific authorities. After 1960 both varieties of authority would find themselves besieged. In the muddied waters ahead, the 1950s would seem like a clear spring, a less complicated era, even an age of innocence. Memory plays tricks that way.

# CHAPTER 8

# *Sexual Revolution*

## *The Myth of the Sixties*

No period in the history of sexuality is more encrusted with legend than the 1960s – which, for Australia at least, is usually understood also to include a slice of the 1970s. The era is conventionally associated with the 'permissive society' and the winning of sexual freedom – when the shackles of fifties conservatism were thrown off and bourgeois morality vanquished.

This '1960s' is not universally applauded; some hold it responsible for most of what is wrong in modern Australian society. 'The permissive '60s and everything that flowed from it', declared National Party leader John Anderson in 2002, saw 'a massive erosion of traditional family values in Australia'. He complained about 'a self-indulgent push for doing whatever feels good, whenever we want to do it, at the cost of far too many of our children'.[1]

The historians seem less certain about the fundamental significance of the decade. They point out that many ideas of the 'sexual revolution' had been championed long before the 1960s. The connection of the 'personal' and the 'political' – so often identified with the new social movements of the era – was already being made by bohemians and radicals in the 1950s. Sexology, meanwhile, had for almost a century been marking out terrain for the pursuit of sexual pleasure, just as new contraceptive technologies widened the gap between reproduction and sex. Agitation for the rights of sexual minorities, which had its origins in sexological investigation, also had a history extending back over many decades.[2]

This chapter and the next explore the years since 1960 in terms of both novelty and continuity. Not only did the period have some characteristics that can be reasonably called revolutionary, but the years since the 1970s have been marked by far-reaching changes in the sexual technologies, practices, politics and values associated with that fabled era. These concluding chapters will stress the fundamental and enduring character of the sixties transformation. While sexual revolution provoked backlash, there would be no turning back.

### *A New Australia?*

In a light-hearted *Bulletin* article published in 1963, Geoffrey Wilmot remarked on 'a strong feeling' among Australians that 'the British are far down the slippery slope to decadence and decay', while their own country was the repository 'of the virtues that once were British'. It wasn't just the loosening of sexual morals that was at issue here but

> all this fancy sex, say the moralists – two-way mirrors, naked slave stuff, flagellation parties and multiple orgies, not to mention the homosexuality for which Britain has long had a reputation in Australia; these are the symptoms of decadence and decay.

Australians, he thought, should not flatter themselves that they would 'play Rome to Britain's Greece in decline. A Mandy to Britain's Christine may be more like it'.[3]

Wilmot's reference here was to Britain's Profumo Affair. On 5 June 1963 John Profumo resigned both from the House of Commons and as war secretary after it was revealed that he had misled parliament over his relationship with Christine Keeler, a showgirl and model whose favours he had been sharing with a Russian diplomat. The ensuing scandal also brought into the spotlight another flamboyant young woman, Mandy Rice Davies. From an Australian point of view, all of this came at a time when Britain seemed to be turning her back on her old empire.[4] The Australian tabloids certainly presented the scandal in a manner that would have led most readers to conclude that there was something deeply wrong with Mother England.[5] Australian schoolchildren, so often astute commentators on current affairs, quickly summed up the situation:

*Half a pound of Mandy Rice,*
*Half of Christine Keeler,*
*Mix it up and what do you get?*
*A very sexy sheila.*[6]

This mixture of sensationalism, disgust, bewilderment and amusement in Australian reaction to the affair might obscure a more significant point; that by the final years of Menzies' long reign, sex was being depicted with increasing prominence and openness in public debate. Yet writing just five years before in 1958, J.D. Pringle, the English expatriate editor of the *Sydney Morning Herald*, had given a different impression. For Pringle, the national treatment of sex was 'healthy, frank, open and often somewhat animal' but there was 'rarely any sense of reserve or sophistication' and, even on the beaches, 'no eroticism'. In Europe the men watched, studied and compared the women; in Australia, 'the handsome, sun-burnt girls play vigorously in the surf or lie on the sand and watch the young men riding the great Pacific waves in to the beach'. It is revealing of this moment on the cusp of the 1960s that Pringle should equate eroticism with European men checking out women, its absence with Australian women looking over young men.[7]

### Learning

The resurgence of VD in the 1960s and rising rates of illegitimacy fuelled renewed interest in sex education, especially as a rising proportion of cases afflicted the young. In Queensland, more than a fifth of VD notifications in 1967 came from teenagers, compared with just one-tenth in the early 1950s, and by the mid-1970s illegitimacy rates were nearly double those of World War II.[8] Rape also seemed more common. In NSW, reported juvenile rape increased eightfold between 1956 and 1969, compared with the trebling of the adult rate. Much of this increase came from gang-rape where, according to one study, boys made 'no attempt to hide their identities and on apprehension seem surprised by the fuss made about "normal" activity'.[9]

While some observers blamed moral permissiveness, others held responsible the mystery in which sex remained shrouded. The Royal Commission on Human Relationships, sitting in the mid-1970s, found high levels of sexual ignorance among Australians. Most children left school without any sex education and what little *was* on offer was plainly inadequate; the odd class or two, possibly slipped into the biology syllabus between lessons on photosynthesis and the function of the aorta. Many parents also remained reluctant to provide their children with instruction. Sex was still something naughty or even dirty, a cause of red faces and awkward glances at the family dinner table. The royal commission's suggested remedy was comprehensive sex and human relationships education in Australian schools as well as for adults, including a 'factual and balanced not condemnatory or judgmental' treatment of homosexuality.[10]

It was not until the 1970s that governments began providing school-based sex, 'human relationships' or 'personal development' classes. Based on the conviction that '[t]o be human is to be sexual', sex education classes sought to develop students' capacities for emotional maturity and responsible, fulfilling sexual expression. These aims had not traditionally figured in classroom teaching; their appearance now reflected the impact of a new pedagogical emphasis on the education of the 'whole' child through the process of self-discovery, and the sexual revolution's placing of the erotic life at the centre of the human personality. Yet while sex education achieved growing community acceptance, conservative organisations such as the Concerned Parents Association lobbied governments to prevent it – with particular success in Queensland, where sex education was banned until the early 1990s.[11] The Royal Commission on Human Relationships' recommendations affirmed many opponents' fears that classes would be used to promote homosexuality.[12] These opponents saw sex education as a conspiracy to thrust the nihilistic philosophy of the sixties sexual revolutionaries on impressionable youngsters. *The Little Red School-Book*, a forthright Danish production translated into English, was one of their favourite targets.[13]

Adolescent masturbation had for many years been generating declining medical and moral concern. Now, some sex-education literature went further in suggesting it was 'quite usual', 'harmless' and 'experienced by most boys', while offering the reassurance that '[i]t seems impossible that anyone can masturbate to excess'. 'If anybody tells you it's harmful to masturbate', proclaimed *The Little Red School-Book*, 'they're lying'.[14] Some sex educators advocated masturbation 'as an important part of the child's sexual development' because it led to acceptance of responsibility for one's 'own sexual arousal'.[15] Wendy McCarthy, a leading sex educator, agreed that there was 'an enormous amount of sexual learning to be had by giving oneself and others permission to masturbate, especially for girls'.[16] Masturbation was becoming swept up in sexual revolution, increasingly understood not so much in Freudian terms as part of a child's sexual development, but as 'a claim to autonomy, to pleasure for its own sake, an escape from the socially prescribed path towards normal adulthood'.[17]

The universities were rapidly swept up in the atmosphere of greater freedom. By the early 1960s the Melbourne University student newspaper, *Farrago*, was regularly discussing a range of sexual issues. Some of this had a distinctly old-fashioned feel about it, such as a 1960 piece on how far a woman should go with her Asian boyfriend. 'It is not a girl's duty or even her right', declared the author, 'to pamper her Asian friend with liberties in order to assure him of his equality. This is degrading'.[18] But there were also signs of change, if something less than sexual revolution. The Student Christian Movement sponsored lectures on 'pre-marital relationships'. The speaker, a doctor, while rejecting 'full physical contact' before marriage, allowed for 'orgasm by manual contact' provided it was accompanied by 'happiness, joy and beauty'.[19] But there were also plenty of letters advocating chastity; one correspondent congratulated the paper for having produced a whole issue without sex in it.[20]

By 1966 *Farrago* was publishing articles on 'Sex and the Single Student: How Not to Be a Mummy'; it contained detailed advice on birth control. An article in the same issue advised new students that 'if you value your virginity too much you may never lose it' and reported that at university, 'The value of virginity slumps a little. People who sleep together are more likely to evoke a slight admiration than condemnation ... that people do sleep together is taken much more for granted'.[21] But a sociological survey of Melbourne University students in 1967 found that many disapproved of premarital sex and the rest 'set stringent conditions for it'. At most, students were inclined to appraise the issue more 'coolly' than they had at school: 'Responsibility to the partner and "real feelings" are in; taboos and submission to authority are out.'[22] Melbourne University, like Sydney, was still running beauty contests but the 1969 winner was soon leading the Women's Liberation Group and active in efforts to end them.[23]

In Sydney, it was a similar story, although the continuing influence of the libertarian tradition there added extra spice. There was an especially provocative address at the new University of NSW in orientation week of 1962 by a psychologist, Peter Kenny – his ideas reputedly included the 'equal right to fornicate or not to fornicate', marriages for homosexuals, and a room to be included in all homes for 'solitary sexual practices'. At Queensland University a young radical, Humphrey McQueen, who published Kenny's views in a newsletter, was suspended and reprimanded by the vice-chancellor.[24] Meanwhile, Sir Stephen Roberts, the vice-chancellor at Sydney University, decided that there would be no further symposiums on sex at his own university as it was not something to be 'discussed in mixed company'.[25] Students showed little patience when a visiting American professor gave a lecture in 1963 on the dangers of pre-marital sex – he was pelted with toilet rolls, fruit and vegetables.[26] At the University of New England in rural Armidale there was student unrest when in 1963 the council banned male and female students from visiting one another in their college rooms. A letter in the student newspaper made it clear enough what was at stake: 'If you're going to have sexual intercourse', it said, 'you'll have it anyway'.[27]

Universities would play a significant role in the emergence of the new politics concerned with 'quality of life' that achieved an ascendancy after 1960. While anti–Vietnam War protest, Aboriginal rights and environmentalism were prominent, it also included a range of matters linked to sex: censorship, contraception, abortion, divorce, women's rights, education and homosexuality. Many demands of the new social movements were, in turn, absorbed into the social-democratic reformism of the Whitlam government (1972–75). The right to sexual fulfilment took its place alongside other claims to rights, soon extending to the handicapped, the aged and children. Doctors, clergy, politicians and bureaucrats who sometimes used their authority to trivialise such claims, or to induce 'shame, guilt and self-disgust' in those articulating them, were condemned as insensitive and inhumane.[28]

### *'The Biggest Topic on Earth': The Contraceptive Pill*
There is a satisfying chronological convenience about the pill's arrival at the beginning of a decade seen as heralding a 'sexual revolution'. But did it inaugurate that revolution? Its most obvious impact, at least

initially, was on married women; but the sexual revolution has been more commonly associated with greater freedom among the young and single. And if the sexual revolution also meant movements to end the oppression of homosexual men and women, how was the pill relevant here?

The pill, in fact, had a massive impact on the lives of millions of Australians. No previous contraceptive technology achieved anything like its almost complete reliability. It largely fulfilled the promise that had been held up in decades of sex-advice literature but never truly realised: sex for pleasure and companionship without fear of pregnancy. And it would have indirect effects even on those, such as gays and lesbians, whose sexual practices ruled out any need for contraception at all.

At first, more modest aspirations attached themselves to the oral contraceptive. Early proponents mainly took for granted that its role was to aid marital 'adjustment', that ill-defined goal of 1950s marriage counselling.[29] But it was soon clear that the pill was opening far broader horizons. When used correctly, it was so effective that it could help liberate women from the tyranny of their own wombs. And the implications of that were truly revolutionary.

In January 1961, just a few months after its US appearance, the pill was released in Australia.[30] The most complete figures on early use are from Melbourne. By 1963 one in ten married women of child-bearing age in that city had a prescription. Falling prices encouraged uptake, a month's supply dropping from £2/3/9 in early 1961 to £1/3/9 in mid-1962. By the early 1970s, six months' supply was just $1.39.[31] One factor especially militated against pill usage: in the early years especially, many women who took it suffered from a variety of unpleasant side effects. Nonetheless, by the mid-1960s, it was being acclaimed in women's magazines as 'changing world history', 'the biggest topic on earth', and 'the greatest talking point since the bomb'.[32]

Some doctors, however, opposed the pill entirely, simply recycling the moral and religious arguments used against contraception for decades, such as that it degraded 'the sexual act in marriage to mere self-gratification'.[33] But the Christian churches themselves were exercising waning control over private behaviour. The decade's 'expressive revolution' promoted a new spirituality that challenged the traditional churches' authority.[34] Even the Catholic Church's sway over the sexuality of younger members was in decline. Catholics who resisted mechanical forms of contraception or chemicals applied at the time of sex felt liberated by the pill. It was clean, clinical and – perhaps most importantly for those raised in a climate of hostility to sex for pleasure – disconnected from the act of sex itself. Revealingly, Catholics were also more attracted to contraceptive techniques that involved the insertion of a Gräfenberg ring or an IUD just once, rather than methods requiring repeated 'sinning'.[35]

The pill could readily be reconciled with the 'modern' Catholic conscience. The Second Vatican Council established by Pope John XXIII in 1962 had unleashed waves of change through the church, and in the flush of excitement, Catholic liberals dared hope it would reconsider its position on contraception – or at least place the pill outside the church's ban on artificial contraception. Although Catholic pill usage lagged behind Protestant, many were taking the oral contraceptive in the 1960s, possibly comforted by the arguments of some Australian priests, theologians and lay intellectuals that it did not breach the church's ban.[36] So, when late in July 1968 John's successor Paul VI issued *Humanae Vitae*, it arrived as a bombshell. The encyclical condemned all forms of birth control except abstinence and the safe period.[37] 'One cannot help wondering what has happened to all the promise that Vatican II seemed to hold', reflected Father Patrick Crudden of the Catholic Education Office in Melbourne.[38] Greg Dening, a Jesuit priest and later a distinguished historian, reflected that *Humanae Vitae* 'turned the moral face of the Church away from the evils of global poverty, of violence within and between nations, of exploitation of the weak, back to the bedroom'.[39]

There was vigorous protest from some lay Catholics, but little public dissent from the clergy.[40] Some such as Dening, who found themselves unable to defend the encyclical, quietly left the priesthood. Father Nicholas Crotty, a moral theologian, was unusual in publicly expressing disapproval, for which he was suspended by Melbourne's Archbishop Knox.[41] Knox himself greeted the encyclical 'with a lively sense of gratitude',[42] but in Sydney Cardinal Gilroy, according to the recollections of priest and historian Edmund Campion, had 'haunted eyes' at a press conference: 'There was too much lead in the saddle bags for this horse to win, and the Cardinal knew it.'[43] But the Cardinal's solemnity did not prevent him from smiling when asked if Catholics using the pill would burn in hell: 'We don't like to say anybody is going to hell', he replied. 'Who are we to judge?'[44] In their statement on the encyclical, the Australian bishops warned Catholics that the ruling was 'authentic and authoritative' and it would be 'a grave act of disobedience' to reject it. Their statement, however, ended with the bishops' prayer 'that husbands and wives may find in bishops and priests Christ-like kindness and understanding in the difficulties of their vocation of marriage'.[45] Under Gilroy's leadership, said the left-leaning *Nation*, the line taken by the Australian hierarchy was 'no show-down and no witch-hunt' but there were certainly priests who felt hounded and bullied.[46]

*Humanae Vitae* drove some believers out of the church while many simply ignored the ban. In Melbourne, the editorial board chairman of the progressive *Catholic Worker* accurately predicted that Australian Catholics were 'likely to give serious loyal attention to the Pope's personal decision and then to follow their own consciences'.[47] A 1970 survey found that the 'consciences' of only 29 per cent of Catholics endorsed Papal teaching on the pill.[48] Many Catholic women now claimed to be taking the pill for medicinal purposes only – for it was found to be healthy in regulating menstruation – and an early 1970s study of Melbourne women reported that 60 per cent of Catholics there had used 'illicit' contraception at one time or another in their lives.[49] Such women were clearly unconvinced by Catholic men's organisations who continued to oppose contraception on the grounds that pregnancy was 'God's greatest gift to man'.[50]

In the 1960s the Catholic Church injected new vigour into the campaign for 'natural family planning'. Unfortunately for their proponents, the methods previously accepted by the church – 'rhythm' and 'temperature'[51] – had become pejoratively known as 'Vatican Roulette' on account of their questionable reliability. Prompted by the Catholic Family Welfare Bureau's marriage counsellor, a Catholic neurologist based in Melbourne named John Billings began research in 1953 that led to the development of the 'Ovulation Method'. Billings was later joined in this effort by his wife, Evelyn, also a doctor, and a mother of nine. The technique they developed required close observation of mucus secretions produced in the cervix – the patterns of which were found to indicate the timing of ovulation – but also depended on a married couple's capacity for periods of abstinence. The Billingses believed that not sex but 'consideration, and the ability to communicate in a non-genital way' were the true foundations of successful marriage. Periodic abstinence, in any case, intensified the subsequent delight of sex.[52]

The idea that the timing of sex should be regulated by vaginal discharges was out of tune with the sexual revolution's privileging of spontaneity, pleasure and mutual desire. Yet the Billings Method was thoroughly 'modern' in the respect it accorded women's knowledge of their own bodies. It assumed their capacity, with the help of science and a considerate husband, to manage marital sexuality, and it relied on their willingness to examine their genitals regularly and talk candidly about them with researchers, doctors and instructors. Rather like an obscene book on which a ban had been lifted, a woman's vagina could now be read by a woman in the interests of a happy Christian marriage. In sum, the Billings Method amounted to an explicit recognition by the Catholic Church that sexual pleasure was critical in a modern marriage, since it took for granted that sex was for something other than producing more of God's children.[53]

Despite this rearguard action, the numbers of women on the pill continued to rise steadily – to a quarter of married Melbourne women by the early 1970s. Indeed, if we exclude the pregnant, those trying to become pregnant and the sterile, the figure rises to almost four in ten.[54] By the late 1960s over two-thirds of married women using contraception under the age of twenty-two were on the pill. For them, 'the pill' and 'contraception' became almost synonymous.[55]

For many married women, the pill largely removed fear of pregnancy; such women were now more able to enjoy their sexuality free from the restraint and fear dictated by less effective contraception. As one Melbourne woman who went on the pill at the beginning of the 1960s recalled, 'At age thirty-nine I began to use the pill … [I]t was wonderful. I felt so fit … I think it was the most marvellous thing that has ever been invented. I thought I could enjoy sex so much more'.[56] Stories of this kind have been underestimated by historians of the sexual revolution preoccupied with the more spectacular and readily observable manifestations of transformation. For a small minority of married people, group sex, partner swapping and open marriages became an alternative to monogamy.[57] But a change of far greater import was the relaxation of a 'culture of abstinence' within marriage itself.[58] People married later and delayed having children longer – but without having to refrain from sex or practise withdrawal. Before the pill, even a careful couple who wanted two children could easily end up with three or four. After the pill, this was much less likely. Perhaps even more radically, women's reproductive systems were no longer so widely assumed to be at the nation's disposal. Earlier in the century, women who limited their fertility were supposedly committing 'race suicide'. Now, the threads that had long tied female sexuality to nation-building were loosened. As a result, media concern in the 1960s about declining birthrates did not translate into a serious case against the pill.

For single women who had increasing access to the pill, new forms of heterosexual experimentation opened up. Nancy, a twenty-year-old bookkeeper living in Sydney in the late 1960s, was from a New England property:

> I've done a lot of thinking, and I'm really too young to get tied down … You never know what's around the corner, and it's more fun hunting than settling. These days, you get on the pill, and you stop worrying. The pill's changed everything. Now, if a girl's over twenty and still a virgin, there's something wrong with her.[59]

Nonetheless, single women found it harder to get the pill. A *Woman's Day* article from 1964 included testimony from one doctor of having been asked for the pill by seventeen- and eighteen-year-old girls with 'no prospect of being married'. 'I've always refused', he added pointedly.[60] But despite some resistance, birth control was becoming both a medical and a private matter. In 1967 the council of the University of New England ruled that the contraceptive pill should be prescribed to its students by an attending doctor 'for medical purposes only and not for purposes of contraception'. But this policy was rescinded in 1969, with council now considering that the matter should be left to 'the professional discretion of the attending doctor'.[61]

Although university surgeries were not always willing to prescribe the pill,[62] as contraceptive services proliferated many young and single women were saved the embarrassment of having to front up to the family doctor. Doris Condon, the Mayor of South Melbourne and co-founder of Victoria's first municipal family planning clinic, told a reporter in 1971 that 'we don't look to see if a woman or girl is wearing a gold ring on her left hand'.[63] Similarly, Peter Hollingworth, Director of Social Services for the Anglican Church's Brotherhood of St Laurence, reported that its family planning clinics prescribed the pill to single women who 'have a special problem of not being able to get married and being fairly committed to someone regarding their sexual drives'. Family planning clinics allowed girls of sixteen or seventeen to have the pill if convinced it was needed, but not for those under sixteen without parental consent.[64] Some parents might well have been willing to give it, happily or otherwise. An eighteen-year-old Sydney Girls High student claimed in the *Bulletin* in 1972 that her mother put her on the pill when she was sixteen, and that half her sixth form class was taking it.[65]

The oral contraceptive raised the prospect that women would find it even harder to resist men's sexual demands. Men could more easily absolve themselves from responsibility for birth control, but the status of the pill as a female contraceptive further undermined their control over reproduction, a matter that evidently worried some doctors.[66] Ethnicity, culture and class also mediated the pill's impact. The oral contraceptive was in the early years taken up predominantly among locally born white women, especially non-Catholics, and migrants from Northern and Western Europe. The uptake was low among Eastern and Southern Europeans, who remained attached to withdrawal.[67] Aboriginal women had their own concerns. The sexual revolution coincided with the development of a new self-confidence among Aboriginal people, a pride in culture and identity, and a vigorous assertion of rights. In view of bureaucrats' earlier plans to breed them out biologically, more recent schemes to absorb them culturally, and the devastation of their family life through child removal, many Indigenous people were hostile to continuing 'white' intervention with their reproductive lives. Shirley Smith ('Mum Shirl'), founder of the Aboriginal Medical Service, complained of forced abortions and sterilisation, and she regarded the newfangled contraceptive technology as a harmful interference with the bodies of Indigenous women: 'They tried to make us stuff those things up us called IUDs, but that's not good either. Doesn't do you no good.' Why was it, these Aboriginal critics asked, that the Family Planning Association received money to promote contraception among Aborigines while the Aboriginal Medical Service was less favoured? Betty Fisher, the SA feminist and Aboriginal rights advocate, told the Royal Commission on Human Relationships: 'Most of us think that the whole purpose of family planning is to stop the growth of Aboriginal people.'[68]

The pill and IUD were most accessible to the better-educated and better-off. However, as the experiences of Aboriginal women revealed, the lives of poor women were also increasingly touched by more reliable contraception. The spread of family planning clinics in the late 1960s and early 1970s – many of them in industrial suburbs – is likely to have increased pill uptake among working-class women, as is its rapidly declining cost.[69] But not all women's lives were transformed. Many tried the pill and went off it. The debate about side effects bubbled on throughout the 1960s and at the end of the decade a widely publicised British report warned of the dangers of blood clots, prompting an immediate drop in usage.[70] Some women turned to the IUD as an alternative, but it too had detrimental consequences for some women. Germaine Greer was not alone among feminists in condemning the pill for its adverse effects on women's health and sexual desire.[71] Nevertheless, improvements in the oral contraceptive during the 1970s saw a recovery in usage.

When researchers at La Trobe University in Melbourne carried out a survey of sexual practice at the beginning of the present century, they found that the pill was still a very popular method of contraception, with more than one-third of women taking it. But 42 per cent of women reported that they were protected from pregnancy either by having had a surgical procedure themselves or by their male partner's vasectomy, choices that were especially common among older couples who had children while young.[72] In the 1960s debates about 'sterilisation' were carried on alongside those on the pill in the *MJA* and although the two forms of contraception were each seen to raise different ethical and legal issues for doctors, at least one aspect was held in common: both involved 'the right to sexual enjoyment without the fear of producing unwanted children'.[73] In each case, the individual right of the patient to control their own fertility was triumphant.

The impact of the new sexual culture was registered in a survey of 1442 Australian women carried out by a visiting American sociologist in 1973. He found that nearly three-quarters had experienced premarital sex, and the average age at which they lost their virginity was eighteen and a half. But younger women were, on this measure, more 'permissive'. Not only did they first engage in sex earlier, younger women also had premarital sex in greater numbers. Ninety-two per cent of married women under twenty-five had engaged in premarital sex, compared with just 38 per cent of those aged over fifty. Younger women who had premarital sex also had, on average, more partners before marriage than older women. Meanwhile, in marital sex, younger women were found to be more likely to initiate sex than older women, had sex more often, and experienced orgasm more frequently. While these results were hardly surprising, the older cohorts did contain many women who wanted *more* sex with their husbands than they were having. Some were dissatisfied with their sexual lives; possibly all those sexological texts of the mid-twentieth century had been sown in fertile soils after all.

Younger women were much more likely to practise oral sex, suggesting that more effective contraception, combined with more open discussion and a growing emphasis on pleasure, was broadening the repertoire of both men and women.[74] But another reason for the rise of oral sex at this time was probably rather mundane: more frequent baths and showers produced cleaner genitals. Even allowing for lower sensitivity to unpleasant odours and tastes earlier in the century, oral sex would have been literally distasteful to most people. Not only were cleaner contraceptives in use by the 1960s, but hot water was available at the turn of a tap in most Australian homes, thereby ending the ritual of the Saturday-evening bath and increasing bodily cleanliness, if not godliness.[75]

At the beginning of the twenty-first century older people, and especially more mature women, were less likely to practise oral sex than the young. But a quarter of all respondents in the national sex survey had done so in their most recent sexual encounter, and nearly four-fifths of the men and two-thirds of women had engaged in fellatio or cunnilingus at least once in their lives.[76] While known to be long significant among male homosexuals, oral sex was now a sufficiently common heterosexual practice to call forth regular columns in women's magazines about how to give perfect fellatio.

### Living Together
In the 1960s marriage was the destiny of all but a small minority of Australians. By 1971, 86 per cent of men and 94 per cent of women were married before their thirty-fifth birthday.[77] Most did so in their early twenties; bachelors, on average, just before they turned twenty-five while their wives were joining them less than a year after their coming of age at twenty-one.[78] For women especially, becoming an

adult was virtually synonymous with getting married. In the mid-1930s the marrying age for bachelors had been twenty-eight, for spinsters twenty-five.

The 1970s, however, would witness the beginning of a reversal of this trend. Couples would come to marry later so that by the end of the 1990s, the median age of a bridegroom was thirty, his wife twenty-eight.[79] The reasons for the change were complex but the increasing incidence of de facto relationships clearly had much to do with it. Men and women had lived together outside legal marriage from the earliest years of settlement. But what had been widely condemned between the Victorian era and the sixties' sexual revolution acquired a new acceptance.

No one knew quite how many Australians were living in de facto partnerships, but all agreed that they were increasing. One calculation suggested a minimum of 34,166 people in 1971, which had jumped four-fold to 131,876 five years later. Opinion polling indicated that public disapproval of such arrangements was also declining. But if 'living together' was a mark of sexual revolution, its incidence once again suggests the uneven impact of change. Those likely to enter de facto relationships were very similar to the groups using modern contraception: the Australian-born and migrants from English-speaking countries. They were also likely to have weak religious affiliations.[80]

One group that had sometimes entered such relationships before the 1970s was men and women separated from a spouse but unable or unwilling to divorce. For this reason, the arrival of no-fault divorce after the passage of the *Family Law Act* in 1975 might have been expected to reduce the number of de facto relationships. That it did not was partly the result of already divorced or separated people entering de facto relationships but not, at least initially, being willing to remarry. A far more significant reason for the rise, however, was its increasing frequency among the young. A minority of the young rejected marriage entirely but most regarded 'living together' as a phase between leaving home and marrying. Many had what amounted to trial marriages, sharing a home and bed with a prospective spouse before entering into a deeper and more permanent commitment. As in the past, couples were delaying marriage because of economic insecurity; but unlike in the past, they were no longer having to delay household formation. The return of mass unemployment and economic insecurity in the 1970s probably discouraged marriage and reproduction, as it had done in the 1930s. But young women were also now better educated and seeking to establish themselves in careers before child-bearing. Twenty-eight per cent of women who married in the years 1973–77 reported having lived with their husband beforehand, which was double the proportion from marriages of the previous five years.[81]

For young people delaying marriage, 'living together' would have been less attractive and less socially acceptable in the absence of more reliable contraception. A trial marriage became something more than a mere trial if it produced children, but the pill, the IUD and easier access to abortion meant that careful couples could avoid such problems. Nevertheless, much of the shame attached to unmarried motherhood was also reduced in the 1970s, as legal marriage had to compete with other socially approved types of sexual relationships. Self-help groups emerged among those who now often referred to themselves as 'single mothers'. The use of this term was part of a larger effort to overcome the stigma that attached to having borne a child out of wedlock, and the discrimination that was its bitter harvest. Such women now often rejected the popular wisdom that single mothers should give up their children for adoption.[82] The Whitlam government's introduction of a supporting mother's benefit in 1973 provided a basic level of financial help, while from 1974 state and territory parliaments passed laws formally abolishing illegitimacy.[83]

Single mothers and their children, however, continued to suffer discrimination. Influenced by a right-wing backlash in the US against black unmarried mothers on welfare, some Australian conservatives professed to believe that young women were deliberately becoming pregnant in order to claim a pension. Those who sought to renew the stigma now turned their attention to the 'immorality' of welfare dependence, and the social irresponsibility of the woman unable to maintain a stable relationship or use contraception effectively. In an era when there had been radical challenges to moral values, the lowly status of the 'pregnant teenager' and the 'unmarried mother' was reinforced, as was social approval of the stable nuclear family as a privileged site of sexual activity.[84]

## The New Feminism

Those who sought to raise the status of single mothers were influenced by a new feminism that demanded a higher status for all women.

Radical women, dissatisfied with the sexism they experienced at the hands of their male fellows in the anti–Vietnam War movement, began holding meetings in the major Australian cities from late 1969 at which they discussed the particular oppression suffered by women. The movement would place women's sexual rights at the heart of its agenda in a way that was distinct from earlier Australian feminisms.[85] Women had the right to sexual pleasure free from fear of pregnancy but would need to assert themselves collectively if they were to realise the full promise of a new technological, social and moral order. So in 1972 the newly formed Women's Electoral Lobby (WEL) made a submission to the Tariff Board arguing for lower duties on imported contraceptives, while feminists lobbied for easier access to effective birth control.[86]

The new feminism was deeply influenced by events, ideas and texts coming from the US, Britain and France, yet the traffic ultimately travelled in both directions, as Australian feminists made their mark internationally. The influential 1966 *Human Sexual Response*, by the American sexologists William Masters and Virginia Johnson, had placed particular stress on women's sexual pleasure in heterosexual coupling derived from stimulation of the clitoris. This emphasis, which seemed to challenge Freud's influential claims concerning the superiority of the vaginal orgasm, could be interpreted to suggest that the penis was less critical to female sexual pleasure than previously assumed in sexology.[87] While some Australian feminists would find the implication that men were irrelevant to sexual pleasure liberating, the new preoccupation with the clitoral orgasm ran into the not inconsiderable problem – if one Sydney gynaecologist is to be believed – that many women did not know what a clitoris was.[88] In any case, Germaine Greer, by then working in England as an academic, was quite unconvinced by all the chatter about clitoral orgasms. Even if the advocates were right, she said in her bestselling 1970 book *The Female Eunuch*, 'a clitoral orgasm with a full cunt is nicer than a clitoral orgasm with an empty one, as far as I can tell at least'. But her main point was that 'a man is more than a dildo'. 'Real gratification', she asserted, 'is not enshrined in a tiny cluster of nerves but in the sexual involvement of the whole person'.

Greer criticised the permissive society's reduction of sexuality to a 'mechanical release involving neither discovery nor triumph, stressing human isolation more dishearteningly than ever before'. If there were women who had only ever experienced clitoral orgasm, it was simply evidence that the whole body had been desexualised. Greer condemned the idea that there was 'a statistically ideal fuck which will always result in satisfaction if the right procedures are followed'. Women needed to avoid the 'last reduction of their humanity' implied in such prescriptions, and instead 'hold out not just for orgasm but for ecstasy'. Part academic text, part manifesto and part self-help manual, *The Female Eunuch* took up a longer tradition of Antipodean sexual radicalism that stretched through the Push, to which Greer had belonged in the early 1960s, and back to William Chidley. Indeed, like Chidley, Greer saw the living vagina as the basis for an active female (hetero)sexuality. A large part of women's battle would be won, she said, if they could 'change their attitude towards sex, and embrace and stimulate the penis instead of *taking* it'.[89] It was partly for this reason that Greer condemned the missionary position, arguing that women should – literally – get on top during intercourse: 'Once you throw a leg over your man, you have made a political gesture.'[90]

Women's Liberation had a tense and ambivalent relationship to the sexual revolution born of a recognition that for some men, the revolutionary struggle was simply an opportunity for more sex. The masculinism of the counter-culture is clear enough in the Australian expatriate Richard Neville's 1970 celebration of sexual revolution, London-style:

When boy meets girl, within minutes of drifting off to a comfortable location, boy can be happily splashing about in girl's cunt, both of them up each other's arses, sucking and fucking with compassionate enthusiasm. No more tedious 'will she or won't she by Saturday?' but a total tactile information exchange, and an unambiguous foundation upon which to build a temporary or permanent relationship. The pot of gold at the end of the rainbow comes first; later one decides whether the rainbow is worth having for its own sake. If the attraction is only biological, nothing is lost except a few million spermatozoa and both parties continue their separate ways. If there is a deeper involvement, the relationship becomes richer, and so does the sexual experience. The way to a girl's mind is through her cunt.[91]

Unlike male libertarians such as Neville, the new feminists recognised sexuality as a site of oppression at the same time as they upheld women's right to sexual pleasure.[92] For instance, Women's Liberation called for an end to sexist advertising and the demeaning representations of women in the public sphere; not because sex should not be publicly depicted but because such images conditioned women for their subjugation and legitimised men's degradation of them.

### Rape and Male Sexuality

A 1968 article on gang-rape in *Man* magazine claimed that 'there are few naturally virile men who go through life … without ever once having attempted sexual relations with a girl against her will'. Yet the male author also believed that women brought it on themselves, since the victim of a pack-rape was often 'physically over-developed for her age and too well-aware of the fact, yet lacking the maturity and experience to control the situation … playing big girls until it … led to disaster'. Girls, he suggested, also tended to invent stories of rape:

> For these reasons, I particularly admire the non-emotional approach most policemen display towards rape victims. Knowing only too well that an emotionally disturbed girl, or one who is afraid of her parents, will yell rape either to attract attention to herself or as an excuse for disobeying her parents, the police usually question an alleged rape victim for at least four hours. During this interrogation – and possibly because they are men – the police attempt to break down the girl's story; get her to admit that she made up the rape story to cover the fact that she was late home.[93]

The matter-of-fact way in which these views were laid out is a fair indication of the mountain faced by feminists who wanted to reform the rape law in the 1970s. Criminologists similarly suggested that in many cases of pack-rape, the victim's conduct was 'such as to strongly encourage, if not invite, the members of these packs to fulfil their ambitions'.[94]

Combating sexual violence emerged as a major preoccupation for many Australian feminists. At a practical level, Women's Liberation groups attracted government funding for women's refuges and rape crisis centres while feminist lawyers argued for reform of rape laws that had hardly moved in their essentials since the Victorian era. Law reformers drew attention to women's reluctance to report rape, harsh treatment of victims by the system, low conviction rates and lenient sentences.[95] Women who reported rape complained of being made by police to feel like 'dirt', judges scolded rape victims for their dress, and barristers defended the relevance of introducing a woman's past sexual conduct into the case for the defence.[96] Some feminists were especially concerned about the legal ambiguity surrounding rape in marriage. Women also demonstrated in the streets against sexual violence towards women, some marching on Anzac Day to protest against rape in war.[97]

The feminist campaigns against rape aimed to transform a law still based on long-standing negative stereotypes of women, such as their 'natural' tendency to deceive. These efforts yielded significant change and a shift of public opinion in favour of victims and against rapists. Feminists argued with some success that rape law should be changed to lay more stress on its violent character, and that the issue of consent should be treated so that it was more sensitive to women's experience of sex.[98] These concerns arose out of police reluctance to press charges when a victim had failed to scream during a rape, or if she lacked highly visible signs of assault on her body. In the 1990s there were several controversies concerning the failure of some male judges to take rape seriously. Some seemed to believe that, in certain instances, 'no' really meant 'yes'. In one notorious case of marital rape in 1993, a judge instructed a jury that there was 'nothing wrong with a husband, faced with his wife's initial refusal to engage in intercourse' to try 'to persuade her to change her mind and that may involve a measure of rougher than usual handling'. Nevertheless, the public outrage about this and other cases showed that sexual assault was being taken more seriously, and that many judges were lagging behind public opinion. By the 1990s convictions were being secured in rape trials that only a decade or two before would have had little prospect of producing such a verdict. One reason for this change is that there was now less scope for defence counsel to introduce evidence of the victim's sexual history, an issue that had long been at the heart of injustices in rape law.[99] The ambiguities regarding rape in marriage were also removed.

For Aboriginal women, especially those living in remote areas, the danger of rape remained very high. According to one Queensland Police estimate from the mid-1990s, Indigenous women in the far north were sixteen to twenty-five times more likely than either Indigenous or non-Indigenous women living elsewhere in the state to become the victims of a sexual assault.[100] Yet when in 1989 the anthropologist Diane Bell raised the issue of intra-racial rape in an article produced with an Aboriginal collaborator, Topsy Nelson, she provoked an acrimonious debate about who is authorised to speak for whom about sexual assault. A group of Aboriginal women replied that white middle-class feminists should mind their own business and steer away from matters 'which can be abused and misinterpreted by racists'.[101] In this way, they dismissed Bell and Nelson's attempt to draw attention to the rape of Aboriginal women by Aboriginal men as just another manifestation of imperialism. The vitriol that rained on Bell especially can only have discouraged further discussion of intra-racial rape; certainly, at any rate, by white feminists.

While the new feminism was sometimes ill-adapted to the circumstances of Aboriginal women, its insistence on women's sexual rights animated the conviction that Australian men needed to embrace a new masculinity. Feminist historians such as Anne Summers in *Damned Whores and God's Police* and Miriam Dixson in *The Real Matilda* connected male sexual behaviour of the 1970s to the broader sweep of Australian history, which they traced back to convict times. This critique of male sexuality centred on the 'ocker', who just wanted to stick 'it' in – feminists condemned hydraulic images of male sex and argued for women's right to sexual pleasure.[102] Some male commentators were also increasingly explicit – and critical – of the attitudes and practices of their own sex. Craig McGregor complained that too many Australian men saw women as 'things to sleep with but not to talk to'.[103] Ronald Conway, a Catholic psychologist and social commentator, was similarly scathing in 1971, asserting that '[t]he sturdy leg that kicks a football often seems less assured when it must straddle the nuptial bed … They appear to have an elementary pelvic concept of sex which tends to bustle them towards vaginal entry with the minimum of delicate preliminaries'.[104] The journalist Suzy Jarratt had no doubt that that the newly permissive Australia was being made primarily by women, who 'expect something more than a five minute grunt and heave. It's orgasm or nothing'. They disliked 'being treated as receptacles or as a pleasant alternative to masturbation'.[105]

## *The Struggle for Abortion Rights*

Feminists demanded safe and effective abortion as part of this larger claim for sexual rights. A woman who sought an abortion should not have her life endangered by an incompetent and unhygienic back-yarder, nor by a doctor who put avoiding prosecution ahead of her safety. She should not be over-charged. She should not be treated like a slut and made to feel as though she 'wasn't worth a pinch of shit'.[106]

Abortion, however, was a more controversial issue than contraception because some Christians equated it with murder, and because its illegality led to corruption. In Melbourne, the campaigns of the late 1960s and early 1970s by the Scottish-born doctor Bertram Wainer helped expose a grubby racket in which abortionists were permitted to carry on their lucrative trade for as long as they paid bribes to police. Wainer's zealotry, compassion and media showmanship led to a 1970 Victorian parliamentary inquiry that did much to expose the dark underside of the abortion business – and resulted in the successful prosecution of several senior policemen – even as it condemned Wainer's credibility as a witness and labelled him a 'grandstander'.[107] In what became known as his 'Winter Offensive' of 1969, Wainer extended his campaign to Sydney, where it was obvious that racketeering also flourished. Soon fearing for his life, the crusader installed a bomb alarm system in his car among other precautions for his personal safety.[108]

A few well-educated middle-class people here and there, less flamboyantly, were also trying to bring to abortion law and practice a greater measure of humanity. Sydney's Wayside Chapel had been quietly assisting women to get abortions since 1964, and from around this time an Abortion Law Reform Association (ALRA) or similar body emerged in all of the states and Canberra.[109] The movement towards the legalisation of abortion in Britain, ultimately achieved through an act of parliament in 1967, provided encouragement, as did shifting public opinion at home. Surveys of the late 1960s and early 1970s indicated that an overwhelming majority believed abortion should be allowed in some circumstances. Even among Catholics there was divergence from their own church's hard line.[110]

The earliest legislative initiatives occurred in WA where a physician and Liberal Party member of the Legislative Council, Gordon Hislop, introduced three unsuccessful private member's bills in 1966, 1968 and 1970. In neighbouring SA, a new law in 1969 provided that a termination was legal if two doctors certified that birth was a risk to the mother's mental or physical health.[111] The right to an abortion, however, was still severely restricted and services were inadequate, not least because the legislation stipulated that the procedure could be carried out only in registered hospitals.[112] For Tasmanian women, abortion provision remained so poor in the 1980s that a trip to Melbourne was nearly obligatory for anyone wanting to terminate a pregnancy.[113]

The Australian Medical Association showed little enthusiasm for a frontal assault on a system that was allowing some of its members to earn vast fortunes at the expense of vulnerable women; however, a few individual doctors were active in challenging the law, sometimes through the ALRA. Some were remarkably frank in recognising abortion as a dirty but necessary business. One full-time abortionist explained that 'to terminate a pregnancy is not a normal way of dealing with the problem. It is a crude way. ... The first time I terminated a pregnancy was quite a moment, just as the first time I killed a man in war was a big moment. But you get over the first instinctive hurdle ... against destroying a living thing. You have a conviction ... that you are doing what has to be done'.[114] Another doctor who supported liberalisation admitted that he still found 'abortion a distasteful operation, particularly once foetal parts are recognizable'.[115] General practitioners routinely referred patients to well-known abortionists – sometimes in return for kickbacks – or they performed the operation themselves. But the lack of legal clarity remained worrying for the many even as it allowed the few to enrich themselves.[116]

In Melbourne, a late 1960s police crackdown led directly to the breaking of this impasse. In raids on surgeries, women were seized from operating tables, and had their vaginas photographed and medical records confiscated. They were also blackmailed into giving evidence against abortionists.[117] But as a direct result, the prosecution of a leading abortionist, Dr Ken Davidson, resulted in the Menhennitt judgment of May 1969. In this landmark case, Justice Menhennitt ruled that abortion was legal where 'necessary to preserve a woman from the serious danger to her life or her physical or mental health ... which the continuance of the pregnancy would entail'.[118] In NSW, a police operation along similar lines led to the Levine judgment of 1971, which further extended the boundaries to include the effects on a woman's mental health of economic and social factors.

These cases in Australia's two most populous states, when combined with the SA legislation, created a more permissive environment for abortion. But in Victoria, reformist doctors complained late in 1971 that the Menhennitt judgment had little real impact.[119] In Queensland, with its deeply conservative and corrupt government led by a devout Lutheran, the first abortion clinic was opened in Brisbane in 1979, thereby inaugurating a campaign of official harassment against doctors and women. The legal status of abortion was still unclear in 1985 when Queensland police raided clinics in Brisbane and Townsville, seizing medical records, a foetus and even some of the plumbing to make their case. Two doctors were later acquitted on the grounds that they had acted in good faith to save the mother's life.[120]

Abortion, more than contraception, is still treated in public debate as a moral issue and in case law, at least, as a medical one. Whereas an adult woman's right to contraception is now largely taken for granted, opponents of abortion contest claims about a woman's right to choose by arguing that from the moment of conception the 'child' achieves a personhood with human rights that need to be balanced against those of the 'mother'. Feminist critics have stressed the continuity between earlier accusations against women of 'race suicide' and conservative complaints of an abortion 'epidemic'.[121]

While early efforts to oppose liberalisation were poorly organised, legislative reform in SA and the landmark cases elsewhere provoked more coherent opposition. The quiet inclusion by the Whitlam government of the termination of a pregnancy on the list of benefits that could be claimed on Medibank, the national health scheme, helped turn abortion into a high-profile issue fought at both the level of national politics and in the more limited jurisdictions of the states and territories. 'Pro-life' associations began appearing in the early 1970s and anti-abortionists have done their best to wind back the legal clock. So hostile were some anti-abortionist tactics that the Royal Women's Hospital in Melbourne took out an injunction in 1986 that banned Right to Life protesters from coming anywhere near the building.[122]

While the Catholic hierarchy and right-wing Christians have been the mainstay of opposition to abortion, other conservatives have sometimes attacked abortion as part of a broader assault on feminism. In the same year as Right to Lifers were banned from the Royal Women's

Hospital, Lauchlan Chipman, a philosopher, complained in the conservative magazine *Quadrant* about US feminists who

> squeal that women will be forced back to the backyard abortionist and the side street butchers. They won't be forced there at all. With the exception of rape victims, they were not forced to have sexual intercourse. They were educated at public expense about contraception, and in many high schools in poor districts contraceptives were … provided free. There are (regrettably …) publicly funded benefits for unmarried mothers. If, with all this, she decides to have her pregnancy terminated by a backyard butcher, that is not force. It is a paradigm case of a woman exercising her right to choose.[123]

Some feminist scholars argue that campaigns against abortion have led to the restriction or even withdrawal of access to services for many Australian women. Yet despite periodic conservative claims about public opinion having turned, there is little support for a greater legal stringency.[124]

### From Prostitutes to Sex Workers

The sexual libertarianism of the 1960s and 1970s had contradictory effects on prostitution. The new emphasis on spontaneity, pleasure and freedom seemed at odds with commercial sex. In an era of liberation, why should any man need to pay for sex? Criminologist Paul Wilson, in an early 1970s study, noticed the role of prostitutes in catering for 'the physically and mentally unattractive in our midst who have no other form of sexual outlet'. The prostitute seemed more like a relic than a cadre of sexual revolution. In an era when orgasm was being held up more than ever as the path to individual self-realisation and even revolutionary emancipation, what was one to make of the prostitute who, when questioned about whether she ever had orgasms, replied: 'About once every six nights. It's just one of those things that happen during work?'[125] 'Inside parlours', reported one former prostitute, 'the greatest contempt is reserved for prostitutes who admit to enjoying it, the greatest self-betrayal is to get turned-on with a guy who's paying you'.[126] 'I would not let myself climax with a client', declared another, 'I deliberately hold it back. On the few occasions when I *have* come with a client

I have felt sick. The thought of enjoying it with someone who has paid me ... ugh. I hate it'. Yet some prostitutes not only reported on-the-job orgasms, but increased satisfaction in their work as a result.[127] 'I wasn't there for sexual pleasure', explained Kate Holden, who worked as a prostitute in Melbourne in the 1990s, but '[i]t would be disingenuous to pretend ... that having sex several times a night I didn't notice if it was good'. She initially shared the hostility of many of her fellow sex workers to having orgasms with clients 'but then, as the opportunities appeared and pleasure seemed more possible, I welcomed the rush of it, the pay-off ... But I remained selective; it was still private'.[128]

The liberalisation apparent in other areas of sexuality did not extend to prostitution in the 1960s. Both in Brisbane and Perth the system of tolerated houses came to an end in the late 1950s as police closed down brothels over which they had previously exercised a close, if informal, supervision. By the 1960s only Kalgoorlie retained the old system of containment based on cooperation between brothel managers and police, and severe restrictions on prostitutes' liberties. In Sydney, there would be occasional raids on illegal brothels, especially just before elections as governments advertised dubious 'law and order' credentials. But the regular appearance in the city of thousands of American servicemen on leave from Vietnam also increased demand for paid sex.

At a time in the early 1960s when the old criminal networks that traditionally dominated Sydney prostitution had all but disappeared, supply was being organised by new entrepreneurs. One Maltese migrant, Joe Borg, set up a lucrative business by buying houses and renting them out to prostitutes, using some of his fellow countrymen as muscle. Although popular with the 'girls' because he charged reasonable rates, Borg's activities caused resentment among some of Sydney's more ruthless criminals. In 1968 he was killed by a bomb planted in his car and rigged up to explode when he turned on the ignition. New legislation was passed later in the year, ostensibly to check the expansion of prostitution and deal with the criminal element. And although the new law did close down the most conspicuous brothels, a more significant outcome was a tightening of the criminal syndicates' grip on the sex industry.[129]

In addition to traditional pub-based prostitution, massage parlours, photographic studios, health clubs, saunas, coffee lounges, fruit shops, escort agencies and even hotel flower services were all used for clandestine prostitution. Sometimes controlled by organised crime, massage parlours were especially significant in spreading prostitution to quiet suburbs that had not previously seen brothels. An import from the west coast of the US, the massage parlour did not always sell the coitus that had been stock-in-trade for traditional prostitution in Australia. In the early days, many provided only hand-relief (masturbation) and in some instances 'massage' actually did mean massage, albeit provided by naked or semi-naked woman.[130]

The massage parlour ultimately became emblematic of the sexual revolution not just because of its novelty, but because it was associated with a broadening of sexual services provided by prostitutes, or 'kinky sex'.[131] One woman who worked in such an establishment in the 1970s recalled most clients as businessmen who wanted a 'half-french' – oral sex without ejaculation – followed by coitus.[132] Where prostitution had once centred on 'straight sex', and most women had refused to engage in anything else, from the 1970s clients demanded and many prostitutes provided oral and anal sex as well as other services catering to a bewildering array of tastes. The trend demanded greater versatility from the sex worker. As one woman commented, 'if a fella wants a good old-fashioned naughty well he has it with his wife or his girlfriend. If they want anything else, see that's what the brothels specialise in'. Sex with a prostitute became less about rapid relief of a genital urge, and more about the enjoyment of a performance, an attempt to buy fulfilment of a fantasy. While consistent with the experimentation of the sexual revolution, this shift might also have partly reflected a changing clientele, in which randy young single males were being replaced by middle-aged and older men, such as husbands pursuing sexual experiences unavailable at home. The spread of increasingly explicit pornography also stimulated new patterns of demand, 'educating' some men in new possibilities. But as crime syndicates exercised greater control, prostitutes were also simply less able to resist clients' demands. Where once a woman who performed oral or anal sex might have been attacked by other prostitutes for making these acts more acceptable, such displays of solidarity were now undermined by the dispersal of services from the inner city to the suburbs and the heroin addiction that led many prostitutes to perform acts they traditionally shunned.[133]

While the massage parlours were novel, more traditional means of selling sex continued. The 'aristocrats' were call girls. Sometimes, they worked out of flats in fashionable suburbs, picking up clients by word-of-mouth and maintaining a list of 'regulars' that ensured a good and fairly safe living. Or they might leave their number with a friendly employee of a hotel or restaurant, who would pass it on to a patron requiring their services. Sex in this case would occur on the premises of the client. For women such as these, the likelihood of arrest was minimal. But at the lower end of this segment of the market, women placed advertisements in newspapers willing to accept their custom, thereby announcing their phone number to all and sundry and increasing the chances of crank-callers and arrest.[134]

At the other end of the status hierarchy were women who hung around pubs, taking drinkers upstairs or out the back for a quickie. In between were the streetwalkers who, although subject to regular arrests by police and violence from some of their clients, continued to ply their trade in difficult times in places such as St Kilda in bayside Melbourne or Sydney's Kings Cross. Some turned to the car in order to solicit clients, but the arrests continued. There were now calls for decriminalisation from civil libertarians, who argued in familiar terms about rights to privacy; but also from feminists, who came round to the view that the oppression of prostitutes, in its dependence on stereotypes of 'good' and 'bad' women, contributed to *all* women's oppression. While legal changes in some Australian states made the prostitute's client liable to punishment, feminists correctly pointed out that in practice the law fell most heavily on women.[135]

Since the 1970s the Australian states and territories have adopted a bewildering variety of legislative strategies for dealing with prostitution. While neither SA nor WA decriminalised at all, Victoria legislated a system of brothel licensing in the mid-1980s at the same time as increasing penalties for street prostitution. But the difficulties of getting official permission to run a brothel, which increased in the mid-1990s, have ensured that most Victorian prostitutes still operate in illegal houses or on the street. NSW adopted a different approach in virtually decriminalising (in 1979), and then partly re-criminalising (in 1983), street-soliciting. In the mid-1990s brothels were effectively legalised, provided they were located discreetly, although in recent years some parliamentarians have tried to bestow more power on local councils to block applications. After massive police corruption was exposed in Queensland in the late 1980s, a new government there responded with harsh laws against both brothels and street-soliciting, but a more relaxed approach to self-employed prostitutes which was later extended to small 'boutique' brothels. There was now a growing tendency to refer to prostitution as an 'industry', and to prostitutes as 'sex workers', partly in recognition of the rights of prostitutes who now included transsexuals, men catering to other men, and men catering to women. In 1996, when the Australian Liquor, Hospitality and Miscellaneous Workers Union began organising them, Australia probably became the first country in the world where prostitutes were unionised.[136]

During the AIDS crisis (see chapter 9), sex workers were identified as a group at serious risk despite the lack of evidence for any infection from this source, thereby continuing a long-standing tradition of seeing prostitutes as a source of contagion. Nevertheless, AIDS added weight to arguments for decriminalisation, so that the threat to public health sex work presented might be met through consultation and cooperation. In the context of AIDS and decriminalisation, prostitutes found it easier to insist that their clients adopt safe practices, notably by using condoms. The negative stereotype of the prostitute as selfish, irresponsible and even half-demented, gave way to a more positive image of the 'sex worker' as a responsible self- and other-regarding working woman.[137] Nevertheless, this attitude did not extend so far in relation to street-walkers, who remained associated in public attitudes and official policy with danger, dirt and disease. It was primarily the brothel worker who was the 'responsible and clean professional'. She, and not the street-walker, was the student using prostitution to pay her way through university, or the mother of two saving up to give her kids a future.[138] Her clients, moreover, were now less likely to be thought of as pathological and recent research would indeed suggest that prostitutes' customers form 'a broad cross-section of men who do not stand out from most other Australians'. About half were between their mid-twenties and forty, most of the others older.[139] Sixteen per cent of men have paid for sex at some time in their lives, but only one per cent of women.[140]

By the 1990s globalisation was reshaping the sex industry. Disembodied forms of sex, delivered on the telephone or the internet, were now an increasingly significant part of the industry. Raelene Frances has also pointed to Australia's place in an international trade that took Australian men on visits to Asian capitals on sex tours, as well as bringing Asian women to Australia to work in often highly exploitative circumstances at the same time as it allowed them to earn a better living than at home.[141] But even in Kalgoorlie the local and the particular were being transformed by forces beyond the community's control. As late as the mid-1990s, one brothel madam there continued to defend that town's containment policy on the grounds that '[t]his is a small town. What happens when one of our clients is taking his wife out for dinner and he looks across the table to see one of our girls waving happily at him? There could be absolute hell to pay'. Both madams and prostitutes had managed to hold the taxman at bay until the 1970s but by then the outside world was closing in on what had been a cosy local racket. Even oral sex made its appearance in the 1970s, in a town renowned for clients who liked it plain and simple. AIDS, court decisions, a nationwide movement for reform of the sex industry and burgeoning agitation for sex workers' rights broke down the sense of prostitution in Kalgoorlie being a law unto itself. In 1995, a quarter of a century after the emergence of Women's Liberation, the town's prostitutes were finally allowed to live in private accommodation and socialise in local hotels.[142]

*Censorship and Pornography*

There had been an overhaul of censorship machinery, accompanied by some liberalisation, in the late 1950s. The federal government created a Literature Censorship Board to consider imported literary works, with the implication that the Minister for Customs would accept its advice, and the department also now had to make public the titles of prohibited publications. In this period, 'almost no significant books were banned', with Nabokov's *Lolita* an exception on the grounds that it would encourage men to seduce teenage girls. From 1960 university libraries could gain permission to buy prohibited books required by their students, but an application from the English Department at the Australian National University to import a library set of *Lolita* was rejected. *Lady Chatterley's Lover* was also banned in the early 1960s, despite a recommendation to the minister from the Literature Censorship Board that it be admitted. Bans on such 'literary' works became rare, if widely publicised.[143]

Liberals initially focused on works with literary merit and argued cautiously that mature adults, being rational creatures, could decide what they would and would not read or view.[144] From the early 1960s, academics, students, writers and intellectuals campaigned against a system that increasingly attracted ridicule. In an age of greater openness about sex, the momentum appeared to be on the side of the anti-censorship lobby. In mid-1963 the Sydney Central Court of Petty Sessions dismissed a charge against a man for having an obscene carving from the Sepik River area of New Guinea in the window of his shop. Press reports were reticent about what had offended the passing constable, but it was actually a vessel in the form of a crouching man, with a penis running from between his legs up into his mouth. This sturdy and substantial member formed a most useful handle for anyone wishing to pour water out of the jug. The magistrate recognised that the carving depicted 'a perverse act' and was in 'extremely bad taste', but ruled that it was not obscene because a statue, unlike a painting or photo, was 'cold in character' and therefore unable to stimulate those vulnerable to the corruption of their morals.[145] In the same year, when a group of Adelaide churchmen complained about a panel discussion on a television program at which a speaker had advocated contraception for schoolgirls, James Darling, the chairman of the ABC, replied: 'That doesn't worry me in the least.'[146]

By the mid-1960s Australia's system of censorship was disintegrating. In an already diverse society undergoing rapid changes in sexual mores, the idea of agreed community standards was absurd. Local publishers, moreover, increasingly produced works that were likely to incur the wrath of the customs department if imported, thereby placing additional pressure on state authorities. Some critics of censorship now asserted more boldly that not only should works with 'artistic' merit be allowed, but sexually explicit material should be available to adults who wanted it. Access to material traditionally suppressed as pornography would, they argued, help educate people about sex and assist them to develop normal – that is, heterosexual – 'interest and practice'. A few radicals went further again in seeing censorship of sex as part of a broader 'sexual repression, maintained through the authoritarian family and monogamous marriage in a capitalist society'.[147]

The young anti-censorship campaigner who made this argument, Wendy Bacon, edited the University of New South Wales newspaper, *Tharunka*, and later an underground paper called *Thor*. Bacon was educated in an exclusive Melbourne private school and then Melbourne

University where she 'fucked because it was anti-establishment to do so'. No one she knew talked much about sex and she had not yet heard of an orgasm. All of this changed when she went to Sydney where in the Push she met people more open and straightforward about sex and relationships and 'it made a dramatic difference to the enjoyment I experienced when fucking'.[148] Bacon deliberately provoked censorship authorities by publishing sexually explicit verse and articles, and regularly found herself in court. 'Just as I had once started fucking to flout social disapproval,' she explained, 'my interest in pornography was stimulated by the opposition we received'. In 1970 several people associated with the production of *Tharunka* found themselves charged with having published an issue containing the poem 'Cunt is a Christian Word'. Outside court on the day of the hearing, Bacon herself was arrested for wearing a nun's habit bearing a line suggested by the poem in question – 'I Have Been Fucked By God's Steel Prick' – and for distributing a reprint. She was later found guilty of the first charge, not guilty of the second, and fined $100 and placed on a two-year good behaviour bond.[149]

In film in the early 1970s, there was a move away from censorship towards classification, with the adoption of the R (restricted) certificate which, for the first time, prohibited anyone under eighteen from seeing certain films but legalised the screening of such films for adults. At the state level, acts of suppression continued. Sex was being dealt with much more explicitly in public – and not just in the student newspapers and fringe magazines which had been defying Australia's censorship laws. Commentators noticed a 'pornography boom', with the emergence of a mass commercial sex industry centred on increasingly explicit and usually imported magazines, sex aids, film screenings, strip shows and the massage parlour with its expanded 'menu' to cater to the needs of the modern, sexually liberated client.[150]

During 1972 shops devoted specifically to the sale of porn opened in several cities, accompanied by official concern about how to deal with hardcore material and the proliferation of sex shops and massage parlours.[151] Bacon made a backhanded tribute to the new openness when she remarked that you could now enter a sex shop in Sydney and buy a magazine containing 'a picture of a lady with the largest cunt you have ever seen', but still with 'exactly the same come-hither look' as she had 'when you could only see her tits'.[152] There was also nudity on stage, as in the musical *Hair*, and in the mainstream cinema, while from 1972 the risqué television series *Number 96* broached previously forbidden topics such as homosexuality. Four-letter words also crept into film and TV, although Graham Kennedy's famous crow-call – 'Faaaaark!' – led to his brief suspension from the airwaves in 1975.[153] New women's magazines offered their liberated female readers male centrefolds and sex advice, while *Forum: The International Journal of Human Relations*, which was based on a British original, took the sexual revolution further, publishing articles on everything in sex from fellatio through to female masturbation, ejaculation control techniques, pornography, cunnilingus, swinging, prostitution, anal sex and genital variations – the latter fully illustrated with an impressive gallery of orifices and appendages. Its letters page was even more wide-ranging, and a powerful testament to the sexual experimentation and openness unleashed in the permissive society; at least among the kinds of folk who read magazines about 'human relations'. The magazine's editorial consultant was 23-year-old Bettina Arndt, then researching female masturbation; she would soon become the country's best known media 'sexpert'.

The political right attacked the sexual revolution for its promotion of divorce, abortion, broken homes, homosexuality, rape and pornography.[154] Peter Coleman, who had written extensively about censorship and argued for liberalisation in the 1960s, came to believe by the mid-1970s that the mass market in pornography was degrading human relationships and that radicals such as Bacon were using the censorship issue as part of a revolutionary attack on authority.[155] The 'sexual revolution', said one conservative, had led to an alarming 'moral confusion and social fragmentation'.[156]

The limits of the new libertarianism, insofar as it related to pornography, were clarified in the late 1970s and early 1980s. With some uncertainty at first, in the second half of the 1970s liberals modified their view that adults had a right to view whatever they wished in private when they accepted that child pornography should be prohibited. Similarly, the growing availability in the early 1980s of pornographic videos that could be screened in one's own home posed a new challenge to Australia's classification system. By this time, feminist arguments that pornography oppressed women were influencing public debate.[157] Pornography, they said, expressed men's power over women in sexual relations. It encouraged men to see women as sex objects. It was sexual harassment and discrimination. It caused violence against women.[158] These ideas exercised some influence over the national debate concerning sexually explicit videos. All states except Queensland had agreed in 1983 to an X classification for pornographic films showing actual – as opposed to simulated – sex. Subsequent debate focused on those films that combined sex with violence, which would be refused classification entirely. In the meantime, in response to a concerted campaign by conservative anti-porn campaigners, the states decided to ban rather than classify X-rated videos. Today, Australians who wish to buy X-rated videos mainly have to do so by mail order from the ACT or the NT. But they do so in large numbers. Thirty-seven per cent of men and 16 per cent of women are likely to have watched an X-rated film in any particular year.[159] As in the case of the smaller number who buy sex from prostitutes, some researchers insisted that 'consumers of pornography are like you and me', unrepresentative of the general population of adult Australians only in being overwhelmingly male. Yet even this was changing, with female consumers making up a growing proportion of the market.[160]

Where sexual libertarians of the 1960s and 1970s saw porn's potential in promoting (male) heterosexual adjustment or revolutionary politics, a new generation of libertarian feminists that emerged in the 1990s, largely centred on Sydney, praised a non-violent, feminist-influenced porn's capacity to liberate both men's and women's sexuality. They criticised the puritanical features of anti-porn feminism, and pointed out that such women found themselves arguing a similar case to those conservative Christians who wished 'to abolish abortion, criminalise homosexuality and dismantle feminism'.[161] Yet many activists of the Women's Liberation era – long before these self-proclaimed 'sex-positive feminists' of the 1990s – had recognised the complexity of pornography as an issue for feminists, refrained from advocating censorship, and were at pains to explain the differences between conservative Christians and feminists when each contemplated sexuality.[162]

At the beginning of the twenty-first century, there were criticisms from some libertarian feminists of a government censorship that was eroding women's hard-won sexual freedoms. Germaine Greer's early 1970s condemnation of 'cunt-hatred' was echoed by complaints in the late 1990s that in order to be passed by the Office of Film and Literature Classification as fit for distribution – in anything other than a sealed plastic bag – pictures of women's vaginas were being 'healed to a single crease'. Moreover, new guidelines introduced for X-rated videos in 2000 meant that various fetishes such as body-piercing, bondage, spanking, fisting, the application of candle wax and 'golden showers' (urination on another's body) were prohibited even when consensual.[163]

There are echoes of the libertarianism of Bacon and Greer – both Sydney Push women – in much of this recent feminist writing.[164] Yet public discussion of feminism and sexuality in the 1990s often laid more emphasis on generational difference and discontinuity. The controversy surrounding the work of another libertarian feminist who came to prominence in the 1970s was a lightning rod for debate about these matters. Helen Garner's 1995 book *The First Stone* explored in a semi-fictional genre a scandal at Melbourne University in which the Master of a residential college was alleged by two students to have fondled them at a social event. Garner argued that unlike the libertarianism of her generation, it was *younger* women who had become straight-laced, puritanical and punitive.[165] In a speech given after the publication of the book, she 'invited' young feminists to

> get real ... [T]o dress to display your body, and then to project all the sexuality of the situation on to men and blame them for it, just so you can continue to feel innocent and put-upon, is dishonest and irresponsible ... If a woman dresses to captivate, she'd better learn to keep her wits about her, for when the wrong fish swims into her net.[166]

Many feminists of Garner's vintage condemned her presentation of this case, suggesting that there was something more complex than mere intergenerational difference at play. The historian Ann Curthoys claimed that Garner was simplistic in her portrayal of intergenerational warfare among feminists and had trivialised the problems of dealing with sexual harassment.[167] After a period in which feminists had been able to celebrate the achievement of much legislation in the 1980s that outlawed sexual discrimination and harassment, it was easy to see evidence of backlash or counter-revolution in these often bitter debates.[168]

*Conclusion*

Was sexual liberation really the road to freedom in a competitive society marked by large inequalities based on class, gender and race? It was at least arguable that so long as these continued, sexual freedom would simply provide new opportunities for large corporations to multiply their millions by exploiting Australians' desire – carefully cultivated by clever advertising – to be sexier than their next-door neighbour. And what of Aboriginal people? What of migrants? The sexual revolution always seemed a very 'Anglo' affair, with the supposedly 'traditional' sexualities of other ethnic and racial groups readily cast as a barrier to liberation.[169] Premarital virginity, for instance, clearly retained its cultural significance for many Southern European migrant families in Australia some time after it had declined in significance for most 'old Australians'. It was reported in the mid-1970s that some Greek-Australian girls were being brought to doctors and 'backyarders' not for abortions, but for hymen restoration operations.[170] Meanwhile, Aboriginal people who had experienced the dislocation of domestic life caused by colonialism were unlikely to find attractive visions of sexual liberation based on a rejection of the bourgeois model of the family.

Class, too, seemed to some liberationists to stand in the way of their long march. In some respects, this suggestion seems odd since, as we have seen in earlier chapters, many working-class people before the 1960s displayed a freer sexuality than all but a bohemian fragment of the middle class. Indeed, one view of the 1960s sexual revolution is of the spread of the sexual mores of this section of working-class youth to an ever wider circle of people, including the young middle class, through the growing influence of mass consumer culture, the declining sway of the churches, and under cover of more reliable and accessible contraception. Yet Germaine Greer claimed that the revolution had made little impact on the working class, who did not practice cunnilingus and were 'still sexually deprived … deeply romantic about the family and … monogamy … deeply sadistic in their expressions of overt sexuality … The permissive society hasn't included the poor or the ugly or the old, and they are still the majority'.[171] Ugliness, and perhaps even poverty and age, were to some extent in the eye of the beholder, but Greer's comments are a reminder that the liberationists' claims to sexual freedom for all sat uneasily beside the realities of difference and diversity in modern Australian society.

Yet lives had also been transformed for the better by the changes that swept over Australian society in the years after 1960. If the revolution in birth control inaugurated by the pill and legal abortion subjected women to the disciplines of the clinic, it also provided the opportunity for an unprecedented sexual and social freedom. And a more open treatment of sex at almost every level of society helped bring an end to the kind of sexual ignorance that had been customary, especially for women, earlier in the century. The sexual revolution left 'a space and a language to speak about sex in a positive and optimistic way'.[172] It had placed sexuality at the very core of identity and if this had the potential to 'weigh like a nightmare on the brain of the living', it could also provide many Australians with a new sense of freedom, pleasure and belonging.

# CHAPTER 9

# *Toleration, Liberation, Backlash*

## *A Kinder Future*

It is 1958, and a criminal law lecture at Sydney University has turned to the vexed subject of 'unnatural offences': 'Whoever commits the abominable crime of buggery, or bestiality, with mankind, or with any animal, shall be liable to penal servitude for fourteen years.' A first-year student, not yet twenty,

> felt the blood rushing to my face. I shuffled my papers. I looked down. Do any of them know? I asked myself. I hope they cannot guess. I could not bear the shame. I should be very, very quiet. Then, maybe, no-one will ever know. No-one will ever guess. I will get through life alone and sexless. But I would rather die than be seen on the front page of the *Mirror*.[1]

More than forty years later, the law student is a High Court Judge. It is the opening ceremony of the sixth Gay Games in Sydney. In front of thousands of spectators and athletes, he delivers the keynote speech, joining with those present 'in the hope and conviction that the future will be kinder and more just than the past':

> Little did my partner Johan [van Vloten] and I think, thirty years ago, as we danced the night away at the Purple Onion, less than a mile from this place, that we would be at the opening of a Gay Games with the Queen's representative and all of you to bear

witness to such a social revolution. Never did we think we would be dancing together in a football stadium. ... [I]f an angel had tapped us on our youthful shoulders and told us of tonight we would have said 'Impossible'. Well, nothing is impossible to the human spirit.

'There will be no U-turns', Michael Kirby predicted.[2]

At the time Kirby was dancing with his partner in the early 1970s, a Sydney doctor, Harry Bailey, was still performing brain operations to help gay men make 'a heterosexual adjustment'. More commonly, practitioners applied hormone and aversion therapies in an effort to 'cure' homosexuality. In aversion therapy, the doctor induced nausea and administered electric shocks from a terminal attached to the patient's neck while screening homosexual films and slides. With an impeccable but cruel logic, heterosexual images would then be shown unaccompanied by drugs or shocks. In some cases, doctors 'cured' the patient's 'illness' by reducing their libido with synthetic oestrogens – an ironic adaptation of a drug more conventionally used to support heterosexual relationships through oral contraception.[3]

While many doctors argued that homosexuality should be treated as a neurosis rather than a sin or crime, a survey published in 1968 found that almost four-fifths of Australians believed that sex in private between consenting males ought to remain a criminal offence. The criminologists who reported these results justly described the 'prognosis for reform' as 'dismal'.[4] As late as 1967, the *Medical Journal of Australia* could still discuss male homosexuality as the 'most prevalent of the sexual deviations' and a way of life that was 'intrinsically lonely and unsatisfying'.[5] But five years later, the Australian and New Zealand College of Psychiatrists issued a clinical memorandum that reported homosexuality was 'not necessarily or commonly associated with neurotic symptoms' but rather 'compatible with good adjustment and a useful and creative contribution ... to society'.[6] Much had happened in that time to transform both the experience of homosexuality and public attitudes towards men and women who lived it.

This chapter will trace the changes that have occurred in the lives of homosexual men and lesbian women in the years since 1960. Like the previous one, it will suggest that while there have been some important continuities such as the persistence of a powerful strain of homophobia, these changes have been truly dramatic. Although gay men and lesbian women continue to experience oppression and discrimination in Australia today, they also enjoy a degree of acceptance and freedom within a heterosexual hegemony that would have been unthinkable in the 1960s. The achievement is something more substantial than the mere tolerance anticipated by liberal law reformers of the 1960s and 1970s, if also less sweeping than the utopian dreams of gay liberationists. Gays and lesbians have been understandably sensitive to signs of a backlash since the breakthroughs of the 1970s and early 1980s, yet anti-gay political mobilisation has been mainly unsuccessful in curbing the gay community's visibility and freedom. In contrast with the late 1960s, most Australians today regard gay or lesbian orientation as a legitimate lifestyle in a more sexually pluralistic society.[7] Indeed, by the early years of the twenty-first century, child sexuality had largely superseded homosexuality as a site of anxiety. While public panic about paedophilia had initially scapegoated the 'predatory' male homosexual, new fears had arisen by the early twenty-first century that no longer belonged to a homophobic agenda.

### From Camp to Gay

In 1972 Dennis Altman, the Australian gay activist, academic and author, called the recently released 'ocker' film *The Adventures of Barry McKenzie* 'the most vicious anti-homosexual film of all time'. He reported that a friend had emerged from the cinema 'scared of being physically assaulted in the street by his fellows in the audience'.[8] Hostility to homosexuality was indeed firmly embedded in Australian culture. Some Australian men still regarded the presence of a 'poofter' in a public place as a standing provocation for a beating or worse. And 'worse' happened late one evening in 1972 when George Duncan, a law lecturer at the University of Adelaide, was assaulted and thrown in the Torrens River. Duncan drowned, and it was soon clear that policemen had killed him.[9]

The Duncan killing increased public sympathy for homosexuals and awareness of the hardships they faced in their daily lives, helping also to galvanise the emergent gay rights movement and liberal advocates of law reform.[10] Arguments for change appeared in the student press, as well as in 'quality' magazines and newspapers, while some doctors, lawyers, judges and even a few clergymen made the case for decriminalisation. Sex between consenting adults in private, they argued, was no business of the state.[11] Meanwhile, the exaggerated heterosexual aggressiveness of Australian men – once celebrated as part of the Australian legend but by the 1970s often parodied as 'ocker-ism' – prompted suggestions in cultural commentary that one found in Australia 'latent homosexuality on an astounding scale'.[12] Mateship received renewed attention from intellectuals: Dennis Altman quoted a man featured in an Australian television program on pack-rape – 'The real fun is doing it with your mates' – as 'a classic statement of oppressed homosexuality and its very sad and severe consequences for this society'.[13]

In 1970 a new and openly homosexual political organisation called the Campaign Against Moral Persecution (CAMP) was formed in Sydney by John Ware, a male homosexual, and Christabel Poll, a lesbian. CAMP rapidly developed into a national organisation of about 1500 members, while its cautious Melbourne branch opted for the more cryptic and less provocative title of Society Five – referring to the five aims of its original program and the 5 per cent of the population thought to be homosexual.[14] CAMP's methods, rhetoric and assumptions initially bore a passing resemblance to the liberals'. The keynote was homosexuals' 'normality': CAMP rejected their image as 'freaks, mental defectives, dangerous perverts, or all three'.[15] On the contrary, Ware assured an interviewer, '[t]he typical homosexual' was 'the man living next door to you whom you might know for years until you began to guess the truth'.[16] But not everyone found this approach persuasive or reassuring. One man wrote to a gay magazine complaining that while he was sympathetic to shattering straight stereotypes about gays, his problem was that his 'very nature' made him 'unable to contribute fully towards eradicating this particular misconception':

> You see, I am a self-evident homosexual, that is effeminate, and any attempt by me to endorse the view that most gays look, act, and dress in a similar way to heterosexuals would be a complete waste of time. I would end up by being a walking contradiction, and worse, I would appear and feel apologetic for the way I look.

This complaint was a reminder that in any politics of representation – and perhaps especially in a field as complex as sexuality – there was exclusion as well as inclusion. Social movements did not have a natural constituency but were rather fields in which a variety of fluid identities coexisted, competed, cooperated – and sometimes found themselves marginalised or even ostracised.[17]

Society Five told its members that if it were 'to expand and exert any influence in the Community, it must be seen to be respectable and legitimate' – made up perhaps of people just like Ware's bloke next door – and 'win support from hetrosexual [sic] quarters … so high standards of conduct and morality are urged on all members'.[18] This Victorian-sounding note of prudence might seem a long way from the sexual revolution's reputed freedom and spontaneity. But in challenging the understanding of homosexuality as a sin, crime or illness, CAMP paved the way for more positive images of same-sex love. Rather than a life stalked by secrecy, sadness and tragedy, it imagined a 'normal' existence for both homosexuals and lesbians: something closer, perhaps, to what gay men and women understood as ordinary heterosexual experience. In sum, their lives should no longer be shadowed by 'the continual fear of exposure, blackmail, being beaten up, robbed and ridiculed'.[19] Why should homosexuals hesitate before showing affection in public? Why should they feel any more inhibited at work in referring to their homosexuality than heterosexuals felt in wearing a wedding ring?[20] At a time when two men could still be arrested for kissing in a public place, these were not trivial concerns but went to the heart of homosexual claims to equality and a satisfying quality of life.[21]

Like other social movements of the 1970s, gay liberation had to negotiate a balance between sameness and difference, immediate goals and utopian dreams. In an especially vivid illustration of the kind of citizenship envisaged by these activists, Poll explained in 1970 that CAMP wanted a world in which 'people's sexual and emotional preferences are no more relevant than the colour of their eyes'.[22] As they articulated their rights in the 1970s, homosexuals habitually made these kinds of comparisons, suggesting that being homosexual was really rather like being left-handed, or having hair of a certain colour. Or it would be; if only society rid itself of its prejudices.[23] Even Altman in public advocate mode could sound a bit like a liberal. As he told an audience of ABC viewers in mid-1972, 'What I really want is for homosexuals to have the same sorts of freedoms that heterosexuals have'.[24] Yet to argue thus in a society where heterosexuality was widely understood as 'natural' was really to envisage something quite radical. In this respect, conservative opponents of gay rights were correct to detect in the movement and moment a revolutionary challenge. Those most vigorous in enforcing 'compulsory heterosexuality' were perhaps better able to see where all this talk of equality and freedom was leading than well-meaning liberals who saw in gays and lesbians only another oppressed minority demanding a fair go.[25]

CAMP did not at first organise demonstrations and protests. It focused instead on the challenges of 'coming out' – that is, offering support for those who took the still bold step of openly declaring their homosexuality – promoting the rational public discussion of homosexuality, and lobbying for changes in the law. Yet notwithstanding its attachment to the liberal model of cautious reform, CAMP pioneered the idea that homosexuals needed to be out and proud if they were to have any real hope of a political breakthrough.[26] A newsletter produced by Society Five linked the personal and political very explicitly, seeing acceptance of one's own homosexuality as the key to a wider transformation in attitudes:

> Hiding our sexuality suggests we are ashamed and afraid of what we are, and only perpetuates the ridiculous myths that have been handed down from generation to generation in blissful ignorance. It is fundamentally up to us to educate people. Let other people see that we are normal well-adjusted human beings, proud of our sexuality and human dignity, and not just a bunch of repressed queens.[27]

These men and women stressed the shared humanity and citizenship between homosexuals and heterosexuals but were moving towards a more ambitious politics. CAMP promoted pride in a gay identity alongside its provision of counselling services, such as Phone-a-Friend for those struggling to come to terms with their sexual orientation. In Melbourne, Society Five also ran a telephone counselling service, as well as pressing for law reform, providing legal and medical referral services, and acting as a forum for the exchange of ideas. Eventually settling into city premises after its Carlton clubrooms were wrecked by a firebug, it housed a dance floor and coffee bar, games area, television room and well-stocked library with reading lounge.[28] Here was the basis for a new form of homosexual sociability, one that was at once private and public, personal and social, discreet yet open.

Organisations such as CAMP and Society Five were sometimes a homosexual's first point of contact with the gay world: they routinely dealt with men and women who were frightened, confused or both. Those who contacted Society Five's secretary in Melbourne included lonely and depressed teenagers, some fresh from a failed relationship with someone of the 'opposite' sex; men and women in their twenties still coming to terms with their sexuality, for whom life was 'lonely & confusing'; the male transvestite who 'would love a man to cook & sew for and look after'; the gay man arrested in a public toilet for loitering with intent; and old-age pensioners, such as the Geelong man looking for 'a clean living chap like myself', or the former Melbourne teacher living in a retirement village who had become 'a chopping-block for frustrated widows'. Many were country people – sometimes married with children – who knew of no homosexuals and sought advice about where they might find them. One young woman living in a NSW country town told the Society Five secretary:

> I' am a very lonely 'bitch' aged 21 year's & yearning for someone to love me ... I haven't many interest's in life but know if the right person came into my life I could learn to love any interest's she might have ...
>
> So if you could be of any assistance at all, I' will include you most certainly in my prayer's.

A middle-aged woman living in North Queensland had her hobbies and friends but found herself 'now just simply missing being with people who talk my language ... It's just simply I'd love to sit down and relax with my kind of people. I find myself thinking how nice it would be to go to a party where I could get up and dance with a girl instead of waiting for some man to ask'. Similarly, a Geelong man in his twenties had friends and activities to keep him busy but only at the price of setting aside a part of himself, a difficulty that even their acceptance of his homosexuality could not overcome: 'The main problem is all my friends are straight. I enjoy their company greatly & appreciated how they have accepted me but I do have many times where I find life sexually very unsatisfying, the reason being I have no camp friends.' He signed off his missive with 'I feel better having written to you as I know you will understand'; and whatever their difficulties, these correspondents received from Society Five's secretary a sympathetic response, even when there was little he could do to help.[29]

The very existence of organisations such as CAMP and Society Five seemed to provide gay men and women with permission to seek a more fulfilling sex life. The boost given to sex for pleasure and companionship by the contraceptive pill and progress in the struggle for abortion rights might also have opened up cultural space for greater experimentation in and acceptance of same-sex relations. Dennis Altman made this connection in his pioneering 1971 study, *Homosexual: Oppression and Liberation*, a book that won him international fame: 'Under the joint impact of technology and the women's movement', he said, 'we are divorcing procreation from sex, and anatomy from role'. Demands for the recognition of homosexuality as a valid form of human relationship seemed 'a logical extension'.[30] Movements such as Women's Liberation and Gay Liberation assumed sexuality as the basis of political identity, mobilisation and rights and rejected the secretiveness that homosexual men and women had previously been forced to endure. In *Homosexual*, Altman presented Gay Liberation as a revolutionary alternative to the tolerance now supported by progressive heterosexual liberals, as well as the older, commercial male homosexual subculture, with its drag queens and 'high premium on momentary and furtive contacts'. Where homosexual men had traditionally been bound together by fear and sexual repression, Gay Liberation was producing 'genuine community' based on pride.[31]

It is not hard to understand the attractions of this approach among men and women struggling to find acceptance in a notoriously homophobic society, yet it created problems of its own. One young gay man complained in 1973 that there was

> almost a ban against getting off with someone else in Gay Liberation … because we have given up the established camp rituals, people just don't get off. And fucking isn't a transcendental thing. You might want to fuck with someone, but you don't dare to approach him, so you get all tense and have another drink.[32]

Another gay male activist of this era recalled that '[p]eople came to meetings wanting to be sluts but the dynamics of the organisation meant you couldn't, really'.³³ Others felt pressure not to 'couple', influenced by Gay Liberation's critique of traditional sex roles. 'It's as if you shouldn't fuck with the same person more than three times a week', complained an obviously frustrated John.³⁴ The 'out and proud' model presented as failures those – often older men and women – whose ways of dealing with their own homosexuality, perhaps carefully negotiated over a lifetime, were unsettled by the openness and assertiveness of the new social movements.

Gay Liberation emerged in Sydney as a distinct organisation when a radical cell of younger student members within CAMP left that organisation in early 1972. A forum on sexual liberation held at the University of Sydney in January, at which both Germaine Greer and Dennis Altman were speakers, was proclaimed by the latter as 'the first appearance … in Australia, of a Gay Liberation group'.³⁵ In these early years 'gay' was an inclusive term that included both men and women, the male homosexual and the lesbian. Following events in Sydney, Gay Liberation groups formed in Melbourne and Adelaide during 1972, and in Perth early in the following year. Melbourne's first gay rights demonstration was provoked by the ABC's cancellation in July 1972 of a current affairs story on Altman's *Homosexual*.³⁶ Protesters captured a sense of the new confidence of the gay moment and, more cheekily, the climate of sexual experimentation of the early 1970s:

> *Two, four, six, eight,*
> *Gay is just as good as straight.*
> *Three, five, seven, nine,*
> *Try it our way just one time.*³⁷

Gay Liberation emphasised the potential fluidity of both sexual behaviours and sex roles once society was liberated by revolution. The idea that all human beings were essentially bisexual was influential, and bisexuality as concept and practice had considerable influence on the sexual radicalism of the period.³⁸ This position created difficult theoretical and practical tensions: if gender roles and sexual identities were artificial – the products of oppressive structures, institutions and values – then 'liberation' would free human beings to be truly human rather than continuing to act the parts in which a repressive society had cast them. But when taken to its logical conclusion, this theory of universal

# THE SEX LIVES OF AUSTRALIANS

bisexuality obliterated the identities on which the politics of liberation rested. Gay Liberation's historic mission was not so much to liberate the homosexual from society's oppression, as to liberate everyone by transcending the artificial differences between the 'homosexual' and the 'heterosexual'.[39] It sought to build community among a long-oppressed sexual minority at the same time as it nurtured a romantic and utopian vision calling for the overthrow of sexual repression. If conventional – and, in their view, artificial – sexual labels and sex roles could be overcome, 'an authentic and liberating sexuality would be revealed'.[40]

### 'Lesbians are Lovely'[41]

In 1960s Australia, there was still limited consciousness of 'lesbianism' as a sexual orientation or of 'the lesbian' as a distinct kind of person. Many young women probably reached adulthood without having heard the word, even if they had vague awareness of the concept. As we have seen in chapter 7, small groups of lesbians engaged in a social life centred on a few sites and organisations, often rubbing shoulders with men who were part of the camp and bohemian world.

Late in 1969 a small group of Melbourne women wrote to the American lesbian organisation known as the Daughters of Bilitis and subsequently set up a group bearing this cryptic name. Its membership was restricted to 'lesbians and female bisexuals 21 years and over' and married women had to produce the written consent of their husbands to belong.[42] In mid-1970, ironically as a means of distancing itself from its more militant American cousin, it changed its name to the very modern-sounding and decidedly unambiguous Australasian Lesbian Movement. In 1970s Melbourne, there was a succession of lesbian organisations, groups, clubs and societies that provided an opportunity for women to socialise, discuss the issues affecting their lives and engage in 'consciousness-raising'. After a 1974 article in a women's magazine on one of these organisations, 'Claudia's Group', it experienced massive, almost overnight growth.[43]

A more politically inclined movement for lesbian rights also emerged during the 1970s, initially alongside gay men in mixed-sex organisations. As many of these women became increasingly dissatisfied with the sexism of some gay men, lesbian feminism developed its own organisational forms and 'women-centred culture'.[44] Robyn

Plaister, a lesbian feminist active in the movement from the early 1970s, recalled that lesbians 'found themselves pushed into a subsidiary role and into being supportive to the men in their push for changes, mainly homosexual rights'.[45] Disagreements also emerged over sexual practice itself. Lesbians were in some cases repelled by the 'promiscuity' of gay men, the assumption that 'fucking a lot' was in itself revolutionary, and gay men's attachment to phallic sexuality and 'beat' life. Male homosexuals, for their part, responded with complaints about 'moralistic' women and made unflattering and unfair comparisons between the attitudes of lesbians and Christian homophobes.[46] At the heart of this divergence was the reality that homosexuals and lesbians had different kinds of erotic lives and different experiences of sexual oppression. It seemed to follow that they also needed different kinds of organisations. Still, many women continued to work alongside men in mixed organisations during the 1970s.[47]

Lesbians were also active in Women's Liberation but here, too, there were tensions. The lesbians who joined Women's Liberation were in a very different position from politically active gay men, who were not required to confront 'hostile heterosexuals' within their own organisations in the way that lesbians sometimes did in the feminist movement. Some lesbians felt that Women's Liberation gave too little attention to their concerns, and even that they were stigmatised by heterosexual women. Yet lesbians provided much of the active membership of Women's Liberation, and they would in due course be prominent in staffing refuges and rape crisis centres.[48]

By 1972 lesbianism was generating its own organisational forms. A CAMP Women's Association (or CWA) – delightfully sharing the same acronym as the venerable and conservative Country Women's Association – was formed in Sydney, while in Melbourne a group calling itself the Radicalesbians, influenced by ideas emerging from Women's Liberation in London, appeared in 1973. Its members called for a 'genderless society', demanded 'liberation' rather than 'equality', and looked forward to the creation of 'a distinct feminist community'. There was suspicion of a sexuality centred on the genitals, for sex was really the '*energy* within all of us'.[49] But the Radicalesbian group, like many lesbian organisations, was short-lived.

Lesbians and their organisations often experienced considerable community hostility. An advertisement containing a telephone number was an open invitation to the crank caller. A Tasmanian community worker reported that any small-town lesbian with 'the intestinal fortitude to express what she is, is immediately trampled by the rush of virile males insisting on showing her the advantages of heterosexual intercourse'.[50] And when a 'Gay Women's Group' began advertising in the *Armidale Express* in 1976 – using just a post office box number and containing the assurance 'All enquiries strictly confidential' – a letter writer in a subsequent issue asked 'why … we have to put up with the advertisement for the Gay Women's Group', adding that '[i]f the Armidale group is as active as the metropolitan ones I fear for our young girls growing up in this city'.[51]

By the 1980s new divisions were beginning to open up among Australian lesbians. The widest were between 'political lesbians', who remained closely associated with liberal and radical feminist campaigns around rape and pornography, and 'sex radicals', who saw themselves as 'putting the sex back into lesbianism'.[52] Like male homosexuality, lesbianism had always posed a direct challenge to the naturalness of heterosexual attraction. As one lesbian put the matter in 1973, 'Even the nicest guys still think that men and women complement each other. And for a guy, a cunt is a nice warm lubricated place for him to come. But it's not the *only* place, not the only way'.[53] Yet by the 1980s there was a growing chorus of complaints about an atmosphere of sex censorship and intolerance among lesbians, a basic confusion of sexism with sex, of penetration with patriarchy. Various forms of fetish, transgression, sexual role-play and performance, including sex with gay men, the consumption of lesbian porn, tattooing, body-piercing, bondage and whipping, were changing the meaning of lesbianism. The 'SM [Sadomasochistic] dykes', as some styled themselves, added an erotic edge to an identity and movement that had become associated with a new puritanism.[54]

### Backlash: Mardi Gras, AIDS and Sexual Counter-Revolution
Polls taken during the 1970s suggested that public opinion was shifting in favour of greater tolerance of gays and lesbians. While it is unlikely that this breakthrough would have occurred without the very public activity of the gay rights movement, it also reflected new attitudes towards sexual privacy. More people were coming to accept the notion

that sexual behaviour between consenting adults was nobody's business but their own, and certainly no proper concern of government.[55] This claim to privacy was a significant manifestation of 'sexual revolution' yet has been underestimated because its roots were in nineteenth-century liberalism rather than late-twentieth-century identity politics. But gay men and women knew that their own sexuality was still widely considered a matter of public concern, and that governments, employers, banks and other organisations discriminated against them. Many found it necessary to maintain their sexuality as a closely guarded secret – to hide their private lives in the workplace, for instance – so as not to bring down on their heads hostility or discrimination. The result might be social isolation, a constant vigilance about revealing too much, or a coldness and reserve that were irritating to others in a society such as Australia where so much value was attached to an easy sociability.

As well as lobbying governments, making submissions to inquiries and working quietly – and sometimes not so quietly – in the churches, schools and universities for a better deal, gay men and women also fought several high-profile cases of blatant discrimination in the mid-1970s. Some activists felt a backlash was gathering momentum and worried that the achievements of the previous decade, as modest as they seemed, would now be wound back. Conservative Christians, in particular, were deeply troubled by public visibility of homosexuality, which they painted as a dire threat to family life. Both in public places, where gay men and women were taunted and bashed, and in the more intimate settings of the family and the workplace, to be gay could still be a traumatic experience. 'I couldn't believe my sexuality could cause so much pain', reflected Tim Conigrave, as he described his parents' efforts to accept his coming out in Melbourne in the late 1970s.[56]

In 1978 Sydney gay and lesbian activists responded to a call from the US for an international day of action to commemorate the famous New York Stonewall Riots of 1969. They organised, for the evening of Saturday 24 June, a street parade or 'mardi gras' in Oxford Street, which was already beginning to overshadow nearby Kings Cross as the centre of Gay Sydney. Amid the revelry some 1000 to 2000 people, many of them in the 'outrageous' costumes they had been encouraged to wear by organisers, emptied out of the bars and assembled for a protest march. They proceeded towards Hyde Park where they encountered the

THE SEX LIVES OF AUSTRALIANS

police. The march then diverted towards Kings Cross and amid brawl-
ing between constabulary and protesters, fifty-three were arrested.
Charges were later either thrown out by the courts or quietly dropped,
but police violence on the evening itself and continuing harassment of
gays in the months afterwards mobilised gay men and women on an
unprecedented scale.[57]

The first gay Mardi Gras opened up 'a whole new period in Australian
lesbian and gay politics'.[58] In particular, there were signs that previously
apolitical cohorts, such as men involved in the burgeoning gay bar
scene, were for the first time being drawn into political involvement.
Gradually, the estrangement between the gay political activist and the
increasingly lively and lucrative commercial gay scene – a gulf which
had helped define early 1970s gay politics – was ending. Gay and lesbian
hotels, discos, nightclubs, booksellers, porn shops, saunas, fuck bars and
other sex-on-premises venues emerged in the major cities through the
1970s to 1990s to cater to gays and, to a lesser extent, lesbians. So, too,
did a lively gay press, with several newspapers and magazines appearing
– and then, often, disappearing – but doing much in the meantime to
create a sense of community. Oxford Street, Sydney, had clothing stores
that catered specifically to a gay clientele tuned into what was *de rigueur*
in San Francisco and New York, but also a 'gay' butcher, ice-cream shop
and even a pharmacy that helpfully sold 'moustache wax and other
gentlemen's grooming aids' to assist gay men in cultivating the butch
appearance that was now fashionable. Sydney became widely recognised as the gay capital of Australia.[59]

Gay venues and shops also emerged in the other capitals and some
regional centres, although provision was sometimes as modest as a single
'gay night' per week at a venue. A group based at Coffs Harbour on the
NSW north coast in the early 1980s met for regular 'picnics, barbecues
and visits to restaurants', including occasional joint events with their
counterparts in Armidale. These men and women aimed for a 'politically
low-key' approach that would 'let coastal gays know that there is a gay
community on the coast which cares about them'.[60] Further south at
Newcastle, and encouraged by local police who presumably wished to
contain the local homosexual population in a single venue, the Star Hotel
made a bar available to a gay and lesbian clientele. It became well known
for its drag shows and was remembered with deep affection by homosexual Novocastrians. One happy lesbian customer recalled:

It was just like a big family. I just walked in the door and everyone was just smiling and happy to see you and asked how you were going. It didn't matter if they didn't know you from a bar of soap … I could go there by myself. And I could go there all day and all night and never, ever feel uncomfortable.

In 1979, when the hotel changed hands and the new licensee decided to clean up the 'hotbed of homos' he had taken over, gay activists picketed the pub.[61]

In tropical Australia, options were more limited. One lonely man wrote to the Society Five from Alice Springs in the mid-1970s seeking help and explaining that '[t]he sense of isolation in a place like this is rather acute'.[62] The scene in Darwin was a little livelier; after Cyclone Tracy in 1974 the Forge Steakhouse was transformed into a nightclub called Dix that ran a gay evening on Mondays and regular drag shows. But Altman was unimpressed by the entertainment on offer when he visited the city some years later. The highlight at the annual gay event held in a local pub, he recalled, was the appearance of an old Sydney drag queen, 'who promptly embarked on a series of racist and sexist jokes'. Still, in the 1980s the local gay community was able to sustain the Boomer Motor Club, a small group which met weekly in members' homes, as well as a Darwin Gay Society that organised a fortnightly event such as a bar night and dance or barbecue. Stonewall Gay Pride Week was held in Darwin for the first time in 1985. When Altman visited Rockhampton in 1993, 'public gay life seemed limited to one night a week at a local pub where two lesbians ran a "gay night" called Club Venus, as reminiscent of the seventies as an Abba revival'.[63] But for gays and lesbians in rural Queensland, where much of the population reviled them, such events could help break down a sense of isolation and vulnerability. By the 1990s gay venues were opening in some of the larger regional towns such as Cairns and Townsville, often established by enterprising Brisbane promoters.[64] And while some gay rights activists worried the movement was 'selling out' to the capitalists, others saw in the new alliances and a commercially viable gay industry an emerging community, or at least the basis for a new sense of belonging.[65]

Gay activists of the early 1970s condemned traditional gender divisions as a key source of homosexual oppression but a decade later new cultural styles imported from the US and embraced by some gay Australian men seemingly accentuated such differences. The 'clone' – in his jeans, tight-fitting shirt and work boots, all encasing a hard muscular body crowned by clipped moustache and short hair – exuded a hyper-masculinity that could seem like a fair impression of an ocker, especially when it was also accompanied by the swilling of beer, ridicule of effeminate male homosexuals, and hostility to women. Some saw in this new enthusiasm for the traditional image of the manly man a concession to the emergent backlash politics of the right; what better way to gain acceptance and get the bullies off your back than to perform a version of masculinity regarded as culturally acceptable? But there also seemed to be a playfulness in the style embraced by these gay men – and, indeed, by the 'lipstick lesbians' who were prominent on the gay scene in the 1990s – that suggested a continuity with the earlier gay movement's questioning of traditional gender roles and images. Some defenders of the clone image celebrated it as a self-confident and public assertion of male homosexuality made possible by Gay Liberation, yet moving beyond the movement's ideological purism.[66] Nonetheless, the stress within the gay 'scene' on youth and beauty raised particular problems for older gay men, who were unable to live up to the ideals of attractiveness increasingly seen to define gayness. Some younger gay men were very intolerant towards the old. As one 75-year-old gay man put it, 'Nobody wants to screw old men. They do not mind being sucked-off by old men. That does not affect them in the way that actually touching them and entering the body of an old man does'.[67]

The new 'macho' culture also contained a strain of racism, which found expression in hostility to Asian men, stereotyped with small penises. 'In today's gay culture it appears that if you can't make someone choke during oral sex you aren't worthy of being gay', complained Kent Chuang, a Sydney gay man born in Hong Kong. Tony Ayres, an Asian-Australian, referred similarly to 'the demoralising feeling that I am, in the eyes of the majority of the gay male population, as undesirable as a woman'. White men attracted to Asians were sometimes dismissed as predatory 'rice queens', being too old and unattractive to get a young white man. The younger Asian men in such relationships were 'potato queens'. Yet the realities of discrimination against Asians meant that there were powerful impulses behind this kind of coupling, as many gay Asians, having internalised the stereotype of the desirable gay man as white, muscular and blond, were reluctant to form relationships among themselves. A few gained acceptance on the gay scene by 'assimilating', which might have included muscling up at the gym, wearing the right kinds of clothes, and, above all, forming a relationship with a young and attractive Anglo-Celtic gay man. Competition between Asian men for the limited number of white men interested in such relationships could be intense, yet paradoxically, Asian men who did show sexual interest in other Asians could receive the epithet 'sticky rice'.[68]

The racism extended to Aboriginal men. '[T]here were many White gays who would not ... be seen walking down the street with an Aboriginal guy', complained one gay Aboriginal man, 'yet these same men wouldn't hesitate to accept a black dick up their arse'. Gay Aboriginal men and women complained of failing to find full acceptance in either the white-dominated gay world or the Indigenous community.[69] Indeed, when the Uniting Church of Australia considered the issue of ordination of gay and lesbian priests at its assemblies in 1997 and 2003, Aboriginal church leaders were prominent among those who opposed the change.[70] But gay groups have formed organisations designed to combat racism and Aboriginal performers have often been prominent at the Gay and Lesbian Mardi Gras.[71]

Mardi Gras, with its potent mix of politics and carnival, epitomised these new and complex fractures, alliances and developments. It has been described as 'the most potent symbol of a change in the politics of desire' and is the country's most public occasion for the performance of a range of 'queer' sexualities.[72] Other Australian cities have had large and successful gay and lesbian festivals, sometimes on a regular basis, but none so popular or spectacular as Mardi Gras, with its colourful floats and costumes, wry humour and cultural confidence. As the festival, including the parade and afterparty, grew in scale and profile – it eventually developed into a month-long program of events – it became even more closely aligned with the commercial Oxford Street gay scene. Meanwhile, as a major tourist event, it has brought millions of dollars into the economy each year and, no doubt partly for this reason, won growing acceptance among heterosexuals. But not everyone in the gay and lesbian community celebrated this transition to something like respectability. Some worried about the apparent evolution of Mardi Gras from an event with a fairly well-defined political agenda into a more diffuse celebration of queerness, a change possibly signified by its controversial removal to the early and warmer time of the year in 1981. And at least one high-profile homosexual man objected to Mardi Gras in principle.

Patrick White and his partner, Manoly Lascaris, met and fell in love in Egypt during the war while White was serving in Royal Air Force intelligence and Lascaris about to enter the Greek army. They moved permanently to Australia in 1948, first living on a small farm at Castle Hill near Sydney, later moving to Centennial Park in the city. By the early 1970s, even before White's Nobel Prize for Literature, they 'were the best-known homosexual couple in the country'.[73] But White refused to openly support the gay rights movement, quipping that he'd 'marched in the streets, but only to get myself a man'.[74] He responded to a request that he offer a message of support for the 1985 celebrations by telling the coordinator that 'as a homosexual I have always detested the Gay Mardi Gras nonsense, particularly since so many non-gay trendies seem to have jumped on the wagon'. 'A lot of screaming queens in Oxford Street will not help the cause for which we shall have to fight', he added in a reference to the AIDS crisis.[75] There are echoes in White's comments of the kinds of objections that 'refined' middle-class homosexuals between the wars had directed at the 'flagrant behaviour' of the 'fairies' and 'queans' in New York and London.[76] It might not be coincidental that White had lived as an expatriate in both cities in the 1930s.

Mardi Gras's political edge, however, has survived, contributed to by continuing discrimination against gay men and women and, ironically, by the politics of the AIDS crisis that so concerned White. As Fiona Nicoll has remarked, if Anzac Day was Australia's 'one day of the year', Mardi Gras has been built up as the 'one night of the year', a national parade that expresses something of the meaning of contemporary Australian life.[77] So central to the meaning of 'gay', 'lesbian' and 'queer' did Mardi Gras become that its decline in the early years of the twenty-first century generated soul-searching about the future of gay culture more generally.[78]

Police harassment of Mardi Gras organisers in the early years derived much of its legitimacy from the continuing illegality of homosexual sex. Of the Australian states only SA had decriminalised homosexuality, in legislation passed in 1975. Earlier legislation, in 1972, had provided limited protection for homosexual acts by allowing men over twenty-one who were hauled before the courts to claim a private and consensual act as a defence.[79] Homosexuality was also decriminalised in the ACT in 1976, but elsewhere, the move towards a more liberal regime appeared to have stalled. A growing number of arrests in Melbourne in 1976–77 and Sydney in 1982–83 helped rejuvenate law reform. Legislation decriminalising homosexual acts passed in Victoria in 1980 and in NSW in 1984.[80] The latter, however, retained a higher age of consent for homosexuals than heterosexuals – it would not be lowered to sixteen, the age that applied to 'straight' sex, until 2003. The homosexual age of consent became an increasingly contentious issue in the 1980s, as opponents of liberalisation sought to associate homosexuality with paedophilia, and the gay rights movement with efforts to promote an 'unnatural' sexual orientation among impressionable youths. These ideas appear to have exercised so much influence on the issue in WA that when its law finally changed in 1990, the homosexual age of consent was set at twenty-one.[81] Decriminalisation also occurred in Queensland at this time but with a peculiar sop to the anxious that legalised male homosexuality for those over sixteen while prohibiting anal sex for anyone under eighteen.[82] That left only Tasmania, where the gay rights movement was galvanised in 1988 by the arrest of 130 of its members at the Salamanca Market in Hobart over several weekends for running a stall. Eventually, activists led by Rodney Croome took the state government all the way to the United Nations Human Rights Committee and in 1994 won a ruling in their favour. In 1997 the Tasmanian Liberal government introduced a bill that, by legalising homosexual acts in the last corner of the nation where they remained a crime, effectively ended a long and tragic chapter in the sexual history of Australia.[83]

By this time, Australia's gay community was already deeply experienced in tragedy of a different kind. Australia's first case of Acquired Immune Deficiency Syndrome (AIDS) was diagnosed in Sydney late in 1982 and reported in May of the following year. The infected man was a visitor from New York. It was quickly noticed in Australia, as in the US, that most of those suffering from the mysterious new disease were gay men. In its early days, the disease was sometimes called the 'Gay Plague', an epithet that reflected and intensified homophobia. There were soon indications within the broader community of panic and discrimination. A schoolteacher and Anglican admitted to me in the mid-1980s that she no longer drank communion wine from the chalice because there were homosexual men in her congregation. Even within the gay community itself, some initially attributed the disease to the 'homosexual lifestyle', suggesting that the male body could only take so much semen from so many different partners.[84] A conservative academic, Geoffrey Partington, attributed AIDS to 'the promiscuous lifestyle among a majority of homosexuals'.[85] This argument also appealed to the conservative clergyman and politician Fred Nile, who laid particular blame on 'the anonymous multiple nature of homosexual perversions'. He called for the closure of all gay bars, discos, bathhouses and saunas, the removal of homosexual teachers from schools, a ban on homosexuals donating blood or semen, and a prohibition on their international travel.[86] While such extreme measures were never seriously contemplated by any Australian government, even today the Red Cross does not permit a blood donation from any man who has had sex with another male in the preceding twelve months. Proposals for mandatory AIDS testing of high-risk groups were popular among heterosexuals in the 1980s. But gay activists argued that this was likely to be counter-productive, creating a false sense of security or even invulnerability among those found to be free of the disease despite previous high-risk behaviour. Compulsory tests would in any case be evaded. They also pointed out that AIDS was blood-borne, so that the kinds of measures used for tuberculosis were not appropriate.[87]

Growing public hysteria was fuelled by sensational media coverage as it became clear during 1984 that HIV-infected blood had been given to some transfusion patients. The director of the Sydney Red Cross Blood Transfusion service called on 'promiscuous homosexuals' to stop donating blood. Already fearing a backlash even before AIDS hit their community, gay men now worried that the crisis was being used to roll back the advances made since the early 1970s.[88] Some commentators detected in the disease the instrument of a sexual counter-revolution that would remake the promiscuous world bequeathed by the 'swinging sixties'.[89] In late 1984 there was further panic when the Queensland health minister announced that three babies had been infected by blood donated by a gay man. 'Die, You Deviate', screamed the headlines of a tabloid newspaper, a sentiment it attributed to the father of one of the babies, who was quoted to the effect 'that the only honourable thing for the murderer' of their child to do was 'commit suicide if he feels as bad about his actions as we are led to believe'.[90] There were even claims that gay men were deliberately contaminating the blood supply. The National Party leader, Ian Sinclair, blamed AIDS on the Hawke Labor government's promotion of homosexuality.[91]

By this stage the federal government was attempting to formulate a strategy for dealing with AIDS. It is indicative of the still marginal nature of gay men and their interests in national politics in the mid-1980s that it took the risk of widespread infection of people *outside* the gay community, through contamination of the blood supply, to get things really moving.[92] Not without controversy or criticism, the Labor government developed an approach that involved members of the gay community working alongside bureaucrats and doctors. Inclusion of community representatives was not always welcomed by professionals, leading to accusations that AIDS policy had been captured by a homosexual clique, but it ensured that policy-making did not become too remote from the realities of everyday life for gay men. Gays were thereby allowed to become instrumental in the effort to save their own lives.[93]

Australia's handling of the AIDS crisis has come to be regarded as an object lesson. Governments mainly rejected a strategy based on mass testing and the isolation of sufferers in favour of a successful campaign to persuade gay men to practise safe sex, through the use of condoms and non-penetrative acts. These campaigns also influenced the broader community, prompting more widespread use of condoms in heterosexual sex as well.[94] In 1987, amid growing fears of infection in the heterosexual community, an advertising campaign depicting AIDS as a ten-pin-bowling Grim Reaper was briefly screened on television. Although criticised by some as an attempt to deflect attention from the connection between AIDS and gay men, Paul Sendziuk has argued that it was an effort by the National Advisory Committee on AIDS 'to manufacture a sense of public urgency' that would persuade governments to give priority to combating the disease.[95] As in the case of fear over the blood supply, the potential impact on heterosexuals was critical. In the hard world of politics, success lay in exploiting the fears of the sexual 'mainstream', not in appealing to its sense of empathy with gay men, sex workers and drug users.

The strategy seemed to have been vindicated by the early 1990s, for AIDS was under control and gay men had modified their sexual behaviour. There had certainly been initial fear and confusion associated with the 'gay lifestyle' theory, and it was reported in 1985 that for many gay men '[p]eriods of celibacy alternate with sexual binges, followed by misery and retreat'. Some male homosexuals, it seemed, believed that they were being told to give up anal sex.[96] Yet, far from ushering in a new puritanism, the AIDS crisis was ultimately used by gay men to assert their sexual rights. As Gary W. Dowsett has argued, the battle for decriminalisation was in large part a battle for the right to engage in sodomy. Not that anal sex was central to the actual sexual practice of all homosexual men; surveys in the early years of the AIDS epidemic found that although most gay men had tried anal sex, only half practised it regularly. Nevertheless, the long-standing association of male homosexuality with a particular sexual act meant that the defence of the right to sodomy had both practical and symbolic dimensions. In these circumstances, a strategy of combating AIDS that undermined the right of gay men to engage in anal sex could not have been anything other than a capitulation.[97]

Yet no such defeat occurred. Rather, a new understanding of gay sexuality emerged in which the quest for pleasure was combined with a novel emphasis on the need for individual responsibility. The image of the hedonistic gay man who lived for instant sexual gratification was powerfully challenged by these new circumstances of the mid-1980s. AIDS politically mobilised a large section of the male homosexual community, and new activities and rituals were devised to cope with the crisis. In the process, AIDS increased the visibility and cohesion of the gay community. Yet the kind of community and activism it encouraged, when mixed with the new 'macho' gay styles and the growing importance of the commercial scene, helped widen the gulf between homosexual men and lesbians.[98]

It also helped gay men find the inspiration and language to convey to a wider audience both the joy and pain of homosexual love, notably through popular memoirs such as John Foster's *Take Me to Paris, Johnny* and Timothy Conigrave's *Holding the Man*.[99] A large part of the cultural significance of these accounts was how, through their adaptation of genres such as romance and tragedy, they reached out to an audience beyond the gay community. They are illustrative of how AIDS, at the same time as it provided homosexuality with greater legitimacy through this universalisation of love and suffering, also contributed a new vocabulary to the public discussion of sexuality in general.[100]

Non-reproductive and therefore transgressive sexual practices such as anal and oral sex, still regarded especially by some older Australians as perversions, could now be depicted and discussed more openly, as they were in gay literature, art, posters and other publicity.[101] What homosexual men did with each other's bodies was hard to avoid in safe-sex publicity.[102] AIDS also added a new and powerful argument in favour of decriminalisation. How could government expect gay men to come forward in a spirit of cooperation to deal with AIDS if their behaviour might lead to arrest and prosecution? These positive outcomes, however, need to be considered alongside the incalculable cost in fear, shame, pain, ravaged bodies, lives lost and sheer grief.[103]

*The Innocence of Children*

AIDS was one site of anti-gay backlash; another was the alleged activities among the young of proselytising homosexuals and paedophiles. At a time when teachers' unions were increasingly taking up the cause of fair treatment of gay and lesbian teachers and rational treatment of homosexuality in schools, it was easy enough for opponents of the permissive society to see in plans for sex education a plot to bring down the Judaeo-Christian order.[104] Any suggestion that homosexuality might have equal validity as a 'lifestyle' with heterosexuality and marriage was likely to generate bitter controversy. One conservative commentator spoke for many more when he remarked that 'if you encourage children to think about homosexuality – and to think about it as a good and acceptable mode of sexuality – then it is highly probable that some children so encouraged will either experiment in homosexuality or adopt it as their sexual "lifestyle"'.[105] Even once the AIDS crisis hit, thereby providing seemingly unassailable arguments for better sex education, there were critics calling for governments to preserve 'school children from homosexual interference with their minds or with their bodies'.[106] More than twenty years later, a classroom exercise in one Sydney school that asked teenagers to imagine growing up heterosexual in a society where everyone was gay was capable of provoking the righteous anger of the tabloid press.[107]

The snide reference to the 'bodies' of schoolchildren was part of a larger set of claims in public debate concerning the 'threat' that homosexuals posed to young people. It emerged during the 1970s as a potent force for anti-gay political mobilisation. Sex between adults and children, however defined, has clearly occurred throughout Australia's history, but before the 1980s, it failed to generate anything like the panic of recent years. An early 1970s Australian sex manual produced by a Sydney doctor asserted that '[d]espite the fantastic publicity that results when an adult allegedly seduces a child … such contacts are relatively rare, and it is even rarer for emotional trauma to result in the child'. Greater mental harm to the child might occur as a result of the 'hysterical reactions of parents, society and the police'.[108] As late as 1981 the criminologist Paul Wilson, referring in an interview with a gay magazine to a recent Queensland case involving one man's 'liaisons with at least 2500 boys' over the course of twenty-five years, argued that 'the effects … were not monumentally bad and in some cases were positively good for some of the boys involved'. Paedophilia, he said, did 'very little harm … to the majority of boys'.[109] Although there is also recent research to suggest that early sexual activity affects children in a variety of ways and is not always harmful, the relaxed attitude in the 1970s stands in stark contrast to more recent popular understandings and the public panic about the danger that paedophiles pose.[110]

Feminist writing on the sexual abuse of children did not associate it with male homosexuality but with patriarchy. Elizabeth Ward, who was active in Women's Liberation in the 1970s and had worked in a Canberra women's refuge, pointed out in a 1984 study that girls comprised the vast majority of child sex-abuse victims, most attacks occurred within the family and heterosexual men were overwhelmingly those most likely to rape children. Fathers who raped their daughters were not 'aberrant males', but rather 'acting within the mainstream of masculine sexual behaviour which sees women as sexual commodities'.[111] It is easy enough to see why such findings should be so disturbing to heterosexual men at a time when male authority in the family and elsewhere was under siege. Yet when the category of 'paedophile' actually emerged in the 1970s and 1980s, he was imagined as a predatory male homosexual. This formulation has been viewed as part of a backlash against the growing visibility of the gay movement, and a defence of an embattled heterosexual masculinity.[112]

The element missing from this story, however, is the response to this backlash of gay men and women themselves. While they had good reason to feel that they were being unfairly targeted, the Freudian roots of so much gay theorising were no better illustrated than in its attitude to the sexuality of children. For liberal advocates of a *laissez-faire* approach to private acts between consenting adults, it was essential to underline that there was a distinction to be made between a paedophile and a homosexual. The drawing of such a contrast was part of the business of creating the persona of the homosexual as an ordinary bloke just like the rest of us, excepting his preference for sex with men, which was his business anyway. But within Gay Liberation itself, this 'consenting adults in private' paradigm was increasingly rejected in favour of sexual liberation based on a rejection of the bourgeois patriarchal family. And the beneficiaries of this liberation would include children and adolescents, whose sexual rights would also be finally recognised. As Altman put it, sex should be transformed into 'a means of expanding contact and creating community' so that 'sexual activity among children would be encouraged rather than ... frowned upon'.[113]

Altman referred to sex '*among* children'. But what of sex between adults and children? Or between adults and post-pubertal adolescents? Homosexual law reform and young people's sexuality were closely entwined, not least because opponents of decriminalisation argued that gay men were prone to assaults on children and to the 'recruitment' of adolescents to their immoral lifestyle. The retention of a higher age of consent for homosexual than heterosexual sex in several Australian jurisdictions illustrated these fears but at the same time undermined the legitimacy of age of consent laws among gay men and women. Homosexual activists argued that these were available to police to persecute 'sexually mature and willing young people' while 'the real sexual abuse of children continues'.[114] As one activist remarked in 1980, 'I will assert as a matter of principle that I have as much right to make a sexual advance at an adolescent if I feel like it as has anybody else, provided that that person has an understanding of what is being proposed and freely consents to it'.[115] But it was this difficult issue of consent that formed the nub of the matter. Although there was a variety of opinion about paedophilia within the gay and lesbian community, some gay men and lesbians saw parallels between the oppression of gays and the persecution of paedophiles, and they came to believe that the latter was a cynical conservative tactic in a campaign against homosexuality.[116] They did not have to look very hard to find evidence to support this case. In 1984 the Delta Task Force of the Victoria Police arrested nine men, all members of a support group which Delta had infiltrated with an informer, for conspiring to corrupt public morals. The courts later threw out all charges for lack of evidence, but by this time whatever doubts remained in the public mind about the connection between homosexuality and paedophilia might have been removed. A member of Delta quoted in the *National Times* claimed that 95 per cent of the situations he had handled involved homosexual men. When asked what would happen if he found evidence of sex between an adult woman and an underage male, his senior officer replied, 'The kid'd probably be as grateful as hell'.[117]

While gay men and women could therefore have been forgiven for sensing a conspiracy against them, the thinking of some activists about this issue also appeared simplistic.[118] For some, sexual liberation implied 'children's rights to be sexual with whoever they choose'.[119] A contributor to *Camp Ink* in 1973 argued that, from a moral point of view, if a child desired 'a sexual relationship with an adult ... the child has at least the same entitlement to choose or refuse; to continue or to discontinue as does an adult'. If there was a seduction problem, it was 'not one of adults who seduce children, but ... one of insufficiently supervised, promiscuous children engaging in the seduction of adults'.[120] A gay male activist thought that society scapegoated 'paedophiles *and* young people' because it refused 'to regard children as autonomous and sexual beings' while another declared that 'at the very heart of the opposition to paedophilia is the belief that children cannot consent' – that they were incapable of rational thought – an attitude he equated with prejudices formerly used to prevent women voting. 'The arguments in favour of paedophilia', he added, 'centre on the way it contributes to the autonomy of the child by reducing its dependence and powerlessness within the family'.[121] Where their opponents saw these arguments about young people's sexual rights as self-serving, gay and lesbian activists drew attention to the oppressive sex roles imposed by the conventional family.

In short, some 1970s libertarians regarded the impulse to protect children from the world of sex as just another pillar of the repressive society, a sad remnant of Victorian puritanism. The advice of one Sydney psychologist certainly flew in the face of conventional understandings of the relationship of adult sex to domestic space: there was no danger in a child seeing parental sexual contact, 'even to the point

of intercourse or orgasm'. This idea was never likely to catch on – it challenged some very long-standing connections between civilised conduct,
adult sexual privacy and the innocence of children – but childhood
sexuality was a subject that generated increasingly intense anxiety.[122]
Governments have become especially sensitive to the political potency
of child sexual abuse. When the NT government released a report in
2007 providing details of sexual abuse of Indigenous children in remote
communities, the Howard government introduced a policy of aggressive bureaucratic and military intervention which included a ban on
pornography.[123] Less was heard of the sexual assault experienced for
generations by adult Aboriginal women, for the rape of grown women
was less effective than that of children in mobilising public support and
drowning out criticism. Similarly, sensational coverage of child sexual
abuse in the churches has obscured the exploitative sexual relations that
have frequently occurred between clergymen and adult women who
trusted them. Australia, like several other western nations, saw the
exposure of many cases of child sexual abuse within religious institutions in the late twentieth century. The difficulties faced by churches in
dealing with this issue have been magnified by the theological failure
of most of them to confront the issue of sexual desire and the survival of
authoritarian structures.[124] In 2003 the Governor-General of Australia
and former Anglican Archbishop of Brisbane, Peter Hollingworth, was
forced to resign following criticisms that he had acted with insufficient
firmness in dealing with clergy in his own diocese who had abused
children.

In the early twenty-first century, a new critique of child sexual
exploitation gathered momentum as it crossed ideological boundaries
and made its way to the heart of political debate. An imperialistic consumerism was giving rise to growing concern about the sexualised
images of the young being used in the cause of corporate profits. The
left-wing columnist and broadcaster Phillip Adams coined the term
'corporate paedophilia' for this phenomenon, while in 2006 the left-
leaning think-tank the Australia Institute published research arguing
that the 'premature sexualisation' of children, especially girls, through
advertising, magazines and television programs, was 'an abuse both of
children and public morality'. The report went so far as to suggest that
premature sexualisation might be playing 'a role in "grooming" children
for paedophiles', both by preparing them for sexual activity with older

people and announcing to paedophiles that children were available for sex.[125] Here, left-wing intellectuals concerned about unrestrained capitalism made common cause with moral conservatives worried about widespread sexual immorality and disorder. The latter complained of 'a sex-soaked culture' that was eroding childhood innocence, but they laid the blame for it not on consumer capitalism so much as the debased values bequeathed by the sexual revolution.[126] In 2008 the Australian Senate responded to this debate with an inquiry into the 'Sexualisation of Children in the Contemporary Media'. While recognising the paucity of evidence and rejecting the more exaggerated and unsubstantiated claims of the Australia Institute, its findings endorsed the case for greater effort by regulators to protect children from likely harm caused by premature sexualisation. In the same year, a new industry code of practice included the provision that advertising 'must not state or imply that Children are sexual beings and that ownership or enjoyment of a Product will enhance their sexuality'.[127]

Participants in this debate have often stressed the apparent novelty of the circumstances faced today by young people, such as rampant consumerism and media saturation. But most concerns they articulated about children's loss of innocence could have come out of almost any time over the last couple of centuries of Australian history. Complaints about young people being 'sexually out of control' seem especially familiar.[128]

It is true that the age at which young people start having sex has declined. The 2003 national survey on sex in Australia found that the median age for the first act of heterosexual intercourse was now sixteen, compared with eighteen for those men born in the 1940s, while for women the drop was even more dramatic, from nineteen to sixteen.[129] Moreover, large numbers of people under twenty – 43 per cent of men and 31 per cent of women – now engaged in oral sex at an earlier age than penetrative sex, where only one in a hundred respondents in their fifties had done things in this order. Oral sex had seemingly become for many teenagers in the early twenty-first century what petting – tongue kissing, breast fondling and genital stimulation – had been to their parents and grandparents: a preliminary to full intercourse.[130] Magazines geared towards teenage girls now advised readers about whether they could perform oral sex while wearing braces on their teeth.

That the sexuality of children had emerged as the site of the most acute anxiety among adults by the early years of the twenty-first century was confirmed in the controversy generated by the photography of the eminent artist Bill Henson during 2008. In May of that year, provoked by media denunciation of an invitation to the opening of an exhibition of Henson's work that contained an image of a naked adolescent girl featured in the show, police raided the Sydney gallery where it was about to open. The exhibition was cancelled and photos seized as evidence in a possible child pornography case against the artist. The Prime Minister, Kevin Rudd, weighed in when questioned on television, describing the photos as 'revolting'. A search for similarly offensive material was conducted in galleries across the country, where Henson's pictures had been displayed for decades without generating complaints. In the end, the police did not pursue a case against either Henson or any of the galleries that displayed his work but, by this time, a moral panic and media frenzy of considerable intensity had acted as a stern warning to any artists contemplating the depiction of a naked child in their work.[131]

## Conclusion

The sexual revolution – whether understood as a phenomenon of the 1960s and 1970s or as a longer historical sweep – placed sexuality at the centre of human experience. Your place in the world flowed from your sexual identity and behaviour. People became fully free – fully human – to the extent that they achieved sexual openness by overcoming the roles and inhibitions imposed by a repressive civilisation. The revolutionaries demanded much of sex – arguably too much – and it is not coincidental that a sense of decline in the cohesion of the gay community has been accompanied by a questioning of the centrality of sex itself to personal identity. It was gay men, of all the revolutionaries, who called on sexuality to bear the heaviest burden in forming their identity and community. But as Robert Reynolds has recently put it, 'We are more than who we choose to bed'.[132]

The rise of 'queer' in the 1990s called into question the liberationist aim of sexual revolution, and the fixed, essential quality of gay and lesbian identities. Imported from the US and arising out of militant AIDS activism, queer included a range of marginalised sexualities – bisexual, transvestite, transsexual, transgender – it seemed anyone who did not identify as heterosexual could find a home there. Yet, paradoxically, queer's proponents advocated a politics in which there was a place for heterosexual desire. Queer, in seeking to overcome the gay/straight divide, inevitably made the gender of one's sexual partner less of a focus.[133] It was partly for that reason resisted by some gay activists of an older generation, who saw in it an attempt to 'devalue affirmation of a homosexual identity'. They worried that queer was too disconnected from real political struggle, that it was too abstract, that it privileged image over the continuing force of oppression in the everyday lives of Australian gays and lesbians.[134] Many younger people, however, have been attracted to queer's culture of inclusiveness and open embrace of a fluidity that they see reflected in the reality of their own lives.

To be gay or lesbian in the twenty-first century was still to suffer oppression. In the early years of this century, the political struggle rapidly shifted to the subject of same-sex marriage, adoption rights and access to fertility treatment. Many queer people, and perhaps especially the young, insist that their relationships should be treated by the state and society 'with the same gravity and respect as any other relationship'.[135] It follows that, like heterosexual couples, they should be allowed to marry. Superficially, their case can appear to belong to the same liberal tradition as the repeal of the laws against sodomy, in which gay men sought equal treatment with other citizens. But in a society where heterosexual coupling is privileged and still widely assumed to be natural, their claims are deeply unsettling to many people beyond conservative Christians. Same-sex marriage has been resisted by both major political parties. At its 2011 national conference, the Labor Party voted to include it in the platform, but also to allow its members a conscience vote when the matter came before parliament. Many comentators believed that this was likely to result in the measure's defeat. Meanwhile, the growing number of lesbians opting for motherhood, while appearing a conservative trend when set beside lesbian SM, actually poses a powerful challenge to widely held assumptions concerning gender roles and the naturalness of the patriarchal family.[136]

Beyond such discrimination, gay people are still subject to verbal and physical abuse and workplace discrimination, and they are still more likely to commit suicide than heterosexuals, especially in rural areas. Michael Kirby's memorable address at the Gay Olympics in 2000 was followed a couple of years later by an episode that exposed the continuing vulnerability of gay men in Australian public life. In 2002 a Liberal Party Senator, Bill Heffernan, under parliamentary privilege accused the High Court Judge of having used a government car to pick up young male prostitutes in Sydney. The documentary 'evidence' was soon exposed as a crude forgery but the incident was deeply distressing for Kirby and Johan van Vloten, his partner of over three decades.

There is an obvious irony in a nation whose stereotypical masculinity is aggressively heterosexual and homophobic having become, by the early years of the third millennium, a benign environment for both gay men and lesbian women by international standards. But the nation that gave the world the Barry McKenzie films also gave it *Priscilla, Queen of the Desert*; Robert Helpmann was graceful before Shane Warne; Mardi Gras holds its own in an informal rivalry with Anzac Day; and even allowing for the cross-dressing of *The Footy Show*, it was surprising to some and delightful to others that the world of rugby league could produce a local gay icon in Ian Roberts. Peter Allen, the grandson of a Tenterfield saddler, was an internationally famous gay celebrity who went to Rio, but still called Australia home.

# *Acknowledgements*

My work on this book began in New England, continued in old England and was completed at the Australian National University in Canberra. I have incurred many debts along the way. At the University of New England (UNE) in Armidale, I benefited from a group of incredibly generous colleagues. I am especially grateful to Alan Atkinson, Howard Brasted, Iain Davidson, the late John Ferry, Erin Ihde, David Kent, David Roberts, Iain Spence, the late Charles Tesoriero and Janis Wilton. The University of New England Sexualities Research Group (UNESEX) was also tremendously supportive. I appreciated the opportunity to present in that forum some of the results of my research and would especially like to thank John Scott, Gail Hawkes and Elizabeth Hale.

This project is also a product of my teaching of a unit at the UNE on *Sexuality in Australian History.* I thank the many students concerned, for their insights and enthusiasm, their generosity in passing on references they came across in their own work, and their intellectual comradeship. I am especially grateful to Robin Hammond, who shared with me many discoveries as she prepared her own study of crime in Sydney between the wars.

Much of the work for this book was carried out 'the old-fashioned way' – between teaching and other university commitments – but the Faculty of Arts at the University of New England provided both some study-leave and welcome financial support in the early stages. Some of the results of Australian Research Council Grant F59700050, 'Bernard O'Dowd and Australian culture: a biographical study', have also been incorporated in the book: I gratefully acknowledge this assistance. I also thank those who helped with the research: Erin Ihde, Lesley McLean, Lyndon Megarrity and Elizabeth Noble. I am grateful to Marie Bongiorno for chasing up some references in Melbourne, and to Trish Wright and Gina Butler for their unfailing friendship and support.

At the Menzies Centre for Australian Studies, King's College London, I would like to thank Carl Bridge, Tim Causer, Ian Henderson and Simon Sleight. Under Carl's headship, the Centre provided a supportive environment in which to carry forward the research and writing. Ian's friendship, collegiality and enthusiasm for this project never faltered, and I am additionally grateful for his guidance on the two post-1960 chapters. Simon passed on many references, shared with me his expertise on colonial Melbourne, and kindly commented on some of the writing on young people. Tim was similarly generous in sharing his great knowledge of convict Australia.

Among my colleagues in the History Department at King's College London, I would especially like to thank Alice Rio and Richard Drayton for inviting me to try out some of my ideas in the History Department and Imperial and World History (Institute of Historical Research) seminars. For similar reasons, I am grateful to Stuart Ward and Mads Clausen at the University of Copenhagen, and Katie Holmes and Lindsey Earner-Byrne at University College Dublin. They were wonderfully hospitable hosts, and I appreciated the opportunity to present papers to them and their colleagues. I also thank Carole Ferrier, Martin Crotty, Marina Larsson and David Roberts, who gave me the chance to try out in print some of my ideas on particular topics explored in this book.

Several friends provided support and advice during a particularly difficult period in this project's gestation. In the first place, I doubt whether the book would have happened at all without John Hirst; I am deeply grateful for his act of faith and friendship. Peter Stanley, with characteristic generosity and wisdom, made available his award-winning *Bad Characters* in advance of its publication and gave valuable feedback on my chapters 5 and 7. He also provided indispensable advice during 2010 in assisting me to tame an increasingly unruly manuscript. Above all, he saw worth in what I was doing. Finally, my ability to see this project through owes much to the support and friendship over many years of Ian Britain, Bridget Griffen-Foley, David Lee, Stuart Macintyre, Humphrey McQueen and Craig Wilcox.

Others commented helpfully on parts of the manuscript, or passed on information about sources. I am especially grateful to Joy Damousi, Tanya Evans, Lisa Featherstone, Libby Gleeson, Margot Harker, Ken Inglis, Ian Johnstone, Phillip Knightley, Josephine Laffin, Kerry Maher, Grant Mansfield, Mark McKenna, Peter McNeil, Ruth Rae, Tim Rowse, Bruce Scates, Babette Smith, Chris Summers, Leigh Summers and Graham Willett. Liz Ross, apart from responding generously to my own work, also shared with me her own research on some of the issues considered in the later chapters of this book. Ian Hancock read and commented on almost the whole manuscript, at absurdly short notice; I am grateful, as ever, for his generosity, friendship and good humour. Barry Smith sent me along several of the paths followed in this book and has always been the most supportive, and non-judgmental, of mentors.

My debts to many institutions, librarians and archivists will be apparent from the endnotes. But I would here like to acknowledge the dedicated assistance I received from the University of Melbourne Archives, the Manuscripts Section of the National Library of Australia, the Australian Lesbian and Gay Archives (especially Gary Jaynes and Graham Willett) and the staff of the Dixson Library at the University of New England.

Chris Feik at Black Inc. has from the beginning shown great enthusiasm for the project, and I would like to thank him, Sophy Williams, Nikola Lusk and the team at Black Inc. for their critical role in seeing the book through to completion. Nikola's great energy, skill and professionalism in editing the manuscript were warmly appreciated, as were Chris's expert eye and sound judgment.

Most importantly of all, there is my family: I thank Angie and Marie Bongiorno, Nina Hetherington, Malcolm and Margaret McLennan, and Amy Bongiorno; Amy was endlessly patient in putting up with the absences occasioned by 'Daddy's work' about the 'olden days'.

Nicole McLennan was there every step of the way. She read and corrected draft chapters, drew my attention to sources and readings, tracked down illustrations and – even when my own faith faltered – never seemed to doubt that this project would have its day. I dedicate this book to her, with all my love.

# Abbreviations

| | |
|---|---|
| ACH | Australian Cultural History |
| ADB | Australian Dictionary of Biography |
| AFS | Australian Feminist Studies |
| AGPS | Australian Government Publishing Service |
| AHS | Australian Historical Studies |
| AIDS | Acquired Immune Deficiency Syndrome |
| AIF | Australian Imperial Force |
| AJPH | Australian Journal of Politics and History |
| ALGA | Australian Lesbian and Gay Archives |
| ALRA | Abortion Law Reform Association |
| ANU | Australian National University |
| AWCL | Australasian White Cross League |
| AWM | Australian War Memorial |
| BCOF | British Commonwealth Occupation Force |
| BL | British Library |
| BPP | British Parliamentary Papers |
| CAMP | Campaign Against Moral Persecution |
| CPD | Commonwealth Parliamentary Debates |
| CUP | Cambridge University Press |
| GCN | Gay Community News |
| H of R | House of Representatives |
| HA | House of Assembly |
| HRA | Historical Records of Australia |
| HRNSW | Historical Records of New South Wales |
| HS | Historical Studies |
| IFR | Institute of Family Relations |
| IUD | Intra-uterine device |
| JACH | Journal of Australian Colonial History |
| JAS | Journal of Australian Studies |
| JHS | Journal of the History of Sexuality |
| JHSSA | Journal of the Historical Society of South Australia |
| JRAHS | Journal of the Royal Australian Historical Society |
| JRH | Journal of Religious History |
| LA | Legislative Assembly |
| LH | Labour History |
| MHJ | Melbourne Historical Journal |

| | |
|---|---|
| MJA | Medical Journal of Australia |
| ML | Mitchell Library, Sydney |
| MUP | Melbourne University Press |
| NEF | New Education Fellowship |
| NHE | New Horizons in Education |
| NHMRC | National Health and Medical Research Council |
| NLA | National Library of Australia |
| NSW | New South Wales |
| NSWBOHP | New South Wales Bicentennial Oral History Project |
| NSWPD | New South Wales Parliamentary Debates |
| NSWPP | New South Wales Parliamentary Papers |
| NT | Northern Territory |
| OUP | Oxford University Press |
| PROV | Public Records Office of Victoria |
| RCACGI | Royal Commission on Alleged Chinese Gambling and Immorality and Charges of Bribery Against Members of the Police Force |
| RCCN | Royal Commission on the Condition of the Natives |
| RCDB | Royal Commission on the Decline of the Birthrate |
| RCES | Royal Commission of Employés in Shops |
| RHA | Racial Hygiene Association |
| SA | South Australia |
| SAPD | South Australian Parliamentary Debates |
| SCCWCM | Select Committee on the Condition of the Working Class of the Metropolis |
| SCPCD | Select Committee on the Bill for the Prevention of Contagious Diseases |
| SCPVD | Select Committee on the Prevalence of Venereal Disease |
| SCT | Select Committee on Transportation |
| SLV | State Library of Victoria |
| SMH | Sydney Morning Herald |
| SRNSW | State Records of New South Wales |
| SUP | Sydney University Press |
| UMA | University of Melbourne Archives |
| UNSWP | University of New South Wales Press |
| UQP | University of Queensland Press |
| UWAP | University of Western Australia Press |
| VD | Venereal Disease |
| VPD | Victorian Parliamentary Debates |
| VPP | Victorian Parliamentary Papers |
| WA | Western Australia |
| WAPD | Western Australian Parliamentary Debates |
| WCTU | Women's Christian Temperance Union |
| WEA | Workers' Educational Association |
| WEL | Women's Electoral Lobby |
| YMCA | Young Men's Christian Association |
| YWCA | Young Women's Christian Association |

# *Endnotes*

## INTRODUCTION

1   Jeffrey Weeks, 'Sexuality and History Revisited', in Weeks, *Making Sexual History*, Polity Press, Cambridge, 2000, p. 139.
2   Roderic Anderson, *Free Radical*, Watson Ferguson & Company, Salisbury (Qld), 2006, p. 122.

## CHAPTER 1

1   *R. v. Marshall and others* [1795] NSWKR 1, *Decisions of the Superior Courts of New South Wales, 1788–1899*, http://www.law.mq.edu.au/research/colonial_case_law/nsw/cases/case_index/1795/r_v_marshall_and_others, and J.F. Nagle, *Collins, the Courts & the Colony: Law and Society in Colonial New South Wales*, University of New South Wales Press (UNSWP), Sydney, 1996, pp. 248–52.
2   Janet Albrechtsen, 'Blind Spot Allows Criminal Barbarism to Flourish', *Australian*, 17 July 2002, p. 11.
3   'Pack, local term', Letters to the Editor, *Australian*, 18 July 2002, p. 10.
4   David Collins, *An Account of the English Colony in New South Wales*, Vol. 1, T. Cadell Jun. and W. Davies, London, 1798, Australian Facsimile Editions No. 76, Libraries Board of South Australia, Adelaide, 1971, April 1795, p. 414.
5   Robert Hughes, *The Fatal Shore: A History of the Transportation of Convicts to Australia, 1787–1868*, Collins Harvill, London, 1987, pp. 88–9; Thomas Keneally, *Australians: Origins to Eureka Volume 1*, Allen & Unwin, Sydney, 2009, p. 89.
6   Grace Karskens, *The Colony: A History of Early Sydney*, Allen & Unwin, Sydney, 2009, pp. 313–31; Carol Baxter, *An Irresistible Temptation: The True Story of Jane New and a Colonial Scandal*, Allen & Unwin, Sydney, 2006.
7   Tim Hitchcock, *English Sexualities 1700–1800*, Macmillan, London, 1997.
8   Thomas Laqueur, 'Orgasm, Generation and the Politics of Reproductive Biology', in Catherine Gallagher and Thomas Laqueur (eds), *The Making of the Modern Body: Sexuality and Society in the Nineteenth Century*, University of California Press, Berkeley, Los Angeles and London, 1987, pp. 1–41.
9   Hitchcock, *English Sexualities*, ch. 3; Rebecca Jennings, *A Lesbian History of Britain: Love and Sex Between Women since 1500*, Greenwood World Publishing, Oxford and Westport, Connecticut, 2007, p. 19.
10  Samuel Marsden to Governor Hunter, 11 August, 1798, in *Historical Records of New South Wales (HRNSW)*, Vol. 3, pp. 439–42. See also Tina Picton Phillips, 'Family Matters: Bastards, Orphans and Baptisms – New South Wales, 1810–1825', *Journal of the Royal Australian Historical Society (JRAHS)*, Vol. 90, Pt 2, 2004, pp. 122–35.
11  Alan Atkinson, 'The Moral Basis of Marriage', *Push from the Bush*, No. 2, November 1978, pp. 104–15.
12  Ann McGrath, 'The White Man's Looking Glass: Aboriginal–Colonial Gender Relations at Port Jackson', *Australian Historical Studies (AHS)* Vol. 24, No. 95, October 1990, pp. 189–206.
13  Collins, *Account*, p. 597.
14  Inga Clendinnen, *Dancing with Strangers*, Text Publishing, Melbourne, 2003, pp. 152–67.

But for a critique of this interpretation, see Shino Konishi, '"Wanton With Plenty": Questioning Ethno-historical Constructions of Sexual Savagery in Aboriginal Societies, 1788–1803', *AHS*, Vol. 39, No. 3, December 2008, pp. 356–72.

15    Collins, *Account*, p. 414.

16    John Pascoe Fawkner, 'Reminiscences of John Pascoe Fawkner', *La Trobe Journal*, No. 3, April 1969, p. 43.

17    James Mudie, Select Committee on Transportation (SCT), Minutes of Evidence, Q. 650–3, p. 40, *British Parliamentary Papers (BPP)*, Crime and Punishment, Transportation, Vol. 2, 1837; Peter Cunningham, *Two Years in New South Wales*, Vol. 2, London, 1827, New Edition, D. S. Macmillan (ed.), Angus & Robertson in association with the Royal Australian Historical Society, Sydney, 1966, p. 186.

18    Henry Reynolds, *The Other Side of the Frontier: Aboriginal Resistance to the European Invasion of Australia*, Penguin Books, Ringwood, 1990, pp. 70–2.

19    Angus R. McGillivery, 'British Convicts, Polynesian Women, and Imperial Designs', *JRAHS*, Vol. 89, Pt 2, December 2003, pp. 179–85.

20    King to Dundas, 10 March 1794, *HRNSW*, Vol. 2, p. 137.

21    John Currey, *David Collins: A Colonial Life*, The Miegunyah Press, Melbourne University Press (MUP), Carlton, 2000; Jonathan King and John King, *Philip Gidley King: A Biography of the Third Governor of New South Wales*, Methuen Australia, North Ryde and North Melbourne, 1981, pp. 39–40, 44, 51–2; Marian Aveling, 'She Only Married to be Free; or, Cleopatra Vindicated', *Push from the Bush*, No. 2, November 1978, p. 121; Richard Johnson, *The Search for the Inland Sea: John Oxley, Explorer, 1783–1828*, MUP, Carlton, 2001, pp. 6, 36–7, 107–8, 150–2.

22    Patricia Grimshaw, Marilyn Lake, Ann McGrath and Marian Quartly, *Creating a Nation*, Penguin Books, Ringwood, 1996 [1994], pp. 33–4.

23    J.P. Fawkner, *Reminiscences of Early Hobart Town 1804–1810*, John Currey (ed.), Colony Press for the Banks Society, Malvern (Vic.), 2007, p. 39.

24    Alison Alexander, *Obliged to Submit: Wives and Mistresses of Colonial Governors*, Montpelier Press, Dynnyrne (Tas.), 1999, ch. 2.

25    Fawkner, *Reminiscences*, p. 49; John Currey (ed.), *Knopwood's Hobart Town Diary 15 February 1804–28 February 1805*, Colony Press, Malvern (Vic.), 2005, pp. 53–4, 78, 84, fn. 82.

26    Alan Atkinson, *The Europeans in Australia: A History, Volume 1: The Beginning*, Oxford University Press (OUP), Oxford, 1997, pp. 132–5.

27    Paula J. Byrne, *Criminal Law and Colonial Subject: New South Wales, 1810–1830*, Cambridge University Press (CUP), Cambridge, 1993, p. 108.

28    Collins, *Account*, pp. 80–1.

29    *R. v. Daniel Gilmore* (1812), in Peter de Waal (ed.), *Unfit for Publication: NSW Supreme Court and Other Bestiality, Buggery & Sodomy Trials 1727–1930*, Vol. 1, self-published, Balmain, 2007, p. 58.

30    Byrne, *Criminal Law and Colonial Subject*, pp. 106–7.

31    *R. v. Hyson* [1796] NSWKR, *Decisions of the Superior Courts of New South Wales, 1788–1899*, http://www.law.mq.edu.au/scnsw/html/R%20v%20Hyson,%201796.htm.

32    *R. v. Reece* [1799] NSWKR 1, *Decisions of the Superior Courts of New South Wales, 1788–1899*, http://www.law.mq.edu.au/research/colonial_case_law/nsw/cases/case_index/1799/r_v_reece.

33    Atkinson, *Europeans*, Vol. 1, p. 121.

34    Hitchcock, *English Sexualities*, p. 62.

35    *R. v. Thomas Hewitt* (1819), in de Waal (ed.), *Unfit*, Vol. 1, p. 63.

36    *Sydney Gazette*, 8 February 1812, [p. 2].

37    See, for instance, *R. v. Francis Wilkinson* (1796) and *R. v. William Taylor and Thomas McLean* (1826) in de Waal (ed.), *Unfit for Publication*, Vol. 1, pp. 41–2 and 73–6.

38    *R. v. Wilson* [1814] NSWKR 1, *Decisions of the Superior Courts of New South Wales, 1788–1899*, http://www.law.mq.edu.au/research/colonial_case_law/nsw/cases/case_index/1814/r_v_wilson.

39    Randolph Trumbach, 'The Birth of the Queen: Sodomy and the Emergence of Gender
      Equality in Modern Culture, 1660–1750' in Martin Duberman, Martha Vicinus and George
      Chauncey Jr (eds), *Hidden from History: Reclaiming the Gay and Lesbian Past*, London, 1991,
      pp. 130–1; Hitchcock, *English Sexualities*, ch. 5 and Rictor Norton, *Mother Clapp's Molly
      House: The Gay Subculture in England 1700–1830*, GMP, Penguin Books, London, 1992.

40    Garry Wotherspoon, 'A Sodom in the South Pacific: Male Homosexuality in Sydney
      1788–1809', in Graeme Aplin (ed.), *A Difficult Infant: Sydney Before Macquarie*, UNSWP,
      Kensington, 1988, p. 98.

41    Kirsty Reid, *Gender, Crime and Empire: Convicts, Settlers and the State in Early Colonial
      Australia*, Manchester University Press, Manchester and New York, 2007.

42    M.J. Belcher, The Child in New South Wales Society 1820–1837, PhD Thesis, University of
      New England, 1982, pp. 121, 147, 149; David Kent and Norma Townsend, 'Some Aspects of
      Colonial Marriage: A Case Study of the Swing Protestors', *Labour History (LH)*, No. 74, May
      1998, pp. 41, 43, 46.

43    Robert Crooke, *The Convict: A Fragment of History*, University of Tasmania Library,
      Hobart, 1958, p. 9.

44    Norma Townsend, 'Penelope Bourke Revisited', *LH*, No. 77, November 1999, pp. 207–18.

45    Kirsten McKenzie, *Scandal in the Colonies: Sydney and Cape Town 1820–1850*, MUP,
      Carlton, 2004, pp. 105, 107.

46    Kirsty Reid, '"Contumacious, Ungovernable and Incorrigible": Convict Women and
      Workplace Resistance, Van Diemen's Land, 1820–1839', in Ian Duffield and James Bradley
      (eds), *Representing Convicts: New Perspectives on Convict Forced Labour Migration*,
      Leicester University Press, London and Washington, 1997, pp. 106–21; Phillip Tardiff,
      *Notorious Strumpets and Dangerous Girls: Convict Women in Van Diemen's Land 1803–1829*,
      Angus & Robertson, North Ryde, 1990.

47    Kay Daniels, *Convict Women*, Allen & Unwin, Sydney, 1998, ch. 8; Raelene Frances,
      *Selling Sex: A Hidden History of Prostitution*, UNSWP, Sydney, 2007, pp. 7–41.

48    Sir Edward Parry, Minutes of Evidence, SCT, Q. 677–8, p. 66, *BPP*, Crime and
      Punishment, Transportation, Vol. 3.

49    Niel Gunson (ed.), *Australian Reminiscences & Papers of L.E. Threlkeld Missionary to the
      Aborigines, 1824–1859*, Vol. 1, Australian Institute of Aboriginal Studies, Canberra, 1974,
      p. 137.

50    John Barnes, Q. 416, p. 48; James Mudie, Minutes of Evidence, SCT, Q. 676–7, p. 42, *BPP*,
      Crime and Punishment, Transportation, Vol. 2.

51    R.H.W. Reece, *Aborigines and Colonists: Aborigines and Colonial Society in New South
      Wales in the 1830s and 1840s*, Sydney University Press (SUP), Sydney, 1974, p. 53.

52    Jillian Oppenheimer, 'Mary Ann Brigg (1834–1905?) as Thunderbolt's Lady – Some
      Account of her Public Life', in J.S. Ryan, assisted by Bruce Cady (ed.), *New England Lives*,
      University of New England in association with the Armidale and District Historical
      Society, Armidale, 1999; 'Colonel Dumaresq, Captain Thunderbolt and Mary Ann Brigg',
      *Push from the Bush*, No. 16, October 1983, p. 19; Carol Baxter, *Captain Thunderbolt & His
      Lady: The True Story of Bushrangers Frederick Ward & Mary Ann Bugg*, Allen & Unwin,
      Sydney, 2011, esp. pp. 1–43.

53    Lyndall Ryan, *The Aboriginal Tasmanians*, Second Edition, Allen & Unwin, Sydney, 1996,
      pp. 67, 69; Vivienne Rae-Ellis, *Black Robinson: Protector of Aborigines*, MUP, Carlton, 1988,
      p. 71; Rebe Taylor, 'Savages or Saviours? – The Australian Sealers and Tasmanian
      Aboriginal Survival', *Journal of Australian Studies (JAS)*, No. 66, 2000, pp. 73–84.

54    John Rintoul (compiler), *Esperance Yesterday and Today*, Esperance Shire Council,
      Esperance, 1964, pp. 12–20.

55    W.N. Clarke, *Perth Gazette*, 7 October 1842, quoted *ibid.*, p. 16.

56    Rebe Taylor, *Unearthed: The Aboriginal Tasmanians of Kangaroo Island*, Wakefield Press,
      Kent Town, 2008 (Second Revised Edition), pp. 28–9, 39–40.

57    Gunson (ed.), *Australian Reminiscences*, Vol. 1, p. 159.

58    Belcher, Child, pp. 159–62.

59  James Belich, *Replenishing the Earth: The Settler Revolution and the Rise of the Anglo-world, 1783–1939*, OUP, Oxford, 2009, pp. 323, 548–9.

60  Belcher, Child, pp. 119, 125–6.

61  Belich, *Replenishing*, pp. 548–9.

62  Edward Gibbon Wakefield, *A Letter From Sydney and Other Writings*, J.M. Dent & Sons, London, 1929 [1829], pp. 52–3.

63  Helen R. Woolcock, *Rights of Passage: Emigration to Australia in the Nineteenth Century*, Tavistock Publications, London and New York, 1986 [1829], pp. 313–14.

64  Bourke to Stanley, 21 January 1834, in *Historical Records of Australia (HRA)*, Series I, Vol. 17 , p. 344.

65  A.J. Hammerton, '"Without Natural Protectors": Female Immigration to Australia, 1832–36', *Historical Studies (HS)*, Vol. 16, No. 65, October 1975, pp. 557–61.

66  Immigration Board Inquiry, Minutes, 12 May 1842– (Sir Charles Napier), No. 34, 42/4246, State Records of New South Wales (SRNSW) 4/1149.1 Immigration 1842–53, Colonial Secretary's Correspondence, Special Bundles.

67  Evidence, in New South Wales, *Minutes of Proceedings of the Immigration Board at Sydney, Respecting Certain Irregularities which Occurred on Board the Ship 'Subraon'*, Government Printer, Sydney, 1848, 20 May 1848, pp. 8, 10, 17, 25, 33, 53; Colonial Secretary, Letters received: Emigration 1848, SRNSW 4/2802.1, MF Reel 2270; Report of the Immigration Board on the case of the Immigrant Ship 'Subraon', 31 October 1848, in *HRA*, Series I, Vol. 26, p. 683; John Ferry, 'The Ferrys, the *Subraon* and the Long Haul to Geelong', *Ancestor*, Vol. 23, No. 1, Autumn 1996, pp. 9–11.

68  Jan Gothard, *Blue China: Single Female Migration to Colonial Australia*, MUP, Carlton, 2001, p. 110 and 'Space, Authority and the Female Emigrant Afloat', *AHS*, Vol. 30, No. 112, April 1999, p. 97.

69  Reid, *Gender*.

70  C.A. Bayly, *Imperial Meridian: The British Empire and the World 1780–1830*, Longman, London and New York, 1989, pp. 207, 235–47.

71  Oliver MacDonagh, 'The Nineteenth-Century Revolution in Government: A Reappraisal', *Historical Journal*, Vol. 1, No. 1, 1958, p. 58 and *Early Victorian Government 1830–1870*, Weidenfeld & Nicolson, London, 1977, pp. 4–6; Joanna Innes, 'Legislation and Public Participation 1760–1830', in David Lemmings (ed.), *The British and Their Laws in the Eighteenth Century*, Boydell Press, Woodbridge, 2005, pp. 102–32.

72  Zoë Laidlaw, *Colonial Connections 1815–45: Patronage, the Information Revolution and Colonial Government*, Manchester University Press, Manchester and New York, 2005, ch. 7.

73  McKenzie, *Scandal*.

74  See Catie Gilchrist, Male Convict Sexuality in the Penal Colonies, 1820–1850, PhD Thesis, University of Sydney, 2004, pp. 54–65, 229–30.

75  Lisa Ford, *Settler Sovereignty: Jurisdiction and Indigenous People in America and Australia, 1788–1836*, Harvard University Press, Cambridge (Mass.) and London, 2010.

76  A.F. Kemp to Bathurst, 11 November 1818, *HRA*, III, Vol. 2, p. 684; see Leonie Mickleborough, *William Sorell in Van Diemen's Land: Lieutenant Governor, 1817–24: A Golden Age?*, Blubber Head Press, Hobart, 2004, p. 104.

77  Marian Aveling, 'Imagining New South Wales as a Gendered Society, 1783–1821', *AHS*, Vol. 25, No. 98, April 1992, pp. 1–12.

78  Bigge to Bathurst, 3 February 1823, *HRA*, III, Vol. 3, pp. 681–5.

79  Johnson, *Search*, pp. 182–3.

80  *HRA*, I, Vol. 13, pp. 72, 43–7.

81  E.A. Slade, Evidence, SCT, Q. 859–914, pp. 52–9, *BPP*, Crime and Punishment, Transportation, Vol. 2. See also evidence of H.W. Parker, Q. 1287–90, pp. 108–9, *BPP*, Crime and Punishment, Transportation, Vol. 3.

82  Max Waugh, *Forgotten Hero: Richard Bourke, Irish Governor of New South Wales 1831–1837*, Australian Scholarly Publishing, Melbourne, 2005, p. 66; James Mudie, *The Felonry of New South Wales*, Lansdowne Press, Melbourne, 1964 [1837], pp. 123–4.

83 John Ritchie, 'Towards Ending an Unclean Thing: the Molesworth Committee and the Abolition of Transportation to New South Wales, 1837–40', *HS*, Vol. 17, No. 67, October 1976, pp. 144–64; J.B. Hirst, *Convict Society and Its Enemies: A History of Early New South Wales*, Allen & Unwin, Sydney, 1983, pp. 26–7; McKenzie, *Scandal*, p. 147; *Norfolk Island 1846: The Accounts of Robert Pringle Stuart and Thomas Beagley Naylor*, Sullivan's Cove, Adelaide, 1979; Ian Brand, *The Convict Probation System: Van Diemen's Land 1839–1854*, Blubber Head Press, Hobart, 1990 and *The Port Arthur Coal Mines 1833–1877*, Regal Publications, Launceston (Tas.), n.d. [c. 1993].

84 Babette Smith, *Australia's Birthstain: The Startling Legacy of the Convict Era*, Allen & Unwin, Sydney, 2008, ch. 8.

85 Timothy James Causer, 'Only a Place For for Angels and Eagles': the Norfolk Island Penal Settlement, 1825–1855, PhD Thesis, King's College London, 2010, pp. 275–6; Catie Gilchrist, 'Space, Sexuality and Convict Resistance in Van Diemen's Land: The Limits of Repression', *Eras Journal*, Edition 6, 2004.

86 Gilchrist, Male Convict Sexuality, pp. 180–4; Reid, *Gender*, chs 5–6; McKenzie, *Scandal*, p. 50 and 'Discourses of Scandal: Bourgeois Respectability and the End of Slavery and Transportation at the Cape and New South Wales, 1830–1850', *Journal of Colonialism and Colonial History*, Vol. 4, No. 3, Winter 2003.

87 H.G. Cocks, *Nameless Offences: Homosexual Desire in the Nineteenth Century*, I.B. Tauris, London and New York, 2003, p. 8.

88 Kay Daniels, 'The Flash Mob: Rebellion, Rough Culture and Sexuality in the Female Factories of Van Diemen's Land', *Australian Feminist Studies (AFS)* Vol. 18, Summer 1993, pp. 133–50 and *Convict Women*, pp. 164–83; Joy Damousi, *Depraved and Disorderly: Female Convicts, Sexuality and Gender in Colonial Australia*, CUP, Melbourne 1997, pp. 69–72.

89 G.R. Lennox, 'A Private and Confidential Despatch of Eardley-Wilmot: Implications, Comparisons and Associations Concerning the Probation System for Convict Women', *Tasmanian Historical Research Association Papers and Proceedings*, Vol. 29, No. 2, June 1982, pp. 80–92. See also Catie Gilchrist, '"The Victim of his own Temerity"? Silence, Scandal and the Recall of Sir John Eardley-Wilmot', *JAS*, No. 84, 2005, pp. 151–61 and Male Convict Sexuality, pp. 224–34.

90 Gilchrist, Male Convict Sexuality, p. 234.

91 Smith, *Australia's Birthstain*, esp. ch. 8.

## CHAPTER 2

1 *Argus*, 28 November 1864, pp. 5–6; 21 December 1864, Supplement, p. 1.

2 Françoise Barrett-Ducrocq, *Love in the Time of Victoria: Sexuality and Desire Among Working-Class Men and Women in Nineteenth-Century London*, tr. John Howe, Penguin Books, New York, 1992, p. 1.

3 *Ibid.*, p. 2; Jeffrey Weeks, *Sex, Politics and Society: The Regulation of Sexuality since 1800*, Second Edition, Longman, London and New York, 1989, ch. 2.

4 Curtis Candler, Addenda to Diary, 23 September 1867, pp. 119–20, MS 9502, State Library of Victoria (SLV).

5 Michael Mason, *The Making of Victorian Sexuality*, OUP, Oxford, 1994, pp. 8–20.

6 David Goodman, *Gold Seeking: Victoria and California in the 1850s*, Allen & Unwin, Sydney, 1994, p. 156.

7 William Howitt, *Land, Labour and Gold or Two Years in Victoria: with Visits to Sydney and Van Diemen's Land*, Lowden, Kilmore, 1972 [1855], p. 94.

8 Goodman, *Gold Seeking*, ch. 5, esp. pp. 163–5; Christina Twomey, '"Without Natural Protectors": Responses to Wife Desertion in Gold-Rush Victoria', *AHS*, Vol. 28, No. 108, April 1997, pp. 22–46.

9 Kate Browning to James Browning, 17 September 1856, Historic Resources Centre Collection, unaccessioned loc. 92/6/3, University of New England and Regional Archives.

10 John Buckley Castieau, Diary, 17 August 1855, in Mark Finnane (ed.), *The Difficulties of*

*My Position: The Diaries of Prison Governor John Buckley Castieau 1855–1884*, National
Library of Australia (NLA), Canberra, 2004, p. 16.

11 Margaret Kiddle, *Men of Yesterday: A Social History of the Western District of Victoria
1834–1890*, MUP, Carlton, 1967, pp. 121–2; and Michael Francis Christie, *Aborigines in
Colonial Victoria 1835–86*, SUP, Sydney, 1979, p. 49.

12 Ian Turner, 'Prisoners in Petticoats: A Shocking History of Female Emancipation in
Australia', in Julie Rigg (ed.), *In Her Own Right: Women of Australia*, Nelson, Melbourne,
p. 8; Raymond Evans, '"Don't You Remember Black Alice, Sam Holt?" Aboriginal Women
in Queensland History', *Hecate*, Vol. 8, No. 2, 1982, pp. 7–21. 'A Ballad of Queensland', the
poem containing this line, is in the *Bulletin*, 26 March 1881, p. 8.

13 Anon., 'Shearer's Song', in Bill Wannan (ed.), *Robust Ribald and Rude Verse in Australia*,
Lansdowne, Melbourne, 1972, p. 49.

14 Bain Attwood, *The Making of the Aborigines*, Allen & Unwin, Sydney, 1989, p. 21.

15 *Ibid*, p. 39 and ' ... In the name of all my Coloured Brethren and Sisters ...': A Biography of
Bessy Cameron', *Hecate*, Vol. 12, Nos 1 and 2, 1986, pp. 9–53.

16 Candler, Addenda to Diary, 17 November 1867, p. 285.

17 Reynolds, *Other Side*, pp. 81–2; Gordon Reid, *A Nest of Hornets: The Massacre of the
Fraser Family at Hornet Bank Station, Central Queensland, 1857, and Related Events*,
OUP, Melbourne, 1982, pp. 62–7.

18 *Moreton Bay Courier*, 9 June 1858, p. 3; *Sydney Morning Herald* (*SMH*), 15 June 1858, p. 3;
and *North Australian*, 2 February 1858, the latter quoted in Reid, *Nest*, p. 94.

19 Reid, *Nest*, p. 95; Henry Reynolds and Noel Loos, 'Aboriginal Resistance in Queensland',
*Australian Journal of Politics and History* (*AJPH*), Vol. 22, No. 2, August 1976, p. 217.

20 Reynolds, *Other Side*, p. 133.

21 Attwood, '"In the name of all my Coloured Brethren and Sisters"', p. 15.

22 Mandy Paul and Robert Foster, 'Married to the Land: Land Grants to Aboriginal Women
in South Australia 1848–1911', *AHS*, Vol. 34, No. 121, April 2003, pp. 48–68.

23 Mark McKenna, *Looking for Blackfellas' Point: An Australian History of Place*, UNSWP,
Sydney, 2002, pp. 79–83.

24 Liz Reed, 'White Girl "Gone Off with the Blacks"', *Hecate*, Vol. 28, No. 1, 2002, pp. 9–22.

25 Milton Lewis, *Thorns on the Rose: The History of Sexually Transmitted Diseases in
Australia in International Perspective*, Australian Government Publishing Service
(AGPS), Canberra, 1998, p. 36; Reece, *Aborigines and Colonists*, p. 54; Kiddle, *Men of
Yesterday*, p. 121.

26 *Portland Guardian*, 10 September 1842, quoted in Lindsey Arkley, *The Hated Protector:
The Story of Charles Wightman Sievwright, Protector of Aborigines 1839–42*, Orbit Press,
Mentone, 2000, pp. 357–8; Jessie Mitchell, 'Corrupt Desires and the Wages of Sin:
Indigenous People, Missionaries and Male Sexuality, 1830–1850', in Ingereth Macfarlane
and Mark Hannah (eds) *Transgressions: Critical Australian Indigenous Histories*,
Aboriginal History Monograph 16, ANU E Press, Canberra, 2007, pp. 229–49, esp. pp. 233–8.

27 Lucy Frost, *A Face in the Glass: The Journal and Life of Annie Baxter Dawbin*, William
Heinemann Australia, Port Melbourne, 1992, pp. 40–1, 47–8, 51, 70, 78–9, 88, 101, 114,
124, 131, 140.

28 Miriam Dixson, *The Real Matilda: Woman and Identity in Australia 1788 to the Present*,
Revised Edition, Penguin Books, Ringwood, 1983 [1976], pp. 197–8.

29 Ross Barber, 'Rape as a Capital Offence in Nineteenth Century Queensland', *AJPH*, Vol. 21,
No. 1, April 1975, pp. 31–41.

30 Carmel Harris, 'The "Terror of the Law" As Applied to Black Rapists in Colonial
Queensland', *Hecate*, Vol. 8, No. 2, 1982, p. 41.

31 Attwood, *Making*, pp. 122–5.

32 Jill Bavin-Mizzi, *Ravished: Sexual Violence in Victorian Australia*, UNSWP, Sydney,
1995, ch. 7.

33 James Mudie, SCT, Q. 650–3, p. 40, *BPP*, Crime and Punishment, Transportation, Vol. 2;
Cunningham, *Two Years*, Vol. 2, p. 186.

34    Kathryn Cronin, *Colonial Casualties: Chinese in Early Victoria*, MUP, Carlton, 1982, p. 19.

35    Victoria, Report of the Select Committee of the Legislative Council on the Subject of
       Chinese Immigration, together with the Proceedings of the Committee and Minutes of
       Evidence, 1856–7, pp. iii–iv, PRO, CO 309/43, Australian Joint Copying Project, Reel 827,
       SLV.

36    Dinah Hales, 'Lost Histories: Chinese-European Families of Central Western New South
       Wales, 1850–80', *Journal of Australian Colonial History (JACH)*, Vol. 6, 2004, pp. 93–112.

37    *Argus*, 16 January 1857, p. 6.

38    Standish, Evidence, Report from the Select Committee upon a Bill for the Prevention of
       Contagious Diseases; together with the Proceedings of the Committee and Minutes of
       Evidence, and Appendices (SCPCD), Victoria, *Votes and Proceedings of the Legislative
       Assembly*, Session 1878, Vol. 1, Q. 104; Rev. W. Young, Report on the Condition of The
       Chinese Population in Victoria, Victoria, *Votes and Proceedings of the Legislative
       Assembly*, 1868, Vol. 3, No. 56, pp. 25, 22.

39    Smith, *Australia's Birthstain*, pp. 328, 372, fn. 27.

40    Report from the Select Committee of the Legislative Council, on the Chinese
       Immigration Bill, Minutes of Evidence, *Journal of the Legislative Council of New South
       Wales*, Session 1858, Vol. 3, Q. 69–72, p. 3; Q. 143–5, p. 5; Q. 59–61, p. 7; Q. 43–4, p. 9; Q.
       21, p. 23. Even the single exception, Captain H.H. Browne, an Immigration Agent,
       admitted that he had never encountered any official accusation of sodomy against a
       Chinese man. See Q. 36–43, p. 13.

41    *SMH*, 7 April 1853, [p. 2], in de Waal (ed.), *Unfit*, p. 246.

42    Russel Ward, *The Australian Legend*, OUP, Melbourne, 1988 [1958], pp. 99–100.

43    Clive Moore, 'The Frontier Makes Strange Bedfellows: Masculinity, Mateship and
       Homosexuality in Colonial Queensland', in Garry Wotherspoon (ed.), *Gay and Lesbian
       Perspectives III: Essays in Australian Culture*, Department of Economic History with the
       Australian Centre for Lesbian and Gay Research, University of Sydney, Sydney, 1996, pp.
       17–44. See also John Rickard, 'Sentimental Blokes', *Meanjin*, Vol. 66, No. 1, 2007, pp. 38–46.

44    Garry Wotherspoon, 'Moonlight and … Romance? The death-cell letters of Captain
       Moonlight and some of their implications', *JRAHS*, Vol. 78, Pts 3 and 4, 1992, pp. 83, 85.

45    John Molony, *Ned Kelly*, Penguin Books, Ringwood, 1989, pp. 210–13 and 286, n. 17;
       Wotherspoon, 'Moonlight', p. 88.

46    Sidney J. Baker, *The Australian Language*, Second Edition, Currawong Publishing,
       Sydney, 1966 [1945], p. 94, quoted in Wotherspoon, 'Moonlight', p. 88; Robert French,
       *Camping by a Billabong: Gay and Lesbian Stories from Australian history*, Blackwattle
       Press, Sydney, 1993, p. 32.

47    Bernard O'Dowd to Walt Whitman, 12 March 1890, in A.L. McLeod (ed.), *Walt Whitman
       in Australia and New Zealand: A Record of His Reception*, Wentworth Press, Sydney, 1964,
       p. 19.

48    Victor Kennedy and Nettie Palmer, *Bernard O'Dowd*, MUP, Carlton, 1954, pp. 39–40.

49    Bernard O'Dowd to Constance Holloway, 2 January 1908, H.H. Pearce Papers, NLA MS
       2765/9/1/13.

50    O'Dowd to Pitt, 1 November 1907, Marie Pitt Papers, Box 22A/1(b), J.K. Moir Collection,
       SLV.

51    Cocks, *Nameless Offences*, pp. 193–4.

52    Bernard O'Dowd, Diary, 21 March 1888. Hugh Anderson's transcription, Hugh Anderson
       Collection of Bernard O'Dowd Materials, Harry Ransom Humanities Research Center,
       University of Texas at Austin, 3.78–3.99.

53    Bernard O'Dowd, Exercise Book, Loose sheet, Bernard O'Dowd Papers,
       MS 7972/7973/8037 Box 2/7, SLV.

54    French (with Garry Wotherspoon), 'More Than Just Friends?', in French, *Camping*, p. 30.

55    French, *Camping*, pp. 39–41; Clive Moore, *Sunshine and Rainbows: The Development of
       Gay and Lesbian Culture in Queensland*, University of Queensland Press (UQP) in
       association with the API Network, St Lucia, 2001, pp. 64–5.

56  George Chauncey, *Gay New York: Gender, Urban Culture, and the Making of the Gay Male World, 1890–1940*, Basic Books, New York, 1994, pp. 80–1, 88–97; Leigh Astbury, *City Bushmen: the Heidelberg School and the Rural Mythology*, OUP, Melbourne, 1985, pp. 100–29.

57  *Wilcannia Times*, 12 October 1882, [p. 2] and *Pastoral Times* (Deniliquin), 21 October 1882, [p. 3], in de Waal (ed.), *Unfit*, Vol. 2, pp. 688–93.

58  Sumner Locke Elliott, *Fairyland*, Harper and Row, New York, 1990, p. 113. See also Sharon Clarke, *Sumner Locke Elliott: Writing Life*, Allen & Unwin, Sydney, 1996, pp. 101–2.

59  Cocks, *Nameless Offences*, ch. 3; Chauncey, *Gay New York*, ch. 5.

60  Moore, *Sunshine*, p. 66. Moore, 'Frontier Makes Strange Bedfellows', pp. 34–7.

61  William James Chidley, *The Confessions of William James Chidley*, S. McInerney (ed.), UQP, St Lucia, 1977, pp. 35–6.

62  *Queen v. Thomas Martin*, Supreme Court, Colony of Victoria, 1868, VPRS 264/5, Public Records Office of Victoria (PROV).

63  Bavin-Mizzi, *Ravished*, p. 123.

64  Moore, *Sunshine*, p. 43; Michael Gilding, *The Making and Breaking of the Australian Family*, Allen & Unwin, Sydney, 1991; Bavin-Mizzi, *Ravished*, pp. 123–4.

65  *Queen v. Thomas Martin*, Supreme Court, Colony of Victoria, 1887, VPRS 264/5, PROV.

66  Robert French, '"Where the Action Was": Archival Sources for Gay History in Australia', in Robert Aldrich and Garry Wotherspoon (eds), *Gay Perspectives: Essays in Australian Gay Culture*, Department of Economic History, The University of Sydney, 1992, pp. 187–8.

67  Walter J. Fogarty, '"Certain Habits": The Development of a Concept of the Male Homosexual in New South Wales Law, 1788–1900', in Aldrich and Wotherspoon (eds), *Gay Perspectives*, pp. 59–76.

68  Chidley, *Confessions*, pp. 60, 164, 175. See also Lucy Chesser, *Parting with My Sex: Cross-Dressing, Inversion and Sexuality in Australian Cultural Life*, SUP, Sydney, 2006, pp. 194–7.

69  Ruth Ford, Contested Desires: Narratives of Passionate Friends, Married Masqueraders and Lesbian Love in Australia, 1918–1945, PhD Thesis, La Trobe University, 2000, pp. 31–48, quotation at p. 48.

70  *Argus*, 20 July 1863, p. 5.

71  *Argus*, 19 August 1862, p. 7.

72  Chesser, *Parting*, p. 190 and 'Cross Dressing, Sexual (Mis)representation and Homosexual Desire, 1863–1893', in David L. Phillips and Graham Willett (eds), *Australia's Homosexual Histories: Gay and Lesbian Perspectives 5*, Australian Centre for Lesbian and Gay Research and the Australian Lesbian and Gay Archives, Sydney and Melbourne, 2000, pp. 16–17; Judith Rodriguez, 'The Original Nosey Alf', *Australian Literary Studies*, Vol. 7, No. 2, October 1975, pp. 176–84.

73  Lucy Chesser, '"A Woman Who Married Three Wives": Management of Disruptive Knowledge in the 1879 Australian Case of Edward De Lacy Evans', *Journal of Women's History*, Vol. 9, No. 4, 1998, pp. 53–77. See also Chesser, 'Cross Dressing', pp. 14–15 and *Parting*, esp. ch. 1.

74  Orlebar, Report, in G.R. Quaife (ed.), *Gold and Colonial Society 1851–1870*, Cassell Australia, Stanmore, 1975, pp. 140–3.

75  Howitt, *Land*, p. 23.

76  *Ibid.*, p. 94.

77  *The Journal of Annie Baxter Dawbin July 1858–May 1868*, Lucy Frost (ed.), UQP in association with the State Library of New South Wales, St Lucia, 1998, 5 July 1863, p. 337.

78  Charles Thatcher, 'Colonial Courtship, or Love on the Diggings', in Charles Thatcher, *Thatcher's Colonial Songs: Forming a Complete Comic History of the Early Diggings*, Cole's Book Arcade, Melbourne, n.d. [Facsimile edition, Libraries Board of South Australia, Adelaide, 1964], p. 8.

79  Lord Robert Cecil, *Lord Robert Cecil's Gold Fields Diary*, Sir Ernest Scott (ed.), MUP, Carlton, 1945, p. 13.

80    Howitt, *Land*, p. 210.

81    Orlebar, Report, p. 38.

82    William Kelly, *Life in Victoria or Victoria in 1853, and Victoria in 1858, Showing the March of Improvement made by the Colony within Those Periods, in Town and Country, Cities and the Diggings*, Vol. 1, No. 6, Historical Reprints Series, Lowden Publishing, Kilmore, 1977 [1859], pp. 186–7, 237; Patricia Grimshaw and Charles Fahey, 'Family and Community in Nineteenth-Century Castlemaine', in Patricia Grimshaw, Chris McConville and Ellen McEwen (eds), *Families in Colonial Australia*, Allen & Unwin, Sydney, 1985, p. 85; William Hopkins, Gold Fields' Commission of Inquiry, Report of the Commission Appointed to Enquire into the Condition of the Gold Fields of Victoria, Q. 3547–8, p. 183, Victorian Legislative Council, *Votes & Proceedings*, 1854–5, Vol. 2.

83    Benjamin Boyce to Father and Mother, 1 February 1844, in Eric Richards, 'A Voice from Below: Benjamin Boyce in South Australia 1839–1846', *LH*, No. 27, November 1974, p. 71.

84    Frost (ed.), *Journal of Annie Baxter Dawbin*, 23 May 1860, p. 173.

85    John Rule, *The Labouring Classes in Early Industrial England, 1750–1850*, Longman, London and New York, 1987, pp. 197–8.

86    Barrett-Ducrocq, *Love*, p. 98.

87    Alan Atkinson, *Camden: Farm and Village Life in Early New South Wales*, OUP, Melbourne, 1992 [1988], p. 133.

88    James George Beaney, *The Generative System and its Functions in Health and Disease*, F.F. Bailliere, Melbourne, 1872, pp. vi–vii.

89    Peter F. McDonald, *Marriage in Australia: Age at First Marriage and Proportions Marrying, 1860–1971*, Australian Family Formation Project Monograph No. 2, Department of Demography, Institute of Advanced Studies, Australian National University (ANU), Canberra, 1975, p. 105.

90    John Ferry, *Colonial Armidale*, UQP, St Lucia, 1999, p. 115.

91    Joseph Elliott, *Our Home in Australia: A Description of Cottage Life in 1860*, The Flannel Flower Press, Sydney, 1984, pp. 7, 15, 21, 27–8, 35, 88, 89.

92    *Australian Medical Journal*, July 1857, pp. 162, 164.

93    Ferry, *Colonial Armidale*, pp. 176–7.

94    *Australian Medical Journal*, January 1862, p. 6.

95    J.H. Palmer, Report from the Select Committee on the Condition of the Working Classes of the Metropolis together with the Proceedings of the Committee, Minutes of Evidence and Appendix (SCCWCM), Q. 1260, pp. 68–9, *Votes and Proceedings of the Legislative Assembly of New South Wales*, 1859–60, Vol. 4.

96    Lynette Finch, *The Classing Gaze: Sexuality, Class and Surveillance*, Allen & Unwin, Sydney, 1993, ch. 3.

97    Standish, SCPCD, Q. 86–9, p. 4.

98    Beaney, *Generative*, p. 84.

99    Palmer, SCCWCM, Q. 1237, p. 67.

100   Beaney, *Generative*, p. 88.

101   Havelock Ellis, Diary 1875–90, Extracts, 24 June 1877, in Geoffrey Dutton, *Kanga Creek: Havelock Ellis in Australia*, Picador, Sydney, 1989, p. 100.

102   Jennings, *Lesbian History of Britain*, p. 28.

103   Beaney, *Generative*, pp. 86–7.

104   *Ibid.*, pp. 94–5, 98–9.

105   Aaron, SCCWCM, Q. 665–6, p. 35.

106   G.B. Hill, SCPCD, Q. 227–9, p. 9.

107   G. Kemp, SCCWCM, Q. 2194, p.134.

108   Kay Daniels, 'Prostitution in Tasmania during the Transition from Penal Settlement to "Civilised" Society', in Kay Daniels (ed.), *So Much Hard Work: Women and Prostitution in Australia*, Fontana/Collins, Sydney, 1984, pp. 29–30.

109   S.W. Mansfield, SCCWCM, Q. 2603, p. 152.

110  Jenny Lee and Charles Fahey, 'A Boom for Whom? Some Developments in the Australian Labour Market 1870–1891', *LH*, No. 50, May 1986, pp. 1–27.

111  Standish, SCPCD, Q. 27, p. 2.

112  Paul de Serville, *Pounds and Pedigrees: The Upper Class in Victoria 1850–80*, OUP, Melbourne, 1991, pp. 60–1; John Lahey, *Damn You, John Christie! The Public Life of Australia's Sherlock Holmes*, SLV, Melbourne, 1993, pp. 20–1.

113  'Prostitution Medically Considered', *Australian Medical Journal*, May 1873, p. 142.

114  *South Australian Parliamentary Debates* (*SAPD*), House of Assembly (HA), 12 November 1884, p. 1702, 13 August 1885, p. 538.

115  Daniels, 'Prostitution in Tasmania', pp. 43–5; Judith Allen, 'The Making of a Prostitute Proletariat in Early Twentieth Century New South Wales', in Daniels (ed.), *So Much Hard Work*, p. 206.

116  Question to Standish, SCPCD, Q. 197, p. 8; *SAPD*, HA, 20 August 1885, p. 603.

117  Graeme Davison, 'Introduction', in Graeme Davison, David Dunstan and Chris McConville (eds), *The Outcasts of Melbourne: Essays in Social History*, Allen & Unwin, Sydney, 1985, pp. 8–10; John Singleton, *A Narrative of Incidents in the Eventful Life of a Physician*, M.L. Hutchison, Melbourne, 1891, pp. 245–69; Shurlee Swain with Renate Howe, *Single Mothers and Their Children: Disposal, Punishment and Survival in Australia*, CUP, Melbourne, 1995, p. 74.

118  Susanne Davies, '"Ragged, Dirty ... Infamous and Obscene": The "Vagrant" in Late-Nineteenth-Century Melbourne', in David Phillips and Susanne Davies (eds), *A Nation of Rogues?: Crime, Law and Punishment in Colonial Australia*, MUP, Carlton, 1994, pp. 144–51.

119  See SCPCD, Q. 480, p. 19; Q. 512, p. 20; Q. 940, p. 37; Q. 1204, p. 46; Q. 1217, p. 47; Q. 1341, p. 52; Q. 1472, p. 58; Q. 1489–90, p. 59.

120  Great Britain's legislation came in three instalments in 1864, 1866 and 1869, while Queensland's laws were passed in 1868 and Tasmania's in 1879.

121  Mary Murnane and Kay Daniels, 'Prostitutes as "Purveyors of Disease": Venereal Disease Legislation in Tasmania, 1868–1945', *Hecate*, Vol. 5, No. 1, 1979, pp. 5–21; E. Barclay, 'Queensland's Contagious Diseases Act, 1868 – "The Act for the Encouragement of Vice" and some Nineteenth Century Attempts to Repeal It Part 1', *Queensland Heritage*, Vol. 2, No. 10, pp. 27–34 and 'Queensland's Contagious Diseases Act, 1868 – "The Act for the Encouragement of Vice" and some Nineteenth Century Attempts to Repeal It Part 2', *Queensland Heritage*, Vol. 3, No. 1, pp. 27–34.

122  Judith Smart, 'Sex, the State and the "Scarlet Scourge": Gender, Citizenship and Venereal Diseases Regulation in Australia during the Great War', *Women's History Review*, Vol. 7, No. 1, 1998, p. 7.

123  Machefer to O'Dowd, n.d. [c. November 1890], Bernard O'Dowd Papers, Box 1/6, SLV.

124  R.F. Hudson, SCPCD, Q. 1569, p. 62; Q. 1597, p. 63; James Dalton, *SCPCD*, Q. 386, p. 15.

125  Evidence, SCPCD, Q. 53, p. 3.

126  Standish, SCPCD, Q. 122–4, p. 5; Susan Horan, '"More Sinned Against than Sinning?" Prostitution in South Australia, 1836–1914', in Daniels (ed.), *So Much Hard Work*, p. 98.

127  Chris McConville, 'The Location of Melbourne's Prostitutes, 1870–1920', *HS*, Vol. 19, No. 74, April 1980, pp. 90–1.

128  See, for instance, *Argus*, 18 September 1860, pp. 5–6; 20 September 1860, p. 5; 9 October 1860, p. 6; 10 October 1860, pp. 5–6; 11 October 1860, p. 6; 2 December 1860, pp. 5–6.

129  Finch, *Classing Gaze*, p. 12 and ch. 2.

130  *Argus*, 23 November 1864, p. 6.

131  *Ibid.*, 19 November 1864, p. 5.

132  *Ibid.* and *Age*, 18, 19, 21, 22 and 23 November 1864.

133  Candler, Addenda to Diary, 24 September 1867, p. 139.

134  Frost (ed.), *Journal of Annie Baxter Dawbin*, 10 July 1864, p. 428.

135  *Argus*, 24 November 1864, p. 4.

136  *Age*, 23 November 1864, p. 4.

# Endnotes

137  Penny Russell, 'A Wish of Distinction': Colonial Gentility and Femininity, MUP, Carlton, 1994, pp. 93, 115–20.

138  Age, 23 November 1864, p. 4.

139  James Curtis, Rustlings in the Golden City, James Curtis [Printer], Ballarat, n.d. [c. 1890], part VII, pp. 3–4; Alex Owen, The Darkened Room: Women, Power, and Spiritualism in Late Nineteenth Century England, Virago Press, London, 1989, pp. 203, 217 and passim.

140  Henry Varley, Lecture to Men on a Vitally Important Subject, Containing Invaluable Information for Young Men, and Those Who Are Married, Varley Bros, Melbourne, 1894, pp. 35–6.

141  Richard Arthur, Purity and Impurity, Australasian White Cross League (AWCL), Purity Series No. 2, George Robertson & Co., Melbourne, n.d., p. 21.

142  de Serville, Pounds and Pedigrees, pp. 138–9.

143  John Stanley James, The Vagabond Papers, MUP, Carlton, 1969, pp. 229, 235; G.B. Hill, SCPCD, Q. 258.

144  Castieau, Diary, 4 May 1855, in Finnane (ed.), Difficulties, p. 10.

145  Candler, Addenda to Diary, 23 September 1867, p. 133.

146  John Russell, Argus, 7 May 1883, quoted in Keith Dunstan, Wowsers, Angus & Robertson, Sydney, 1974 [1968], pp. 24–5.

147  Candler, Addenda to Diary, 10 November 1867, pp. 276–7.

148  Ibid., 6 October 1867, pp. 221–2.

149  Deana Heath, Purifying Empire: Obscenity and the Politics of Moral Regulation in Britain, India and Australia, CUP, Cambridge, 2010, pp. 129–30.

150  E. Graeme Robertson, 'Melbourne's Public Anatomical and Anthropological Museums, and the Jordans', Medical Journal of Australia (MJA), 4 February 1956, pp. 165–7, 169–71.

151  Russell, Wish, p. 93.

152  Candler, Addenda to Diary, 24 September 1867, p. 153; 23 September 1867, pp. 134–5, 128–9.

153  Penny Russell, '"For Better or for Worse": Love, Power and Sexuality in Upper-Class Marriages in Melbourne, 1860–1980', AFS, Vol. 7/8, Summer 1988, pp. 11–26, quotation at p. 18.

154  Russell, Wish, p. 93.

155  I have corrected Candler's slight misquotation: Thomas Moore, Moore's Poetical Works, Complete in One Volume, Longman, Brown, Green & Longmans, London, 1853, p. 386.

156  Candler, Addenda to Diary, 23 September 1867, pp. 132, 135.

157  Frost (ed.), Journal of Annie Baxter Dawbin, 10 July 1864, p. 428.

158  Michael Clarke, 'Big' Clarke, Queensberry Hill Press, Carlton, 1980, pp. 68–9.

159  Clarke, 'Big' Clarke, pp. 68ff.

160  Beaney, Generative, pp. 294, 296.

161  Ibid., p. 34.

162  Alexander Paterson, The Male Generative Function in Health and Disease, Second Edition, L. Bruck, Medical Publisher, Sydney, 1887, p. 51.

163  Ibid., pp. 51–2.

164  Walter Balls-Headley, The Evolution of the Diseases of Women, Smith, Elder & Co., London, 1894, pp. 2, 34.

165  A.W. Martin, Henry Parkes: A Biography, MUP, Carlton, 1980, p. 422.

166  Queen v. Thomas Martin, Supreme Court, Colony of Victoria, 1887, VPRS 264/5, PROV.

167  Candler, Addenda to Diary, 11 August 1867, p. 28.

168  Havelock Ellis, 'My Life: From Chapter Three [Australia]' [first published 1940], in Dutton, Kanga Creek, p. 187.

169  Candler, Addenda to Diary, 6 October 1867, pp. 221–2.

170  de Serville, Pounds and Pedigrees, pp. 54, 65, 130; Ann Galbally, Redmond Barry: An Anglo-Irish Australian, MUP, Carlton, 1995, p. 174; Candler, Addenda to Diary, 2 December 1867, p. 317.

171  Frost (ed.), Journal of Annie Baxter Dawbin, 1 January 1864, p. 377; 16 June 1864, p. 422 and p. 408, n. 108; Simon Cooke, 'Candler, Samuel Curtis', in Christopher Cunneen with

Jill Roe, Beverley Kingston and Stephen Garton (eds), *Australian Dictionary of Biography (ADB) Supplement 1580–1980*, MUP, Carlton, 2005, p. 64.

172 Galbally, *Redmond Barry*, pp. 68, 101.

173 Martin, *Henry Parkes*, pp. 321, 378–80.

174 Margaret Glass, *Charles Cameron Kingston: Federation Father*, The Miegunyah Press at MUP, Carlton, 1997, esp. pp. 43–51.

175 Charles Francis, 'Stawell, Sir William Foster (1815–1889)', Bede Nairn (ed.), *ADB*, Vol. 6: 1851–1890 R–Z, MUP, Carlton, 1976, p. 175.

176 Young, *Sir William Foster*, p. 8. See also Galbally, *Redmond Barry*, pp. 71–2.

177 Candler, Addenda to Diary, 2 December 1867, p. 315.

178 Ellis, 'My Life', in Dutton, *Kanga Creek*, p. 167.

179 *Ibid.*, p. 193 and *passim*.

180 Ellis, Diary, 1 September 1877, in *ibid.*, p. 103.

181 Ellis, 'My Life', in *ibid.*, p. 215.

182 Geoffrey Dutton, 'Introduction', in *ibid.*, p. 16.

183 Ellis, 'My Life', in *ibid.*, pp. 196, 208.

184 *Ibid.*, pp. 211–12, 217.

## CHAPTER 3

1 Clive Moore, 'Colonial Manhood and Masculinities', *JAS*, No. 56, 1998, p. 37.

2 Balls-Headley, *Evolution*, pp. 12, 22.

3 Chidley, *Confessions*, p. 15.

4 William James Chidley, 'The Answer', in Bill Hornadge, *Chidley's Answer to the Sex Problem*, Review Publications, Dubbo, 1971, p. 56.

5 For Chidley, see Mark Finnane, 'Sexuality and Social Order: The State versus Chidley', in Sydney Labour History Group, *What Rough Beast? The State and Social Order in Australian History*, Allen & Unwin/The Australian Society for the Study of Labour History, Sydney, 1982, pp. 192–219 and 'The Popular Defence of Chidley', *LH*, No. 41, November 1981, pp. 57–73; Robert Darby, 'William Acton's Antipodean Disciples: A Colonial Perspective on His Theories of Male Sexual (Dys)function', *Journal of the History of Sexuality (JHS)*, Vol. 13, No. 2, 2004, pp. 173–82.

6 Finnane, 'Popular Defence', pp. 68–9.

7 William Saumarez Smith, Evidence, and Charles Mackellar's question to W.W. Rutledge, in *New South Wales Royal Commission on the Decline of the Birthrate and on the Mortality of Infants in New South Wales (RCDB)*, Vol. 2, Minutes, Evidence, Exhibits, Index, NLA microform (mfm) N69, Q. 6349 and Q. 6461, pp. 219, 226.

8 T.P. Lucas, *Do Thyself No Harm: A Lecture to Men By Dr T.P. Lucas Delivered to Young Men's Christian Association, Melbourne*, Mason, Firth & McCutcheon [Printers], Melbourne, 1885, pp. 43ff.

9 Varley, *Lecture to Men*, p. 32.

10 Marilyn Lake, 'The Politics of Respectability: Identifying the Masculinist Context', *HS*, Vol. 22, No. 86, 1986, pp. 116–31.

11 *Ibid.*, p. 129–30.

12 *Ibid.*, p. 130.

13 John Rickard, *H.B. Higgins: The Rebel as Judge*, Allen & Unwin, Sydney, 1984, pp. 66–7.

14 Judith A. Allen, *Rose Scott: Vision and Revision in Feminism*, OUP, Melbourne, 1994, pp. 90–2.

15 Pat Quiggin, *No Rising Generation: Women & Fertility in Late Nineteenth Century Australia*, Australian Family Formation Project Monograph No. 10, Department of Demography, Research School of Social Sciences, ANU, Canberra, 1988, pp. 21, 37.

16 *Ibid.*, p. 3; Lado T. Ruzicka and John C. Caldwell, *The End of Demographic Transition in Australia*, Australian Family Formation Project Monograph No. 5, Department of Demography, Institute of Advanced Studies, ANU, Canberra, 1977, p. 8.

17  Ruzicka and Caldwell, *End of Demographic Transition*, p. 9.

18  Quiggin, *No Rising Generation*, p. 118.

19  Simon Szreter, *Fertility, Class and Gender in Britain, 1860–1940*, CUP, Cambridge, 1996, pp. 389–424.

20  Hera Cook, *The Long Sexual Revolution: English Women, Sex, and Contraception 1800–1975*, OUP, Oxford, 2004 and Cook, 'Unseemly and Unwomanly Behaviour: Comparing Women's Control of Their Fertility in Australia and England from 1890 to 1970', *Journal of Population Research*, Vol. 17, No. 2, 2000, pp. 134–5; Szreter, *Fertility*, pp. 389–424.

21  Mark Girouard, *The Return of Camelot: Chivalry and the English Gentleman*, Yale University Press, New Haven and London, 1981.

22  Alexander Paterson, *Physical Health of Woman: Useful Knowledge for Maiden, Wife, and Mother*, Edwards, Dunlop and Co., Sydney, 1890, pp. 71–3, 79–83; Paterson, *Male Generative Function*, p. 51.

23  Cook, 'Unseemly and Unwomanly Behaviour', p. 135; Quiggin, *No Rising Generation*, p. 32; Margaret Anderson, 'No Sex Please We're Demographers: Nineteenth Century Fertility Decline Revisited', in Joy Damousi and Katherine Ellinghaus (eds), *Citizenship, Women and Social Justice: International Historical Perspectives*, History Department, University of Melbourne, Melbourne, 1999, p. 254.

24  Hugh Jackson, 'Fertility Decline in New South Wales: The Mackellar Royal Commission Reconsidered', *AHS*, Vol. 23, No. 92, April 1989, pp. 260–73.

25  Angus McLaren, *Birth Control in Nineteenth-Century England*, Croom Helm, London, 1978, esp. chs. 1, 12 and 13.

26  Peter Coleman, *Obscenity, Blasphemy, Sedition: 100 Years of Censorship in Australia*, Angus & Robertson, Sydney, 1974, pp. 53–7.

27  Frank M.C. Forster and Nigel H. Sinnott, 'Joseph Symes, H.K. Rusden and the Knowlton Pamphlet', *Atheist Journal*, Vol. 8, No. 4, pp. 9–11.

28  Stewart Warren, *The Wife's Guide and Friend*, Fifth Edition, Saunders & Co., Melbourne, 1898, p. v; *RCDB*, Vol. 2, p. 271; *RCDB*, Vol. 1, Report, p. 17.

29  *Truth* (Sydney), 26 May 1895, p. 8.

30  Brettena Smyth, *Limitation of Offspring*, Eighth Edition, self-published, Melbourne, 1893, pp. 19, 26.

31  Paterson, *Physical Health of Woman*, pp. 123–4.

32  *RCDB*, Vol. 2, Q. 2934, p. 89.

33  Dr R. Scot Skirving, *ibid.*, Q. 3157–60, pp. 97–8.

34  Dr W.J.S. McKay, *ibid.*, Q. 3312–16, 3325, pp. 104–5.

35  Brettena Smyth, *What Every Woman Should Know, Diseases Incidental to Women. Their Cause, Prevention and Cure, by Mrs B. Smyth, Being the Substance of a Lecture delivered at the Town Hall, North Melbourne*, H.J. Prender, Melbourne, 1895, p. 42.

36  Lyn Finch and Jon Stratton, 'The Australian Working Class and the Practice of Abortion 1880–1939', *JAS*, No. 23, November 1988, p. 48.

37  Dr R. Arthur, *RCDB*, Vol. 2, Q. 5250, pp. 179–80.

38  Dr C.W. Morgan, *ibid.*, Q. 1086, p. 27.

39  Patricia Sumerling, 'The Darker Side of Motherhood: Abortion and Infanticide in South Australia 1870–1910', *Journal of the Historical Society of South Australia (JHSSA)*, No. 13, 1985, p. 113.

40  Janet McCalman, *Sex and Suffering: Women's Health and a Women's Hospital: The Royal Women's Hospital, Melbourne 1856–1996*, MUP, Carlton, 1999, pp. 128–9.

41  Finch and Stratton, 'The Australian Working Class'; Judith Allen, 'Octavius Beale Re-considered: Infanticide, Babyfarming and Abortion in NSW 1880–1939', in Sydney Labour History Group, *What Rough Beast?*, pp. 111–29.

42  Sumerling, 'Darker', pp. 113–14.

43  *Ibid.*, p. 117.

44  Report from the Select Committee on Law Respecting Practice of Medicine and Surgery; together with the Proceedings of the Committee, Minutes of Evidence, and Appendices,

*Journal of the Legislative Council of New South Wales*, Session 1887–8, Vol. XLIII, Part IV, Report, p. 8; A.R. Wilkinson, Evidence, Q. 2172–2184, pp. 80–1; R.H. Willis, Evidence, Q. 2532–4, 2554–5, pp. 93–4; Appendix G8, p. 130.
45  *Truth* (Sydney), 26 May 1895, p. 8.
46  *Ibid.*, 10 November 1895, p. 8.
47  McCalman, *Sex and Suffering*, p. 128.
48  Kevin J. Fraser, 'Dr. L.L. Smith's Entrepreneurial Medical Practice in Victorian Melbourne', in H. Attwood, R. Gillespie and M. Lewis (eds), *New Perspectives on the History of Medicine: First National Conference of the Australian Society of the History of Medicine 1989*, University of Melbourne and the Australian Society of the History of Medicine, Medical History Unit, University of Melbourne, Parkville, 1990, pp. 143–62; Philippa Martyr, *Paradise of Quacks: An Alternative History of Medicine in Australia*, Macleay Press, Sydney, 2002, pp. 121–2.
49  Allen, 'Octavius Beale Re-considered'; Judith A. Allen, 'The Trials of Abortion in Late Nineteenth and Early Twentieth Century Australia', in David Walker with Stephen Garton and Julia Horne (eds), *Crimes and Trials*, an issue of *Australian Cultural History (ACH)*, No. 12, 1993, pp. 87–99; and Swain with Howe, *Single Mothers*, pp. 36–47 and ch. 5.
50  Finch and Stratton, 'The Australian Working Class'.
51  Smyth, *Limitation*, pp. 26, 24.
52  J. Spence, *RCDB*, Vol. 2, Q. 2308, p. 65.
53  Marjorie Johnston with John Wippell, *Ansell: Portrait of an International Company*, Ansell International, Glen Waverley, 1990, pp. 4–5; Geoffrey Blainey, *Jumping Over the Wheel*, Allen & Unwin, Sydney, 1993, pp. 237–9.
54  McLaren, *Birth Control*, p. 222.
55  Sergeant George Jeffes, *RCDB*, Vol. 2, Q. 5343, p. 183; *North Melbourne Advertiser*, 21 October 1892, in Smyth, *What Every Woman*, n.p.
56  *Truth* (Sydney), 26 May 1895, p. 8; Smyth, *Limitation*, n.p.
57  John Hore, Sub Inspector (No. 2 Division, Fitzroy), 11 November 1909, Age of Consent Report 1909, Chief Secretary's Files, PROV, VPRS 1226/PO, Box 107.
58  T.A. Coghlan, *The Decline of the Birth-Rate of New South Wales and Other Phenomena of Child-Birth: An Essay in Statistics*, William Applegate Gullick, Government Printer, Sydney, 1903, pp. 7–8.
59  Age of Consent Report 1909, Chief Secretary's Files, PROV, VPRS 1226/PO, Box 107; Swain with Howe, *Single Mothers*, p. 21.
60  Varley, *Lecture to Men*, p. 23.
61  *Ibid.*, pp. 29–30.
62  *RCDB*, Vol. 2, Q. 5619, p. 183.
63  *RCDB*, Vol. 2, Q. 6130, p. 216.
64  Quiggin, *No Rising Generation*, pp. 74, 77 and *passim*.
65  G.B. Hill, SCPVD, Q. 204, p. 8.
66  H.W. Sainsbury, 6 November 1909, Age of Consent Report 1909, Chief Secretary's Files, PROV, VPRS 1226/PO, Box 107.
67  F.T.W. Ford, SCPVD, Q. 1357–8, p. 53.
68  J. Duncan, Report of the Shops and Factories Commission; together with Minutes of Proceedings, Evidence, and Appendices, Q. 4837, p. 130, South Australia, *Parliamentary Papers*, 1892, Vol. 2, No. 27.
69  *Truth* (Sydney), 18 April 1897, p. 8.
70  *RCDB*, Vol. 2, Q. 3070, p. 94.
71  W.H. Soul, *ibid.*, Q. 1557, p. 10.
72  H.S. Brothwood, *ibid.*, Q. 1273, p. 33. On blushing, see Russell, *Wish*, p. 110.
73  See, for example, H.S. Levy, Evidence, *RCDB*, Vol. 2, Q. 744, p. 17.
74  *Truth* (Sydney), 11 August 1895, p. 8.
75  Dr A. Watson-Munro, *RCDB*, Vol. 2, Q. 2678, p. 79.
76  Beaney, *Generative System*, pp. 141, 144, 148.

77    Paterson, *Physical Health of Woman*, pp. 130–2.

78    McLaren, *Birth Control*, pp. 126–7, 132, 136.

79    Beaney, *Generative*, p. 143.

80    Neville Hicks, 'This Sin and Scandal': *Australia's Population Debate 1891–1911*, ANU Press, Canberra, ACT and Norwalk, Conn., 1978, pp. 68–71.

81    *RCDB*, Vol. 2, Q. 5496–525, pp. 187–8.

82    Judith Allen, '"Our Deeply Degraded Sex" and "The Animal in Man": Rose Scott, Feminism and Sexuality 1890–1925', *AFS*, Vol. 7/8, Summer 1988, pp. 65–91.

83    Bessie Harrison Lee, *Marriage and Heredity*, Fourth Edition, J.J. Howard [Printer], Melbourne, 1894, pp. 8, 43, 55; Patricia Grimshaw, 'Bessie Harrison Lee and the Fight for Voluntary Motherhood', in Marilyn Lake and Farley Kelly (eds), *Double Time: Women in Victoria – 150 Years*, Penguin Books, Ringwood, 1985, pp. 139–47.

84    Allen, *Rose Scott*, pp. 181–2.

85    Louisa Lawson, 'The Divorce Extension Bill or, The Drunkard's Wife', *Dawn*, March 1890, in Olive Lawson (ed.), *The First Voice of Australian Feminism: Excerpts from Louisa Lawson's* The Dawn *1888–1895*, Simon & Schuster Australia in association with the New Endeavour Press, Brookvale and St Peters, 1990, pp. 53–4.

86    W.C. Windeyer, *Ex Parte Collins: A Judgment*, published by the author, Sydney, 1889, p. 13.

87    *Woman's Voice*, 18 May 1895, in Jan Roberts and Beverley Kingston (eds), *Maybanke: A Woman's Voice: The Collected Work of Maybanke Selfe-Wolstenholme-Anderson 1845–1927*, Ruskin Rowe Press, Avalon Beach, n.d. [c. 2001], pp. 136–7.

88    *Woman's Voice*, 29 June 1895, in Roberts and Kingston (eds), *Maybanke*, p. 142, also quoted in Susan Magarey, *Passions of the First Wave Feminists*, UNSWP, Sydney, 2001, pp. 67–8. See also Susan Sheridan, 'The *Woman's Voice* on Sexuality', in Susan Magarey, Sue Rowley and Susan Sheridan (eds), *Debutante Nation: Feminism Contests the 1890s*, Allen & Unwin, Sydney, 1993, pp. 114–24.

89    Janette M. Bomford, *That Dangerous and Persuasive Woman: Vida Goldstein*, MUP, Carlton, 1993, pp. 28–9.

90    Catherine Helen Spence, *A Week in the Future*, Hale & Iremonger, Sydney, 1987 [first published 1888–89], pp. 39, 79; Magarey, *Passions*, pp. 77–8.

91    See, for example, George Black, 'Malthusianism, New & Old: An Inquiry into the Alleged Decline of the Birthrate', clippings, n.d. [after 1903], George Black File, Evatt Collection, Flinders University, South Australia.

92    J.A. Andrews, *What is Communism?*, Bob James (ed.), Backyard Press, Prahran, n.d., pp. 106–7.

93    O'Dowd to Constance Holloway, 13 December 1905, H.H. Pearce Papers, NLA MS 2765/9/1/10; *Bookfellow*, 21 February 1907.

94    *Tocsin*, 4 November 1897.

95    Edward M. Curr, *The Australian Race: Its Origin, Languages, Customs, Place of Landing in Australia, and the Routes by Which It Spread Itself over That Continent*, Volume I, John Farnes, Government Printer, Melbourne, 1886, p. 72.

96    [Rosamond Benham], *Sense About Sex, By A Woman Doctor*, The Century [Printer], Adelaide, 1905, p. 48.

97    *The Victorian Law Reports, 1907*, pp. 112–17; *The Wayside Goose*, 30 June 1906.

98    *Argus*, 9 October 1911, p. 7; 16 October, 1911, p. 9; *Truth* (Melbourne), 14 October 1911, p. 6.

99    Finnane, 'Popular Defence'.

100   Letter from Archibald Strong, date obscured, 1916, in William James Chidley Papers, Mitchell Library (ML) MS 143/8, p. 663; Strong to O'Dowd, 8 October 1911, H.H. Pearce Papers, NLA 2765/9/1/3; *Argus*, 9 October 1911, p. 7; *Truth* (Melbourne), 14 October 1911, p. 6.

101   See for example, 40 Vic. No. 544, *An Act for More Effectually Preventing the Sale of Obscene Books, Pictures, Prints, and Other Articles*, 24 October 1876 and 43 Vic. No. 24, *An Act for More Effectually Preventing the Sale of Obscene Books, Pictures, Prints, and Other Articles*, 22 April 1880; and Coleman, *Obscenity*, prologue and pp. 96–7.

102  15 Vic. No. 4, *An Act for the More Effectual Prevention of Vagrancy, and for the Punishment of Idle and Disorderly Persons, Rogues, and Vagabonds, and Incorrigible Rogues, in the Colony of New South Wales*, 1 December 1851.

103  David Day, *Smugglers and Sailors: The Customs History of Australia 1788–1901*, AGPS, Canberra, 1992, pp. 240, 285.

104  Coleman, *Obscenity*, pp. 3–6.

105  Heath, *Purifying Empire*, ch. 4, esp. pp. 101–7.

106  *Age*, 3 August 1894, p. 3.

107  David Day, *Contraband and Controversy: The Customs History of Australia from 1901*, AGPS, Canberra, 1996, pp. 104–6; Lahey, *Damn You, John Christie!*, pp. 217–18; Coleman, *Obscenity*, pp. 6–8.

108  Day, *Contraband*, p. 104.

109  John F. Williams, *The Quarantined Culture: Australian Reactions to Modernism 1913–1939*, CUP, Melbourne, 1995; Heath, *Purifying Empire*, p. 129.

110  Day, *Contraband*, p. 104; Joe Rich, 'G.W.L. Marshall-Hall and the Meaning of Indecency in Late Victorian Melbourne', *JAS*, No. 23, November 1988, pp. 67–9.

111  Chidley, *Confessions*, p. 47.

112  Lisa Z. Sigel, 'Filth in the Wrong People's Hands: Postcards and the Expansion of Pornography in Britain and the Atlantic World, 1880–1914, *Journal of Social History*, Vol. 33, No. 4, 2000, pp. 859–85.

113  Day, *Contraband*, pp. 103–4; Coleman, *Obscenity*, pp. 113–14; Ford, 'Contested Desires', pp. 31–48; Patrick White, *Flaws in the Glass: A Self-Portrait*, Jonathan Cape, London, 1981, pp. 43–4; Lahey, *Damn You, John Christie!*, p. 220; Jill Julius Matthews, 'Blue Movies in Australia: A Preliminary History', *NFSA Journal*, Vol. 2, No. 3, 2007, pp. 2–4.

114  John Hetherington, *Norman Lindsay: The Embattled Olympian*, OUP, Melbourne, 1973, pp. 57–60, 101–3. The plates of this book show both paintings (between pp. 96 and 97).

115  Heath, *Purifying Empire*, pp. 129–31.

116  Allen, 'Octavius', p. 127.

117  Heath, *Purifying Empire*, pp. 131–2, 137–8.

118  Allen, 'Octavius', p. 111.

119  *An Act to Suppress Indecent and Obscene Publications*, 23 July 1900, Act No. 2, 1900, S. 4 and *An Act to Amend the Indecent Publications Act, 1900*, 22 September 1900, Act No. 27, 1900, S. 1.

120  *An Act to Amend the* Crimes Act *1890 and for Other Purposes*, No. 1231, 23 December 1891, S. 57.

121  *RCDB*, Vol. 2, p. 70.

122  Day, *Contraband*, p. 114.

## CHAPTER 4

1  Lyn Finch, 'Seduction and Punishment', *Hecate*, Vol. 16, Nos 1/2, 1990, pp. 8–22; Jill Roe, 'Chivalry and Social Policy in the Antipodes', *HS*, Vol. 22, No. 88, April 1987, pp. 395–410.

2  Sterling, quoted in Anna Blainey, The 'Fallen' are Every Mother's Children: The Woman's Christian Temperance Union's Campaigns for Temperance, Women's Suffrage and Sexual Reform in Australia, 1885–1905, PhD Thesis, La Trobe University, 2000, p. 153; *Age*, 28 August 1893, p. 6; Harrison Lee, *Marriage and Heredity*, p. 41; *Victorian Parliamentary Debates (VPD)*, Legislative Council, 27 August 1891, pp. 1289–91; 2 September 1891, pp. 1326–32.

3  Richard Arthur, *The Training of Children in Purity: A Booklet for Parents*, Purity Series No. IV, George Robertson, Melbourne, n.d.

4  Richard White, *Inventing Australia: Images and Identity, 1688–1980*, Allen & Unwin, Sydney, 1981, ch. 3.

5  James, 'The Outcasts of Melbourne', in *The Vagabond Papers*, pp. 30–1, 40.

6   Jill Bavin-Mizzi, 'Understandings of Justice: Australian Rape and Carnal Knowledge
    Cases, 1876–1924', in Diane Kirkby (ed.), *Sex, Power and Justice: Historical Perspectives of
    Law in Australia*, OUP, Melbourne and New York, 1995, pp. 19–20.
7   Finch, *Classing Gaze*, pp. 61–3; Bavin-Mizzi, *Ravished*, pp. 95–7; Keith Thomas, 'The
    Double Standard', *Journal of the History of Ideas*, Vol. 20, No. 2, April 1959, pp. 213–16.
8   Teresa Brennan and Carole Pateman, '"Mere Auxiliaries to the Commonwealth": Women
    and the Origins of Liberalism', *Political Studies*, Vol. 27, No. 2, p. 196.
9   Royal Commission on Employés in Shops (*RCES*), Report on the Operation of the
    Victorian Factory Act 1874, p. vi, in *Victorian Parliamentary Papers* (*VPP*), Session 1884,
    Vol. 2, No. 18.
10  Charles Olden, *'The Protection of Girls and Young Women and the Legislative Repression of
    Vice Generally.' A Lecture Delivered to Men Only in the Protestant Hall, Sydney, August 4$^{th}$
    1885, by Charles Olden, under the Auspices of the Committee of the New South Wales
    Social Purity Society, and Published at the Society's Request. Together with an Introductory
    Address by the Chairman the Right Rev. Dr Barry, Primate of Australia*, Sydney, 1885, p. 25.
11  Sergeant Nugent (Port Melbourne Station), 11 November 1909, Age of Consent Report,
    1909, Chief Secretary's Files, PROV, VPRS 1226/PO, Box 107.
12  Evidence, Report of the Shops and Factories Commission; together with Minutes of
    Proceedings, Evidence, and Appendices, Q. 11510–19, p. 276, in *Proceedings of the
    Parliament of South Australia*, Vol. 2, No. 37.
13  *SAPD*, HA, 28 July 1885, p. 373.
14  Allen, '"Our deeply degraded sex "', pp. 65–91.
15  Jim Jose, 'Legislating for Social Purity, 1883–1885: the Reverend Joseph Coles Kirby and
    the Social Purity Society', *JHSSA*, No. 18, 1990, pp. 119–34.
16  Richard Phillips, 'Imperialism and the Regulation of Sexuality: Colonial Legislation on
    Contagious Diseases and Ages of Consent', *Journal of Historical Geography*, Vol. 28, No. 3,
    2002, pp. 344–6.
17  H.W. Jackson, *Contagious Diseases Acts as Measures of Social Reform, A Public Lecture
    Delivered by Dr H.W. Jackson, at the Request of the Committee of the New South Wales
    Social Purity Society, on Monday Evening, 13th November, 1882. The Very Rev. Dean of
    Sydney in the Chair*, F. Cunninghame [Printers], Sydney, 1882, pp. 10, 22.
18  SCPCD, Q. 197, p. 8; Q. 584, p. 23; Q. 786, p. 31; Q. 1857–9, p. 72.
19  Employés in Shops Commission, Second Progress Report, Evidence, Q. 853, p. 33, *VPP*,
    Legislative Assembly (LA), Second Session, 1883, Vol. 2, No. 16.
20  *SAPD*, HA, 11 August 1885, p. 482.
21  *Ibid.*, 18 August 1885, p. 576.
22  *South Australian Register*, 22 September 1885, p. 7.
23  *SAPD*, HA, 18 August 1885, p. 575. See also *SAPD*, HA, 8 December 1885, pp. 1812–13,
    1815; *South Australian Register*, 22 September 1885, p. 7.
24  James George Beaney F.R.C.S., *Spermatorrhoea in its Physiological, Medical, & Legal
    Aspects*, Walker, May & Co., Melbourne, 1870.
25  *Australian Medical Journal*, July 1860, p. 234.
26  Alan Hunt, 'The Great Masturbation Panic and the Discourses of Moral Regulation in
    Nineteenth- and Early Twentieth-Century Britain', *JHS*, Vol. 8, No. 4, 1998, p. 595.
27  Richard Arthur, *The Choice Between Purity and Impurity*, AWCL, Sydney, n.d., pp. 1–2.
28  See *ibid.*; Dr Richard Arthur, *The Innocence of Children*, S.D. Townsend [Printer], Sydney,
    1894; *Age*, 28 August 1893, pp. 5–6.
29  AWCL, *A Talk to a Boy, by a Doctor*, Australasian White Cross League, Sydney, n.d.
30  A.A. Lendon, quoted in Jim Jose, 'Sex Education, the Family and the State in Early Twentieth
    Century South Australia', *History of Education Review*, Vol. 27, No. 1, 1998, p. 40.
31  Quoted in Kerreen M. Reiger, *The Disenchantment of the Home: Modernizing the
    Australian Family 1880–1940*, OUP, Melbourne, 1985, p. 182.
32  Thomas W. Laqueur, *Solitary Sex: A Cultural History of Masturbation*, Zone Books, New
    York, 2003, p. 52.

33    Charlie Fox, *Working Australia*, Allen & Unwin, Sydney, 1991, p. 80.

34    Frances, *Selling Sex*, p. 133.

35    Martin Crotty, *Making the Australian Male: Middle-Class Masculinity 1870–1920*, MUP, Carlton, 2001, pp. 183, 185.

36    David Walker, 'Continence for a Nation: Seminal Loss and National Vigour', *LH*, No. 48, May 1985, pp. 1–14.

37    Varley, *Lecture to Men*, pp. 3, 6.

38    Dr Howard Freeman and Dr Wallace, *Rescued at Last: Being Clinical Experiences on Nervous and Private Diseases, by Sydney's Leading Specialists*, n.p., Sydney, 1898, pp. 1, 9, 14, 18, 165, 133, 161, 21, 31, 34, 35; Peter J. Phillips, *Kill or Cure: Lotions, Potions, Characters and Quacks or Early Australia*, Greenhouse Publications, Richmond (Vic.), 1984, pp. 36–53.

39    Dr Bottrell, *At Once or Never! A Pamphlet with a Purpose*, C.E. Fuller [Printer], Sydney, n.d., pp. 5–6.

40    Lisa Featherstone, 'Pathologising White Male Sexuality in Late Nineteenth-Century Australia through the Medical Prism of Excess and Constraint', *AHS*, Vol. 41, No. 3, 2010, pp. 347–50.

41    Arthur, *Training of Children*, p. 25; Darby, 'William Acton's Antipodean Disciples', p. 172.

42    Dr Alexander Paterson, *Nervous Debility: An Essay*, F. Cunninghame [Printers], Sydney, 1889, pp. 15, 18–19.

43    Walker, 'Continence', p. 6.

44    Paterson, *Nervous Debility*, pp. 28–31.

45    Percy Grainger, 'Mrs L[owrey] and My Early London Days (1945)', in Malcolm Gillies, David Pear and Mark Carroll (eds), *Self-Portrait of Percy Grainger*, OUP, New York, 2006, p. 97.

46    Machefer to O'Dowd, n.d. [c. November 1890], Bernard O'Dowd Papers, Box 1/6, SLV.

47    Chidley, *Confessions*, pp. 27, 47, 97, 133.

48    David Walker, 'Youth on Trial: The Mount Rennie Case', *LH*, No. 50, May 1986, pp. 28–41; Simon Sleight, The Territories of Youth: Young People and Public Space in Melbourne, c. 1870–1901, PhD Thesis, Monash University, 2008, pp. 152–5.

49    Bavin-Mizzi, *Ravished*, p. 165; George Morgan, 'The *Bulletin* and the Larrikin: Moral Panic in Late Nineteenth Century Sydney', *Media International Australia*, No. 85, November 1997, pp. 20–1.

50    Bavin-Mizzi, *Ravished*, ch. 6.

51    Sleight, Territories, pp. 149, 155.

52    George Higinbotham, *Argus*, 28 February 1889, p. 11, quoted in Bavin-Mizzi, *Ravished*, p. 162.

53    Quoted in Walker, 'Youth on Trial', p. 38.

54    *VPD*, Legislative Council, Vol. 63, 2 September 1890, p. 1329.

55    *Truth* (Sydney), 1 March 1895, p. 4.

56    *SAPD*, HA, 12 November 1884, pp. 1702–3.

57    SCPCD, Q. 521, p. 21; SCPCD, Q. 672, p. 26.

58    *SAPD*, HA, 18 August 1885, p. 542.

59    *Ibid.*, 20 August 1885, p. 604.

60    Judith A. Allen, *Sex & Secrets: Crimes Involving Australian Women Since 1880*, OUP, Melbourne, 1990, pp. 45–88; Bavin-Mizzi, *Ravished*, chs 1–3.

61    Bavin-Mizzi, *Ravished*, ch. 3.

62    Sergeant McGillicuddy, 3061, Malvern, 10 November 1909, Age of Consent Report, 1909, Chief Secretary's Files, PROV, VPRS 1226/PO, Box 107.

63    *South Australian Register*, 22 September 1885, p. 7; 55 VIC., No. 24, 1891, Part I, s. 4. *Criminal Law Amendment Act. Criminal Law. An Act to Make Better Provision for the Protection of Women and Girls, and for Other Purposes.*

64    Jessica Horton, 'The Case of Elsie Barrett: Aboriginal Women, Sexuality and the Victorian Board for the Protection of Aborigines', *JAS*, Vol. 34, No. 1, March 2010, pp. 1–18.

65    *An Act to Amend the* Crimes Act *1890 and for Other Purposes*, 23 December 1891, 55 VICT., No. 1231, s. 6.

66    Bavin-Mizzi, *Ravished*, pp. 89–90.

67    Theo G. Grano to Constance Holloway, 12 January 1907, H.H. Pearce Papers, NLA MS 2765/9/1/3; *Ararat Advertiser*, 11 January 1907; *Stawell News and Pleasant Creek Chronicle*, 10 January 1907; Denton Davenport Miller, otherwise known as Denton Davenport and Emma Brown, Marriage Certificate, District of Stawell, State of Victoria, 12 January 1907, No. 98 in Register, No. 637.

68    T.A. Coghlan, *Decline of the Birth-Rate*, pp. 7–12.

69    Henry Finlay, *To Have But Not to Hold: A History of Attitudes to Marriage and Divorce in Australia 1858–1975*, The Federation Press, Leichhardt and Annandale, 2005, *passim*.

70    Blainey, The 'Fallen', p. 148.

71    Allen, *Sex & Secrets*, pp. 77–80; *Crimes (Girls' Protection) Act*, No. 2, 1910, s. 2; Bomford, *That Dangerous and Persuasive Woman*, pp. 101, 132–3; Deborah Tyler, 'The Case of Irene Tuckerman: Understanding Sexual Violence and the Protection of Women and Girls, Victoria 1890–1925', *History of Education Review*, Vol. 15, No. 2, 1986, pp. 56–9.

72    Arthur, *Choice*, p. 10.

73    Blainey, The 'Fallen', pp. 155, 171–3.

74    Quoted in Frank Bongiorno, *The People's Party: Victorian Labor and the Radical Tradition 1875–1914*, MUP, Carlton, 1996, p. 102.

75    *Bulletin*, 1 May 1880, quoted in Kate Bagnall, 'Across the Threshold: White Women and Chinese Hawkers in the White Colonial Imaginary', *Hecate*, Vol. 28, No. 2, 2002, p. 19. See also J.C. Watson, 6 September 1901, *Commonwealth Parliamentary Debates (CPD)*, House of Representatives (H of R), Vol. 4, p. 4634.

76    Evidence, Report of the Royal Commission on Alleged Chinese Gambling and Immorality and Charges of Bribery Against Members of the Police Force, (RCACGI), Q. 13589, p. 374, *Votes and Proceedings of the Legislative Assembly of New South Wales*, 1891–92, No. 272-a, Vol. 8.

77    Sandi Robb, 'Myths, Lies and Invisible Lives: European Women and Chinese Men in North Queensland 1870–1900', *Lilith*, 12, 2003, pp. 101–2.

78    *CPD*, III-3502–4, 7 August 1901, in D. Gibb, *The Making of 'White Australia'*, Victorian Historical Association, West Melbourne, 1973, p. 101.

79    *CPD*, H of R, Vol. 4, 6 September 1901, p. 4633.

80    *Ibid.*, p. 4665.

81    *Ibid.*, p. 5246.

82    Minutes of Evidence, Report from the Select Committee on Common Lodging Houses, Q. 261, p. 9 and Q. 476, p. 16, *Votes and Proceedings of the Legislative Assembly of New South Wales*, No. 396-a, 1875–6, Vol. 6.

83    SCPCD, Q. 1652, p. 64.

84    Bagnall, 'Across the Threshold', p. 21.

85    SCPCD, Q. 1032, p. 40.

86    *Commonweal* (Melbourne), 23 July 1892, p. 2.

87    *Truth* (Sydney), 20 September 1896, p. 5.

88    Report, RCACGI, p. 21.

89    'Chinese Camps. (Reports Upon.)', *Votes and Proceedings of the Legislative Assembly of New South Wales*, 1883–1884, No. 351, Vol. 11, pp. 1–6. See also RCACGI, Q. 13903, 13963, pp. 386–7.

90    Jan Ryan, '"She Lives with a Chinaman": Orient-ing "White" Women in the Courts of Law', *JAS*, No. 60, March 1999, pp. 149–59; Sue Davies, 'Working their way to Respectability: Women, Vagrancy and Reform in Late Nineteenth Century Melbourne', *Lilith*, No. 6, 1989, p. 55; Robb, 'Myths, Lies and Invisible Lives'.

91    Royal Commission on the Condition of the Natives (RCCN), Western Australia. *Minutes and Votes and Proceedings of the Parliament*, 1905, Vol. 1, Q. 463, p. 53.

92   Henry Reynolds, *North of Capricorn: The Untold Story of Australia's North*, Allen & Unwin, Sydney, 2003, pp. 136–42, 152–7.
93   *Ibid.*, p. 136. See also Regina Ganter, *Mixed Relations: Asian-Aboriginal Contact in North Australia*, University of Western Australia Press (UWAP), Crawley, 2006, pp. 72–3.
94   RCCN, Q. 1288, p. 86.
95   Frances, *Selling Sex*, pp. 80–8.
96   Report, RCCN, p. 25.
97   RCCN, Q. 333, p. 48.
98   *Ibid.*, Q. 1780, p. 105; Q. 1218, p. 83.
99   *Ibid.*, Q. 628–30, p. 59.
100  *Ibid.*, Q. 1405–7, p. 90.
101  *Ibid.*, Q. 1766, p. 104.
102  J.B. Gribble, *Dark Deeds in a Sunny Land or Blacks and Whites in North-West Australia*, Bob Tonkinson (ed.), UWAP with Institute of Applied Aboriginal Studies, Western Australian College of Advanced Education, Nedlands/Mt. Lawley, 1987 [1905], p. 51.
103  Su-Jane Hunt, 'The Gribble Affair: A Study in Colonial Politics', in *ibid.*, pp. 62–73. See also Christine Halse, *A Terribly Wild Man*, Allen & Unwin, Sydney, 2002, pp. 12–14.
104  RCCN, Q. 1187, p. 82; Chesser, *Parting*, pp. 107–12.
105  RCCN, Q. 1592, p. 95.
106  Quoted in Ann McGrath, 'The Golden Thread of Kinship: Mixed Marriages between Asians and Aboriginal Women during Australia's Federation Era', in Penny Edwards and Shen Yuanfang (eds), *Lost in the Whitewash: Aboriginal-Asian Encounters in Australia, 1901–2001*, Humanities Research Centre, ANU, Canberra, 2003, p. 43.
107  Archibald Meston, Special Commissioner under Instructions from the Queensland Government, 'Report on the Aboriginals of Queensland', in Queensland, *Votes & Proceedings of the Legislative Assembly*, Session 1896, Vol. IV, C.A. 85–1896, pp. 9, 13–14.
108  Regina Ganter and Ros Kidd, 'The Powers of Protectors: Conflicts Surrounding Queensland's 1897 Aboriginal Legislation', *AHS*, Vol. 25, No. 101, October 1993, pp. 536–54.
109  Heather Goodall, *Invasion to Embassy: Land in Aboriginal Politics in New South Wales, 1770–1972*, SUP, Sydney, 2008, pp. 141–3.
110  Attwood, *Making*, p. 99.
111  Katherine Ellinghaus, 'Regulating Koori Marriages: The 1886 Victorian *Aborigines Protection Act*', *JAS*, No. 67, 2001, pp. 22–9.
112  R. Brough Smith, *The Aborigines of Victoria: With Notes Relating to the Habits of the Natives of Other Parts of Australia and Tasmania Compiled from the Various Sources for the Government of Victoria*, John Currey O'Neil, Melbourne, 1972 [1878], pp. lx, lxvii; Gregory D. Smithers, *Science, Sexuality, and Race in the United States and Australia 1780s–1890s*, Routledge, New York, 2009, pp. 90–4, 171–5; Russell McGregor, 'An Aboriginal Caucasian: Some Uses for Racial Kinship in Early Twentieth Century Australia', *Australian Aboriginal Studies*, No. 1, 1996, pp. 11–20.
113  Horton, 'The Case of Elsie Barrett'.
114  Halse, *Terribly Wild Man*, pp. 81–7.
115  Laurie Moore and Stephan Williams, *The True Story of Jimmy Governor*, Allen & Unwin, Sydney, 2001, pp. 138–40.
116  *Ibid.*, pp. 18–19, 27.
117  Ganter and Kidd, 'The Powers of Protectors', pp. 536–54; Regina Ganter, 'Living An Immoral Life – "Coloured" Women and the Paternalistic State', *Hecate*, Vol. 24, No. 1, 1998, pp. 13–40.
118  McGrath, 'Golden Thread of Kinship'.
119  D.C.S. Sissons, '*Karayuki-san:* Japanese Prostitutes in Australia, 1887–1916, I and II, *HS*, Vol. 16, No. 68, April 1977, pp. 323–41 and Vol. 16, No. 69, October 1977, pp. 474–88; Susan Jane Hunt, *Spinifex and Hessian: Women's Lives in North-Western Australia 1860–1900*, UWAP, Nedlands, 1986, ch. 5, esp. p. 125; Elaine McKewon, *The Scarlet Mile:*

*A Social History of Prostitution in Kalgoorlie, 1894–2004*, UWAP, Crawley, 2005, p. 12 and ch. 2; Frances, *Selling Sex*, pp. 47–60.

120  *CPD*, H of R, Vol. 4, 12 September 1901, p. 4835.

121  Quoted in Raymond Evans, '"Soiled Doves": Prostitution and Society in Colonial Queensland – An Overview', *Hecate*, Vol. 1, No. 2, July 1975, p. 13.

122  David Walker, *Anxious Nation: Australia and the Rise of Asia 1850–1939*, UQP, St Lucia, 1999, p. 134.

123  Raelene Frances, 'Sex Workers or Citizens? Prostitution and the Shaping of "Settler" Society in Australia', *International Review of Social History*, 44, 1999, Supplement, pp. 105–22.

124  *Ibid.*, p. 104.

125  Hilary Golder and Judith Allen, 'Prostitution in New South Wales 1870–1932: Re-structuring an Industry', *Refractory Girl*, Nos 18/19, December 1979–January 1980, pp. 17–24; Judith Allen, 'The Making of a Prostitute Proletariat in Early Twentieth Century New South Wales', in Kay Daniels (ed.), *So Much Hard Work*, pp. 192–232.

126  N. Gleeson, Criminal Investigation Branch, Memo to the Chief Commissioner of Police, Melbourne, 10 November 1909, F9331, Age of Consent Report, 1909, Chief Secretary's Files, PROV, VPRS 1226/PO, Box 107.

127  Senior Constable A.J. Sims, Carlton, 11 November 1909; Constable E.W. Sharpe, Carlton, 11 November 1909, *ibid.*

128  McConville, 'The location of Melbourne's prostitutes', pp. 86–97 and 'From "Criminal Class" to "Underworld"', in Davison, Dunstan and McConville (eds), *Outcasts*, pp. 69–90.

129  Raelene Davidson [now Frances], 'Dealing with the "Social Evil": Prostitution and the Police in Perth and on the Eastern Goldfields, 1895–1924', in Daniels (ed.), *So Much Hard Work*, pp. 162–91. See also McKewon, *Scarlet Mile*, ch. 3, esp. pp. 39, 47.

130  Allen, 'Making', p. 210.

131  F.B. Smith, 'Labouchere's Amendment to the Criminal Law Amendment Bill', *HS*, Vol. 17, No. 67, October 1976, p. 165.

132  Cocks, *Nameless Offences*, pp. 17, 30–1.

133  Gilding, *Making*, p. 99.

134  Jill Bavin-Mizzi, '"An Unnatural Offence": Sodomy in Western Australia from 1880–1900', in Charlie Fox (ed.), *Historical Refractions: Studies in Western Australian History*, Vol. 14, 1993, p. 113.

135  *SMH*, 7 July 1887, p. 12, in de Waal (ed.), *Unfit*, Vol. 1, p. 11; *Argus*, 7 July 1887, p. 8.

136  Chesser, *Parting*, ch. 6.

137  Moore, *Sunshine*, p. 74.

138  Bruce Baskerville, '"Agreed to Without Debate": Silencing Sodomy in "Colonial" Western Australia, 1870–1905', in Robert Aldrich and Garry Wotherspoon (eds), *Gay and Lesbian Perspectives IV: Studies in Australian Culture*, Department of Economic History and Australian Centre for Lesbian and Gay Research, The University of Sydney, Sydney, 1998, p. 98; Adam Carr, 'Policing the "Abominable Crime" in Nineteenth Century Victoria', in Phillips and Willett (eds), *Australia's Homosexual Histories*, p. 34.

139  Yorick Smaal, 'Coding Desire: The Emergence of a Homosexual Subculture in Queensland, 1899–1914', *Queensland Review*, Special Issue: *Queer Queensland*, Yorick Smaal and Belinda McKay (eds), Vol. 14, No. 2, 2007, p. 20.

140  Chauncey, *Gay New York*, p. 136; Graeme Davison, 'Sydney and the Bush: an Urban Context for the Australian Legend', *HS*, Vol. 18, No. 71, October 1978, pp. 191–209.

141  Quoted in Bavin-Mizzi, '"An Unnatural Offence"', p. 106.

142  David Marr, 'After the Fall', *SMH*, *Spectrum*, 25 November 2000, pp. 1, 4–5.

143  *Truth* (Sydney), 7 April 1895, p. 5.

144  Robert Aldrich, *Colonialism and Homosexuality*, Routledge, New York and London, 2003, p. 239; Marr, 'After the Fall', p. 4.

145  *Age*, 28 May 1895, p. 4.

146  *R. v. James Joseph Alphonsus Neiland* (1895), in de Waal (ed.), *Unfit*, Vol. 2, pp. 934–5, 938,

943–4; Jill Julius Matthews, 'Reflections on Gay and Lesbian Activism', in Aldrich and Wotherspoon (eds), *Gay and Lesbian Perspectives IV*, pp. 26–7.

147   Featherstone, 'Pathologising', pp. 345–7 and 'Even More Hidden from History? Male Homosexuality and Medicine in Turn-of-the-Century Australia', in Yorick Smaal and Graham Willett (eds), *Out Here: Gay and Lesbian Perspectives VI*, Monash University Publishing, Melbourne, 2011, pp. 56–68.

148   Rev. F.B. Meyer, *The Vestibule of Girl-Life: A Letter to Young Girls*, AWCL, Sydney, n.d.

149   Jennings, *Lesbian History of Britain*, p. 50.

150   Quiggin, *No Rising Generation*, pp. 62–3.

151   Ann Vickery, 'Lesbia Harford's Romantic Legacy', in Maryanne Dever, Sally Newman and Ann Vickery, *The Intimate Archive: Journeys Through Private Papers*, NLA, Canberra, 2009, pp. 103–4.

152   *Century* (Adelaide), 23 January 1901, p. 5.

153   Karen McLeod, *Henry Handel Richardson: A Critical Study*, CUP, Cambridge, 1985, pp. 85–6, 91.

154   Lesley A. Hall, '"The English Have Hot-Water Bottles": The Morganatic Marriage between Medicine and Sexology in Britain since William Acton', in Roy Porter and Mikulás Teich (eds), *Sexual Knowledge, Sexual Science: The History of Attitudes to Sexuality*, CUP, Cambridge, 1994, p. 350.

155   Havelock Ellis, 'Sexual Inversion', in Havelock Ellis, *Studies in the Psychology of Sex*, Vol. 1, Pt 4, Random House, New York, 1942, p. 287.

156   Chris Waters, 'Havelock Ellis, Sigmund Freud and the State: Discourses of Homosexual Identity in Interwar Britain', in Lucy Bland and Laura Doan (eds), *Sexology in Culture: Labelling Bodies and Desires*, Polity Press, Cambridge, 1998, p. 168; Jeffrey Weeks, *Coming Out: Homosexual Politics in Britain from the Nineteenth Century to the Present*, Quartet Books, London, 1990, pp. 62, 64.

157   Percy Grainger, 'Read This If Ella Grainger or Percy Grainger Are Found Dead Covered with Whip Marks (1932)', in Gillies, Pear and Carroll (eds), *Self-Portrait*, p. 123, also quoted in David Pear, 'The Passions of Percy', *Meanjin*, Vol. 62, No. 2, 2003, p. 64.

158   Grainger, 'Notes of Whip-Lust (1948)', in Gillies, Pear and Carroll (eds), *Self-Portrait*, p. 167.

159   John Bird, *Percy Grainger*, Currency Press, Sydney, 1999, p. 155. See also Grainger to Karen Holten, 19 March 1909, in Kay Dreyfus (ed.), *The Farthest North of Humanness: Letters of Percy Grainger 1901–14*, Macmillan, South Melbourne, 1985, p. 275.

160   Ruth Ford, '"The Man-Woman Murderer": Sex Fraud, Sexual Inversion and the Unmentionable "Article" in 1920s Australia', *Gender and History*, Vol. 12, No. 1, April 2000, pp. 164, 191, n. 34; Chesser, *Parting*, p. 274.

161   Bird, *Percy Grainger*, p. 57.

162   Grainger, 'To Whoever Opens the Package Marked "Do Not Open until 10 Years after My Death" (1956)', in Gillies, Pear and Carroll (eds), *Self-Portrait*, p. 161.

163   Percy Grainger to Rose Grainger, 9 November 1911 and 10 November 1908, in Dreyfus (ed.), *Farthest North*, pp. 243–4.

164   Quoted in Eileen Dorum, *Percy Grainger: the man behind the music*, I.C. and E.E. Dorum, Melbourne, 1986, p. 77.

165   Edward Carpenter, 'The Intermediate Sex', in David Fernbach and Noël Greig (eds), *Edward Carpenter, Selected Writings, Volume 1: Sex*, GMP, London, 1984, pp. 190, 215.

166   White, *Flaws*, pp. 34–5, 80–1, 113, 135, 153–4; White to Geoffrey Dutton, 17 September 1980, in David Marr (ed.), *Patrick White Letters*, Random House, Sydney, 1994, p. 537 and Marr, *Patrick White: A Life*, Random House, Sydney, 1991, pp. 75–6, 581–2.

167   Letter to Carpenter, 26 September 1914, MSS 376/1, Carpenter Papers, Sheffield Archives, England. See also Sylvia Martin, *Passionate Friends: Mary Fullerton, Mabel Singleton & Miles Franklin*, Onlywomen Press, London, 2001.

168   Gail Reekie, '"She Was A Lovable Man": Marion/Bill Edwards and the Feminisation of Australian Culture', *Journal of Australian Lesbian Feminist Studies*, No. 4, June 1994,

pp. 43–50; Ruth Ford, "'The Man-Woman Murderer'", pp. 158–96; Chesser, *Parting*, ch. 9
and pp. 314–17; *Truth* (Sydney), 10 October 1920, p. 10.
169    Lewis, *Thorns on the Rose*, chs 2 and 3.

# CHAPTER 5

1    *Armidale Express*, 17 November 1914, p. 7; *Age*, 2 November 1914, p. 7; 11 November 1914,
p. 8; Judith Smart, "'Poor Little Belgium" and Australian Popular Support for War
1914–1915', *War & Society*, Vol. 12, No. 1, May 1994, pp. 33, 35–7; C.P. Barreira, "'Myth of
Poor Little Belgium" as Mainspring: A Remark', *Flinders Journal of History and Politics*,
Vol. 19, 1997, p. 60.
2    Quoted in Philippa Levine, *Prostitution, Race, and Politics: Policing Venereal Disease in the
British Empire*, Routledge, New York and London, 2003, p. 168.
3    *Age*, 9 November 1914, p. 10.
4    Day, *Contraband*, p. 126; Andrew Pike and Ross Cooper, *Australian Film 1900–1977:
A Guide to Feature Film Production*, OUP, Melbourne, 1998, pp. 80–1.
5    Quoted in Helen Doyle, 'Allegations of Disloyalty at Koroit during World War I', in Philip
Bull, Frances Devlin-Glass and Helen Doyle (eds), *Ireland and Australia, 1798–1998:
Studies in Culture, Identity and Migration*, Crossing Press, Sydney, 2000, p. 168.
6    Quoted in Raymond Evans, *Loyalty and Disloyalty: Social Conflict on the Queensland
Homefront, 1914–18*, Allen & Unwin, Sydney, 1987, pp. 96–7.
7    M. McKernan, *Australians in Wartime: Commentary and Documents*, Thomas Nelson,
Melbourne, 1984, p. 39; Wayne Murdoch, "'Disgusting Days" and "Putrid Practices":
Reporting Homosexual Men's Lives in the *Melbourne Truth*, during the First World War',
in Aldrich and Wotherspoon (eds), *Gay and Lesbian Perspectives IV*, pp. 124, 127, 129.
8    *Truth* (Melbourne), 29 April 1916, p. 3. Most references to the Melbourne edition of *Truth*
concerning homosexuality in this chapter and chapter 6 are from Wayne Murdoch,
'Homosexuality and the Melbourne *Truth*: An Annotated Listing, 1913–45', in Phillips and
Willett (eds), *Australia's Homosexual Histories*, pp. 177–221.
9    *Truth* (Melbourne), 5 August 1916, p. 5.
10    *Teaching of Sex Hygiene: Report of a Conference Organised by the Workers' Educational
Association of New South Wales and Held in the Union Hall, Sydney University on
November 23, 24 and 15, 1916*, Second Edition, Workers' Educational Association (WEA),
Sydney, 1918, p. 83.
11    *Truth* (Melbourne), 5 August 1916, p. 5.
12    Stephen Garton, *The Cost of War: Australians Return*, OUP, Melbourne, 1996, pp. 50–1;
A.B. Facey, *A Fortunate Life*, Penguin Books, Ringwood, 1985, p. 275.
13    Kosmas Tsokhas, *Making a Nation State: Cultural Identity, Economic Nationalism and
Sexuality in Australian History*, MUP, Carlton, 2001, p. 165; Gary Simes, 'The Language of
Homosexuality in Australia', in Aldrich and Wotherspoon (eds), *Gay Perspectives*, p. 41.
14    Barry Pearce, *Elioth Gruner 1882–1939*, Art Gallery of New South Wales, Sydney, 1983,
pp. 8, 19. There are further references to male homosexuals in the AIF in 'Interview
with anonymous male about sexual behaviour during 1930s', Interviewed by Larraine
Stevens, 15–22 July 1982, NLA ORAL TRC 2404 Int.No. 1200, p. 2; John Lee, 'Male
Homosexual Identity and Subculture in Adelaide Before World War II', in Aldrich and
Wotherspoon (eds), *Gay Perspectives*, p. 102; and Herbert M. Moran, *Viewless Winds:
Being the Recollections and Digressions of an Australian Surgeon*, Peter Davies,
London, 1939, pp. 53–4.
15    Peter Stanley, *Bad Characters: Sex, Crime, Mutiny, and Murder and the Australian Imperial
Force*, Pier 9, Millers Point, 2010, ch. 33.
16    D.A. Kent, 'The Anzac Book and the Anzac legend: C.E.W. Bean as Editor and Image-
Maker', *HS*, Vol. 21, No. 84, April 1985, pp. 376–90.
17    Quoted in Alistair Thomson, *Anzac Memories: Living with the Legend*, OUP, Melbourne,
1994, p. 80.

18  C.A. Hemsley, Diary, 27 August, 30 September, 1 October 1916, Australian War Memorial (AWM) PR 85/295.

19  See Suzanne Brugger, *Australians and Egypt 1914–1919*, MUP, Carlton, 1980, pp. 65–8.

20  C.A. Hemsley, Diary, 8 October 1916.

21  R.C. Hunter to Mother and Father, Letter, 25 July 1915, AWM 1 DRL 367, File No. 12/11/1329.

22  A.G. Butler to Mrs Butler, 1 December 1914, 1 January 1915, Col. A.G. Butler Papers, AWM 3DRL 7100, File No. 419/8/1.

23  Dudley McCarthy, *Gallipoli to the Somme: The Story of C.E.W. Bean*, John Ferguson, Sydney, 1983, pp. 91–5; John F. Williams, *Anzacs, the Media and the Great War*, UNSWP, Sydney, 1999, pp. 59–63.

24  Quoted in Levine, *Prostitution, Race, and Politics*, pp. 167–8.

25  Brugger, *Australians and Egypt*, pp. 145–7; Richard White, 'Sun, Sand and Syphilis: Australian Soldiers and the Orient Egypt 1914', in *Australian Perceptions of Asia*, an issue of *ACH*, No. 9, 1990, pp. 60–2

26  Quoted in Levine, *Prostitution, Race, and Politics*, p. 156; Brugger, *Australians and Egypt*, pp. 145–7.

27  *MJA*, 11 September 1915, p. 250.

28  A.G. Butler, *The Australian Army Medical Services in the War of 1914–1918*, Vol. I, AWM, Melbourne, 1938, p. 74.

29  E.M. Andrews, *The Anzac Illusion: Anglo-Australian Relations during World War I*, CUP, Cambridge, 1993, p. 184.

30  Lewis, *Thorns on the Rose*, p. 160.

31  Quoted in R.T. Beckett, 'An Imperial Force?' The AIF in the United Kingdom 1914–1918, PhD Thesis, University of London, 2008, pp. 274–5 and Levine, *Prostitution, Race, and Politics*, p. 150.

32  Butler, *Australian Army*, Vol. I, pp. 58, 77; A.G. Butler to Mrs Butler, 29 November 1914, Butler Papers.

33  Hunter to Mother and Father, 25 July 1915, AWM1 DRL 367, File No. 12/11/1329.

34  White, 'Sun, Sand and Syphilis', pp. 59–62.

35  Richard White, 'The Soldier as Tourist: The Australian Experience of the Great War', *War & Society*, Vol. 5, No. 1, May 1987, pp. 63–77.

36  Hunter to Mother and Father, 25 July 1915, AWM1 DRL 367, File No. 12/11/1329.

37  Brugger, *Australians and Egypt*, p. 64.

38  Hunter to Mother and Father, 25 July 1915, AWM1 DRL 367, File No. 12/11/1329; A.H.T. Mountain, Extracts from Letters, 26 March 1915, AWM 2DRL 95, File No. 12/11/1424.

39  H.D. Grant, Diary, 22nd Day at Sea, 1917, AWM PR 00009, File No. 91/0141.

40  Butler, *Australian Army*, Vol. I, p. 76.

41  H.D. Grant, Diary, 22nd Day at Sea, 1917, AWM PR 00009, File No. 91/0141.

42  Stanley, *Bad Characters*, pp. 28–9.

43  Butler, *Australian Army*, Vol. I, p. 77.

44  *Ibid.*, p. 486, n. 23.

45  *Ibid.*, Vol. 3, pp. 153–4, 173.

46  See National Archives of Australia, Series B 539, AIF 125/1/1012, Disposal of Remains of Late Major General Sir W.T. Bridges. I am grateful to Steve Hart of Canberra for copies of this file with his own summary, 19 August 2003.

47  Levine, *Prostitution, Race, and Politics*, p. 151; Robert A. Hall, *The Black Diggers: Aborigines and Torres Strait Islanders in the Second World War*, Allen & Unwin, Sydney, 1989, p. 1.

48  Quoted in Butler, *Australian Army*, Vol. 3, pp. 159–60.

49  Report of the AWCL for the Twelve Months Ending 31st Dec., 1915, unpublished typescript, n.d. [1916] [NLA]; Butler, *Australian Army*, Vol. 1, p. 774, and Vol. 3, p. 155; Eric Evans, *So Far from Home: The Remarkable Diaries of Eric Evans, an Australian Soldier During World War I*, Kangaroo Press, East Roseville, 2002, p. 113.

50  Quoted in Levine, *Prostitution, Race, and Politics*, p. 155.

## Endnotes

51    Hunter to Mother and Father, 15 October 1915, AWM 1 DRL 367, File No. 12/11/1329.
52    Joanna Bourke, *An Intimate History of Killing: Face-to-Face Killing in Twentieth-Century Warfare*, Granta Books, London, 1999, p. 13. See also pp. 31–45.
53    Quoted in Bill Gammage, *The Broken Years: Australian Soldiers in the Great War*, Penguin Books, Ringwood, 1975, p. 97.
54    Ruth Rae, *Veiled Lives: Threading Australian Nursing History into the Fabric of the First World War*, The College of Nursing, Burwood (NSW), 2009, p. 367.
55    Katie Holmes, 'Day Mothers and Night Sisters: World War I Nurses and Sexuality', in Joy Damousi and Marilyn Lake (eds), *Gender and War: Australians at War in the Twentieth Century*, CUP, Melbourne, 1995, pp. 43–59.
56    J. Maxwell, *Hell's Bells and Mademoiselles*, Angus & Robertson, Sydney and London, 1939 [1932], pp. 37–8, 93.
57    Evans, *So Far From Home*, pp. 137–8, 158–9.
58    G.D. Mitchell, *Backs to the Wall*, Angus & Robertson, Sydney, 1937, p. 167.
59    James Curran, 'Bonjoor Paree!: The First AIF in Paris, 1916–1918', *JAS*, No. 60, March 1999, pp. 18–26.
60    Mitchell, *Backs to the Wall*, pp. 168–70.
61    Carol Fallows, *Love & War: Stories of War Brides from the Great War to Vietnam*, Bantam Books, Sydney, 2002, p. 40, ch. 2.
62    Maxwell, *Hell's Bells*, pp. 81–2; Fallows, *Love & War*, pp. 36–9.
63    Larry Anthony to Mother, 13 January 1916, in Doug and Margot Anthony (eds), *Letters Home to Mother from Gallipoli and Beyond: Diaries and Letters of Sapper Hubert Anthony*, Allen & Unwin, Sydney, 2009, p. 219.
64    Anonymous Soldier to Brother, 8 June 1917, AWM PR 87/153, File No. 419/036/009.
65    Margot Strickland, *Angela Thirkell: Portrait of a Lady Novelist*, Duckworth, London, 1977, pp. 40–3, 64; Lance Thirkell, *Melbourne and London: A Childhood Memoir*, Angela Thirkell Society, London, 2000, pp. 1–47.
66    Graham McInnes, *The Road to Gundagai*, The Hogarth Press, London, 1985 [1965], pp. 18, 37–8.
67    G.L.A. Thirkell, Diary, 25, 30 March, 11 May, 15 July 1917, AWM 3 DRL 2719, File No. 419/103/12.
68    C.A. Hemsley, Diary, 18 October 1916.
69    Beckett, 'An Imperial Force', pp. 281–2; Lewis, *Thorns on the Rose*, pp. 162–3; Levine, *Prostitution, Race, and Politics*, pp. 160–5.
70    Stanley, *Bad Characters*, ch. 46.
71    Curran, '"Bonjoor Paree!"', p. 24.
72    Levine, *Prostitution, Race and Politics*, p. 166.
73    Stanley, *Bad Characters*, p. 82.
74    H.R. Williams, *The Gallant Company: An Australian Soldier's Story of 1915–18*, Angus & Robertson, Sydney, 1933, p. 45.
75    Maxwell, *Hell's Bells*, pp. 153, 28, 41, 148.
76    Hunter to Mother and Father, 8 April 1916.
77    Fallows, *Love & War*, pp. 39–41, 64.
78    Stanley, *Bad Characters*, passim.
79    S.M. Scott (ed.), *Corporal Jones' War: The Diary of an ANZAC*, Black Swan Press, Curtin University of Technology, Perth, 2005, p. 135 (26 May 1917).
80    Evans, *So Far From Home*, pp. 28, 248.
81    *Ibid.*, pp. 50, 165–6, 236.
82    Mitchell, *Backs to the Wall*, pp. 163–5, 275, 280.
83    Maxwell, *Hell's Bells*, pp. 266–7.
84    Stanley, *Bad Characters*, p. 242.
85    F.B. Smith, 'If Australia Had Not Participated in the Great War? An Essay on the Costs of War', in Craig Wilcox assisted by Janice Aldridge (eds), *The Great War: Gains and Losses – Anzac and Empire*, AWM and ANU, Canberra, 1995, p. 180.

86   Lois [Marion Piddington], *Via Nuova or Science & Maternity*, Dymock's Book Arcade, Sydney, 1916, p. 8; Ann Curthoys, 'Eugenics, Feminism, and Birth Control: The Case of Marion Piddington', *Hecate*, Vol. 15, No. 1, 1989, pp. 73–89.

87   Diana H. Wyndham, Striving for National Fitness: Eugenics in Australia 1910s to 1930s, PhD Thesis, University of Sydney, 1996, p. 75. A version of this thesis has been published as Diana Wyndham, *Eugenics in Australia: Striving for National Fitness*, Galton Institute, London, 2003.

88   Dr Henry Waterman Swan, *Facultative Motherhood Without Offence to Moral Law: Every Woman's Right to Motherhood*, Australasian Authors' Agency, Melbourne, 1918, pp. 6, 22, 11–12, 21, 20.

89   Sigmund Freud to Marion Piddington, 19 June 1921, Piddington Papers, NLA MS 1158; H. McQueen, 'Freud – Letter to Our Sub Continent', *Bowyang*, No. 4, August–September 1980, pp. 140–3. The campaign for celibate motherhood is explored in Wyndham, 'Striving', pp. 72–80.

90   Andrews, *Anzac Illusion*, p. 183; Fallows, *Love & War*, pp. 95–100; Butler, *Australian Army*, Vol. 3, p. 186, n. 36.

91   Michael McKernan, *The Australian People and the Great War*, Nelson, West Melbourne, 1980, pp. 90–2.

92   Judith Smart, 'The Great War and the "Scarlet Scourge": Debates about Venereal Diseases in Melbourne During World War I', in Judith Smart and Tony Wood (eds), *An ANZAC Muster: War and Society in Australia and New Zealand, 1914–18 and 1939–45: Selected Papers*, Monash publications in History: 14, Clayton, 1992, pp. 58–85.

93   Marilyn Lake, 'Frontier Feminism and the Marauding White Man', *JAS*, No. 49, 1996, pp. 12–20.

94   Everitt Atkinson and William J. Dakin, *Sex Hygiene and Sex Education*, Angus & Robertson, Sydney, 1918, pp. 89–90.

95   *Ibid.*, p. 107.

96   Julie Tisdale, 'Venereal Disease and the Policing of the Amateur in Melbourne during World War I', *Lilith*, No. 9, 1996, pp. 33–50.

97   Minutes of Evidence, Progress Report from the Select Committee on Prevalence of Venereal Diseases; together with the Proceedings of the Committee and Minutes of Evidence and Appendices (SCPVD), *New South Wales Parliamentary Papers (NSWPP)* 1915, Vol. 5, Q. 1242, p. 62.

98   *Ibid.*, Q. 864–6, p. 44; Q. 973–4, p. 49; Q. 1544–7, p. 76; Q. 1580, p. 78; Lisa Featherstone, *Let's Talk About Sex in Australia: Histories of Sexuality in Australia from Federation to the Pill*, Cambridge Scholars Publishing, Newcastle upon Tyne, 2011, p. 105.

99   SCPVD, Q. 753, p. 40.

100  Featherstone, *Let's Talk About Sex*, p. 101.

101  Smart, 'Sex, the State and the "Scarlet Scourge"'; Judith Smart, 'Feminists, Labour Women and Venereal Disease in Early Twentieth Century Melbourne', *AFS*, Vol. 15, 1992, pp. 25–40 (in which the quoted passages are found at p. 71); Bruce Scates and Raelene Frances, *Women and the Great War*, CUP, Melbourne, 1997, pp. 123–9.

102  *MJA*, 10 July 1915, p. 33.

103  Marilyn Lake, *Getting Equal: The History of Australian Feminism*, Allen & Unwin, Sydney, 1999, pp. 49–213.

104  *Teaching of Sex Hygiene*, p. 2. See also *Proceedings of the University of Sydney Society for Combating Venereal Diseases: I: Inaugural Addresses*, December 1916, esp. pp. 12–13 and SCPVD, Q. 2421, p. 125.

105  J. Smyth, 'Sex Education for Boys', in *Teaching of Sex Hygiene*, p. 175.

106  Atkinson and Dakin, *Sex Hygiene*, pp. 99, 103.

107  *Teaching of Sex Hygiene*, pp. 91–2.

108  G. Logan, *Sex Education in Queensland: A History of the Debate 1900–1980*, Historical Perspectives on Contemporary Issues in Queensland Education No. 2, Information and Publications Branch, Department of Education, Queensland, Brisbane, 1980, pp. 12, 15,

17–20; *Report of the Australasian White Cross League for the Period of Fifteen Months from 1st January, 1916 to 31st March, 1917*, AWCL, Sydney, n.d. [1917], NLA.

109　SCPVD, Q. 2296–8, pp. 120–1; Q. 2345, p. 121; Q. 2470, p. 128. Bligh was not permitted to speak at Sydney Grammar: see Q. 2393–6, p. 124.

110　Bishop Long, in *Teaching of Sex Hygiene*, p. 101.

111　*Teaching of Sex Hygiene*, pp. 89, 69.

112　SCPVD, Q. 2362, p. 123.

113　Logan, *Sex Education*, p. 3.

114　*Teaching of Sex Hygiene*, pp. 80, 85.

115　Zoë Benjamin, 'Preventive Training for Young Children in Relation to Sexual Control', in *ibid.*, p. 147.

116　J. Smyth, 'Sex Education for Boys', in *ibid.*, p. 177.

117　*Ibid.*, pp. 80–1, 87.

118　White, *Flaws*, p. 11.

119　'Chief Secretary's Department. Legislative Assembly. Question Answered in the Legislative Assembly on 26/9/16 Respecting Mr. Chidley', in SRNSW, Chief Secretary's Correspondence, Special Bundles, 1916, Chidley 1, 5/5298.

120　Chief Secretary to Cabinet, 6 October 1916, CS16 3643; Under Secretary to The Acting Under Secretary, Department of the Attorney General and of Justice, 12 October 1916; E.B. Harkness, note on file, 18 December 1916, 16. 3647, 18 Dec., in SRNSW, Chief Secretary's Correspondence, Special Bundles, 1916, Chidley 1, 5/5298.

121　*Evening News*, 28 December 1916, clipping in SRNSW, Chief Secretary's Correspondence, Special Bundles, 1916, Chidley 1, 5/5298; McInerney, 'Introduction', in Chidley, *Confessions*, pp. xxx–xxxi.

122　Ellis, quoted in McInerney, 'Introduction', p. xviii; Chidley to Ellis, 5 December 1899, Chidley Papers, ML MSS 143/8, pp. 361–8.

123　Chidley Papers, Carpenter to Chidley, n.d. [copy], ML MSS 143/7, pp. 9–11; Chidley to Ellis, 27 August 1900, ML MSS 143/8, pp. 423–5; Chidley to Ellis, 5 December 1899, ML MSS 143/8, pp. 361–8; Carpenter to Chidley [Copy], 20 January 1903, ML MSS 143/7, pp. 11–15.

124　Chidley to Ellis, 5 December 1899, Chidley Papers, ML MSS 143/8, pp. 361–8.

125　Finnane, 'Sexuality and the Social Order', p. 209.

# CHAPTER 6

1　Facey, *Fortunate Life*, p. 284.

2　Marina Larsson, *Shattered Anzacs: Living with the Scars of War*, UNSWP, Sydney, 2009, pp. 135–6.

3　Paul G. Dane, 'The Psycho-neuroses of Soldiers and Their Treatment', *MJA*, 25 April 1925, pp. 427–30; Joy Damousi, *Freud in the Antipodes: A Cultural History of Psychoanalysis in Australia*, UNSWP, Sydney, 2005, pp. 50–2.

4　'Morons, Morals and Mentality', *MJA*, 17 May 1919, pp. 406–7.

5　W.A.T. Lind, 'The Sex Instinct and Its Disorders', *MJA*, 6 August 1927, pp. 182–5, partly quoted in G. McBurnie, Constructing Sexuality in Victoria 1930–1950: Sex Reformers Associated with the Victorian Eugenics Society, PhD Thesis, Monash University, 1989, p. 172.

6　Freud, however, was less willing to abandon the idea that female inverts were masculine.

7　Sigmund Freud, *On Sexuality: Three Essays on the Theory of Sexuality and Other Works*, Penguin Books, London, 1991, pp. 53, 58–61, 48.

8　J.V. McAree, 'Sex and Its Influence in the Causation of Mental Psychoses', Australian Medical Congress (British Medical Association), Transactions of the First Session Melbourne, 12–17 November 1923, *Supplement to the MJA*, 14 June 1924, p. 420.

9　Walker, 'Continence', p. 9 and 'Mind and Body', in Bill Gammage and Peter Spearritt (eds), *Australians 1938*, Fairfax, Syme and Weldon Associates, Broadway (NSW), 1987, pp. 223–34.

10    Chauncey, *Gay New York*, pp. 111–27, 353–4.

11    *Truth* (Melbourne), 4 October 1919, p. 2.

12    *Truth* (Melbourne), 9 April 1921, p. 7.

13    *Truth* (Sydney), 27 February 1921, p. 7; *Truth* (Brisbane), 6 March 1921, p. 10.

14    *Truth* (Melbourne), 9 April 1921, p. 7; *Truth* (Brisbane), 6 March 1921, p. 10.

15    Alfred J. Briton, *The Book of Life*, Health & Physical Culture Publishing, Sydney, 1933, pp. 76–7.

16    Garry Wotherspoon, *'City of the Plain': History of a Gay Sub-culture*, Hale & Iremonger, Sydney, 1991, p. 54; Simes, 'Language of Homosexuality'.

17    Fabio Cleto (ed.), *Camp: Queer Aesthetics and the Performing Subject: A Reader*, Edinburgh University Press, Edinburgh, 1999, esp. Susan Sontag, 'Notes on "Camp"' (1964), pp. 53–65.

18    Simes, 'Language of Homosexuality', p. 46.

19    Marr, *Patrick White*, chs 7–10; Chauncey, *Gay New York*, chs 4 and 10; Matt Houlbrook, *Queer London: Perils and Pleasures in the Sexual Metropolis, 1918–1957*, University of Chicago Press, Chicago and London, 2005, ch. 8.

20    Elliott, *Fairyland*, pp. 101–2; Clarke, *Sumner Locke Elliott*, pp. xv–xviii and ch. 4.

21    Moore, *Sunshine*, pp. 67–102; Wotherspoon, *'City of the Plain'*, ch. 1; Lee, 'Male Homosexual Identity', pp. 100–1.

22    Lee, 'Male Homosexual Identity', pp. 108–11.

23    Graham Carbery, 'Some Melbourne Beats: A "Map" of a Subculture from the 1930s to the 1950s', in Aldrich and Wotherspoon (eds), *Gay Perspectives*, pp. 131–45; Wotherspoon, *'City of the Plain'*, pp. 64–9.

24    Murdoch, '"Disgusting Days" and "Putrid Practices"', pp. 123–4.

25    *Labor Daily*, 19 January 1931, p. 1.

26    Wotherspoon, *'City of the Plain'*, p. 47.

27    Catherine S., interview with John Shields, 25 March 1987, NSW Bicentennial Oral History Collection (NSWBOHC), ML MS 5163, 32/2/21–30, p. 30.

28    Frank M., interview with Marjorie Biggins, 3 and 27 May 1987, NSWBOHC, ML MS 5163, 40/2/35–7, pp. 35–6.

29    Edwards was rumoured to be the illegitimate son of C.C. Kingston (see ch. 2). Reece Jennings, 'Rex v. Edwards: A Politician and the Law', *JHSSA*, No. 8, 1980, pp. 92–8; Suzanne Edgar, 'Edwards, Albert Augustine', in Bede Nairn and Geoffrey Serle (eds), *ADB: Volume 8: 1891–1939 Cl–Gib*, MUP, Carlton, 1981, pp. 415–16.

30    Adrian Dixson, 'Adrian Finds His Avalon', in Garry Wotherspoon (ed.), *Being Different: Nine Gay Men Remember*, Hale & Iremonger, Sydney, 1989 [1986], p. 76; Elliott, *Fairyland*, pp. 147–8.

31    Anderson, *Free Radical*, p. 28.

32    Robert V. Storer, *A Survey of Sexual Life in Adolescence and Marriage*, Science Publishing, Melbourne, 1932, pp. 96, 187, 122, 187–8, 190.

33    Lind, 'Sex Instinct and Its Disorders', pp. 184–5.

34    McAree, 'Sex and Its Influence', p. 419.

35    *Truth* (Melbourne), 31 July 1920, p. 8, quoted in Ford, 'Contested Desires', p. 87; Ruth Ford, '"Lady-Friends" and "Sexual Deviationists": Lesbians and Law in Australia, 1920s–1950s', in Kirkby (ed.), *Sex Power and Justice*, pp. 36–42.

36    Carbery, 'Some Melbourne Beats', p. 131.

37    Ford, Contested Desires, *passim*.

38    Judith Keene, 'Aileen Palmer's Coming of Age', in Barbara Caine, E.A. Grosz and Marie de Lepervanche (eds), *Crossing Boundaries: Feminisms and the Critique of Knowledges*, Allen & Unwin, Sydney, 1988, esp. pp. 180–1.

39    Sally Newman, 'Silent Witness? Aileen Palmer and the Problem of Evidence in Lesbian History', *Women's History Review*, Vol. 11, No. 3, 2002, p. 513.

40    Sally Newman, 'Body of Evidence: Aileen Palmer's Textual Lives', *Hecate*, Vol. 26, No. 1, 2000, p. 12. See also Newman, 'Aileen Palmer's Textual Lives', in Dever, Newman and Vickery, *Intimate Archive*, pp. 133–76.

41   Edith Young to Vance Palmer, 23 October 1948, Palmer Papers, NLA 1174/1/7511-12.

42   Liz Conor, 'The Flapper in the Heterosexual Scene', *JAS*, No. 71, 2001, pp. 44, 47.

43   Liz Conor, *The Spectacular Modern Woman: Feminine Visibility in the 1920s*, Indiana University Press, Bloomington and Indianapolis, 2004, p. 183 and *passim*.

44   *Ibid.*, pp. 73-4, 237.

45   Catriona Elder, '"The Question of the Unmarried": Some Meanings of Being Single in Australia in the 1920s and 1930s', *AFS*, Vol. 18, Summer, 1993, pp. 159, 151.

46   Lake, *Getting Equal*, pp. 56-7.

47   Conor, *Spectacular*, p. 216.

48   Jessie Urquhart, 'The Waiting', *Australian Woman's Mirror*, 23 December 1924, pp. 4, 59.

49   Karen Twigg, 'The Role of the "Local Dance" in Country Courtship of the 1930s', in *But Nothing Interesting Ever Happened to Us: Memories of the Twenties and Thirties in Victoria*, Victorian Branch of the Oral History Association of Australia, Melbourne, 1986, p. 20.

50   Twigg, 'Role', pp. 17-27; Brian Lewis, *Sunday at Kooyong Road*, Hutchison of Australia, Richmond (Vic.), 1976; Janet McCalman, *Journeyings: The Biography of a Middle-class Generation 1920-1990*, MUP, Carlton, 1993, pp. 191-2.

51   Catriona Elder, '"It Was Hard for Us to Marry Aboriginal"': Some Meanings of Singleness for Aboriginal Women in Australia in the 1930s', *Lilith*, No. 8, Summer 1993, pp. 114-37.

52   Conor, *Spectacular*, ch. 6.

53   Jackie Huggins, '"Firing On in the Mind": Aboriginal Women Domestic Servants in the Inter-War Years', *Hecate*, Vol. 13, No. 2, 1987-88, p. 20.

54   Elder, '"It Was Hard for Us to Marry Aboriginal"', pp. 120-2.

55   Fiona Paisley, *Loving Protection? Australian Feminism and Aboriginal Women's Rights, 1919-1939*, MUP, Carlton, 2000. See also Lake, *Getting Equal*, ch. 5.

56   Anna Haebich, *For Their Own Good: Aborigines and Government in the South West of Western Australia 1900-1940*, Second Edition, UWAP, Nedlands, 1992, pp. 328, 337, 339.

57   *Western Australian Parliamentary Debates* (*WAPD*), Legislative Council, Vol. 97, 13 October 1936, p. 1065.

58   *Ibid.*, 29 September 1934, pp. 823, 822.

59   *Ibid.*, 13 October 1936, p. 1067.

60   *Ibid.*, 13 October 1936, p. 1068; 14 October, p. 1106.

61   *Ibid.*, 14 October 1936, p. 1107.

62   *Ibid.*, 13 October 1936, p. 1069.

63   *Ibid.*, 14 October 1936, p. 1109.

64   Patricia Jacobs, 'Science and Veiled Assumptions: Miscegenation in WA 1930-1937', *Australian Aboriginal Studies*, No. 2, 1986, p. 18.

65   Commonwealth of Australia, *Aboriginal Welfare, Initial Conference of Commonwealth and State Aboriginal Authorities held at Canberra, 21st to 23rd April, 1937*, pp. 10, 14, 17; McGregor, 'Aboriginal Caucasian'.

66   Russell McGregor, '"Breed out the Colour" or the Importance of Being White', *AHS*, Vol. 33, No. 120, October 2002, pp. 286-302; Tony Austin, 'Cecil Cook, Scientific Thought and "Half-Castes" in the Northern Territory 1927-1939', *Aboriginal History*, Vol. 14, Pt 2, pp. 104-22.

67   Victoria Haskins, '"A Better Chance"? – Sexual Abuse and the Apprenticeship of Aboriginal Girls under the NSW Aborigines Protection Board', *Aboriginal History*, Vol. 28, 2004, p. 53.

68   Raymond Evans, 'Aborigines', in D.J. Murphy, R.B. Joyce and Colin A. Hughes (eds), *Labor in Power: The Labor Party and Governments in Queensland 1915-57*, UQP, St Lucia, 1980, p. 346; Commonwealth of Australia, *Aboriginal Welfare*, pp. 8, 20.

69   Quoted in Huggins, '"Firing On"', p. 16. See also Thom Blake, *A Dumping Ground: A History of the Cherbourg Settlement*, UQP, St Lucia, 2001, pp. 132-3.

70   Rani Kerin, 'Dogging for a Living: Aborigines and "Undesirables" in South Australia', in Bain Attwood and Tom Griffiths (eds), *Frontier, Race, Nation: Henry Reynolds and Australian History*, Australian Scholarly Publishing, North Melbourne, 2009, pp. 136-56.

71  Alexander C.T. Geppert, 'Divine Sex, Happy Marriage, Regenerated Nation: Marie Stopes's Marital Manual *Married Love* and the Making of a Best-seller, 1918–1955', *JHS*, Vol. 8, No. 3, 1998, pp. 389–433.

72  Th. H. Van de Velde, *Ideal Marriage: Its Physiology and Technique*, William Heinemann (Medical Books), London, 1937 [1928], p. 172.

73  Jessamyn Neuhaus, 'The Importance of Being Orgasmic: Sexuality, Gender, and Marital Sex Manuals in the United States, 1920–1963', *JHS*, Vol. 9, No. 4, October 2000, pp. 447–73; Marie Carmichael Stopes, *Married Love: A New Contribution to the Solution of Sex Difficulties*, 9th Edition, G.P. Putnam's Sons, London, 1921, pp. 48, 57, 61–3, 67, 70, 73–5, 80–1, 84, 92.

74  Marion Piddington to Marie Stopes, 24 March [1924]; 21 March 1926; 7 June 1926; 1 June 1926, Marie Stopes Papers, British Library (BL), MS 58572.

75  Kathleen B., interview, NSWBOHP, ML MS 5163, 122/2/16.

76  Leigh Summers, The Transmission of Misogyny: Sex Advice Literature in Mid-Twentieth Century Australia, BA (Hons) Thesis, Department of History and Politics, James Cook University of North Queensland, 1992, p. 2.

77  Curthoys, 'Eugenics, Feminism, and Birth Control', pp. 73–89.

78  Piddington to Stopes, 10 March 1919, BL MS 58572.

79  *Ibid.*, 27 April 1922; 1 June 1926; 24 January 1928, BL MS 58572.

80  Finch, *Classing Gaze*, p. 140; Reiger, *Disenchantment*, pp. 187–9.

81  Marion Piddington, *Tell Them! Or the Second Stage of Mothercraft: A Hand-book of Suggestions for the Sex-Training of the Child*, Moore's Book Shop, Sydney, 1926, pp. 49–50.

82  Piddington to Stopes, 21 March 1926, BL MS 58572.

83  Frank M.C. Forster, 'Haire, Norman', in John Ritchie (ed.), *ADB, Volume 14: 1940–1980 Di–Kel*, MUP, Carlton, 1996, pp. 353–4; Weeks, *Coming Out*, pp. 139–40, 151–5; Ivan Crozier, '"All the World's a Stage": Dora Russell, Norman Haire, and the 1929 London World League for Sexual Reform Congress', *JHS*, Vol. 12, No. 1, January 2003, pp. 16–37 and 'Becoming a Sexologist: Norman Haire, the 1929 London World League for Sexual Reform Congress, and Organizing Medical Knowledge about Sex in Interwar England', *History of Science*, Vol. 39, Pt 3, No. 125, September 2001, pp. 299–329.

84  This paragraph, and that which precedes it, is dependent on Crozier, '"All the World's a Stage"' and 'Becoming a Sexologist'. The quotation at the end of the paragraph is at p. 22 of '"All the World's a Stage"'.

85  McBurnie, Constructing Sexuality, pp. 173, 219–31; Damousi, *Freud in the Antipodes*, pp. 69–73.

86  Lisa Featherstone, '"Fitful Rambles of an Unruly Pencil": George Southern's Challenge to Sexual Normativity in 1920s Australia', *JHS*, Vol. 19, No. 3, September 2010, pp. 389–408.

87  G.W.R. Southern, *Making Morality Modern: A Plea for Sexual Reform on a Scientific Basis Addressed To Working People*, Self-Published, Mosman, 1934, pp. 47, 50.

88  Reiger, *Disenchantment*, pp. 185–6.

89  *The Guide to Virile Manhood*, Father and Son Welfare Movement and League of Youth and Honor, Sydney, 1935, p. 16.

90  Grant Rodwell, 'Curing the Precocious Masturbator: Eugenics and Australian Early Childhood Education', *JAS*, No. 59, 1998, pp. 82–92.

91  Norman Haire, *Hymen or the Future of Marriage*, Kegan Paul, Trench, Trubner & Co., London, 1927, pp. 46, 50.

92  Laqueur, *Solitary Sex*, pp. 22–3, 391–2

93  Storer, *Survey*, pp. 113–14.

94  Stephen Garton, 'Eugenics', in Graeme Davison, John Hirst and Stuart Macintyre (eds), *The Oxford Companion to Australian History*, OUP, Melbourne, 1998, pp. 226–7.

95  *Smith's Weekly*, 30 January 1932, p. 16; 20 February 1932, p. 19; 23 January 1932, p. 23.

96  Haire, *Hymen*, pp. 30–1, 37, 90–1, 94–5, 32.

97  Ellen Warne, 'Sex Education Debates and the Modest Mother in Australia, 1890s to the 1930s', *Women's History Review*, Vol. 8, No. 2, 1999, p. 320.

98    Jim Jose, 'The White Cross League and Sex Education in SA State Schools 1916–1929',
      *JHSSA*, No. 24, 1996, p. 53.
99    Logan, *Sex Education in Queensland*, pp. 22–3.
100   Jim Davidson, *A Three-Cornered Life: The Historian WK Hancock*, UNSWP, Sydney, 2010,
      p. 32.
101   'Sex Education', *Australian Woman's Mirror*, 27 December 1927; Edith Howes, *The
      Cradle Ship*, Cassell and Company, London, Toronto, Melbourne and Sydney, 1930
      [1916], pp. 150–2.
102   Margaret Conley, '"Citizens – Protect your birthright!" The Racial Hygiene Association of
      New South Wales', *Bowyang: Work on Changing Australia*, No. 6, 1981, pp. 8–12.
103   RHA, Executive, Minutes, 1 June 1931, Ruby Rich Papers, NLA MS 7493, Box 68.
104   Conley, '"Citizens"', p. 11.
105   Johnston with Wippell, *Ansell*, p. 19.
106   John C. Caldwell, Christabel Young, Helen Ware, Donald Lavis and Anh-Thu Davis,
      'Knowledge, Attitudes, and Practice of Family Planning in Melbourne, 1971', *Studies in
      Family Planning*, Vol. 4, No. 3, March 1973, p. 54. For British developments, see Kate
      Fisher, '"She Was Quite Satisfied with the Arrangements I Made": Gender and Birth
      Control in Britain 1920–1950', *Past and Present*, No. 169, November 2000, pp. 161–93 and
      Kate Fisher and Simon Szreter, '"They Prefer Withdrawal": The Choice of Birth Control in
      Britain, 1918–1950', *Journal of Interdisciplinary History*, Vol. 34, No. 2, Autumn 2003, pp.
      263–91. For Stopes and Haire, see Judith A. Allen, 'Cultural Genealogies of Anovulation:
      Revisiting Abortion, the Pill and Feminist Sexual Politics', in Catherine Kevin (ed.),
      *Feminism and the Body: Interdisciplinary Perspectives*, Cambridge Scholars Publishing,
      Newcastle Upon Tyne, 2009, pp. 8–28.
107   RHA, General Secretary's Report for Year Ending June 30th 1935, ML.
108   Conley, '"Citizens"', p. 10.
109   Ruby Rich, interview, 12 December 1976, De Berg Tapes 994–5, transcript, p. 13,369, NLA.
110   Jane Foley, The Eugenics Society of Victoria and Its Role in the Birth Control Controversy
      of the 1930s, BA (Hons) Thesis, Department of History, University of Melbourne, 1980;
      McBurnie, Constructing Sexuality, pp. 112–20; Kelvin Churches, '120 Years of Abortion in
      Melbourne', *Age, Review*, 24 April 1976, p. 14; Victor H. Wallace, 'Family Planning in
      Melbourne', *MJA*, 29 March 1969, pp. 706–7 and 'Vasectomy', *MJA*, 27 January 1973, p. 212.
111   Piddington to Stopes, 12 August 1931, BL MS 58572.
112   Marion Piddington, *Institute of Family Relations, 91 Phillip Street, Sydney*, Circular, 1
      January 1933, Bessie Rischbieth Papers, NLA 2004/12/1718.
113   Piddington to Ada Bromham, 27 August 1931, Bessie Rischbieth Papers, NLA
      2004/12/1701; Piddington to Stopes, 1, 7 June 1926, BL MS 58572.
114   Piddington to Stopes, 24 January, 22 June, 19 November 1928, 7 January 1929, BL MS 58572.
115   Gwenda Davey, 'My Childhood', unpublished autobiography, in Gwyn Dow and June Factor
      (eds), *Australian Childhood: An Anthology*, McPhee Gribble, Ringwood, 1991, p. 252.
116   Jim Comerford, interviewed by Marjorie Higgins, 15 May 1987, NSWBOHP, ML MS 5163,
      54/2/22-23.
117   Gillian Colclough, '"Innocent, Not Ignorant": Oral Recall of Sexual Knowledge and
      Conduct by Early Twentieth Century North Queensland Women', *JAS*, Vol. 34, No. 1,
      March 2010, pp. 79–93.
118   Ivy T., interviewed by Claire Williams, 18 February 1987, NSWBOHP, ML MS 5163,
      15/1/33.
119   Jan Carter, *Nothing to Spare: Recollections of Australian Pioneering Women*, Penguin
      Books, Ringwood, 1983, p. 55.
120   Lewis, *Sunday*, p. 28; Amy Joy Jarrott, 'It's Wonderful to See a Return to the Natural and
      Happy State': Women, Work and Domesticity in World War II and Post-War Australia,
      BA (Hons) Thesis, History, University of Queensland, 2006, p. 128, n. 113.
121   Amanda Kaladelfos, 'Murder in Gun Alley: Girls, Grime and Gumshoe History', *JAS*,
      Vol. 34, No. 4, December 2010, pp. 471–84.

122   *Truth* (Sydney), 31 August 1924, p. 1; *New South Wales Parliamentary Debates* (*NSWPD*), LA, Vol. 96, 2 September 1924, pp. 1654–5, 1639, 1648; *SMH*, 2 September 1924, p. 13.

123   *Truth* (Melbourne), 13 June 1925, p. 9.

124   H. Leaver, 'Mental Aspects of Gynaecology', *MJA*, 15 December 1934, pp. 773–4.

125   J.W. Springthorpe, Diary (Vol. 10), 16 December 1922, SLV MS 9898.

126   P.U.H., 'Birth Control', [*West Australian*], [13] December 1934, clipping in Bessie Rischbieth Papers, NLA MS 2004/12/1763.

127   'Birth control. Request for free clinics. Minister Not Impressed', clipping, 26 November 1939, in Bessie Rischbieth Papers, NLA MS 2004/12/1870.

128   David Potts, *The Myth of the Great Depression*, Scribe, Melbourne, 2006, pp. 233, 252–3, 312, 313.

129   Betty Moffitt, '"Hello Mother, Hello Father": The Family Scene', in Rigg (ed.), *In Her Own Right*, pp. 75–6.

130   Stefania Siedlecky and Diana Wyndham, *Populate and Perish: Australian Women's Fight for Birth Control*, Allen & Unwin, Sydney, 1990, pp. 25–8; J.C. Caldwell and H. Ware, 'The Evolution of Family Planning in Australia', *Population Studies*, Vol. 27, 1973, p. 31.

131   Allen, *Sex & Secrets*, pp. 158–68.

132   Pawang, 'Unborn Australians', *Bulletin*, 17 January 1940, p. 8.

133   Norman Haire, 'Abortion in Australia', *Journal of Sex Education*, Vol. 2, No. 4, February–March 1950, pp. 173–4.

134   Allen, *Sex & Secrets*, p. 166.

135   Churches, '120 Years of Abortion', p. 13.

136   Janet McCalman, *Struggletown: Portrait of an Australian Working-Class Community*, Penguin Books, Ringwood, 1988, pp. 130–1.

137   McCalman, *Sex and Suffering*, pp. 216–17.

138   Churches, '120 Years of Abortion', p. 13.

139   Anonymous male, interviewed by Larraine Stevens about sexual behaviour during 1930s, 15–22 July 1982, NLA ORAL TRC 2404 Int.No.-1200, p. 1. A Belgian woman was charging £5 in the 1930s according to this man's testimony.

140   Barbara Baird, 'The Self-Aborting Woman', *AFS*, Vol. 13, No. 28, 1998, pp. 323–37; Nicole Moore, '"Me Operation:" Abortion and Class in Australian Women's Novels, 1920s–1950', *Hecate*, Vol. 22, No. 1, 1996, pp. 27–46.

141   Siedlecky and Wyndham, *Populate and Perish*, p. 74.

142   J.W. Springthorpe, Diary (Vol. 9), 1 September 1921, SLV MS 9898.

143   *West Australian*, 7 December 1934, p. 16.

144   Ina Bertrand, 'Education or Exploitation: The Exhibition of "Social Hygiene" Films in Australia'. *Continuum: Journal of Media & Cultural Studies*, Vol. 12, No. 1, 1998, pp. 31–46.

145   R.S. Wallace and W. Cresswell O'Reilly, 'Commonwealth Film Censorship, Report for the Year 1925', *Commonwealth Parliamentary Papers* (*CPP*) 1926–27–28, No. 21, Vol. 5, p. 6.

146   Wallace and O'Reilly, 'Commonwealth Film Censorship, Report for the Year 1926', *CPP* 1926–27–28, No. 105, Vol. 5, p. 4.

147   Wallace and O'Reilly, 'Commonwealth Film Censorship, Report on the Work for the Year 1927', *CPP* 1926–27–28, No. 223, Vol. 5, p. 5.

148   Quoted in Day, *Contraband*, p. 177.

149   Piddington to Stopes, n.d. [postmarked 11 May 1923; received 15 June 1923]; 'Banned Books', clipping [*Age*, 24 May 1923], in Piddington–Stopes Correspondence, p. 36; Piddington to Stopes, 18 June [1923]; Piddington to Stopes, 3 July [1923]; *CPD*, undated extract [1923], in Piddington–Stopes Correspondence, p. 43, BL MS 58572.

150   Nicole Moore, 'Treasonous Sex: Birth Control Obscenity Censorship and White Australia, *AFS*, Vol. 20, No. 48, November 2005, pp. 319–42.

151   Coleman, *Obscenity*, pp. 13–14.

152   *Labor Daily*, 16 January 1930, p. 1; 14 February 1930, p. 1.

153   Hetherington, *Norman Lindsay*, pp. 168–9, 185–9; Norman Lindsay to Leslie Meller, June

1931, in R.G. Howarth and A.W. Baker (eds), *Letters of Norman Lindsay*, Angus & Robertson, Sydney, 1979, pp. 302–3.

154  Norman Lindsay, *Creative Effort: An Essay in Affirmation*, Published for the Author by Art in Australia, Sydney, 1920, p. 245.

155  A.D. Hope, 'Introduction', in Norman Lindsay, *Siren and Satyr: The Personal Philosophy of Norman Lindsay*, Sun Academy Series, South Melbourne, 1976, p. 5.

156  *VPD*, LA, Vol. 104, 10 August 1938, pp. 702–3; *Truth* (Melbourne), 13 August 1938, pp. 1, 4.

157  Quoted in Deana Heath, 'Literary Censorship, Imperialism and the White Australia Policy', in Martin Lyons and John Arnold (eds), *A History of the Book in Australia 1891–1945*, UQP, St Lucia, 2001, p. 79. See also Heath, *Purifying Empire*, pp. 95, 102.

158  Raelene Frances, 'White Slaves' and White Australia: Prostitution and Australian Society, Eighth Annual History Lecture for the History Council of NSW delivered 15 September 2003 at Museum of Sydney, History Council of NSW, Sydney, 2003, p. 22.

159  Frances, 'White Slaves', pp. 19–26; 'Sex Workers', pp. 108–22; and *Selling Sex*, ch. 14. See also Day, *Contraband*, pp. 214–16; *Truth* (Melbourne), 21 November 1936, p. 10; 28 November 1936, p. 1; 5 December 1936, p. 9.

160  *MJA*, 28 April 1923, p. 479.

161  Robin Lesley Hammond, Young Men with Guns: Crooks, Cops and the Consorting Law in 1920s–1930s Sydney, MA (Hons) Thesis, University of New England, 2008.

162  Larry Writer, *Razor: A True Story of Slashers, Gangsters, Prostitutes and Sly Grog*, Pan Macmillan, Sydney, 2001, p. 26; Allen, *Sex & Secrets*, p. 169.

163  Writer, *Razor*, p. 55; Alfred W. McCoy, *Drug Traffic: Narcotics and Organized Crime in Australia*, Harper & Row, Sydney, 1980, p. 125.

164  Writer, *Razor*, pp. 95, 31; McCoy, *Drug Traffic*, p. 142.

165  Golder and Allen, 'Prostitution in New South Wales', pp. 17–24.

166  *Ibid.*, p. 21; Potts, *Myth of the Great Depression*, pp. 102–3, 208, 233; Frances, *Selling Sex*, p. 223; Alfred W. McCoy, 'Crime: Two Cities and their Syndicates: A Comparative Urban History of Organised Crime', in Jim Davidson (ed.), *The Sydney–Melbourne Book*, Allen & Unwin, Sydney, 1986, p. 107.

167  Bill Jenkings with Norm Lipson and Tony Barnao, *As Crime Goes by …The Life and Times of "Bondi" Bill Jenkings*, Ironbark Press, Randwick, 1992, p. 135.

168  Writer, *Razor*, p. 185; B.W. Higman, *Domestic Service in Australia*, MUP, Carlton, 2002, p. 169.

169  Peter Kirkpatrick, *The Sea Coast of Bohemia: Literary Life in Sydney's Roaring Twenties*, UQP, St Lucia, 1992, ch. 10.

170  Frances, *Selling Sex*, p. 222.

171  *New South Wales Police Criminal Register*, Supplement to *New South Wales Police Gazette*, 10 May 1933, Walter Naughton, No. 112, SRNSW 1/3326. My thanks to Robin Hammond for this reference.

172  McCoy, 'Crime', pp. 97–100.

173  David Horner, *Blamey: The Commander-in-Chief*, Allen & Unwin, Sydney, 1998, pp. 80–3.

174  Frances, *Selling Sex*, chs 12 and 13.

## CHAPTER 7

1  John Murphy, *Imagining the Fifties: Private Sentiment and Political Culture in Menzies' Australia*, UNSWP/Pluto Press, Sydney, 2000, p. 56.

2  N.M. Gibson, 'V.D. and the Army', *Salt*, Vol. 2, No. 7, 16 February 1942, p. 27; Allan S. Walker, *Clinical Problems of the War*, AWM, Canberra, 1952, pp. 264–5.

3  Gibson, 'V.D. and the Army', pp. 24–8. See also 'There's Fighting on the Second Front' and Gibson, 'The Second Front: Venereal Disease', *Salt*, Vol. 2, No. 5, 2 February 1942, pp. 1, 23–6; Gibson, 'Gonorrhoea and Syphilis at Work', *Salt*, Vol. 2, No. 6, 9 February 1942, pp. 23–7; 'V.D. Spreads', *Salt*, Vol. 6, No. 7, 7 June 1943, pp. 1–6.

4   John Barrett, *We Were There: Australian Soldiers of World War II Tell Their Stories*,
    Penguin Books, Ringwood, 1988, pp. 266–7, 354, 360–1, 365. For sulphonamides, see
    Lewis, *Thorns on the Rose*, pp. 248–9 and N.M. Gibson, 'Control of Venereal Disease in
    the Army', *MJA*, 26 September 1942, p. 291.
5   Barrett, *We Were There*, p. 352.
6   Lawson Glassop, *The Rats in New Guinea*, Horwitz Publications, London, Melbourne and
    Sydney, 1969 [1963], p. 61.
7   Stephen Williams, 'Non-Gonococcal Urethritis in Australian Troops Stationed in
    Borneo', *MJA*, 18 May 1946, p. 694.
8   Michael McKernan, *This War Never Ends: The Pain of Separation and Return*, UQP, St
    Lucia, 2001, pp. 138, 163.
9   Hank Nelson, *Prisoners of War: Australians under Nippon*, ABC Books, Sydney, 2001
    [1985], pp. 25–6. See also Barrett, *We Were There*, p. 367.
10  A.E. Coates, 'Clinical Lessons from Prisoner of War Hospitals in the Far East (Burma and
    Siam)', *MJA*, 1 June 1946, p. 759. See also C.R. Boyce, 'A Report on the Psychopathic States of
    the Australian Imperial Force in the Malayan Campaign', *MJA*, 7 September 1946, p. 341.
11  Dr V.H. Wallace Patient History Cards, 3. Sexual Problems – Male and Female,
    1938–1954, Random, Victor Wallace Papers, Accession No. 77/65, LS 3/30/6, University of
    Melbourne Archives (UMA).
12  McKernan, *This War Never Ends*, pp. 138, 163.
13  Barrett, *We Were There*, p. 345; James Wood, *The Forgotten Force: The Australian Military
    Contribution to the Occupation of Japan, 1945–1952*, Allen & Unwin, Sydney, 1998, pp. 69,
    93–103, 107, 111–15; Joanna Bourke, *Rape: A History from 1860 to the Present Day*, Virago,
    London, 2007, pp. 357–8; Robin Gerster, *Travels in Atomic Sunshine: Australia and the
    Occupation of Japan*, Scribe, Melbourne, 2008, pp. 86–7, 103–18, 136–7, 206, 211–13, 221,
    266.
14  Michael Sturma, 'Loving the Alien: The Underside of Relations between American
    Servicemen and Australian Women in Queensland, 1942–1945', *JAS*, No. 24, May 1989,
    pp. 4–5.
15  E. Daniel Potts and Annette Potts, *Yanks Down Under: The American Impact on
    Australia*, OUP, Melbourne, 1985, pp. 146–51; Frances, *Selling Sex*, pp. 249–52.
16  Roberta Perkins and Garry Bennett, *Being a Prostitute: Prostitute Women and Prostitute
    Men*, Allen & Unwin, Sydney, 1985, p. 61.
17  McCoy, *Drug Traffic*, p. 161.
18  Libby Connors, Lynette Finch, Kay Saunders and Helen Taylor, *Australia's Frontline:
    Remembering the 1939–45 War*, UQP, St Lucia, 1992, pp. 154–6.
19  McCoy, *Drug Traffic*, pp. 163–4.
20  Rosemary Campbell, *Heroes and Lovers: A Question of National Identity*, Allen & Unwin,
    Sydney, 1989, p. 57.
21  Sturma, 'Loving the Alien', p. 4; Marilyn Lake, 'The Desire for a Yank: Sexual Relations
    between Australian Women and American Servicemen during World War II', *JHS*, Vol. 2,
    No. 4, 1992, pp. 621–33.
22  Sturma, 'Loving the Alien', pp. 3–17; Allen, *Sex & Secrets*, pp. 218–25.
23  Ivan Chapman, *Private Eddie Leonski: The Brownout Strangler*, Hale & Iremonger, Sydney,
    1982; Kate Darian-Smith, *On the Home Front: Melbourne in Wartime 1939–1945*, OUP,
    Melbourne, 1990, p. 222.
24  Robert Milliken, *Lillian Roxon: Mother of Rock*, Thunder's Mouth Press, New York, 2005
    [2002], p. 24.
25  Dymphna Cusack and Florence James, *Come in Spinner*, Angus & Robertson, North Ryde,
    1988 [1951], p. 38.
26  Campbell, *Heroes and Lovers*, pp. 64, 71–3, 78, 83; '"Lounge Lizzy" is on the Prowl', *Salt*,
    Vol. 11, No. 6, 19 November 1945, pp. 1–4; Lyn Finch, 'Consuming Passions: Romance and
    Consumerism during World War II', in Damousi and Lake (eds), *Gender and War*, ch. 5.
27  Quoted in Lake, 'Desire for a Yank', p. 627.

28    Darian-Smith, *On the Home Front*, p. 211.

29    Lawson Glassop, *We Were the Rats*, Currey O'Neil, South Yarra, 1982 [1944], p. 72.

30    *Truth* (Sydney), 23 January 1944, p. 20.

31    Sean Brawley and Chris Dixson, 'Jim Crow Downunder? African American Encounters with White Australia, 1942–1945', *Pacific Historical Review*, Vol. 71, No. 4, November 2002, pp. 622–3; Kay Saunders and Helen Taylor, 'The Reception of Black American Servicemen in Australia during World War II: The Resilience of "White Australia"', *Journal of Black Studies*, Vol. 25, No. 3, January 1995, pp. 331–48.

32    Robert A. Hall, *The Black Diggers: Aborigines and Torres Strait Islanders in the Second World War*, Allen & Unwin, Sydney, 1989, pp. 127, 156.

33    'V.D. Spreads', p. 2.

34    W.J. Thomas, *Plain Words: A Guide to Sex Education*, N.S.W. Bookstall Co., Sydney, 1943, pp. 77, 66; Monica Dux, '"Discharging the Truth": Venereal Disease, the Amateur and the Print Media, 1942–1945', *Lilith*, Vol. 10, 2001, p. 79.

35    Gibson, 'Control of Venereal Disease', p. 290.

36    *MJA*, 17 October 1942, p. 367; Kay Saunders and Helen Taylor, '"To Combat the Plague": The Construction of Moral Alarm and State Intervention in Queensland During World War II', *Hecate*, Vol. 14, No. 1, 1988, pp. 13–14.

37    'The Parliamentary Joint Committee on Social Security: Sixth Interim Report on a Comprehensive Health Scheme', *MJA*, 17 July 1943, p. 49.

38    Report of Committee of Inquiry Regarding Sexual Offences, 1944, *Queensland Parliamentary Papers*, 1944–45, p. 8.

39    'Dr Wykeham Terriss' [Norman Haire], 'Shaving Heads not Remedy', *Woman*, 28 August 1944, p. 9.

40    Lewis, *Thorns on the Rose*, pp. 250, 259.

41    K.G. Basavarajappa, 'Pre-marital Pregnancies and Ex-nuptial Births in Australia, 1911–66', *Australian and New Zealand Journal of Sociology*, Vol. 4, No. 2, October 1968, pp. 126–45, esp. pp. 143–4.

42    'Morals and the War', *MJA*, 3 October 1942, p. 324.

43    'Venereal Diseases and Their Prevention: Some Recent Pronouncements', *MJA*, 9 October 1943, p. 299. See also *MJA*, 6 March 1943, p. 222.

44    Thomas, *Plain Words*, pp. 78, 80–1.

45    'Sex Hygiene Courses for Children', *New Horizons in Education* (*NHE*), Vol. 2, No. 4, December 1941, p. 15.

46    Report of Committee of Inquiry Regarding Sexual Offences', pp. 16–17.

47    McBurnie, Constructing Sexuality, pp. 78–9, 174–5.

48    Lotte Fink, *The Child and Sex*, Angus & Robertson, Sydney, 1945, p. 41.

49    Florence Kenny, *The Guide Through Girlhood*, Father and Son Welfare Movement and League of Youth and Honour, Sydney, 1945, pp. 27, 28, 30.

50    Thomas, *Plain Words*, pp. 50, 52; McBurnie, Constructing Sexuality, pp. 233, 252.

51    Victor H. Wallace, 'South Melbourne Lecture 5', 30 August 1949, pp. 10–11, WEA Lectures by V.H. Wallace, Second Series, V.H. Wallace Papers, 4/3/1, UMA.

52    Wickham Terrace was the Brisbane street in which many medical specialists had their practices.

53    Alison Bashford and Carolyn Strange, 'Public Pedagogy: Sex Education and Mass Communication in the Mid-Twentieth Century', *JHS*, Vol. 13, No. 1, January 2004, pp. 71–99; Enid Lyons, *Among the Carrion Crows*, Rigby, Adelaide, 1972, p. 85; Norman Haire to Guy Natusch, 11 May 1946, Norman Haire Papers, University of Sydney, Box 3.4.

54    Terriss [Haire], 'Pre-marriage Advice', *Woman*, 23 June 1947, p. 38.

55    Lyons, *Among the Carrion Crows*, p. 88.

56    Terriss [Haire], 'Promiscuity Always a Danger', *Woman*, 8 March 1943, p. 8, 'Nature Demands a Penalty', *Woman*, 2 October 1944, p. 12, 'Value of Early Marriages', *Woman*, 9 October 1944, p. 9, 'Marriage that Failed', *Woman*, 12 May 1947, p. 38 and 'Need for Control', *Woman*, 4 August 1947, p. 38.

57    Norman Haire, *Sex Problems of To-day*, Second Edition, Angus & Robertson, Sydney and London, 1943, pp. 25–6.

58    Terriss [Haire], 'Think of Your Partner', *Woman*, 4 November 1946, p. 38.

59    Terriss [Haire], 'Group-Therapy for Frigidity', *Woman*, 11 September 1950.

60    Terriss [Haire], 'Equality in Marriage', *Woman*, 20 January 1947, p. 38.

61    Terriss [Haire], 'Frigidity in Women', *Woman*, 27 November 1950.

62    Terriss [Haire], 'Problems of Adolescence (2)', *Woman*, 11 March 1946, p. 38.

63    Haire, *Sex Problems of To-day*, p. 84.

64    H.M. North, 'Sexual Problems of Childhood and Adolescence', *MJA*, 14 September 1946, p. 378.

65    *Guide to Virile Manhood*, Ninth Edition, Father and Son Welfare Movement of Australia, Melbourne, Sydney and Brisbane, 1957, pp. 23–4; *A Guide to Manhood*, Father and Son Welfare Movement of Australia, Melbourne, Sydney, Brisbane and Adelaide, 1959, pp. 22–3.

66    *Age*, 2 September 1942, p. 3.

67    *MJA*, 9 October 1943, p. 307.

68    National Health and Medical Research Council (NHMRC), Interim Report on the Medical Aspects of the Decline of the Birth Rate, adopted by the NHMRC at its eighteenth session, 22–24 November 1944, *MJA*, 10 February 1945, pp. 156–9; Julie Harvey, 'The Truth about Mothers and Babies? The NHMRC and the Declining Birth Rate', *MHJ*, Vol. 27, 1999, p. 41; McBurnie, Constructing Sexuality, pp. 124–46.

69    Haire, *Sex Problems of To-day*, p. 29.

70    *Sun*, 8 March 1945 and F.E. Ward, 'Race Suicide', *Daily Telegraph*, 27 November 1944, clippings in Haire Papers 2.24.

71    'Population Unlimited?', *The Nation's Forum of the Air*, broadcast on its National Network by the Australian Broadcasting Commission, Vol. 1, No. 2, 23 August 1944, p. 10, Haire Papers, Box 2.24.

72    C. Mayne, *Exit Australia*, Third Edition Revised, Australian National Secretariat of Catholic Action, Melbourne, n.d., pp. 3, 27–9, 37–40, 54.

73    Haire, *Sex Problems of To-day*, p. 42 and 'Abortion in Australia', p. 174.

74    Victor Wallace, *Women and Children First*, OUP, Melbourne, 1946, pp. 107, 49.

75    Jo Wainer (ed.), *Lost: Illegal Abortion Stories*, MUP, Carlton, 2006, pp. 19–28, 39–46, 47–59, 151–4, and *passim*.

76    Barbara Baird, *'I had one too …': An Oral History of Abortion in South Australia before 1970*, Women's Studies Unit, Flinders University of South Australia, Bedford Park, 1990, pp. 49, 63, 76.

77    Lisa Featherstone, 'Sexy Mamas? Women, Sexuality and Reproduction in Australia in the 1940s', *AHS*, Vol. 36, No. 126, October 2005, pp. 234–52; Angus McLaren, *Twentieth-Century Sexuality: A History*, Blackwell Publishers, 1999, p. 7; Marilyn Lake, 'Female Desires: The Meaning of World War Two', *AHS*, Vol. 24, No. 95, 1990, pp. 267–84.

78    Caldwell and Ware, 'Evolution', p. 16.

79    Murphy, *Imagining*, p. 60; McBurnie, Constructing Sexuality, p. 178.

80    Dr V.H. Wallace Patient History Cards, 3. Sexual Problems – Male and Female, 1938–1954, Random, Wallace Papers, LS 3/30/6, UMA.

81    Jarrott, 'It's Wonderful to See a Return to the Natural and Happy State', pp. 99–100, 113, 115.

82    A. James Hammerton and Alistair Thomson, *Ten Pound Poms: Australia's Invisible Migrants*, Manchester University Press, Manchester and New York, 2005, pp. 105, 185.

83    Glenda Sluga, Bonegilla Reception and Training Centre: 1947–1971, MA Thesis, University of Melbourne, 1985, pp. 61, 66–7, 69, 133, 227.

84    Bain Attwood, *Rights for Aborigines*, Allen & Unwin, Sydney, 2003, p. 158.

85    Peter McDonald, Lado Ruzicka and Patricia Pyne, 'Marriage, Fertility and Mortality', in Wray Vamplew (ed.), *Australians: Historical Statistics*, Fairfax, Syme & Weldon Associates, Broadway (NSW), 1987, pp. 43, 46–47; Murphy, *Imagining*, p. 56 and ch. 4; Garton, *Cost of War*, pp. 107–8; James Walter, 'Designing Families and Solid Citizens: The Dialectic of Modernity and the Matrimonial Causes Bill, 1959, *AHS*, Vol. 32, No. 116,

April 2001, pp. 53, 48–9; Finlay, *To Have But Not To Hold*, p. 317; McBurnie, 'Constructing Sexuality', pp. 211, 219, 193–208.

86    Milliken, *Lillian Roxon*, p. 57.

87    Dr V.H. Wallace Patient History Cards, 3. Sexual Problems – Male and Female, 1938–1954, Random, Wallace Papers, LS 3/30/6, UMA. For a discussion of this body of evidence, see McBurnie, Constructing Sexuality, pp. 257–69.

88    Ross Laurie, 'Fantasy Worlds: The Depiction of Women and the Mating Game in Men's Magazines in the 1950s', *JAS* No. 56, 1998, pp. 116–24; Richard White, 'The Importance of Being *Man*', in Peter Spearritt and David Walker (eds), *Australian Popular Culture*, Allen & Unwin, Sydney, London, 1979, ch. 8.

89    McBurnie, Constructing Sexuality, pp. 255, 267.

90    *Man*, November 1956, p. 80.

91    Cassandra Pybus, *Seduction and Consent: A Case of Gross Moral Turpitude*, Mandarin, Port Melbourne, 1994, p. 16.

92    Peter McPhee, *'Pansy': A Life of Roy Douglas Wright*, MUP, Carlton, 1999, pp. 117, 124 129.

93    Nevill Drury, *Pan's Daughter: The Strange World of Rosaleen Norton*, Collins, Sydney, 1988, p. 85.

94    John L. Holmes, 'Eugene Goossens in Sydney: His Rise and Fall', *Quadrant*, 213, Vol. 29, No. 7, July 1985, pp. 57–60.

95    *Sun* (Sydney), 13 March 1956, p. 1; James Cockington, *Banned: Tales from the Bizarre History of Australian Obscenity*, ABC Books, Sydney, 2001, p. 137; Carole Rosen, *The Goossens: A Musical Century*, Andre Deutsch, London, 1993, pp. 340–1.

96    *Sun-Herald* (Sydney), 11 March 1956, p. 1.

97    *Sun* (Sydney), 15 March 1956, p. 3.

98    *Truth* (Sydney), 25 March 1956, p. 2; Cockington, *Banned*, p. 145; Rosen, *Goossens*, pp. 364–7; Renée Goossens, *Belonging: A Memoir*, ABC Books, Sydney, 2003, p. 182.

99    *Sun* (Sydney), 23 March 1956, p. 1; *Truth* (Sydney), 25 March 1956, p. 14; *SMH*, 23 March 1956, p. 5.

100   Stephen Garton, *Histories of Sexuality*, Equinox, London, 2004, pp. 211, 217, 220–1.

101   Matthews, 'Blue Movies', pp. 5–9.

102   Matthews, 'Blue Movies'; Anne Coombs, *Sex and Anarchy: The Life and Death of the Sydney Push*, Viking/Penguin, Ringwood, 1996, pp. 193, 196–7.

103   Christine Wallace, *Greer: Untamed Shrew*, Pan Macmillan, Sydney, 1997, pp. 56–7.

104   The foregoing discussion, and my discussion of the 'Drift' and 'Push' generally, draws on Coombs, *Sex and Anarchy*; Wallace, *Greer*, ch. 4; and John Docker, *Australian Cultural Elites: Intellectual Traditions in Sydney and Melbourne*, Angus & Robertson, Sydney, 1974, ch. 8.

105   Quoted in Wallace, *Greer*, p. 91.

106   Judy Ogilvie, *The Push: An Impressionist Memoir*, Primavera, 1995, Leichhardt, p. 114.

107   Wallace, *Greer*, p. 83.

108   Quoted in Coombs, *Sex and Anarchy*, p. 82.

109   Wallace, *Greer*, pp. 52–3.

110   *Just Friends?*, Fourth Edition, Guide Series No. 5, Father and Son Welfare Movement of Australia, n.d., pp. 33–4.

111   Jon Stratton, *The Young Ones: Working-Class Culture, Consumption and the Category of Youth*, Black Swan Press, Perth, 1992, pp. 83–4, 104, 118.

112   Stanley Cohen, *Folk Devils and Moral Panics: The Creation of the Mods and Rockers*, Paladin, St Albans, UK, 1973 [1972].

113   Swain with Howe, *Single Mothers*, pp. 50, 88–90, 139–49.

114   John Braithwaite and Michelle Barker, 'Bodgies and Widgies: Folk Devils of the Fifties', in Paul R. Wilson and John Braithwaite (eds), *Two Faces of Deviance: Crimes of the Powerless and the Powerful*, UQP, St Lucia, 1978, p. 29.

115   A.E. Manning, *The Bodgie: A Study in Abnormal Psychology*, A.H. and A.W. Reed, Wellington, 1958, p. 68.

116   *Truth* (Sydney), 26 January 1958, p. 48.

117   Manning, *Bodgie*, pp. 20, 19.
118   *Truth* (Sydney), 28 April 1957, p. 14.
119   *Truth* (Sydney), 13 April 1958, p. 61.
120   Malcolm Muggeridge, 'An Evening With The Bodgies Of Melbourne', *SMH*, 2 April 1958, p. 2.
121   Stratton, *Young Ones*, ch. 5.
122   *Truth* (Sydney), 11 February 1951, p. 3.
123   Manning, *Bodgie*, pp. 15, 19–20, 37, 41.
124   North, 'Sexual Problems', p. 378.
125   Carbery, 'Melbourne Beats', pp. 138, 141, 144.
126   Hazel Hawke, *My Own Life*, Text Publishing Company, Melbourne, 1995 [1992], p. 40.
127   Graeme Davison with Sheryl Yelland, *Car Wars: How the Car Won Our Hearts and Conquered Our Cities*, Allen & Unwin, Sydney, 2004, p. 54.
128   *Truth* (Sydney), 10 February 1952.
129   *Truth* (Sydney), 27 March 1955, p. 12. For the relationship between the availability of cars and gang-rape, see G. D. Woods, 'Some Aspects of Pack Rape in Sydney', *Australian and New Zealand Journal of Criminology*, Vol. 2, No. 2, June 1969, pp. 111–13; Ross Barber, 'An Investigation into Rape and Attempted Rape Cases in Queensland', *Australian and New Zealand Journal of Criminology*, Vol. 6, No. 4, December 1973, p. 227.
130   For an alternative account more sympathetic to Orr, see John B. Polya and Robert J. Solomon, *Dreyfus in Australia*, Fast Books, Glebe, 1996, p. 112.
131   W.F. Connell, E.P. Francis, Elizabeth E. Skilbeck and a Group of Sydney University Students, *Growing Up in an Australian City: A Study of Adolescents in Sydney*, Australian Council for Educational Research, Melbourne, 1963, pp. 131–3.
132   Richard Zachariah, 'Cars "Promoted as Sex Symbols"', *Age*, 5 June 1967, p. 3.
133   *Crowd*, 19 February 1958, p. 7.
134   Davison with Yelland, *Car Wars*, pp. 102–4.
135   Robert S. Close, *Love Me Sailor*, Horwitz Publications, London, Melbourne and Sydney, 1969 [1945]; Nicole Moore, 'Obscene and Over Here: National Sex and the *Love Me Sailor* Obscenity Case', *Australian Literary Studies*, Vol. 20, No. 4, October 2002, pp. 316–29.
136   Coleman, *Obscenity*, pp. 117–30; J.A. Iliffe, 'The Australian "Obscene Publications" Legislation of 1953–55', *Sydney Law Review*, Vol. 2, No. 1, January 1956, pp. 134–9 and 'Transport Publishing Company Ltd. (and Others) v. Literature Board of Review', *Sydney Law Review*, Vol. 2, No. 2, January 1957, pp. 374–9.
137   Iliffe, 'Transport Publishing', esp. pp. 375, 377; Walter B. Campbell, 'Censorship of Literature in Queensland', *University of Queensland Law Journal*, Vol. 3, No. 3, December 1958, pp. 244–57; Coleman, *Obscenity*, pp. 123–30.
138   Mark Finnane, 'Censorship and the Child: Explaining the Comics Campaign', Vol. 23, No. 92, April 1989, p. 240.
139   Josie Arnold, *Mother Superior Woman Inferior*, Dove Communications, Blackburn (Vic.), 1985, p. 192.
140   Hammerton and Thomson, *Ten Pound Poms*, pp. 185–6.
141   Caldwell and Ware, 'Evolution', pp. 16, 18, 25.
142   *Truth* (Sydney), 18 March 1956, p. 38.
143   *Truth* (Sydney), 31 March 1957, p. 13.
144   *Truth* (Sydney), 6 January 1957, p. 8.
145   Siobhan McHugh, *The Snowy: The People behind the Power*, William Heinemann Australia, Port Melbourne, 1989, pp. 171–81.
146   Noel Tovey, *Little Black Bastard: A Story of Survival*, Hodder, Sydney, 2004, esp. ch. 5; Cassi Plate, 'The Letters of Costas Tachtsis and Carl Plate', *Heat*, 23 New Series, 2010, pp. 117–38.
147   Barbara Sullivan, *The Politics of Sex: Prostitution and Pornography in Australia Since 1945*, CUP, Cambridge, 1997, pp. 117, 39, 45–52.
148   Manning, *Bodgie*, p. 47.
149   *Truth* (Sydney), 1 December 1957, p. 54.
150   *Truth* (Sydney), 15 June 1958, p. 11.

151 Garry Wotherspoon, '"The Greatest Social Menace Facing Australia": Homosexuality and the State in NSW during the Cold War', *LH*, No. 56, May 1989, pp. 15–28 and '*City of the Plain*', ch. 3. See also 'Sexual Behaviour in the Human Male', *MJA*, 16 October 1948, p. 469.

152 Wotherspoon, '*City of the Plain*', p. 81.

153 Anne Blair, *Ruxton: A Biography*, Allen & Unwin, Sydney, 2004, p. 104.

154 Anderson, *Free Radical*, pp. 1–50.

155 Garry Wotherspoon, 'Comrades-in-Arms: World War II and Male Homosexuality in Australia', in Damousi and Lake (eds), *Gender and War*, pp. 205–7.

156 *Truth* (Sydney), 9 January 1944, p. 11.

157 Glassop, *Rats in New Guinea*, p. 21, in Joan Beaumont (ed.), *Australia's War 1939–45*, Allen & Unwin, Sydney, 2000 [1996], p. 153.

158 A.J.M. Sinclair, 'Psychiatric Aspects of the Present War', *MJA*, 3 June 1944, p. 509.

159 A.T. Edwards, 'Some Remarks on Psychotic Ex-Servicemen', *MJA*, 25 May 1946, p. 738.

160 John O'Donnell, 'John's Story', in Wotherspoon (ed.), *Being Different*, p. 47.

161 Elliott, *Fairyland*, pp. 174–6.

162 Moore, *Sunshine and Rainbows*, ch. 7; Wotherspoon, '*City of the Plain*', ch. 2 and 'Comrades-in-Arms', ch. 12.

163 Moore, *Sunshine and Rainbows*, p. 108.

164 Carbery, 'Some Melbourne Beats', pp. 134–5.

165 Yorick Smaal, 'Friends and Lovers: Social Networks and Homosexual Life in War-time Queensland, 1938–1948', in Smaal and Willett (eds), *Out Here*, pp. 168-87.

166 Wotherspoon, '*City of the Plain*', p. 81.

167 Neuhaus, 'Importance', p. 470.

168 Wotherspoon, '"Greatest Social Menace"', p. 19.

169 Graham Willett, 'The Darkest Decade: Homophobia in 1950s Australia', in John Murphy and Judith Smart (eds), *The Forgotten Fifties: Aspects of Australian Society and Culture in the 1950s*, MUP/AHS (Special Issue: Vol. 28, No. 109, October 1997), p. 127.

170 For the experiences of one young Melbourne man in this period, including his prosecution for homosexual offences, see Tovey, *Little Black Bastard*.

171 Wotherspoon, '*City of the Plain*', ch. 3 and '"Greatest Social Menace"'. For an alternative view of the effects of repression, see Willett, 'Darkest Decade'.

172 Jim Wafer, Erica Southgate and Lyndall Coan, *Out in the Valley: Hunter Gay and Lesbian Histories*, Newcastle History Monograph No. 15, Newcastle Region Library, 2000, pp. 60–79.

173 Graeme Blundell, *King: The Life and Comedy of Graham Kennedy*, Pan Macmillan, Sydney, 2003, p. 161.

174 Bridget Griffen-Foley, *Sir Frank Packer: The Young Master*, HarperBusiness, Sydney, 2000, pp. 272–3.

175 *Just Friends?*, p. 8.

176 *The Guide to Virile Manhood*, Ninth Edition, Guide Series No. 2, Father and Son Welfare Movement of Australia, Melbourne, 1957, p. 25.

177 'Are They Feminine? Who, and Why, Are the AWAS?', *Salt*, Vol. 7, No. 12, 14 February 1944, pp. 1–5.

178 Ruth Ford, 'Lesbians and Loose Women: Female Sexuality and the Women's Services during World War II', in Damousi and Lake (eds), *Gender and War*, pp. 93, 95–8; 'Disciplined, Punished and Resisting Bodies: Lesbian Women and the Australian Armed Services, 1950s–60s', *Lilith*, No. 9, Autumn 1996, pp. 53–77.

179 Tovey, *Little Black Bastard*, chs. 6–7, esp. p. 122.

180 Lucy Chesser, Negotiating Subjectivities: The Construction of Lesbian Identities in Melbourne, 1960–1969, BA (Hons) Thesis, Department of History, University of Melbourne, 1993 and 'Australasian Lesbian Movement, "Claudia's Group" and Lynx: "Non-Political" Lesbian Organisation in Melbourne, 1969–1980', *Hecate*, Vol. 22, No. 1, 1996, pp. 70–1. For lesbian social life in Sydney in the 1960s, see Rebecca Jennings and Sandra Mackay, *Out and About: Sydney's Lesbian Social Scene 1960s–1980s*, Pride History Group, Sydney, 2009, esp. pp. 5–20.

181    Rebecca Jennings, 'The Gateways Club and the Emergence of a Post-Second World War Lesbian Subculture', *Social History*, Vol. 31, No. 2, May 2006, pp. 206–25.
182    *Guide to Womanhood: A Reliable Sex Education Book for Young Women 15 Years and Over*, Father and Son Welfare Movement of Australia Inc. Mother and Daughter Section, Sydney, 1963, p. 29.
183    *The Guide Through Teen Years*, Fifth Edition, Guide Series No. 4, Father and Son Welfare Movement of Australia, Sydney, 1957, p. 25.
184    *SMH*, 22 April 1959, p. 5.

## CHAPTER 8

1      *SMH*, 17 June 2002, p. 3.
2      Garton, *Histories of Sexuality*, ch. 11.
3      Geoffrey Wilmot, 'A Broadside for Britannia: Could It Not Happen Here?', *Bulletin*, 3 August 1963, pp. 15–16.
4      Frank Knopfelmacher, 'England Made Them', in 'Three Lessons from the Profumo Affair', *Bulletin*, 6 July 1963, pp. 31–2.
5      *Daily Mirror* (Sydney), 14 June 1963, p. 29.
6      Ian Turner, *Cinderella Dressed in Yella*, Heinemann Educational, Melbourne, 1971, p. 91. I have corrected the spelling of the word 'sheila' ('shiela' in original).
7      John Douglas Pringle, *Australian Accent*, Chatto and Windus, London, 1965 [1958], pp. 24, 38–40.
8      Logan, *Sex Education in Queensland*, pp. 39–40.
9      Anne Deveson, *Australians at Risk*, Cassell Australia, Stanmore, 1978, pp. 158, 161; Paul G. Ward and Greg Woods, *Law and Order in Australia*, Angus & Robertson, Sydney, 1972, p. 93.
10     Deveson, *Australians at Risk*, ch. 6, esp. pp. 168, 192.
11     Logan, *Sex Education in Queensland*, ch. 6; John Scott, '"Children Ask the Damnedest Questions!": Sex(uality) Education as a Social Problem', in Gail Hawkes and John Scott (eds), *Perspectives in Human Sexuality*, OUP, South Melbourne, 2005, pp. 175–85; Ian Hunter, 'Laughter and Warmth: Sex Education in Victorian Secondary Schools', in Peter Botsman and Ross Harley (eds), *Sex, Politics & Representation*, Local Consumption Publications, Sydney, 1984, pp. 55–81.
12     Steven Angelides, 'The Continuing Homosexual Offensive: Sex Education, Gay Rights and Homosexual Recruitment', in Shirleene Robinson (ed.), *Homophobia: An Australian History*, Federation Press, Annandale and Leichhardt, 2008, pp. 172–92.
13     Soren Hansen and Jesper Jensen, *The Little Red School-Book*, tr. Berit Thornberry, Thor Publications, Kensington (NSW), 1973; Iola Hack, 'Hecklers challenge school sex course', *Age*, 13 July 1972, p. 3.
14     Quoted in Rosemary Auchmuty, 'The Truth About Sex', in Peter Spearritt and David Walker (eds), *Australian Popular Culture*, Allen & Unwin, Sydney, London, 1979, p. 187.
15     Deveson, *Australians at Risk*, pp. 204–5.
16     Quoted in Gael Knepfer, *Sex in Australia*, J & G Publishing, Milsons Point, 1984, p. 7.
17     Laqueur, *Solitary Sex*, pp. 397, 413; http://www.melbournewankers.com.au/history.html.
18     *Farrago*, 18 March 1960, p. 4.
19     *Ibid.*, 5 May 1961, p. 6.
20     *Ibid.*, 5 August 1960, p. 4.
21     *Ibid.*, 7 March 1966, pp. 4–5.
22     Graham Little, *The University Experience: An Australian Study*, MUP, Carlton, 1970, pp. 162–4.
23     Katy Reade, 'Recognising and Constructing an Identity: the Beginnings of the Women's Liberation Movement in Melbourne', *MHJ*, Vol. 24, 1996, p. 32.
24     *Honi Soit* (Sydney), 27 March 1962, p. 1; 31 July 1962, pp. 1, 3; Malcolm I. Thomas, *A Place of Light & Learning: The University of Queensland's First Seventy-five Years*, UQP, St Lucia, 1985, pp. 303–4.

25   *Honi Soit*, 5 June 1962, p. 1.

26   *Daily Telegraph* (Sydney), 21 June 1963, p. 3.

27   Matthew Jordan, *A Spirit of True Learning: The Jubilee History of the University of New England*, UNSWP, Sydney, 2004, pp. 187–91.

28   Deveson, *Australians at Risk*, pp. 196, 201, 210–11.

29   R.S.W. [Roger S. Wurm], 'Fundamental Relationships in Family Life', *MJA*, 17 April 1965, p. 601. See also Patricia Johnson, 'Woman Doctor Discusses the Pill', *Australian Women's Weekly*, 28 October 1964, p. 7.

30   For the pill's development, see Elizabeth Siegel Watkins, *On the Pill: A Social History of Oral Contraceptives 1950–1970*, The John Hopkins University Press, Baltimore and London, 1998.

31   Donald R. Lavis, *Oral Contraception in Melbourne, 1961–1971*, Australian Family Formation Project Monograph No. 3, Department of Demography Institute of Advanced Studies, ANU, Canberra, 1975, p. 22; *MJA*, 21 July 1962, pp. xxii–xxiii; *Australian Financial Review*, 9 July 1963, p. 9; R.S.W. [Roger S. Wurm], 'Fundamental Relationships', p. 601.

32   '10 Top Australian Doctors Debate the Pill', *Woman's Day*, 28 September 1964, p. 4; Lillian Roxon, 'Why My Pill Is Safe', *Woman's Day*, 26 October 1964, pp. 20–21; Anne Goldie, 'A Doctor Answers the Critics of the Pill', *Woman's Day*, 21 June 1965, pp. 4–5; Johnson, 'Woman Doctor'.

33   *MJA*, 4 May 1963, p. 675; 5 September 1964, p. 391; 3 April 1965, p. 523.

34   David Hilliard, 'The Religious Crisis of the 1960s: The Experience of the Australian Churches', *JRH*, Vol. 21, No. 2, June 1997, esp. p. 227.

35   Caldwell and Ware, 'Evolution', pp. 23–5.

36   Lavis, *Oral Contraception in Melbourne*, p. 42; 'A Catholic Case for the Pill', *Bulletin*, 11 July 1964, pp. 38–41.

37   Val Noone, 'The Church and the Pill: Irish and Australian debates of the 1960s', in Richard Davis et al. (eds), *Irish-Australian Studies: Papers Delivered at the Eighth Irish-Australian Conference, Hobart, July 1995*, Crossing Press, Sydney, 1996, p. 462.

38   *Australian*, 1 August 1968, p. 1.

39   Greg Dening, *Beach Crossings: Voyaging across Times, Cultures, and Self*, University of Pennsylvania Press, Philadelphia, 2004, p. 111.

40   'After the Encyclical', *Nation*, 31 August 1968, p. 7.

41   Hilliard, 'Religious Crisis', p. 219; *Age*, 12 August 1968, p. 1.

42   Quoted in Josephine Laffin, Matthew Beovich: Archbishop of Adelaide, PhD Thesis, University of Adelaide, 2006, pp. 363–4.

43   Edmund Campion, *Rockchoppers: Growing Up Catholic in Australia*, Penguin Books, Ringwood, 1982, p. 20.

44   *Age*, 31 July 1968, p. 1.

45   *Catholic Weekly* (Sydney), 8 August 1969, in Patrick O'Farrell (ed.) assisted by Deidre O'Farrell, *Documents in Australian Catholic History, Volume II: 1884–1968*, Geoffrey Chapman, London, 1969, pp. 413–14.

46   'After the Encyclical', p. 8.

47   *Age*, 30 July 1968, p. 2.

48   Patrick O'Farrell, *The Catholic Church and Community in Australia: A History*, Nelson, West Melbourne, 1977, p. 414.

49   Caldwell and Ware, 'Evolution', p. 24.

50   Deveson, *Australians at Risk*, p. 235.

51   The 'rhythm method' was based on research that had by the 1930s more accurately identified the days of the cycle in which women were most likely to be fertile or infertile. The 'temperature method' had similarly located periods of likely maximum and minimum fertility, according to changes in a woman's body temperature.

52   John Billings, 'The Quest – Leading to the Discovery of the Billings Ovulation Method', *Bulletin of the Ovulation Method Research and Reference Centre of Australia*, Vol. 29, No. 1, March 2002, pp. 18–28, at http://www.woomb.org/omrrca/bulletin/vol29/no1/TheQuest.pdf;

John J. Billings, *The Ovulation Method: The Achievement of Avoidance of Pregnancy by a Technique Which Is Reliable and Universally Acceptable*, Seventh Edition, Advocate Press, Melbourne, 1983, pp. xv, 3–4; Deveson, *Australians at Risk*, pp. 230–1.

53  Billings, *Ovulation Method*, p. 4; Evelyn L. Billings, John J. Billings and Maurice Catarinich, *Atlas of the Ovulation Method: The Mucus Patterns of Fertility and Infertility*, Third Edition, Advocate Press, Melbourne, 1979, pp. 8–9, 40.

54  Lavis, *Oral Contraception*, pp. 22–3, 90; Rodney P. Shearman, 'The Mechanism of Action of Oral Contraceptives and their Side Effects in Clinical Practice', *MJA*, 16 January 1965, p. 68; *MJA*, 13 February 1965, p. 243.

55  Caldwell and Ware, 'Evolution', pp. 22, 16.

56  McCalman, *Sex and Suffering*, p. 324.

57  'After Wife-Swapping – The Group Scene?', *Man*, June 1971, pp. 10–11, 45; 'Swinging', in Katie Holmes and Marilyn Lake (eds), *Freedom Bound II: Documents on Women in Modern Australia*, Allen & Unwin, Sydney, 1994, pp. 170–1.

58  Szreter, *Fertility*, ch. 8.

59  Sandra Hall, 'The Girls in Their Summer Dresses: Four Profiles', in Rigg (ed.), *In Her Own Right*, p. 33.

60  '10 Top Australian Doctors'.

61  University of New England, Council, Minutes, 11 December 1967, Minute Book 2442, Source Book 9100; 8 September 1969, Minute Book 2833, Source Book 12,304. These meetings dealt with reports of the Student Health Committee held 30 November 1967 and 22 July 1969, University of New England and Regional Archives.

62  *Uni Sex: A Study of Sexual Attitudes and Behaviour at Australian Universities*, Eclipse Paperbacks, Dee Why West, 1972, p. 20.

63  *Age*, 3 March 1971, p. 8.

64  *Age*, 21 July 1971, p. 8.

65  *Bulletin*, 1 January 1972, p. 40.

66  *MJA*, 4 May 1963, p. 675; 2 October 1971, p. 731.

67  Caldwell and Ware, 'Evolution', pp. 16, 25–6.

68  Deveson, *Australians at Risk*, pp. 298, 317; Verity Burgmann, *Power and Protest: Movements for Change in Australian Society*, Allen & Unwin, Sydney, 1993, p. 121.

69  John Leeton and Janet Paterson, 'Family Planning in Melbourne: A Medical–Social Project', *MJA*, 8 March 1969, p. 538; Carl Wood, N. de Mestre, R. MacKenzie, M. Barson and E. Lewis, 'Birth Control Survey in a Lower Social Group in Melbourne', *MJA*, 27 March 1971, p. 692; Margaret Raphael, 'The Role of "The Pill" in the Work Force', *MJA*, 16 October 1971, p. 813.

70  Siedlecky and Wyndham, *Populate and Perish*, pp. 44–5.

71  Germaine Greer, 'Contraception – 1972', *Sunday Times*, 12 March 1972, in Greer, *The Madwoman's Underclothes: Essays and Occasional Writings 1968–85*, Picador/Pan Books, London, 1986, pp. 105–7.

72  Juliet Richters and Chris Rissel, *Doing It Down Under: The Sexual Lives of Australians*, Allen & Unwin, Sydney, 2005, pp. 77–9.

73  Ian Edwards, 'Winning a New Freedom: The Right to Surgical Sterilisations', *Australian Quarterly*, Vol. 51, No. 1, March 1979, p. 92; *MJA*, 20 April 1963, p. 599; 17 August 1963, pp. 283–5; 7 September 1963, pp. 428–9; 21 September 1963, p. 516; 28 September 1963, p. 558; 6 February 1971, p. 347.

74  Robert R. Bell, *The Sex Survey of Australian Women*, Sun Books, Melbourne, 1974, chs. 5–8, *passim*.

75  Graeme Davison, 'Down the Gurgler: Historical Influences on Australian Domestic Water Consumption', in Patrick Troy (ed.), *Troubled Waters: Confronting the Water Crisis in Australia's Cities*, ANU E Press, Canberra, 2008, pp. 49–50.

76  Richters and Rissel, *Doing It Down Under*, pp. 7–9.

77  New South Wales Law Reform Commission, *De Facto Relationships: Issues Paper*, 1981, p. 14.

78  McDonald, Ruzicka and Pyne, 'Marriage', p. 46.

79  Australian Bureau of Statistics, *Year Book Australia, 2008*, http://www.abs.gov.au/
    ausstats/abs@.nsf/0/D5F4805AD4C3E03ECA2573D2001103E0?opendocument.

80  New South Wales Law Reform Commission, *Report on De Facto Relationships*, June 1983,
    pp. 41–3, 47, 53–4; Siew-Ean Khoo, *Living Together: A Report Using Australian Family
    Formation Project Data Prepared for the Australian Institute of Family Studies*,
    Australian Institute of Family Studies Working Paper No. 10, Collins Dove, Melbourne,
    1986, pp. 5, 10–11.

81  Khoo, *Living Together*, p. 5 and *passim*; NSW Law Reform Commission, *Report on De Facto
    Relationships*, ch. 3.

82  Swain with Howe, *Single Mothers*, ch. 9.

83  Stephanie Charlesworth, 'The Impact of the *Victorian Status of Children Act* 1974 on the
    Legal and Social Rights of Children Born to Unmarried Parents', *University of Tasmania
    Law Review*, Vol. 8, No. 2, 1985, pp. 195–207.

84  Swain with Howe, *Single Mothers*, pp. 207–8; Gail Reekie, *Measuring Immorality: Social
    Inquiry and the Problem of Illegitimacy*, CUP , Cambridge, 1998, *passim*.

85  Marilyn Lake, 'Sexuality and Feminism: Some Notes in their Australian History', *Lilith*,
    No. 7, Winter 1991, p. 36.

86  'Contraceptives Duty under Fire', *Age*, 26 July 1972, p. 6; 'Protecting the Contraceptive',
    *Age*, 27 July 1972, p. 9.

87  William H. Masters and Virginia E. Johnson, *Human Sexual Response*, Little, Brown and
    Company, Boston, 1966, ch. 5; Gail Hawkes, *Sex & Pleasure in Western Culture*, Polity
    Press, Cambridge, 2004, pp. 164–5.

88  Deveson, *Australians at Risk*, p. 196.

89  Germaine Greer, *The Female Eunuch*, Paladin, London, 1972 [1970], pp. 307, 42–5.

90  Germaine Greer, 'Getting Out from Under', *Forum*, Vol. 1, No. 4, 1973, p. 9. See also
    Greer, 'Ladies Get on Top for Better Orgasms', *Tharunka*, Family Issue, 28 July 1971.

91  Richard Neville, *Play Power*, Jonathan Cape, London, 1970, p. 92.

92  Lake, 'Sexuality', pp. 29–45.

93  Des Mahon, 'The Anatomy of a Pack Rape', *Man*, December 1968, p. 98.

94  Barber, 'Investigation', pp. 228–9.

95  Gail Mason, 'Reforming the Law of Rape: Incursions into the Masculinist Sanctum', in
    Kirkby (ed.), *Sex, Power and Justice*, pp. 51–2.

96  Deveson, *Australians at Risk*, pp. 173, 178.

97  Adrian Howe, 'Anzac Mythology and the Feminist Challenge', *Melbourne Journal of
    Politics*, Vol. 15, 1983–04, pp. 17–23.

98  Mason, 'Reforming', pp. 53–60.

99  Regina Graycar and Jenny Morgan, 'A Quarter Century of Feminism in Law: Back to the
    Future', *Alternative Law Journal*, Vol. 20, 1999, p. 2, http://www.austlii.edu.au/au/journals/
    AltLJ/1999/20.html.

100 Melanie Heenan, 'Just "Keeping the Peace": A Reluctance to Respond to Male Partner
    Sexual Violence', *Issues: Australian Centre for the Study of Sexual Assault*, No. 1, March
    2004, http://www.aifs.gov.au/acssa/pubs/issue/i1pdf/acssa_i1_introduction.pdf.

101 Diane Bell and Topsy Napurrula Nelson, 'Speaking about Rape is Everyone's Business',
    *Women's Studies International Forum*, Vol. 12, No. 4, 1989, pp. 403–16; Jackie Huggins et al.,
    'Letter to the Editor', *Women's Studies International Forum*, Vol. 14, No. 5, 1991, pp. 506–7.

102 Anne Summers, *Damned Whores and God's Police: The Colonization of Women in
    Australia*, Penguin Books, Ringwood, 1975; Dixson, *Real Matilda*, pp. 31–2.

103 Craig McGregor, *Profile of Australia*, Ringwood, Penguin, 1968 [1966], p. 61.

104 Ronald Conway, *The Great Australian Stupor: An Interpretation of the Australian Way of
    Life*, Sun Books, Melbourne, 1971, pp. 124–5.

105 Suzy Jarratt, *Permissive Australia*, Jack de Lissa, Sydney, 1970, pp. 48, 51.

106 Deveson, *Australians at Risk*, p. 258

107 Bertram Wainer, *It Isn't Nice*, Alpha Books, Sydney, 1972, pp. 138–9.

108 *Digger*, 26 August–9 September [1972], pp. 6–8; 9–23 September [1972], pp. 8–10; Gideon

Haigh, *The Racket: How Abortion Became Legal in Australia*, MUP, Carlton, 2008.

109 'Abortion', *Forum*, Vol. 1, No. 5, 1973, p. 9.

110 D. Chappell and P.R. Wilson, 'Public Attitudes to the Reform of The Law Relating to Abortion and Homosexuality, Part I', *Australian Law Journal*, Vol. 42, 30 August 1968, pp. 121–4; J. Caldwell and H. Ware, 'Australian Attitudes towards Abortion: Survey Evidence', in Nicholas Haines (ed.), *Abortion: Repeal or Reform?*, Australian National University Centre for Continuing Education, Canberra, 1972, pp. 10–21, 41–91.

111 Jill Blewett, 'The Abortion Law Reform Association of South Australia 1968–73', in Jan Mercer (ed.), *The Other Half: Women in Australian Society*, Penguin Books, Ringwood, 1975, pp. 377–94.

112 Lyndall Ryan, 'Abortion in South Australia 1970–1991', *Refractory Girl*, No. 41, December 1991, pp. 2–4.

113 Lyndall Ryan and Margie Ripper, 'Women, Abortion and the State', *JAS*, No. 37, 1993, pp. 78–80.

114 Quoted in Paul Wilson, *The Sexual Dilemma: Abortion, Homosexuality, Prostitution and the Criminal Threshold*, UQP, St Lucia, 1971, p. 33.

115 *MJA*, 26 August 1972, p. 513.

116 Tony McMichael, 'The Law in Victoria', in Tony McMichael (ed.), *Abortion: The Unenforceable Law: The Reality of Unwanted Pregnancy and Abortion in Australia*, Abortion Law Reform Association of Victoria, Melbourne, 1972, p. 18.

117 McMichael, 'The Law in Victoria', p. 19.

118 John Warhurst and Vance Merrill, 'The Abortion Issue in Australia: Pressure Politics and Policy', *Australian Quarterly*, Vol. 54, No. 2, Winter 1982, p. 120.

119 'A Statement on Abortion in Victoria', *MJA*, 6 November 1971, pp. 982–3.

120 Karen Coleman, 'The Politics of Abortion in Australia: Freedom, Church and State', *Feminist Review*, No. 29, Spring 1988, pp. 82, 93–6; Siedlecky and Wyndham, *Populate and Perish*, pp. 90–1, 98; Rebecca M. Albury, *The Politics of Reproduction: Beyond the Slogans*, Allen & Unwin, Sydney, 1999, pp. 66, 122.

121 Barbara Baird, 'Maternity, Whiteness and National Identity: The Case of Abortion', *AFS*, Vol. 21, No. 50, July 2006, pp. 197–221; Margie Ripper and Lyndall Ryan, 'The Role of the "Withdrawal Method" in the Control of Abortion', *AFS*, Vol. 13, No. 28, 1998, pp. 313–22; Albury, *Politics of Reproduction*, p. 116.

122 Judy McVey, 'The Right to Life Offensive Since 1969', *Hecate*, Vol. 9, Nos 1–2, 1983, pp. 35–43; McCalman, *Sex and Suffering*, p. 339.

123 Lauchlan Chipman, 'Abortion: Time to Turn Back the Clock', *Quadrant*, No. 221, Vol. 30, No. 4, April 1986, p. 33.

124 Katharine Betts, 'Attitudes to Abortion in Australia: 1972 to 2003, *People and Place*, Vol. 12, No. 4, 2004, pp. 22–7.

125 Wilson, *Sexual Dilemma*, pp. 75, 153, 71.

126 Dorothy Johnston, 'Prostitution: One Experience', in Daniels (ed.), *So Much Hard Work*, p. 353.

127 Roberta Perkins, *Working Girls: Prostitutes, Their Life and Social Control*, Australian Institute of Criminology, Canberra, 1991, pp. 10, 218–21; Miraca Gross, 'Prostitutes: Interviews with Three Australian Working Women', *Forum*, Vol. 6, No. 8, 1978, pp. 15–16, 19.

128 Kate Holden, *In My Skin: A Memoir*, Text Publishing, Melbourne, 2005, pp. 192–3.

129 Marcel Winter, *Prostitution in Australia*, Purtaboi Publications, Balgowlah, 1976, pp. 96–100.

130 *Ibid.*, pp. 49, 65–75; Frances, *Selling Sex*, p. 256.

131 Roberta Perkins, 'Being and Becoming "Working Girls": An Oral History of Prostitutes in Sydney 1935–1985', in John Shields (ed.), *All Our Labours: Oral Histories of Working Life in Twentieth Century Sydney*, UNSWP, Sydney, 1992, pp. 174, 186.

132 Roberta Perkins, 'Working Girls in "Wowserville": Prostitute Women in Sydney since 1945', in Richard Kennedy (ed.), *Australian Welfare: Historical Sociology*, Macmillan,

South Melbourne, 1989, p. 373.

133   Frances, *Selling Sex*, pp. 267–71.

134   *Ibid.*, pp. 252–68; Winter, *Prostitution*, pp. 75–80; Steve Dombray, 'The Changing Face of Australia's Call Girls', *Man*, June 1967, pp. 29–30.

135   Ken Buckley, 'Rooting for Prostitutes', *Forum*, Vol. 2, No. 5, 1974, pp. 17–20; Sullivan, *Politics of Sex*, pp. 152–9, 165.

136   Sullivan, *Politics of Sex*, pp. 180–97, 204–27; Frances, *Selling Sex*, ch. 16; John Scott, 'A Labour of Sex? Female and Male Prostitution', in Hawkes and Scott (eds), *Perspectives in Human Sexuality*, pp. 233–53, esp. p. 237.

137   Frances, *Selling Sex*, ch. 16; Paul Sendziuk, *Learning to Trust: Australian Responses to AIDS*, UNSWP, Sydney, 2003, ch. 8.

138   John Scott, 'Prostitution and Public Health in New South Wales', *Culture, Health and Sexuality*, Vol. 5, No. 3, 2003, p. 289.

139   Roberta Perkins, '"How Much Are You, Love?" The Customer in the Australian Sex Industry', *Social Alternatives*, Vol. 18, No. 3, July 1999, p. 38.

140   Richters and Rissel, *Doing It Down Under*, p. 100.

141   Frances, *Selling Sex*, pp. 284–7.

142   McKewon, *The Scarlet Mile*, pp. 136–7.

143   Coleman, *Obscenity*, pp. 21–3, 44–7; Hall Greenland, '"The Protectors"', *Honi Soit*, 24 March 1964, p. 4.

144   Sullivan, *Politics of Sex*, pp. 44, 75–96.

145   *Bulletin*, 6 July 1963, p. 9; *Daily Telegraph*, 25 June 1963, p. 13; Phillip Knightley, 'Australian Writers in Britain and "Expatriatism"', *Changing Australia: The Biennial Conference of the British Australian Studies Association*, Royal Holloway, University of London, 2–5 September 2008 and email to the author, 2 September 2009.

146   *Daily Telegraph*, 15 June 1963, p. 7.

147   Sullivan, *Politics of Sex*, pp. 88, 133; Wendy Bacon, 'Opening Statement', in Ann Turner (ed.), *Censorship*, Heinemann Educational Australia, South Yarra, 1975, pp. 20, 25, 32; Wendy Bacon, 'From P.L.C. to Thor', in *Uni Sex*, p. 46.

148   Bacon, 'From P.L.C. to Thor', pp. 46–7.

149   Donald Horne, *Time of Hope: Australia 1966–72*, Angus & Robertson, Sydney, 1980, p. 20; Wendy Bacon, 'From P.L.C. to Thor', pp. 44, 48, 50–1.

150   Winter, *Prostitution*, pp. 66–72; Matthews, 'Blue Movies', pp. 7–8.

151   Sullivan, *Politics of Sex*, pp. 137–8.

152   Bacon, 'From P.L.C. to Thor', p. 62.

153   Blundell, *King*, ch. 22.

154   Michael Barnard and Lauchlan Chipman, 'Two Views of the Sexual Revolution', *Quadrant*, July 1982, pp. 8, 16.

155   Peter Coleman, 'Opening Statement', in Turner (ed.), *Censorship*, pp. 48, 52.

156   Barnard, 'Two Views', p. 11.

157   Sullivan, *Politics of Sex*, pp. 166–80.

158   Catharine Lumby, *Bad Girls: The Media, Sex and Feminism in the '90s*, Allen & Unwin, Sydney, 1997, pp. xxii, 51, 110 and ch. 2; Mary Spongberg, 'Prostitution and Pornography: The Debate between Radical and Libertarian Feminists', *Lilith*, No. 7, Winter 1991, pp. 46–70.

159   Richters and Rissel, *Doing It Down Under*, p. 39.

160   Paul Wilson, *Dealing with Pornography: The Case against Censorship*, UNSWP, Sydney, 1995, p. 30; Alan McKee, Katherine Albury and Catharine Lumby, *The Porn Report*, MUP, Carlton, 2008, p. 26. For female porn users, see *Porn Report*, pp. xii, 21, 26–7, 39, 45–6 and ch. 5.

161   Sullivan, *Politics of Sex*, p. 133; Lumby, *Bad Girls*, pp. xv, 97, 108; McKee, Albury and Lumby, *Porn Report*, p. 22 and *passim*.

162   See, for instance Rosemary Pringle, 'The Dialectics of Porn', *Scarlet Woman*, No. 12, 1981, pp. 3–10; Beatrice Faust, *Women, Sex and Pornography*, Penguin Books, Ringwood, 1982 [1980].

163 Helen Vnuk, *Snatched: Sex and Censorship in Australia*, Vintage, Milsons Point, 2003, pp. 26–7, 123.

164 Apart from Lumby's work, see Kath Albury, *Yes Means Yes: Getting Explicit about Heterosexuality*, Allen & Unwin, Sydney, 2002.

165 Helen Garner, *The First Stone: Some Questions about Sex and Power*, Picador, Sydney, 1995.

166 Helen Garner, 'The Fate of the First Stone', *The Sydney Papers*, Spring 1995, p. 37.

167 Ann Curthoys, 'Helen Garner's *The First Stone*', *AFS*, Vol. 21, Autumn 1995, pp. 203–11.

168 Jenny Morgan, 'Sexual Harassment: Where Did It Go In 1995', in Jenna Mead (ed.), *Bodyjamming*, Vintage, Milsons Point, 1997, pp. 101–15.

169 Rosi Braidotti, 'Remembering Fitzroy High', in Mead (ed.), *Bodyjamming*, pp. 133–47.

170 Miraca Gross, 'When in Rome ....?', *Forum*, Vol. 5, No. 11, October 1977, pp. 28–35 and 'The Greeks in Australia, *Forum*, Vol. 5, No. 12, December 1977, pp. 21–6.

171 'Greer on Revolution': A discussion between Germaine Greer, Ian Turner and Chris Hector recorded in Melbourne, February 1972, *Overland*, Nos 50–1, Autumn 1972, p. 48.

172 Jill Julius Matthews (ed.), *Sex in Public: Australian Sexual Cultures*, Allen & Unwin, Sydney, 1997, p. xii.

## CHAPTER 9

1 Michael Kirby, 'Remembering Wolfenden', *Meanjin*, Vol. 66, No. 3, 2007, pp. 135–6.

2 Michael Kirby, 'Speech at the Opening Ceremony of the Gay Games VI at Aussie Stadium, Sydney, 2 November 2002', in Sally Warhaft (ed.), *Well May We Say ... The Speeches That Made Australia*, Black Inc., Melbourne, 2004, pp. 553–6.

3 Pip Porter, 'The Gay Crowds See a Silver Lining', *Forum*, Vol. 2, No. 7, 1974, p. 26; William S. Rowe, 'The Treatment of Homosexuality and Associated Perversions by Psychotherapy and Aversion Therapy', *MJA*, 30 September 1967, pp. 637–8.

4 Robert Reynolds, *From Camp to Queer: Re-making the Australian Homosexual*, MUP, Carlton, 2002, pp. 11–20; *MJA*, 25 August 1962, p. 321; D. Chappell and P.R. Wilson, 'Public Attitudes to the Reform of The Law Relating to Abortion and Homosexuality Part II', *Australian Law Journal*, Vol. 42, 30 September 1968, pp. 175–80, esp. p. 179.

5 'Male Homosexuality', *MJA*, 30 September 1967, p. 652.

6 Deveson, *Australians at Risk*, p. 319.

7 Michael Flood and Clive Hamilton, 'Mapping Homophobia in Australia', in Robinson (ed.), *Homophobia*, pp. 16–38.

8 *Nation Review*, 11–17 November 1972, in Dennis Altman, *Coming Out in the Seventies*, Penguin Books, Ringwood, 1980, pp. 36, 38.

9 Three policemen were charged in 1987, but only two brought to trial. Both were acquitted of manslaughter. See Tim Reeves, 'The 1972 Debate on Male Homosexuality in South Australia', in Robert Aldrich (ed.), *Gay Perspectives II: More Essays in Australian Gay Culture*, Department of Economic History, The University of Sydney, 1994, pp. 149–92.

10 Graham Willett, *Living Out Loud: A History of Gay and Lesbian Activism in Australia*, Allen & Unwin, Sydney, 2000, pp. 87–9.

11 Graham Willett, 'Mostly Harmless: Liberalism and Homosexuality in Australia in the 1960s', in Martin Crotty and Doug Scobie (eds), *Raiding Clio's Closet: Postgraduate Presentations in History 1997*, The History Department, Melbourne University, Parkville, 1997, pp. 105–16. See also Claude Forell, 'Time for Liberation of the "Gay" People', *Age*, 20 July 1972, p. 8.

12 Conway, *Great Australian Stupor*, p. 144.

13 Dennis Altman, 'Forum on Sexual Liberation', in Altman, *Coming Out*, pp. 16–17.

14 Steven Angelides, 'Authenticating Sexuality: Gay Liberation and the Truth of Sex', *MHJ*, Vol. 22, 1992–93, p. 60; Moore, *Sunshine and Rainbows*, p. 165.

15 Ware, quoted in Willett, *Living Out Loud*, p. 35.

16 *Australian*, 10 September 1970, p. 3, quoted in Denise Thompson, *Flaws in the Social Fabric: Homosexuals and Society in Sydney*, Allen & Unwin, Sydney, 1985, p. 16.

17  Paul Davies, 'Effeminate Rights', *Gay Community News (GCN)*, November 1980, p. 5.
18  'Five: A Society for the Rights of Individuals', Monthly Newsletter No. 5, July 1972, John Vergona Papers, Acq 2009-0043, Folder 2, Australian Lesbian and Gay Archives (ALGA), Melbourne.
19  Brian Lindberg, quoted in Deveson, *Australians at Risk*, p. 332.
20  John Ware, 'Twelve Months Past', *Camp Ink*, September 1971, pp. 4–6.
21  *GCN*, November 1979, pp. 3–5.
22  Christabel Poll, 'Gay Lib', *Old Mole*, 26 October 1970, quoted in Willett, *Living Out Loud*, p. 45 and Reynolds, *From Camp to Queer*, p. 32.
23  Deveson, *Australians at Risk*, pp. 327–8, 332.
24  'Labor "May Change Morals Laws"', *Age*, 4 July 1972, p. 4.
25  Adrienne Rich, 'Compulsory Heterosexuality and Lesbian Existence', *Signs*, Vol. 5, No. 4, Summer 1980, pp. 631–60.
26  Reynolds, *From Camp to Queer*, p. 35.
27  'Melbourne Scene', 8 August 1972, pp. 7–8, Vergona Papers, Folder 2, ALGA.
28  'Concerning Society Five', Leaflet, n.d., Society Five Papers, Box 13, ALGA.
29  All quotations come from letters in Society Five Papers, Boxes 11 and 13, ALGA.
30  Dennis Altman, *Homosexual: Oppression and Liberation*, Penguin Books, Harmondsworth and Ringwood, 1973 [1971], p. 233.
31  Altman, *Homosexual*, pp. 107, 229; Jeffrey Weeks, 'Dennis Altman and the Politics of (Homo)Sexual Liberation', in Weeks, *Making Sexual History*, pp. 75–85, esp. pp. 79–80.
32  *Digger*, 8 September – 6 October 1973, p. 6.
33  Ken Davis, quoted in Robert Reynolds, *What Happened to Gay Life?*, UNSWP, Sydney, 2007, p. 27.
34  *Digger*, 8 September – 6 October 1973, p. 6.
35  Altman, 'Forum on Sexual Liberation', in *Coming Out*, pp. 16, 18.
36  Willett, *Living Out Loud*, pp. 62–3 and 'Gay Lib. interview banned by ABC', *Age*, 6 July 1972, p. 3.
37  'Gay Lib grows angry at ABC', *Age*, 13 July 1972, p. 12.
38  See, for instance, *Digger*, 2–16 December [1972], p. 3.
39  Dennis Altman, *Defying Gravity: A Political Life*, Allen & Unwin, Sydney, 1997, p. 66; Altman, *Homosexual*, p. 239.
40  Reynolds, *From Camp to Queer*, p. 78.
41  See *Refractory Girl*, Lesbian Issue, Summer 1974.
42  Sue Wills, 'Inside the CWA – The Other One', *Journal of Australian Lesbian Feminist Studies*, No. 4, June 1994, p. 6.
43  Chesser, 'Australasian Lesbian Movement', pp. 69–91; Willett, *Living Out Loud*, pp. 36–8.
44  Willett, *Living Out Loud*, pp. 65–6, 68; Gisela Kaplan, *Meagre Harvest: The Australian Women's Movement 1950s–1990s*, Allen & Unwin, Sydney, 1996, p. 98.
45  Robyn Plaister, in Beverley Symons and Rowan Cahill (eds), *A Turbulent Decade: Social Protest Movements and the Labour Movement, 1965–1975*, Sydney Branch, Australian Society for the Study of Labour History, Newtown, 2005, p. 40.
46  Thompson, *Flaws*, pp. 67–9.
47  Willett, *Living Out Loud*, pp. 64–5.
48  Lake, *Getting Equal*, pp. 241–7.
49  'The Melbourne Gay Women's Group', in Mercer (ed.), *The Other Half*, pp. 441–5; *Vashti's Voice*, No. 4, July 1973 and No. 5, Nov/Dec 1973, in *Voices of Vashti Anthology: Melbourne Women 1972–1981*, n.d. [1981], pp. 80–1.
50  Deveson, *Australians at Risk*, p. 340.
51  *Armidale Express*, 14 January 1976, p. 17; 19 January 1976, p. 2.
52  Robyn, 'Guess Who's Coming to Power', *Campaign*, 14 February 1984. See also Willett, *Living Out Loud*, p. 256.
53  Jenny, quoted in *Digger*, 8 September – 6 October 1973, p. 7.
54  Kimberly O'Sullivan, 'Dangerous Desire: Lesbianism as Sex or Politics', in Matthews (ed.),

*Sex in Public*, pp. 114–26; McKee, Albury and Lumby, *Porn Report*, ch. 5.

55    *Age*, 23 April 1970, p. 7.

56    Timothy Conigrave, *Holding the Man*, Penguin Books, Ringwood, 1998, p. 105.

57    Clive Faro with Gary Wotherspoon, *Street Seen: A History of Oxford Street*, MUP, Carlton, 2000, pp. 233–7; Graham Carbery, *A History of the Sydney Gay and Lesbian Mardi Gras*, Australian Lesbian and Gay Archives Inc., Parkville, 1995, pp. 7–17.

58    Willett, *Living Out Loud*, p. 138.

59    Faro with Wotherspoon, *Street Seen*, chs 7–8; Willett, *Living Out Loud*, ch. 11; Shirleene Robinson, 'On the Frontline: The Queer Press and the Fight Against Homophobia', in Robinson (ed.), *Homophobia*, pp. 193–217.

60    *GCN*, October 1981, p. 36.

61    Wafer, Southgate and Coan, *Out in the Valley*, pp. 98–127, 240–1.

62    Letter to Society Five, 11 August 1975, Society Five Papers, Box 13, ALGA.

63    Dino Hodge, *Did You Meet Any Malagas? A Homosexual History of Australia's Tropical Capital*, Little Gem Publications, Nightcliff, 1993, pp. 43, 110–11; Altman, *Defying Gravity*, pp. 105–6; Sim Lee, 'A Journey with Support', in Wotherspoon (ed.), *Being Different*, pp. 213–21.

64    Moore, *Sunshine and Rainbows*, pp. 143–7, 199–210.

65    Willett, *Living Out Loud*, p. 147.

66    'Clones and the Question of Liberation', *Campaign*, January 1981, in Craig Johnston, *A Sydney Gaze: The Making of Gay Liberation*, Schiltron Press, Sydney, 1999, pp. 68–73, esp. p. 72; Willett, *Living Out Loud*, p. 146; Faro with Wotherspoon, *Street Seen*, pp. 244, 251–2; Reynolds, *What Happened to Gay Life?*, p. 47.

67    Peter Robinson, *The Changing World of Gay Men*, Palgrave Macmillan, Houndmills, 2008, p. 174.

68    *Ibid.*, p. 87; Kent Chuang, 'Using Chopsticks to Eat Steak', in Peter A. Jackson and Gerard Sullivan (eds), *Multicultural Queer: Australian Narratives*, Harrington Park Press, Binghamton, NY, 1999, pp. 37, 41. In the same volume, Damien Ridge, Amos Hee and Victor Minichiello, '"Asian" Men on the Scene: Challenges to "Gay Communities"', pp. 43–68, esp. pp. 53, 58 and 'China Doll – The Experience of Being a Gay Chinese Australian', pp. 89, 91–2.

69    Gays and Lesbians Aboriginal Alliance, 'Peopling the Empty Mirror: The Prospects for Lesbian and Gay Aboriginal History', in Aldrich (ed.), *Gay Perspectives II*, pp. 8, 17–19.

70    'The Uniting Church in Australia and Homosexuality', http://www.religioustolerance. org/hom_uoz.htm.

71    Wendy Brady, 'Colour Bars', in Craig Johnston and Paul van Reyk (eds), *Queer City: Gay and Lesbian Politics in Sydney*, Pluto Press, Annandale, 2000, pp. 21–7.

72    Faro with Wotherspoon, *Street Seen*, pp. 236–7; Fiona Nicoll, *From Diggers to Drag Queens: Configurations of Australian National Identity*, Pluto Press, Annandale, 2001, ch. 7.

73    Marr, *Patrick White*, p. 527.

74    *Ibid.*, p. 583.

75    Patrick White to Jim Jenkins, 28 December 1984, in Marr (ed.), *Patrick White Letters*, p. 600.

76    Chauncey, *Gay New York*, pp. 103, 298; Houlbrook, *Queer London*, pp. 195–6, 206–7.

77    Nicoll, *From Diggers to Drag Queens*, p. 193.

78    Reynolds, *What Happened to Gay Life?*, esp. pp. 1–8.

79    Reeves, '1972 Debate on Male Homosexuality in South Australia'; Malcolm Cowan and Tim Reeves, 'The "Gay Rights" Movement and the Decriminalisation Debate in South Australia, 1973–1975', in Aldrich and Wotherspoon (eds), *Gay and Lesbian Perspectives IV*, pp. 164–93.

80    Willett, *Living Out Loud*, ch. 9; Johnston, *Sydney Gaze*, p. 152.

81    Willett, *Living Out Loud*, pp. 161–5, 227–31.

82    Moore, *Sunshine and Rainbows*, pp. 183–7; Willett, *Living Out Loud*, pp. 219–24.

83    Willett, *Living Out Loud*, pp. 231–7; Alan Berman, 'The Repeal of the Sodomy Laws in Tasmania in 1997 and the Status of Homophobia in Contemporary Australia', in Robinson (ed.), *Homophobia*, pp. 236–53.

84    Sendziuk, *Learning to Trust*, pp. 1–2, 12–15; Adele Horin, 'Gay Life After AIDS', *National Times*, 8–14 November 1985, pp. 9–10.
85    Geoffrey Partington, 'How to Guard Children against AIDS', *Bulletin*, 18 December 1984, p. 36.
86    Fred Nile, *The Facts on AIDS – 'The Gay Plague'*, Supplement to Australian Christian Solidarity, n.d. [c. 1984], n.p.
87    Sendziuk, *Learning to Trust*, esp. chs 1–5.
88    Paul Sendziuk, 'Bad Blood: The Contamination of Australia's Blood Supply and the Emergence of Gay Activism in the Age of AIDS', *JAS*, No. 67, 2001, pp. 78–9.
89    Hiram Caton, 'The AIDS Apocalypse', *Quadrant*, No. 217, Vol. 29, No. 11, November 1985, p. 27; Horin, 'Gay Life'.
90    Willett, *Living Out Loud*, p. 168; Robinson, 'On the Frontline', p. 206.
91    Sendziuk, *Learning to Trust*, pp. 57–8.
92    John Ballard, 'Australia: Participation and Innovation in a Federal System', in David L. Kirp and Ronald Bayer (eds), *AIDS in the Industrialized Democracies: Passions, Politics, and Policies*, Rutgers University Press, New Brunswick (NJ), 1992, p. 134.
93    Sendziuk, *Learning to Trust*, ch. 4; Altman, *Defying Gravity*, p. 192.
94    Dennis Altman, 'The Most Political of Diseases', in Eric Timewell, Victor Minichiello and David Plummer (eds), *AIDS in Australia*, Prentice Hall, Sydney, 1992, pp. 349–58; Ballard, 'Australia', pp. 134–67.
95    Sendziuk, *Learning to Trust*, p. 147.
96    Horin, 'Gay Life'.
97    Gary W. Dowsett, *Practicing Desire: Homosexual Sex in the Era of AIDS*, Stanford University Press, Stanford, California, 1996, pp. 37, 80.
98    *Ibid., passim* and Gary W. Dowsett, 'Sexual Conduct, Sexual Culture, Sexual Community: Gay Men's Bodies and AIDS', in Matthews (ed.), *Sex in Public*, pp. 81–2; Robinson, 'On the Frontline', p. 207.
99    John Foster, *Take Me to Paris, Johnny*, Black Inc., Melbourne, 2003 [1993]; Conigrave, *Holding the Man*.
100   Alan Sandison, '*Holding the Man*: Tragedy and the Literature of AIDS', in Ken Stewart and Shirley Walker (eds), *'Unemployed at Last': Essays on Australian Literature to 2002 for Julian Croft*, CALLS, Centre for Australian Studies, University of New England, Armidale, 2002, pp. 187–209.
101   Altman, 'Most Political of Diseases', pp. 66–8; Ted Gott, 'Where the Streets Have New Aims: The Poster in the Age of AIDS', in Ted Gott (compiler), *Don't Leave Me This Way: Art in the Age of AIDS*, National Gallery of Australia, Thames & Hudson, Melbourne 1994, pp. 186–211.
102   Dowsett, 'Sexual Conduct', p. 89.
103   Sendziuk, *Learning to Trust*, p. 223.
104   Graham Willett, '"Proud and Employed": The Gay and Lesbian Movement and the Victorian Teachers' Unions in the 1970s', *LH*, No. 76, May 1999, pp. 78–94.
105   Andrew Lansdown, 'Homosexuals on the Offensive', *Quadrant*, No. 154, Vol. 24, No. 6, June 1980, pp. 29–30.
106   Partington, 'How to Guard Children against AIDS', p. 39.
107   *Daily Telegraph*, 6 June 2005, pp. 1 and 2; 7 June, 2005, p. 19.
108   'Dr Twinkle', *Sex is for Everybody*, Nelson, Melbourne, 1971, pp. 27, 29.
109   '"As a Community We Are Terrified of Paedophilia": An Interview with Author Paul Wilson', *GCN*, September 1981, pp. 28, 30.
110   See, for instance, Sally V. Hunter, 'Constructing a Sense of the Self Following Early Experiences with Adults: a Qualitative Research Study', *Psychotherapy in Australia*, Vol. 13, No. 4, August 2007, pp. 12–21.
111   Elizabeth Ward, *Father–Daughter Rape*, The Women's Press, London, 1984, pp. 80, 194–5, 201.
112   Stephen Angelides, 'The Emergence of the Paedophile in the Late Twentieth Century',

*AHS*, Vol. 36, No. 126, October 2005, pp. 272–95.

113  Altman, *Homosexual*, pp. 100, 104.

114  Alison Thorne and Bronwyn Levy, 'Politics, Paedophilia and Free Speech: The Witch Hunt Continues', *Hecate*, Vol. 11, No. 2, 1985, p. 72. See also Graham Carbery, 'Paedophilia – The Case for Consistency', *GCN*, October 1981, p. 39.

115  Adam Carr, 'Out of the Woodwork: George Small's Crusade Against the Sodomites', *GCN*, November 1980, p. 15.

116  Graham Willett, 'Paedophilia and Public Morals', *GCN*, August 1981, p. 19; 'Paedophilia: An Editorial', *GCN*, September 1981, p. 24; Warren Talbot, 'Paedophilia: The Case for Caution', *GCN*, September 1981, p. 26 and 'Paedophilia', *GCN*, October 1981, p. 8.

117  Susanna Rodell, 'The Men Who Love Children', *National Times*, 8–14 November 1985, pp. 18–19. The article is quoted in Thorne and Levy, 'Politics', p. 70.

118  The debate within the gay and lesbian communities about paedophilia is examined from a hostile perspective in Andrew Lansdown, 'Paedophile Liberation and the Radical Homosexuals', *Quadrant*, No. 204, Vol. 28, No. 9, September 1984, pp. 47–53.

119  Thorne and Levy, 'Politics', pp. 72–3.

120  Gary Baldi, 'On the Seduction of Children, *Camp Ink*, Vol. 3, No. 3, 1973, p. 5.

121  Carbery, 'Paedophilia'; Graham Willett, 'Consenting Children: One More Crack in the Wall?', *GCN*, September 1981, pp. 24–5.

122  Deveson, *Australians at Risk*, p. 205.

123  *Ampe Akelyernemane Meke Mekarle 'Little Children are Sacred'*, Report of the Northern Territory Board of Inquiry into the Protection of Aboriginal Children from Sexual Abuse, Northern Territory Government, Darwin, 2007.

124  Muriel Porter, *Sex, Power & the Clergy*, Hardie Grant Books, South Yarra, 2003, pp. 7–8, 130–2.

125  Emma Rush and Andrea La Nauze, *Corporate Paedophilia: Sexualisation of Children in Australia*, The Australia Institute, Discussion Paper Number 90, October 2006, pp. vii–ix and 23.

126  Miranda Devine, 'Kids Exposed to Sex Too Soon', *SMH*, 15 April 2007, http://www.smh.com.au/news/miranda-devine/kids-exposed-to-sex-too-soon/2007/04/14/1175971410574.html.

127  The Senate, Standing Committee on Environment, Communications and the Arts, *Sexualisation of Children in the Contemporary Media*, June 2008, http://www.aph.gov.au/SENATE/committee/eca_ctte/sexualisation_of_children/report/report.pdf, *passim* and p. 57.

128  *Ibid.*, p. 22.

129  That is, half the respondents who were 15–19 years old first had sex when they were either aged sixteen or younger.

130  Chris E. Rissel et al., 'Sex in Australia: First Experiences of Vaginal Intercourse and Oral Sex among a Representative Sample of Adults', *Australian and New Zealand Journal of Public Health*, Vol. 27, No. 2, April 2003, pp. 131–7; Richters and Rissel, *Doing it Down Under*, pp. 1–4.

131  David Marr, *The Henson Case*, Text, Melbourne, 2008.

132  Reynolds, *What Happened to Gay Life?*, p. 194.

133  Steven Angelides, 'The Queer Intervention: Sexuality, Identity, and Cultural Politics', *Melbourne Journal of Politics*, Vol. 22, 1994, pp. 66–88.

134  Johnston, *Sydney Gaze*, pp. 230–1.

135  Quoted in Reynolds, *What Happened to Gay Life?*, p. 188.

136  Barbara Baird, 'The L Word: Histories, Theories, and Contemporary Stories of Lesbianism', in Hawkes and Scott (eds), *Perspectives in Human Sexuality*, p. 77.

# *Index*